TAKEN BY STORM

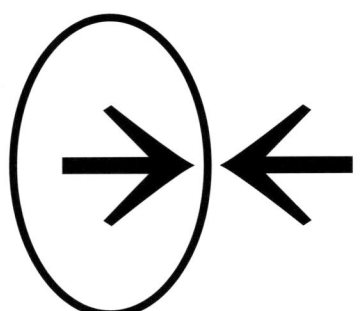

TAKEN BY STORM

THE ALBUM ART OF STORM THORGERSON

A RETROSPECTIVE

COMPILED BY STORM THORGERSON AND PETER CURZON

This book is dedicated to coupledom and to these couples in particular
for their spiritual and practical support: Trudy McGuiness & Del Rowe,
Sue & Merck Mercuriades, Jane & Brad Faine, Bob & Jan Ezrin,
Luke & Lizzie Thornton and of course to coupling in general.

Text by STORM THORGERSON
Book Design by PETER CURZON & STORM THORGERSON
with LEE BAKER
Editing by DAVID GALE & CHRIS CHARLESWORTH
Typing by ROXANA WOODS
Research by DANIEL ABBOTT
Print Outs by MARK PHIPPS & JERRY SWEET

Exclusive Distributors, Music Sales Limited, 14/15 Berners Street, London, W1T 3LJ.

Music Sales Corporation, 257 Park Avenue South, New York, NY 10010, USA.

Macmillan Distribution Services, 53 Park West Drive, Derrimut, Vic 3030, Australia.

Printed by: Kyodo, Singapore
A catalogue record for this book is available from the British Library.
Visit Omnibus Press on the web at www.omnibuspress.com

Several images from this book can be purchased as fine art prints via:
www.stormthorgerson.com

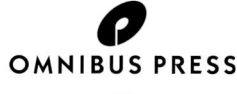

OMNIBUS PRESS

VISION ON

PREFACE

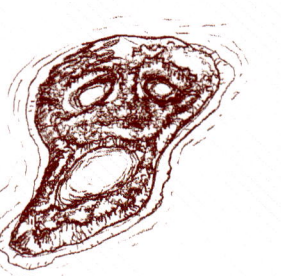

'NO MAN IS AN ISLAND' when all is said and Donne - the work in this book could not be executed by one person alone, but is the result of sundry collaborations – some long lasting and complex, some short and straight forward, involving partners, prop makers, designers, illustrators, photographers, actors and models, printers and retouchers, drivers, helpers, friends and so on, who should all rightfully be acknowledged and thanked.

Firstly, Aubrey Powell more affectionately known as Po, co-founder and equal partner in the Hipgnosis studio with whom numerous album covers were concocted, produced and successfully delivered to an expectant Seventies music world along with posters, single sleeves, videos, books, etc. and without whom nothing would have been remotely the same, Peter Christopherson the third and later partner in Hipgnosis; honorary fourth member George Hardie; Richard 'Granny' Evans, Colin Chambers, Richard Manning and others seriously too numerous to mention.

Secondly, Peter Curzon, long suffering colleague and design confidante in StormStudios, a loose and

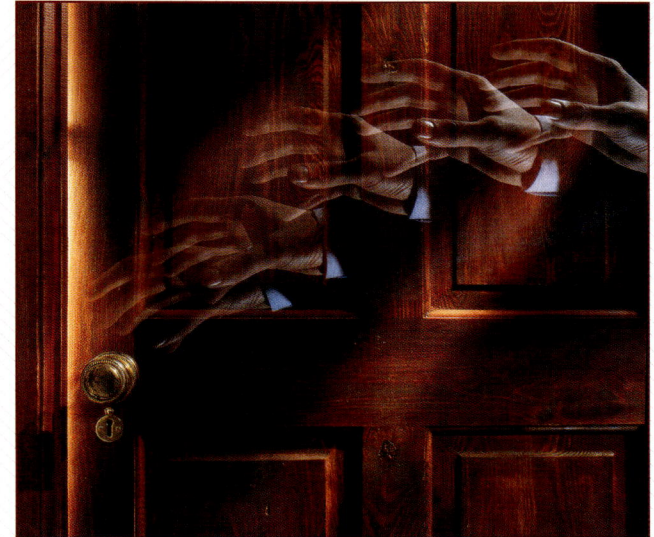

changing affiliation of designers and photographers guilty of producing still more album covers, posters, single sleeves, books, etc, etc over the last fifteen years. The affiliates include photographers Rupert Truman and Tony May, designers Finlay Cowan, Daniel Abbott, Sam Brooks, Jon Crossland and Lee Baker, retouchers Badger and Jason Reddy, prop makers Jez Clarke and John Robertson not to forget Keith Breeden then designer now portrait painter. You are all acknowledged and deeply thanked, that's for sure.

July 06

PS The usual apologia - The views in this book are those of the deranged author only and no other parties, for which the author accepts culpability and responsibility. Also blah-de-blah, tried damnedest to avoid errors and omissions, but if through inadvertency there are any outstanding the author humbly apologises blah-de-blah. Oh, and also for a patchy memory, I nearly forgot.

Foreword

I HAVE KNOWN STORM intermittently and sometimes philosophically for the last five years. When we first met it occurred to me that he is one of the most bloody minded and stubborn grumpy sods I have ever met! He speaks his mind and has a stoic disposition, which is bold and a rarity in this fickle industry, but one which garners respect. The pursuit of his own vision, which on occasion bypasses all external input can be difficult for some to handle. However his reasoning, delivered with a mordant even waspish wit and a dogged attitude, ensures you come round to his point of view. I'm sure he feels that he knows best and is therefore merely protecting the artist from a potential error of judgement by philistines like me! For that I, and I'm sure many others, sincerely thank him.

Is Storm simply a clever manipulator of the visual cortex or is he actually tapping into vast reservoirs of the unknown by tuning into frequencies outside the five sense reality that imprison the rest of us and producing translated broadcasts from parallel universes which we are left to ponder and attempt to reason? I believe the latter, but maybe his real motives will never be known...

Seriously though, this collection of work shows why his name and style will remain as recognisable yet mystifying, as timeless but relevant as ever.

(Is that ok Storm? Can we have our negs back now?)

Matt Bellamy

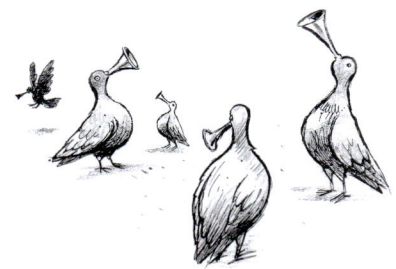

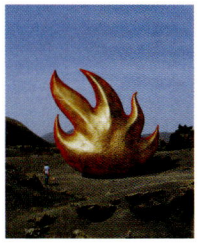

INTRODUCTION

Welcome, dear viewer, to this book of music-related images. Now that I'm an old fart, this book legitimately constitutes a kind of retrospective containing small chunks of work from the Seventies, the Eighties and the Nineties and a large chunk from now, the 21st Century. This disproportion is because previous decades have been dealt with more fully in earlier books, though they are mostly out of print.

Half of *Taken By Storm* is what I modestly call the 'best' of past work and half is the 'best' of recent work. The use of the word 'best' begs, of course, a few questions. What does it mean? The best of what ,you might well ask? And the best according to whom? The best by what criteria? Okay, okay, it's a loose phrase for heaven's sake, and it means the images which we like best - "we" being yours truly and my colleagues Peter Curzon, Dan Abbott and Lee Baker, none of whom has a jaundiced eye now, do they? However contaminated our view, we know what we like. And if all else failed, and they didn't agree with me, I resorted to insult and ridicule.

The images herewith have been for the most part designed as album covers for musical recordings, be they vinyl, CD, single bag, cassette, minidisc or cartridge (remember those?). The designs mostly saw the light of day, *i.e.* were published and have remained, usually for years, as the covers of the albums or singles they first adorned.

The order of images is random because most other orders felt unsatisfying or imposed. Chronological is ordinary and misleadingly developmental; 'thematic' is too clustered and obsessive and hence prone to repetition; by 'category' is too format driven; 'alphabetically' is self-evidently too predictable; so random it is - we might get some surprise juxtapostions, you never know. In addition, random feels more arty, more left hemisphere. Random allows greater 'dipability', random is in the end ordered, for a book is finite.

We are egomaniac purists and have returned to source artwork wherever feasible, in order to reproduce the images as well as possible. We have stripped them when appropriate of text, titles, names, company logos, catalogue numbers and anything else that might 'intrude' on our creations. They are, after all, our babies and must remain unsullied (would you sully your baby?).

I hope you enjoy exploring our offerings half as much as we did producing them.

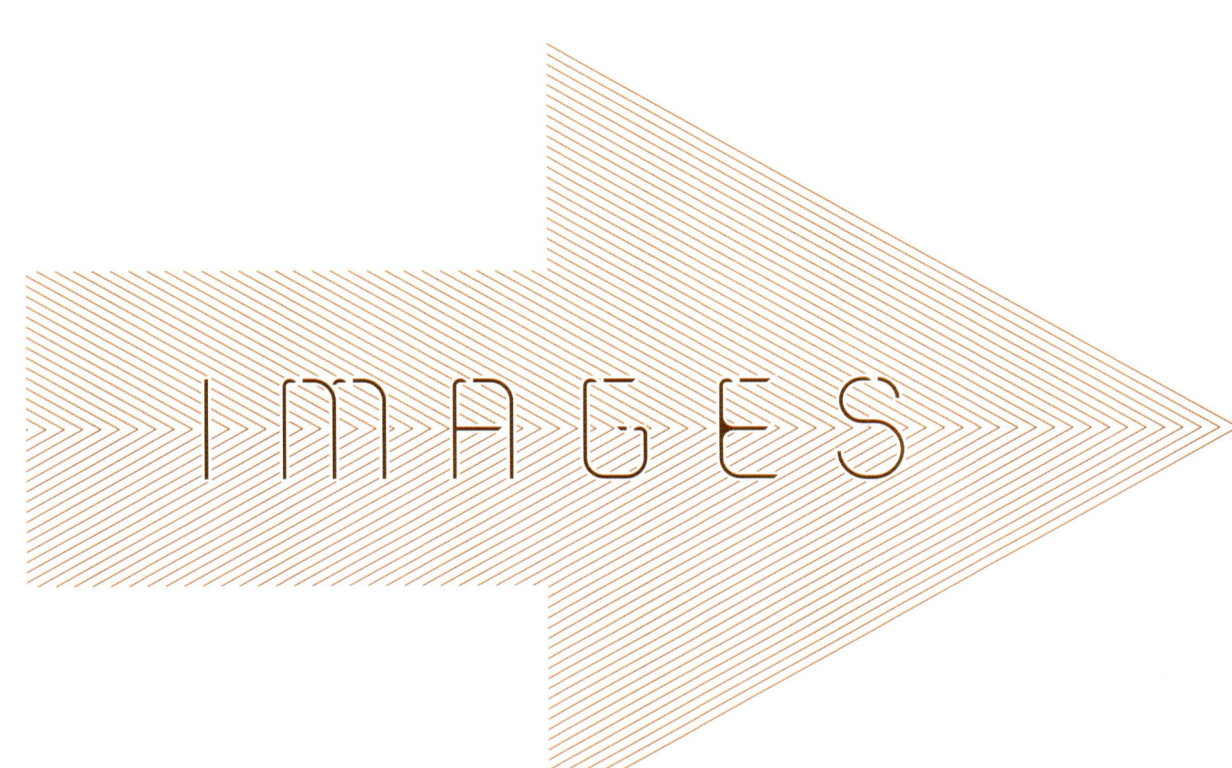

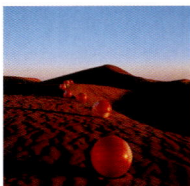

ELEGY I don't often dream images – more's the pity, it would make life easier – but I did dream this one. I find that the twilight zone between wakefulness and sleep (either going to sleep or waking in the morning) very fruitful for ideas, a time when the mind drifts in reverie but is conscious enough to record and embellish. When this image 'popped' into view in the brain I had been listening to the music. I had envisaged a desert where the vastness and atmosphere felt appropriate, but the scene was too empty. An addition was quickly made, namely an unending line of red footballs stretching into the distance as if they might cross the whole desert… which is almost what it was – we drove to the Sahara in a small van full of red plastic balls, placed them in a line trying to avoid footprints and took a picture just as the sun went down (which accounts for the shadows). A sort of land art project – totally outrageous but worked a treat. I hope Keith Emerson and co liked it as much as we did.

Why red footballs you might ask. I asked the same question but got no answer. It's what popped into my mind as I listened to the music, so balls are relevant but without explanation. Which is not all that could be said about balls, not by a long stretch.

*The Nice **Elegy** Vinyl front Charisma 1971 Design & Photos Hipgnosis Location Zagora, Morocco*

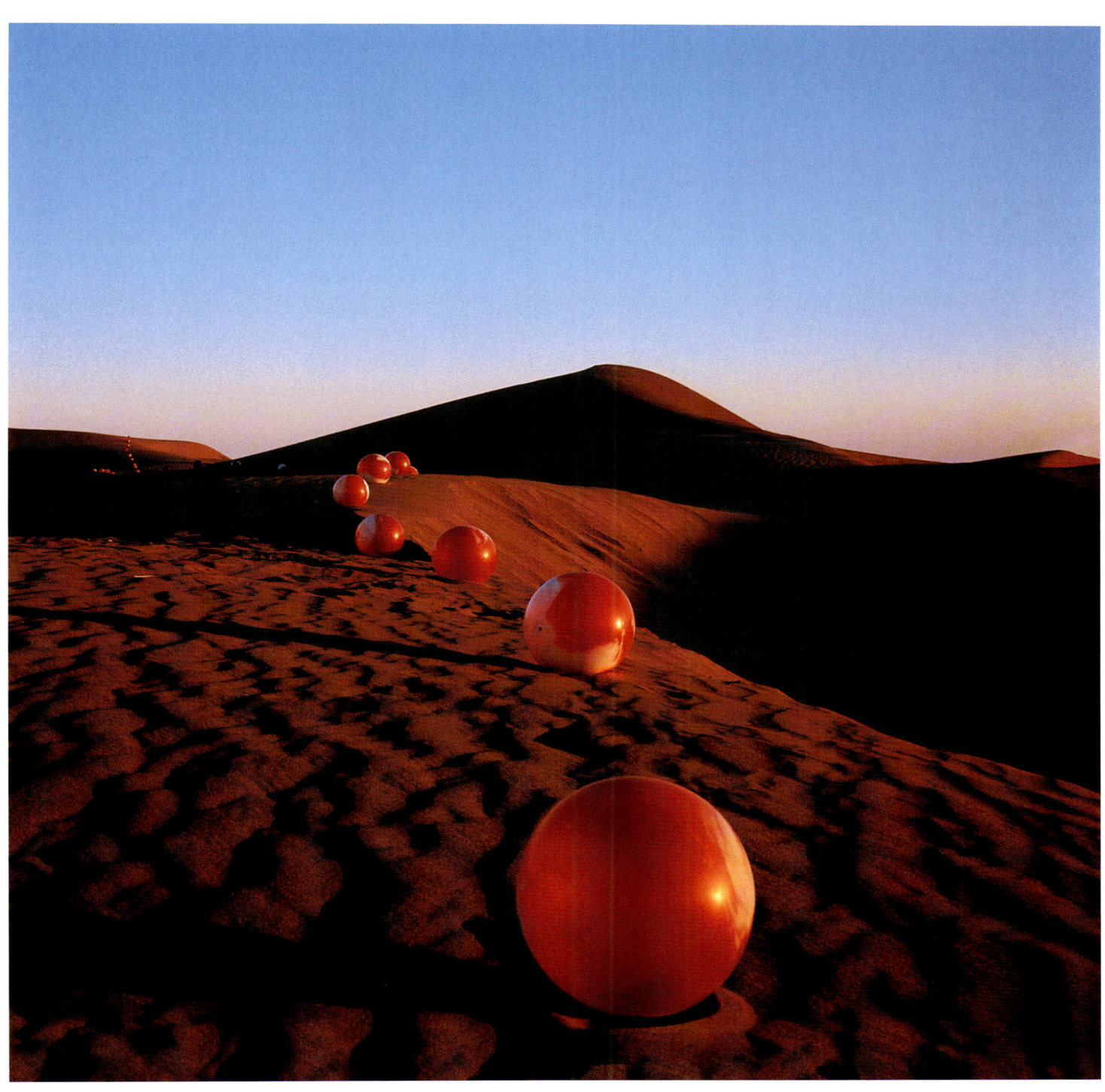

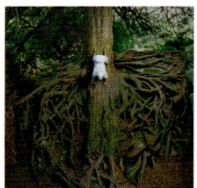

THE WIDOW Sometimes I'm embarrassed about how straightforward some things are. I'm not thinking of the relationships between designer and musician which are invariably complex: immensely satisfying on the one hand and equally torturous on the other. At the time of designing this image we were getting on well with the Mars Volta...well...hmmmm...reasonably well. I'm not sure they liked this picture that much, but it did appear in their CD booklet for Frances The Mute and was also used for the cover of their single, 'The Widow'.

The straightforwardness came in the derivation. Frances The Mute was based on a convoluted story about an orphan who, when coming of age, decided to search for his real parents. The music on the album was like the soundtrack to a movie never made and the story of this movie was, in essence, a man searching for his roots. Looking for his roots, huh? And where are roots if not in the ground? Or at the bottom of a plant or tree? And there you have it, a man crawling down a tree towards the roots. I know you're thinking this is stupid, as I did until I spotted, in a book, a tree with amazing aerial roots, something like a mangrove or a banyan tree. The picture also reminded me of Tolkien, who is portrayed sitting amongst some aerial roots in a place called Puzzle Wood, not unlike Middle Earth.

I don't know about you, dear reader, but I think trees are incredible. They are wondrous things, one of the ten best things on the planet, functional, beautiful, varied and invariably uplifting. Suddenly this idea didn't seem quite so daft. I imagined some kind of Indian ritual, where the famous tree-crawler has to shimmy his way down the tree from top to bottom, not the other way around, for he is trying to find his roots, not reach the sky.

And this amazing tree is for real, and turned out not to be in exotic Costa Rica nor Madagascar as I had anticipated, but near Gatwick Airport, 50 not so exotic miles south of London. These are the aerial roots of a yew tree, which originally clung to a large rock to support the trunk and branches, but over the years had lost its top soil, washed away by water that exposed its root system, now resembling branches rather than roots.

The Mars Volta **The Widow** *CD single front Universal 2004*
Design & Photos StormStudios Location Wakehurst, Sussex

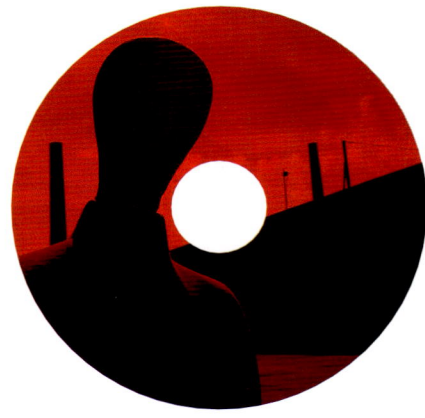

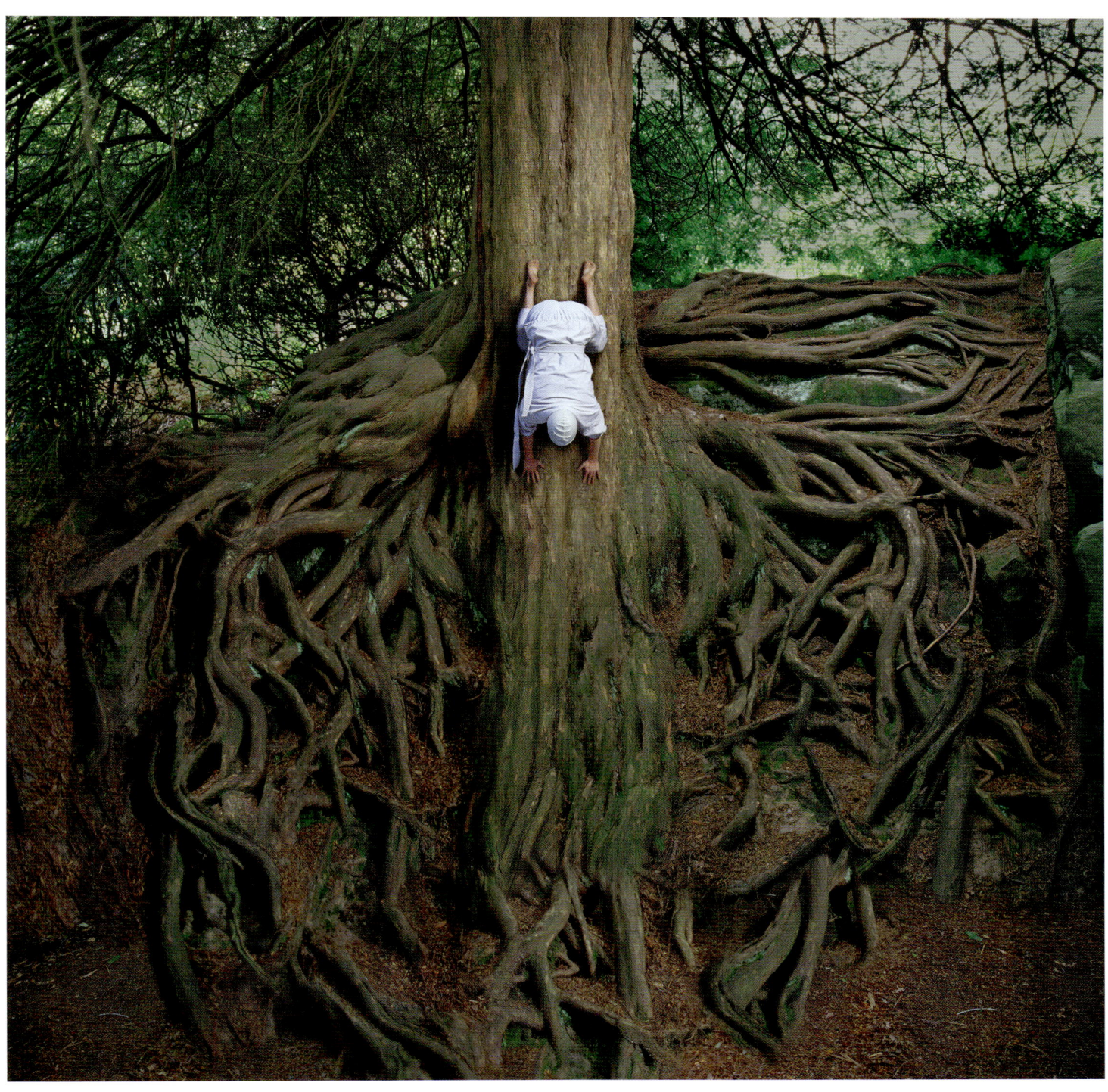

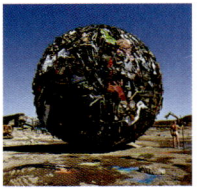

STOMP 442 Stomp 442 by Anthrax was a seriously minimal record of unencumbered heavy rock. No messing here. A very large ball of scrap metal which could roll around the urban landscape accruing lots of additional scrap as it went about its business, seemed equally forthright, especially if it was very big. The figure in the picture shows the size. In reality it is his pet ball which he has 'mentally' brought to heel. A ball as a big as a house, composed of a large number of car parts – hubcaps, radiators, fenders, exhausts, etc, all of fixed, real size.

The sculpture was built solely for this photograph and was made in sections then hung by a crane. The visual elusiveness of a sphere is such that the viewer cannot tell if it's solid since the back of the sphere cannot be seen. In addition, each segment of a sphere has the same curvature, thus our sculpture is in fact one half of a quadrant which is rotated in position, photographed each time and then joined in the computer. It is, I stress, a real ball but not all real at the same time, though you wouldn't know this unless I told you. And you don't believe everything I say anyway.

*Anthrax **Stomp 442** CD album front Electra 1995*
Design & Photos StormStudios Location Beckton, London

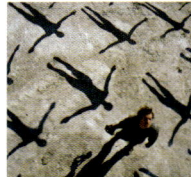

ABSOLUTION Commissions come in many different ways, and this one arrived via the very wonderful Internet, insomuch as Dom, the intrepid drummer of Muse, discovered a rough on our website which he thought might work for them.

We met with Dom and agreed that we should try and render our pencil sketch as a real event: shadows of flying people spread across the ground as if cast by a squadron of flying craft, magical beings swooping over the Earth to the amazement of the viewer on the ground looking up. It is as though he is witnessing some mystical event, a visitation of strange beings, which can only be inferred by us, the viewers of the picture, because all we see is shadows, whereas the viewer in the picture sees them for real, gliding serenely overhead. He is deeply moved and experiences a kind of absolution as one might in the presence of a such a miraculous sight.

The other thing I hoped the band liked as much as I did is the pattern made by the shadows which has, I feel, the appeal of all patterns, namely the symmetry, but not the meaningless repetition of wall paper. I had imagined that these flying beings were like the strange creatures out of a children's story by Maurice Sendak, whose illustrations I much admired. It seemed important to maintain a texture in the ground, holes, pebbles, striations, etc, to provide a 3-D backcloth upon which the shadows could fall. A chalkpit was deemed appropriate since Muse had spent much of their teenage years hanging out in the chalkpits near their Devon homes. Doing what? I'd like to know.

In pursuit again of the avowed philosophy of 'doing it for real' we made cut-out shapes from hardboard and fixed them on top of tall poles, took them to a chalkpit near London and photographed them in strong sunlight, thus to cast definite shadows. All very well you might think, except for the typical, crappy English weather, unpredictable yet grey, which meant we had to shoot this three times.

I felt 'absolved' through endeavour.

*Muse **Absolution** CD album front East West 2003*
Design & Photos StormStudios Location Buntingford, Essex

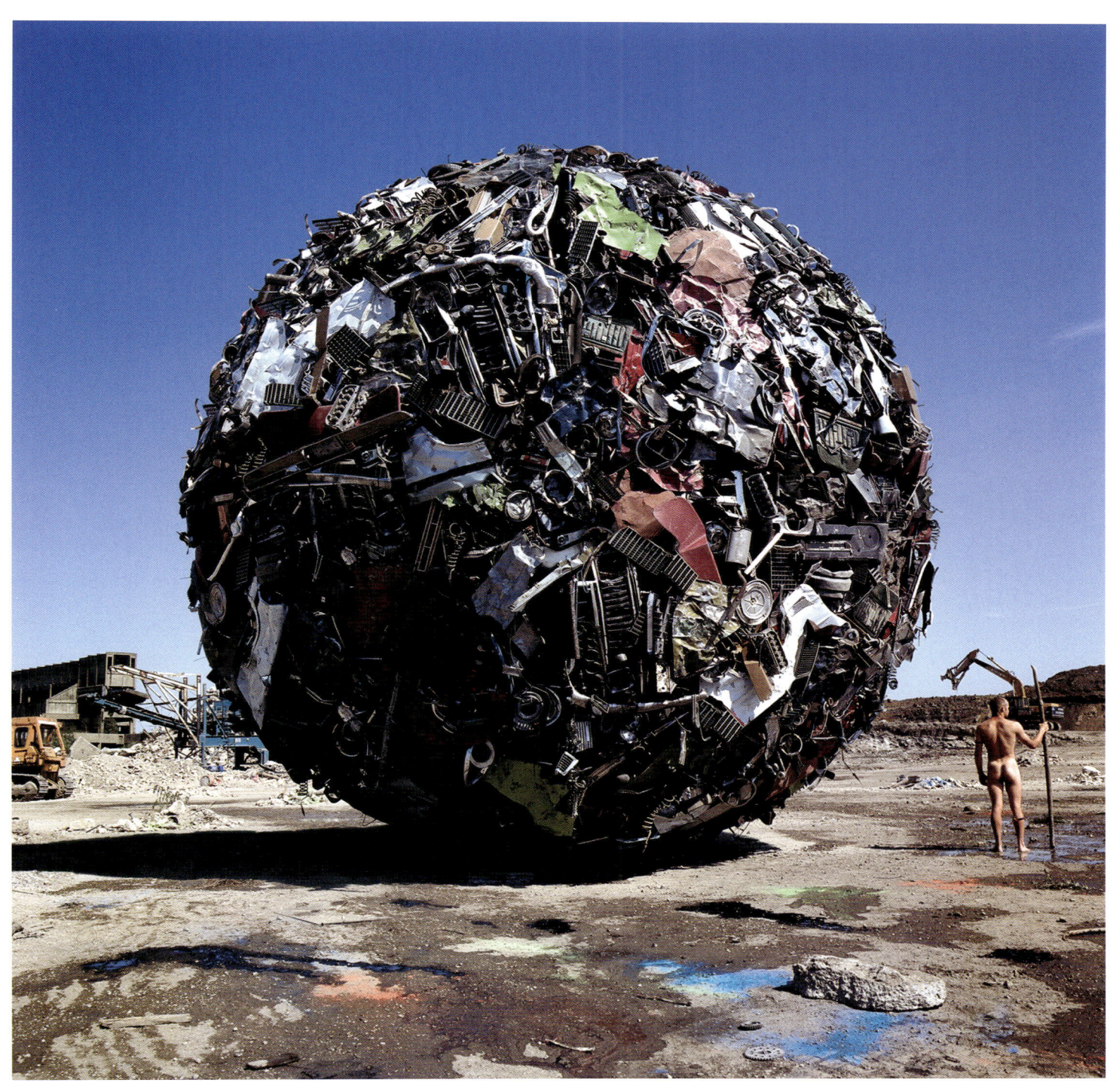

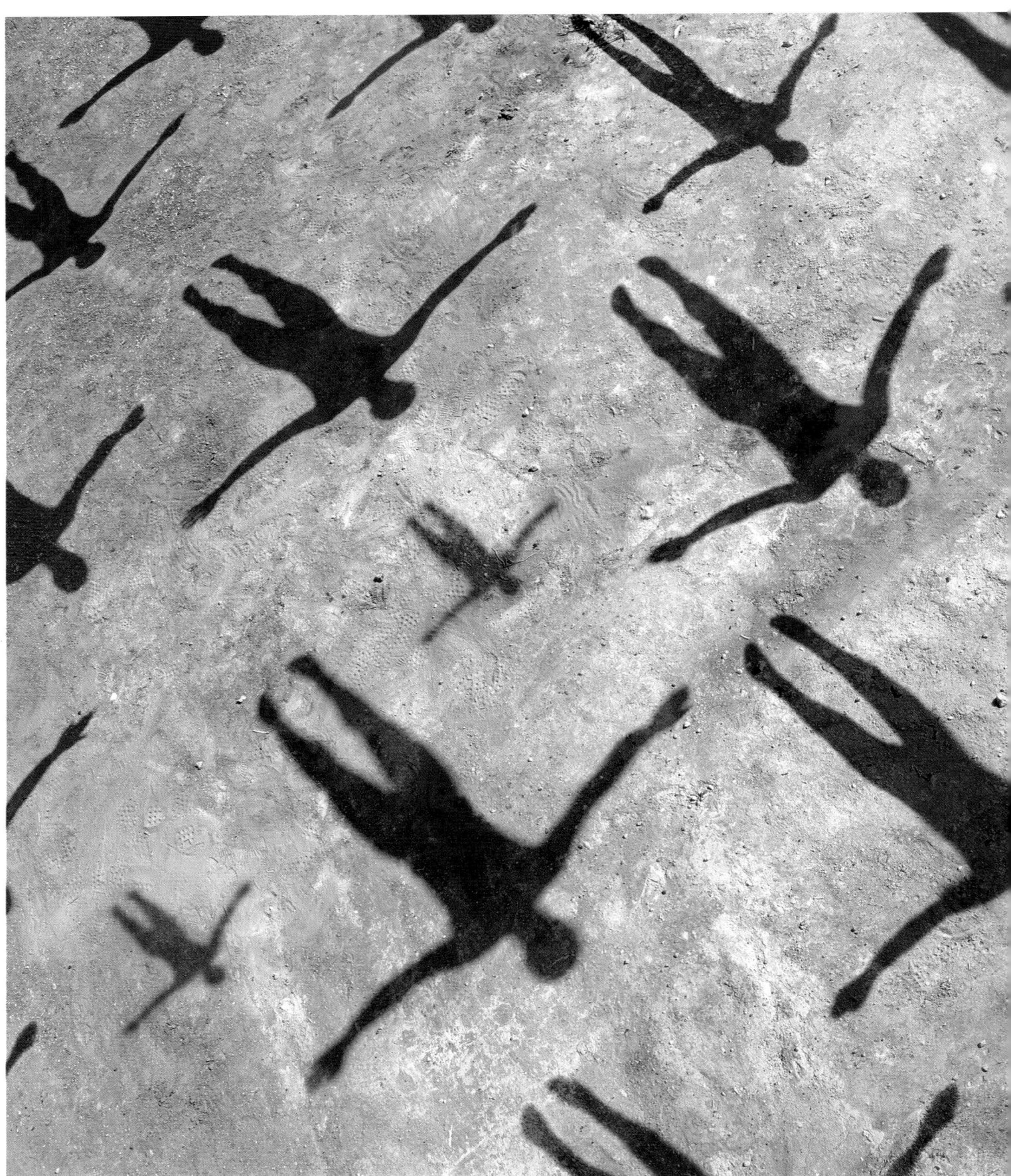

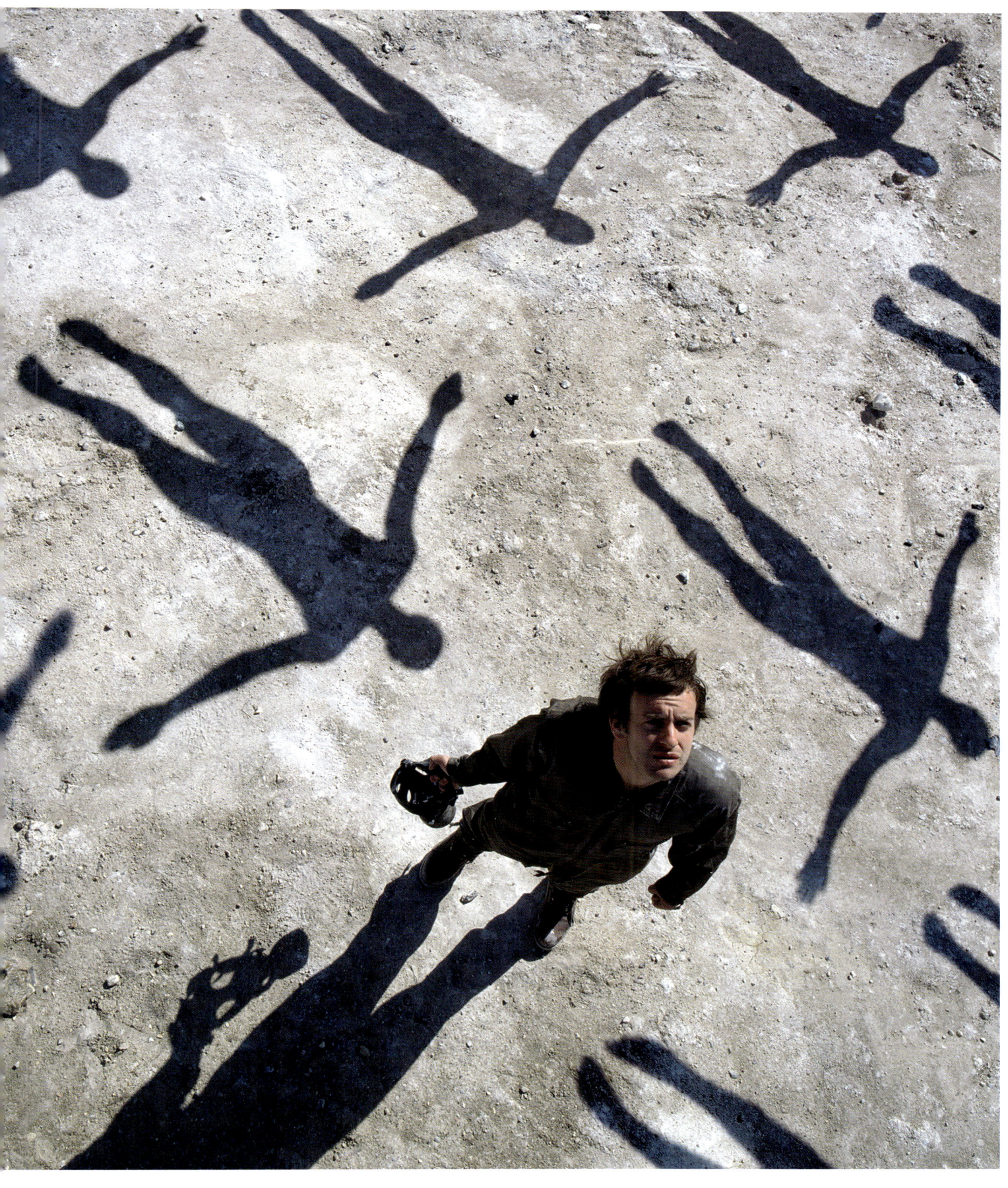

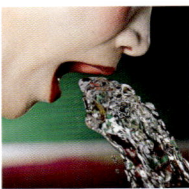

CORRELATIONS I knew that the cosmic guitar overdubs of Manuel Gottsching, aka Ashra, colliding and eliding as they did, one upon another in a cascade, had to be represented by water, but this is not much of an insight since water is a rather large topic and can be interpreted in a gazillion ways. We took as a cue a moment from everyday life, namely someone drinking from a water fountain. It seemed promising not unlike Peter Gabriel's car (pg.63) or the Billy Karloff image (pg.85), just an ordinary event isolated by photography and further highlighted by the framing, turning the commonplace into the special.

I thought the spuming water from the fountain had suggestive overtones, especially if it was one of those very vertical fountains which fall back on itself, presenting a clearly phallic shape. If in addition the person drinking was a woman, bending down to the spume, it would be even more suggestive, if not positively rude. However, the rudeness would be tempered in part by the coolness of the water, especially if lit carefully and backlit to add a glacial quality. If the woman were pale and Japanese, perhaps it would add still more iciness to the image and thus the finished piece would contain a contrasting mixture of hot and cold, of rudeness and rationality.

I think that I'm also fond of this picture for its use of the square. Although album covers are stimulating to design, because of the music, the lack of product placement, and the relative artistic freedom, the downside is that it invariably involves a square, be it vinyl or CD. This is a given though and I'm no crybaby, so sometimes we must make the best use of the square, which I think this design does in an economical way. The image was photographed in the Hipgnosis studio, and required a hose, a supply of water, a Japanese girl, coloured paper, and flash lighting.

On further inspection, I sometimes imagine that the water is conscious or a bit like an animal, craning forward to penetrate the woman's mouth...

'Penetrate'? I dunno, sex again.

Ashra **Correlations** *Vinyl front Virgin 1979 Design & Photos Hipgnosis*

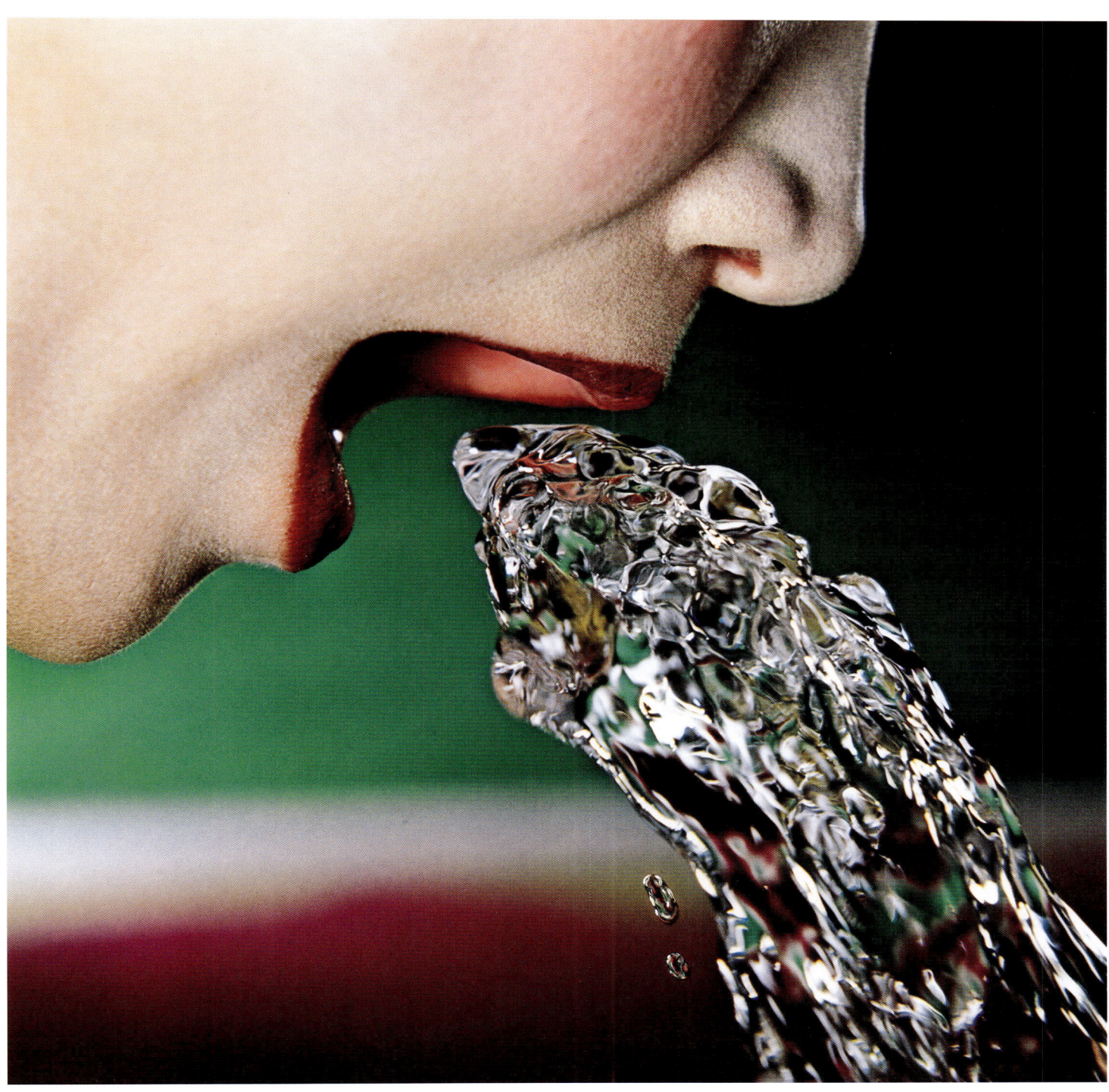

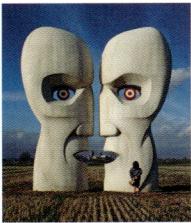

THE DIVISION BELL These stone statues were a variant of the metal statues (see pgs. 64-65), and were for the same album. Because Pink Floyd liked both metal and stone heads we ended up making both of them and using them on different formats. I consider, unashamedly, this to be one of the best things I've ever done, can I say that? Not so much for the dialogue with the viewer and not so much for the implication of a third absent face, a spiritual face i.e. that of Syd Barrett, formed by the two eyes looking at you, rather than at each other, but more because the statues themselves, designed with wild-eyed Keith Breeden, were very imposing in their own right, majestic, elegant and monolithic, standing eerily in the fens of East Anglia.

*Pink Floyd **The Division Bell** Cassette EMI 1994 Design Storm Thorgerson & Keith Breeden Photos Tony May & Storm Thorgerson Location Streatham, Ely*

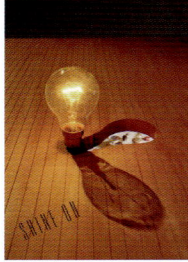

HALL OF FAME A preoccupation of people in the visual field (as opposed to the cornfield) is what is the nature of an object, visually speaking? Does an object change because of perspective? Or angle? Is an object defined by its contours, or by its shadow, or its reflection? These child-like obsessions become realised in pictures (see *Inside Out*, pg.154, and *Stomp 442* pg.17). In this instance the object was a light bulb plus its shadow, and a hole in the ground, cut in the shape of the light bulb (light bulbs are also a preoccupation, see *On Air* pg.144 and *Ignoto* pg.116). Being a preoccupation doesn't mean we have any thing perceptive to say about it: it only means it reappears in some of our images. In this instance it seemed most appropriate for Pink Floyd, as a congratulatory advert for their induction into the UK *Hall of Fame*. The transparency of the light bulb and of its shadow and its hole, corresponded nicely with the transparency of the whole *Hall of Fame* shenanigans. As Pete Townshend pointed out in his ceremony speech, there was no actual physical hall... it was just an invention for TV. The whole thing smelt like a sham, so why was he there? Why was I there? Why was there a light bulb?

*Pink Floyd **Hall Of Fame** Print Ad EMI 2005 Design & Photos StormStudios*

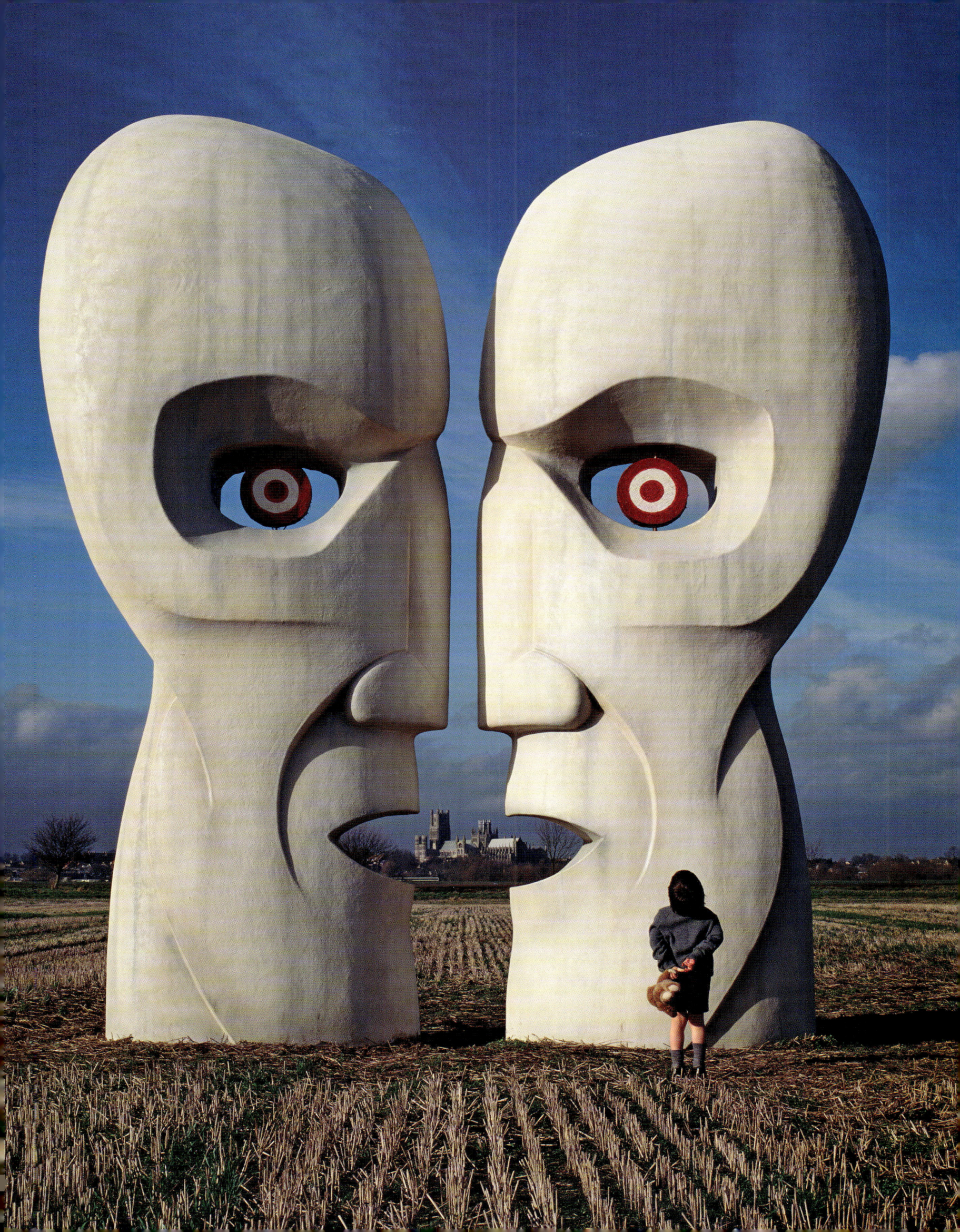

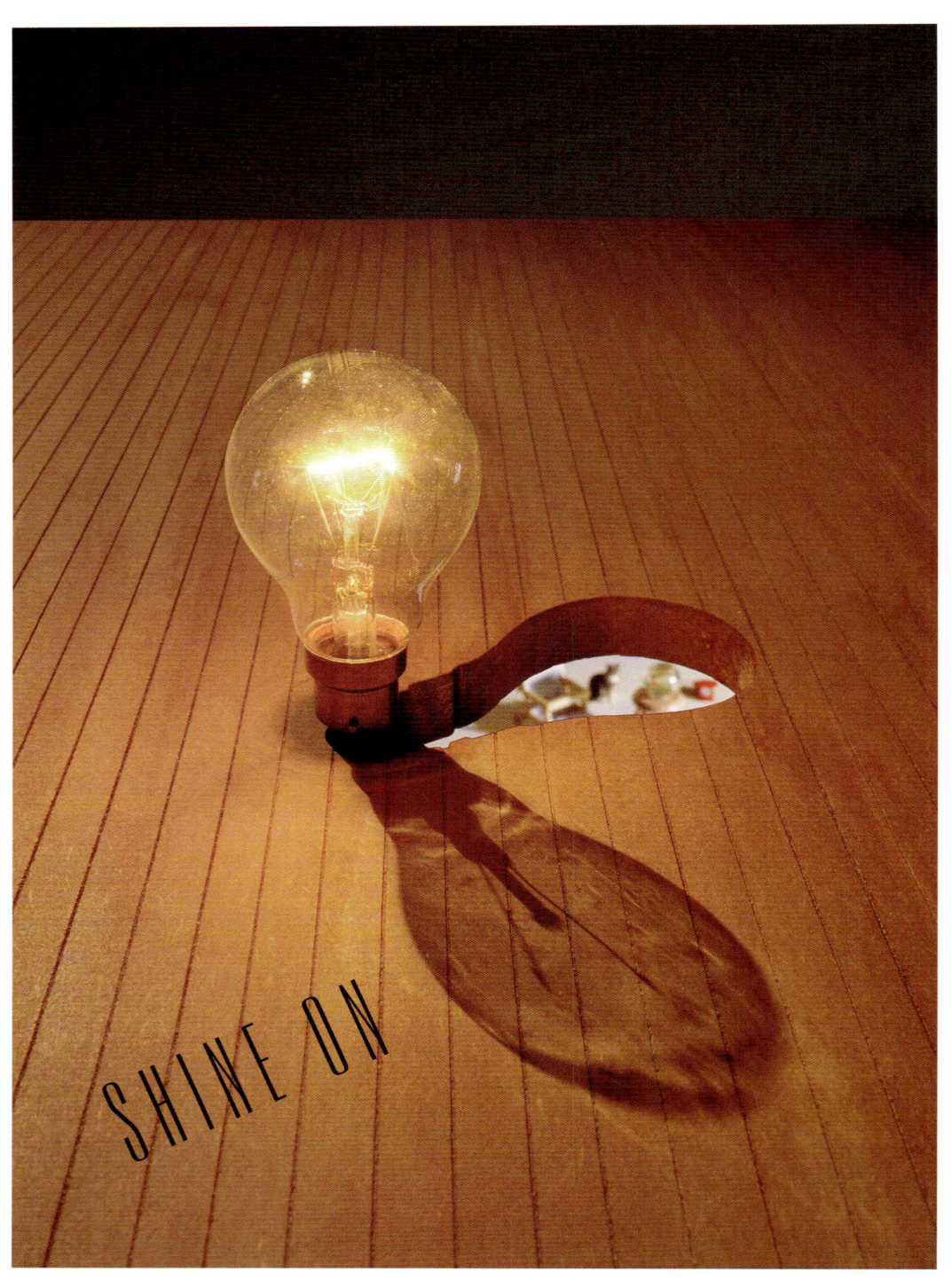

SHINE ON

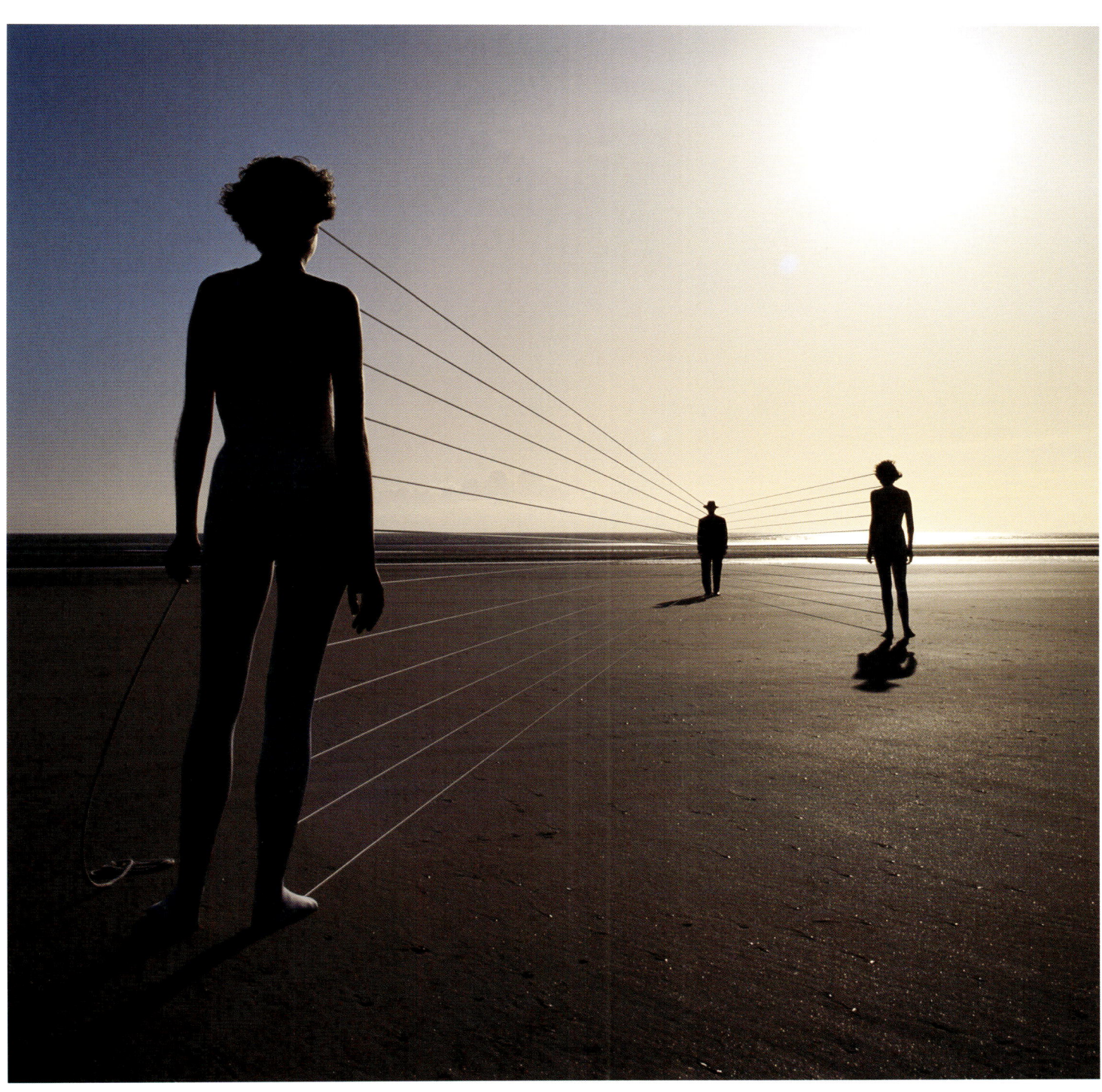

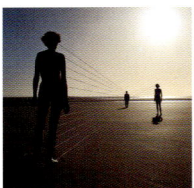

KINDRED SPIRIT Fritz Kreisler played wonderful classical violin throughout the Twenties and Thirties. He was a virtuoso much admired by musicians and public alike. Two particular aspects marked him out. Firstly, he played like an angel; secondly, he composed pieces but pretended they were not his own. He attributed them instead to obscure (and sometimes fictitious) baroque composers, and so he could insert them into his concert programme without disturbance. Credit was not the issue.

At the other end of the violin spectrum is the one and only (thank God) Nigel Kennedy – modern phenomenon, enfant terrible, soccer crazy, hard drinking genius, seemingly sharing with Kreisler only one particular quality – the ability to play beautifully. He made an album of Kreisler tunes and favourite concert pieces called *Kindred Spirit*. And it was fantastic: truly a beautiful thing.

I designed the album cover around the twin muses in Kreisler's life – playing and composing – and pictured them as female shapes, or silhouettes (in deference to the two major women in his life). They were connected to the one source, Kreisler himself, by means of strings – strings of the violin, of course, but also strings of attachment. The whole image was intended to be minimal, geometric and elegant. A dash of mystery perhaps, but mostly cool and classical. Tony May took an excellent backlit photo at Camber Sands on the South Coast of England late in the afternoon with perfect winter sun. We loved it. Nigel said he loved it. What could go wrong?

I should have known that Nigel is frighteningly unpredictable. I had worked with him before. And what he did was unpredictably unpredictable. He completed the album, but decided that he didn't, on reflection, want to release it at all. And then, in 1998, just as predictably he changed his mind and released the album after all. However he replaced my picture with a photo of himself, the swine, which was pretty depressing – but quite predictable.

*Nigel Kennedy **Kindred Spirit** EMI 1995 CD album front, unreleased Design & Photos StormStudios Location Camber Sands*

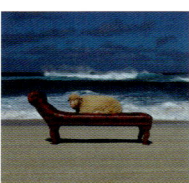

LOOK HERE This picture of a sheep on a psychoanalytic couch was designed as a poster insert for 10cc's 1980 album *Look Here*. The band had asked for 'something different'. I never really have a clear idea of what that expression means. Does it mean something new? Something different from what we had done previously? Something different from every album cover that ever existed? In my more truculent mood I decided to take them literally and suggest something without imagery, without imagery? Bit like shooting myself in the foot. I suggested that the album cover was verbal, like a newspaper headline, large fractured text, no imagery.

I thought that it was more engaging to ask a question and between us we came up with 'Are you normal?' as if the viewer were barmy, which somehow applied to the intrinsic madness of rock'n'roll, of 10cc, of my good self or 10cc's fans. We started, however, with a t-shirt, the front of which asked 'Are you coming?' visible on approach while the back asked, 'Are you going?' I thought this was kind of neat, geographically speaking.

Of course this whole thrust backfired because the album had 'Are you normal?' on the front but this wasn't the title, it was *Look Here*, so it all became a trifle confusing. Anyway, the question, 'Are you normal', led to the idea of normalcy and what could be more normal than a sheep, all of whom tend to follow each other. But to be normal you'd need a lengthy dose of psychotherapy, hence the sheep on the couch is undergoing intensive treatment, set against the vast sea of the unconscious, namely the wild ocean.

The most incongruous aspect of this saga was that the record company wanted us to shoot in Brighton or North Wales whereas we were rather keen on Hawaii... Think about it... the rollers in Brighton would be non-existent and the light in North Wales would be crap. Fortunately 10cc believed in us, or disbelieved in record companies, and thought that Hawaii would be a damn good idea, albeit terribly indulgent. The real question was would Hawaii have sheep? But since we were very organised at Hipgnosis we rang them up first and they did, but we forgot to ask if they had a couch. But Po, who had gone to Hawaii, lucky devil, had the good sense to get the couch custom made in Honolulu and took this fabulous photo with the aid of force fed valium and a bunch of dogs to keep the sheep in position. What could be more normal?

*10cc **Look Here** Poster Phonogram 1980 Design & Photos Hipgnosis Location Hawaii*

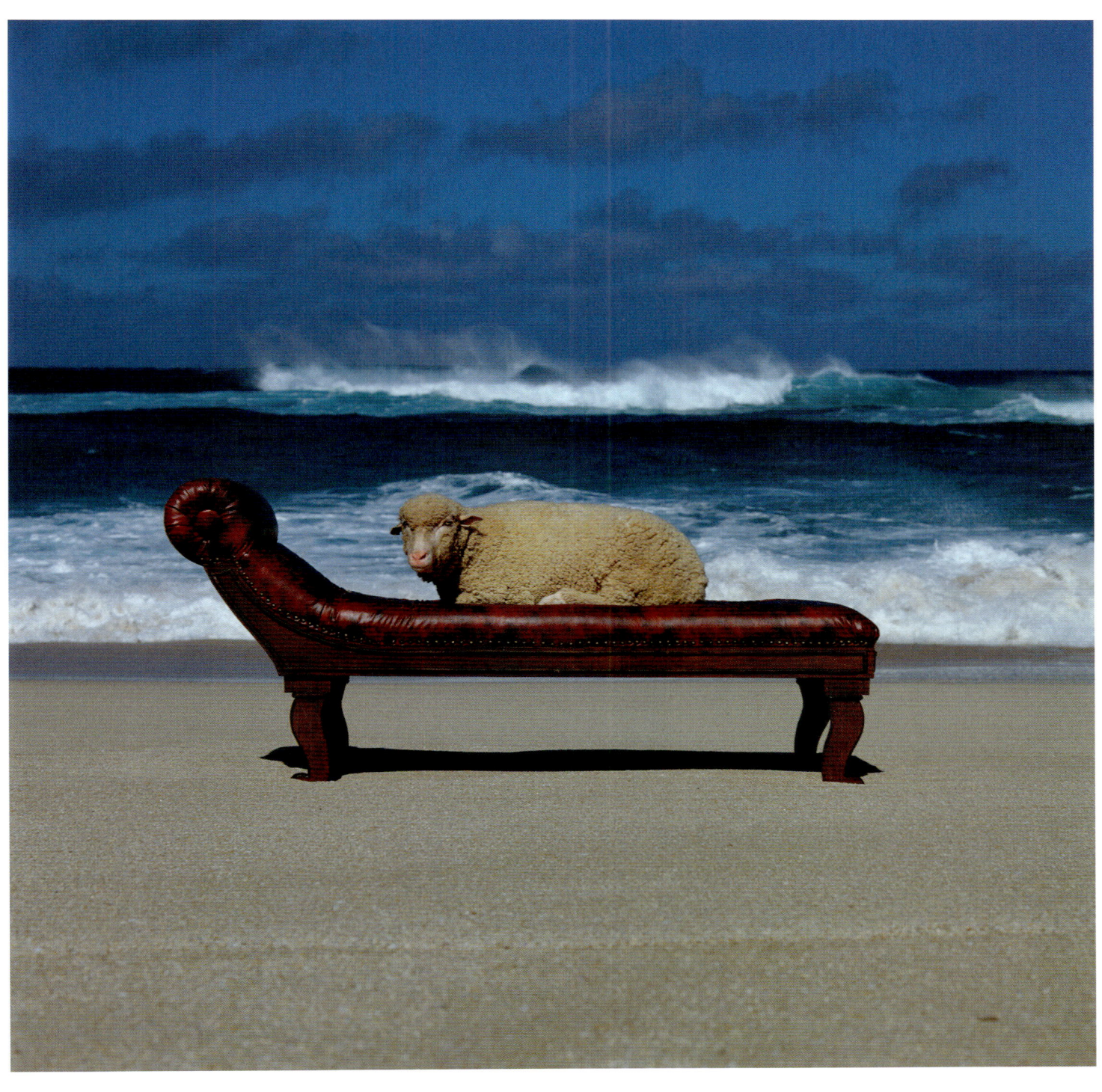

ARE YOU NORMAL

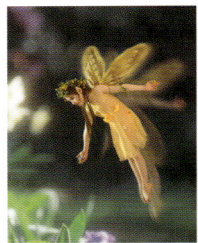

BELIEVE We decided to suggest to Believe Media – a commercial and video production company in L.A. – that they consider a composite logo. Not one symbol or image or logo type but a collection of images. These images could be used separately to indicate the different departments (commercials, videos, invoices, website, etc) or all together for the company as a whole. The images for the seven letters of Believe. Seven images but on one theme, different but related. First idea was seven insubstantial things, things that were clearly present but were easily disrupted, such as reflections, rainbow, shadow. Phenomena that exist but are insubstantial, intangible, kind of there but not there. The second set of suggestions shown here were phenomena alleged to exist but perhaps requiring some degree of belief rather than knowledge. A phenomenon, you could ask, 'Do you believe in..." fairies for example, or in aliens, or in ghosts, or in levitation, or in out of body experiences, or even mermaids. By representing such questionable items as photographs along with an instruction to believe added a further dimension, hopefully of irony, *i.e.* are aliens and fairies, real objects or merely objects of belief. Obviously, they are real otherwise we couldn't photograph them – the camera never lies, as the say in LA, and they should know ha ha la la.

Believe Company Logo 2000 Design & Photos StormStudios

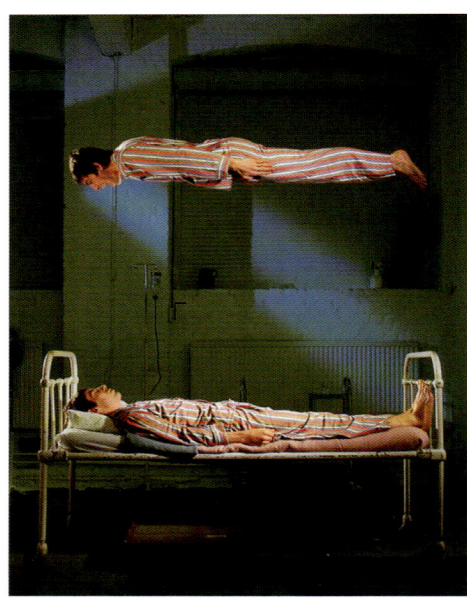

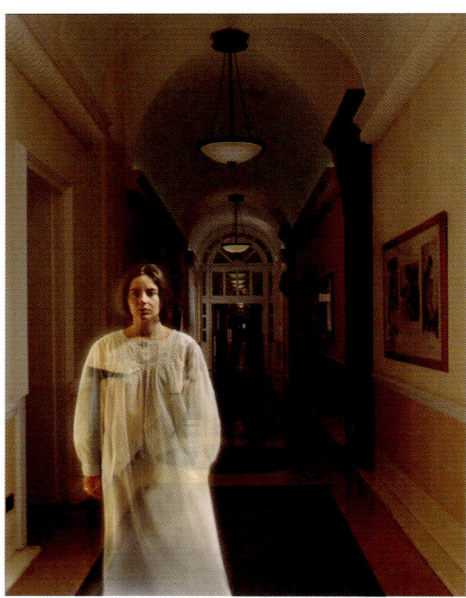

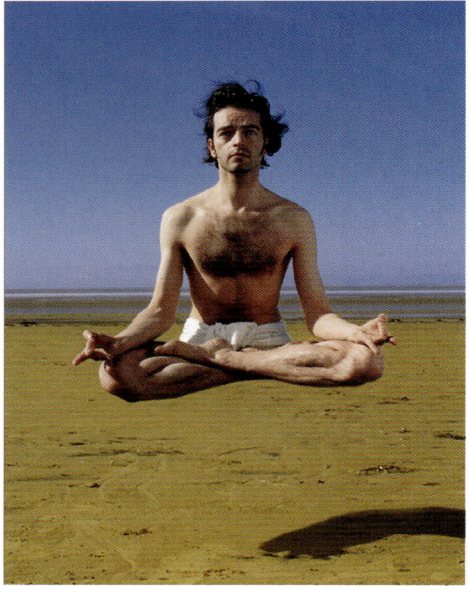

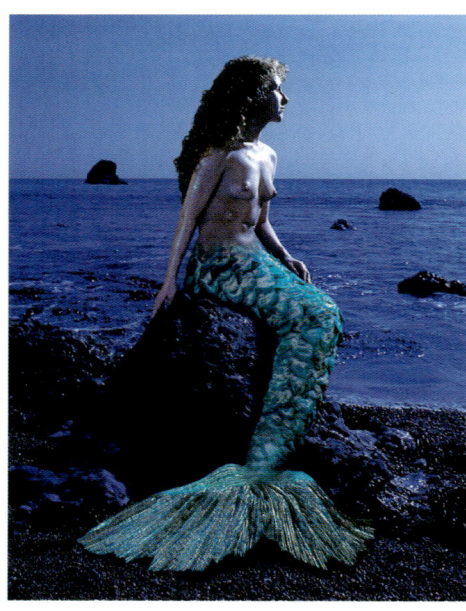

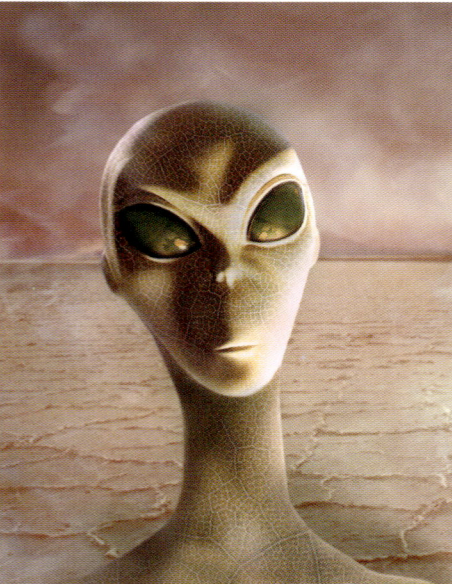

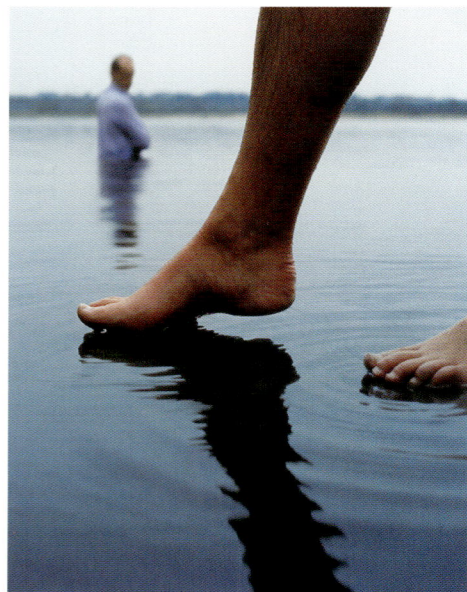

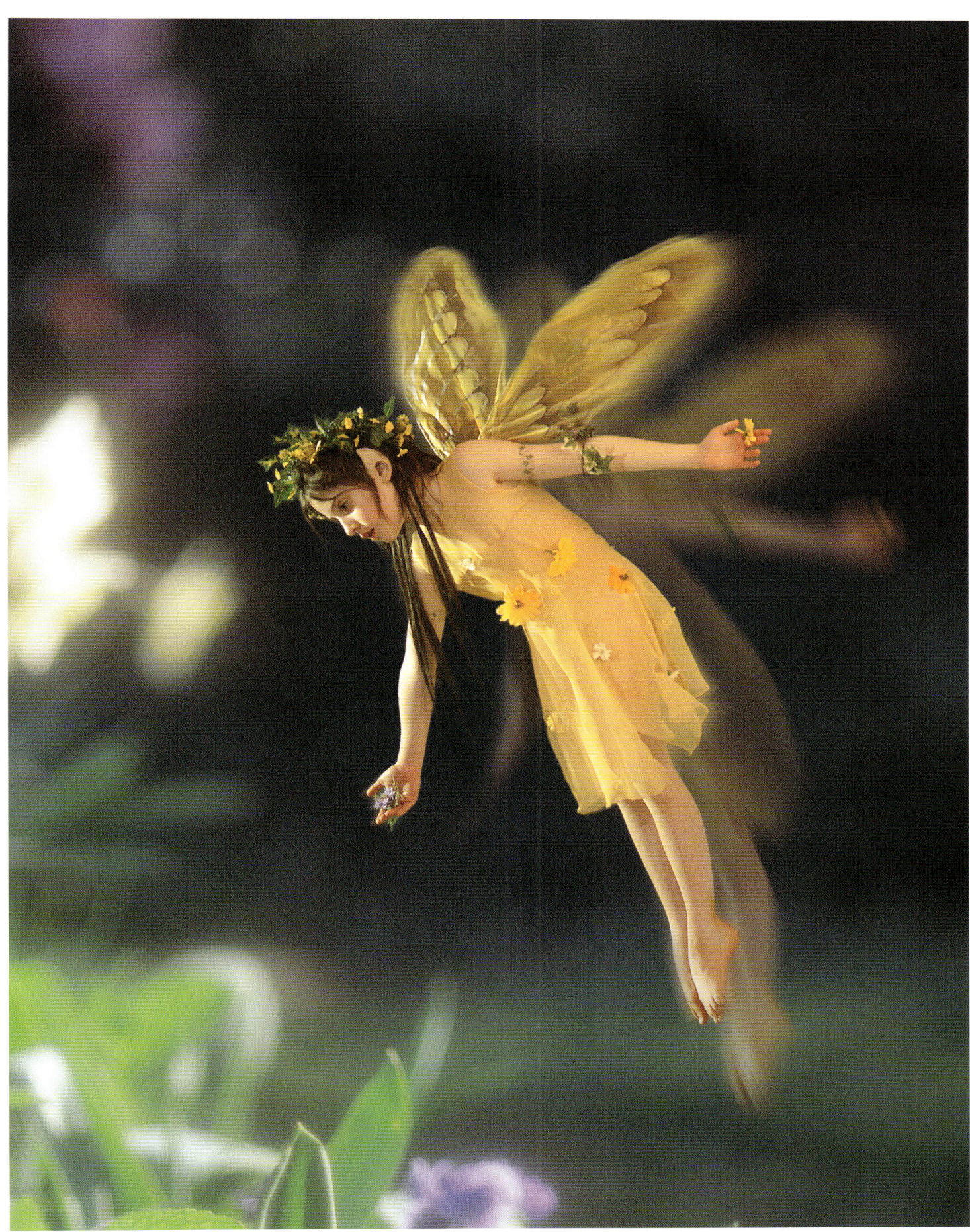

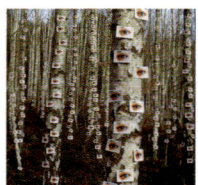

GASOLINE Memory is a devilish thing, a slippery thing, you think you got it down and then it eludes you, like trying to catch a fish with bare hands. This image of eyes on trees is an exterior installation – hundreds of photos of eyes attached temporarily to silver birch trees, but its derivation I am not so sure about. Being an image of romance (romantic obsession) and paranoia, it could easily have come from the lyrics of 'Catherine Wheel'. Alternatively I dimly recall a lateral association with the phrase 'the walls have ears' (more paranoia) so the trees have eyes but why trees? I don't know, though I remember that they had to be sliver birches, not some other tree, which may have been a simple visual preference (an obscure inspiration from the likes of Ansel Adams or Edward Weston, fond of photographing silver birches or aspens in morning light). I guess it could be the contrast of tree trunk and background since those pioneering photographers often preferred to work in black and white. Such a contrast also worked better in dull English light whereas brown trees would not have stood out and would instead look unnecessarily gloomy. Either way Rupert and Sam made a sterling effort to adorn every tree in sight making, I think, an effective and eye catching (oh my) image.

Catherine Wheel **Gasoline** *CD single Columbia 2000*
Design & Photos StormStudios Location Virginia Water

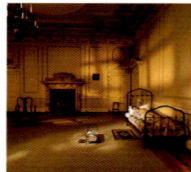

VIRTUAL LIFERS (overleaf) had so little money, God bless them, that we had to do it at cost, but insisted that there would be no changes to the artwork whatsoever! Power Crazed Designer strikes again! The idea of this image is a cross between the Victorian notion of the Homunculus - the interior voice of conscience characterised as another entity inside ourselves – and Borges' writing about the dreamer – does the dreamer dream dreams or do the dreams dream the dreamer? Is the little man in the little bed dreaming about the big man in the big bed or vice versa? Who is really in charge? Who precedes whom?

This idea of the voice in the head, of there being possibly another person inside oneself is commonplace, I have one watching me as I type this now. You have one don't you? For schizophrenics and religious zealots, and the odd rock'n'roll star, the voice within is so powerful it can overtake, whereas for the majority, hopefully, this voice is a comfort, an ally, keeps good company and may even keep some of us on the straight and narrow.

Silent Buddahs **Virtual Lifers** *CD front Paradise Productions 2000*
Design & Photos StormStudios Location Richmond, London

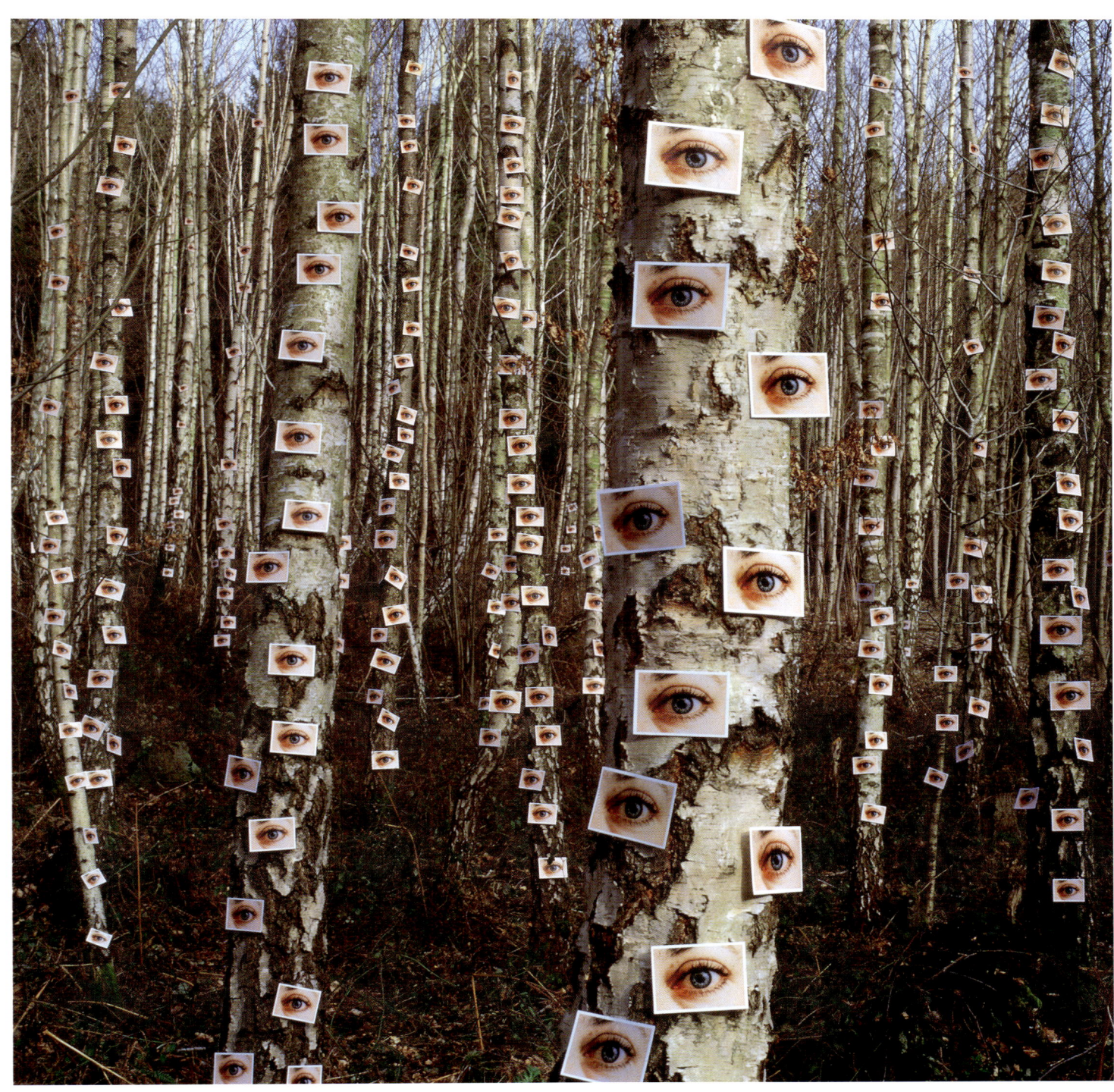

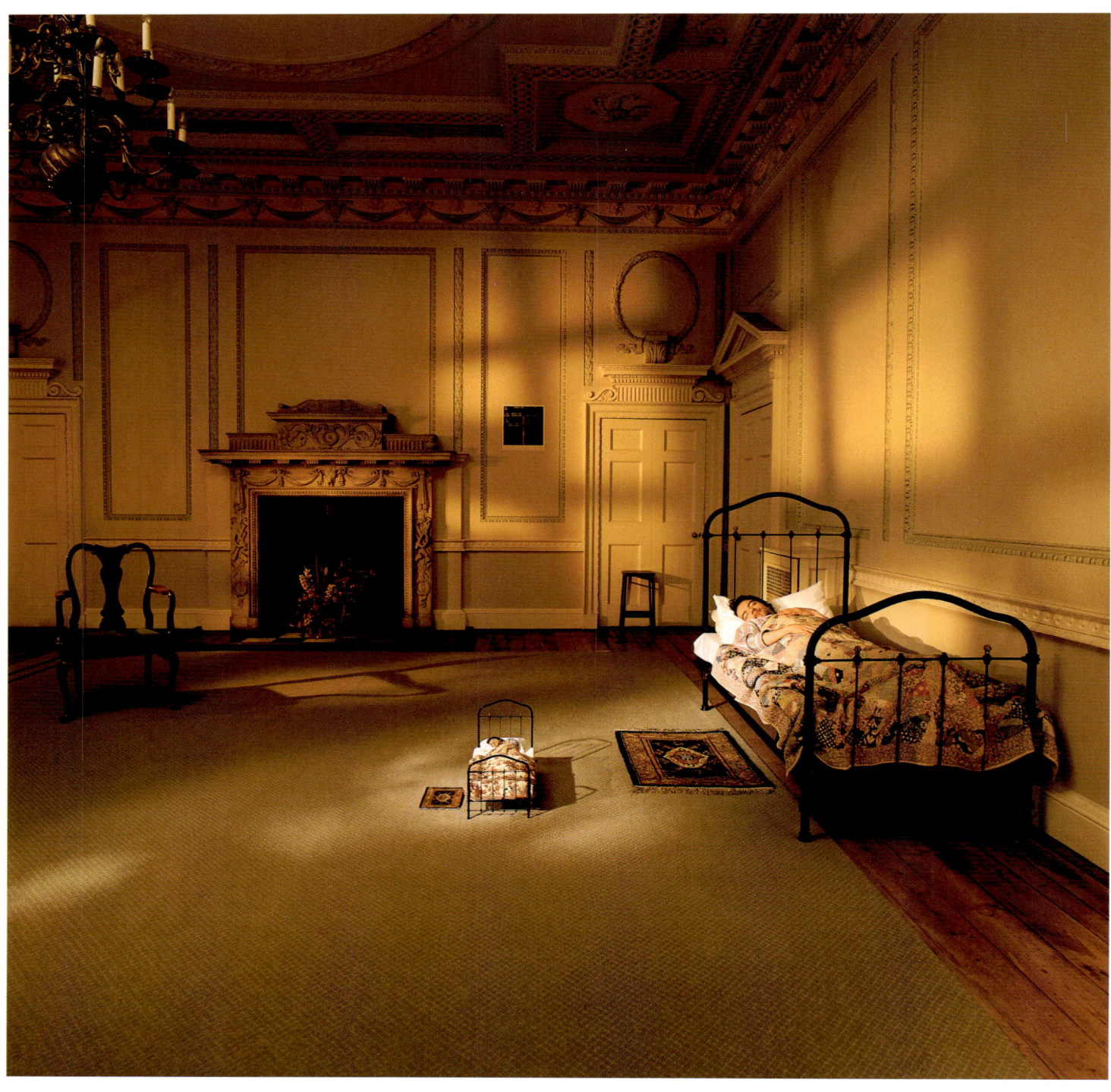

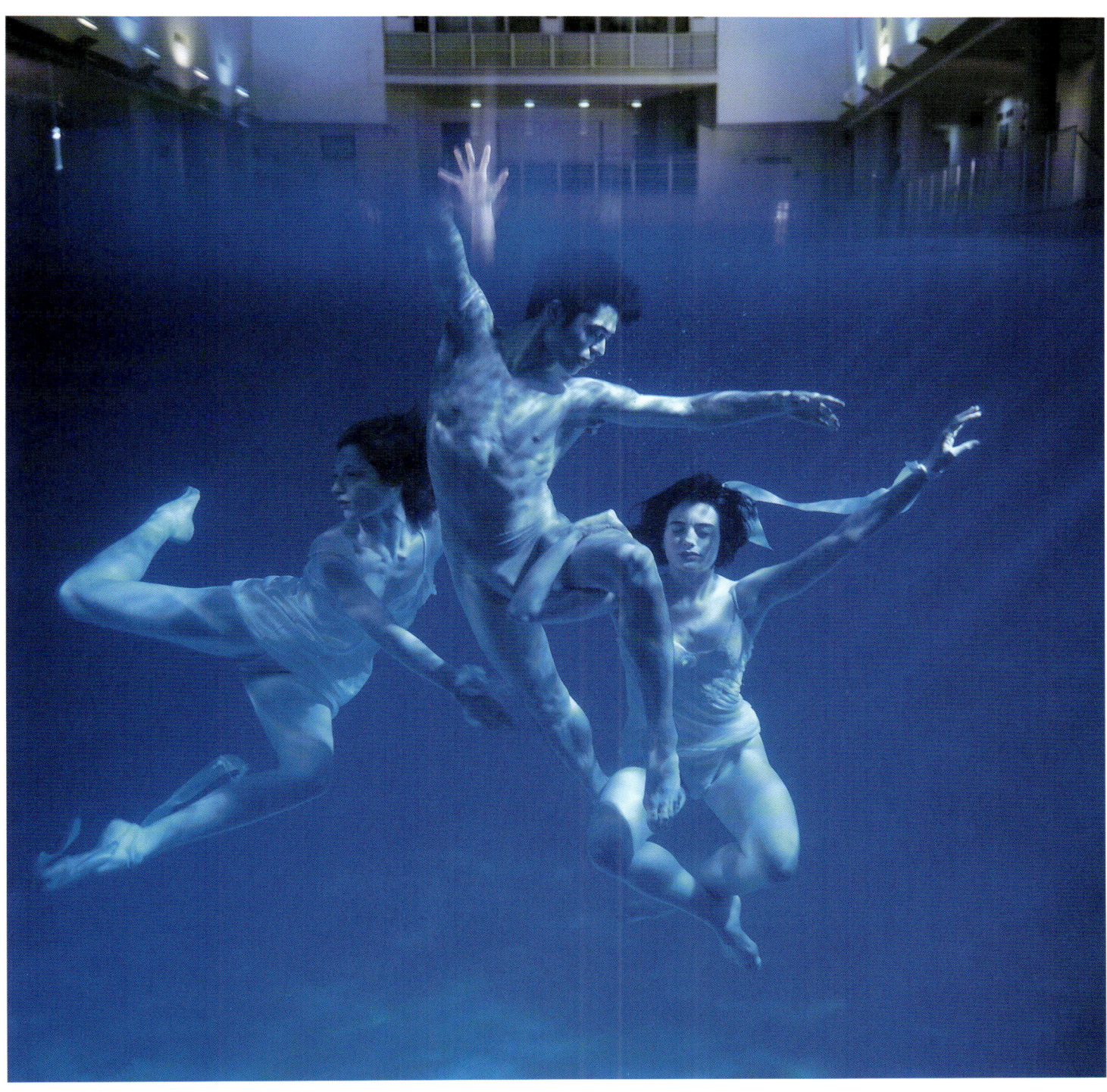

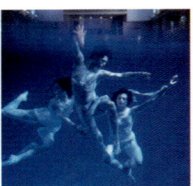

CHROME The music is the starting point for all design ideas and we played it over and over again in varying circumstances. We read and re-read the lyrics. And we talked, scribbled, thought hard, and gradually accumulated snippets, doodles and phrases which evolved by further discussion and thinking into more concrete ideas and recognisable sketches. 'Tip of the iceberg' was a phrase that recurred. But how to show the tip of something when the rest of it is hidden? There has to be a large part unseen, otherwise how can it be the tip of anything? The tip of an iceberg is only knowable from history, not from the data at hand, which is why they are so dangerous. Thus our 'iceberg' must be viewable in entirety yet its tip highlighted – hence water is the medium, as it is for a real iceberg, since it is transparent and one can see the tip (hand) above the surface with the bodies visible below. Bodies dressed in white like ice and triangular in outline again like an iceberg which therefore required dancers in formation. With me so far?

We found a location in Central London (the university swimming pool in Malet Street), hired some powerful tungsten lights, and devised a cunning method for taking the actual photographs.

The underwater camera was discarded because of lack of quality/definition incurred by the intervening glass of the protective housing. We could not shoot through a porthole below the surface (though the location had one) because it was just a bit too far beneath the surface, so we used an ordinary rectangular fish tank held near the the edge of the pool and submerged three quarters in the water, forming an air pocket, or rather a glass window or porthole of our own, now at water level. A junior bathysphere. By lying on the poolside our photographer Tony May could lean over and down into the fish tank with his usual trusty Hasselblad and take pictures as normal, except for a contorted position creating a certain discomfort, and plenty of complaint.

Chrome is unashamedly a favourite of ours, a good and appropriate idea realised through resolute endeavour, cooperative teamwork and a large slice of luck. The disembodied hand is actually the outstretched hand of the male dancer briefly visible above the water line. This is the tip of the iceberg, the tip of the three dancers, who are floating below the water level. The lapping water at the edge of our fishtank operated like a natural wipe and provided a double exposure, thus the hand is exposed out of water and the bodies exposed underwater. It amounted to an enormous slice of luck, unlike the most famous iceberg in history.

*Catherine Wheel **Chrome** CD front Fontana 1993*
Design & Photos StormStudios Location Malet Street, London

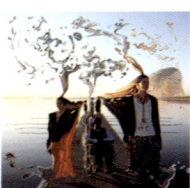

TELEVATORS A single release taken from The Mars Volta's fantastical album *Deloused In The Comatorium* needed a fantastical, haunting design. The music was echoey, moody and seemed to consist of elongated notes and chords, along with a recurring line of lyric 'Did you see the curse that flew right by you?', all of which made me think of ghostly, extended, fluid figures, originally intended to look like Munch but ending up more like Dali. The girls are the ghosts or 'curse' floating past the suicidal hero in the wheelchair. The jetty was chosen to help tell the story of what was (at the far end) and what is (near the camera) and also to refer to the bridge from which the tragic hero in the Mars Volta story threw himself. And just to cap it all, the light – low, strong winter sun in the calm waters of the lake – added greatly to the Scandinavian vibe, as in Munch, even though it later became like Dali. One good painter deserves another, or, as they say, one good Turner deserves anotherer.

*The Mars Volta **Televators** CD front Universal 2004*
Design & Photos StormStudios Location Heathrow, London

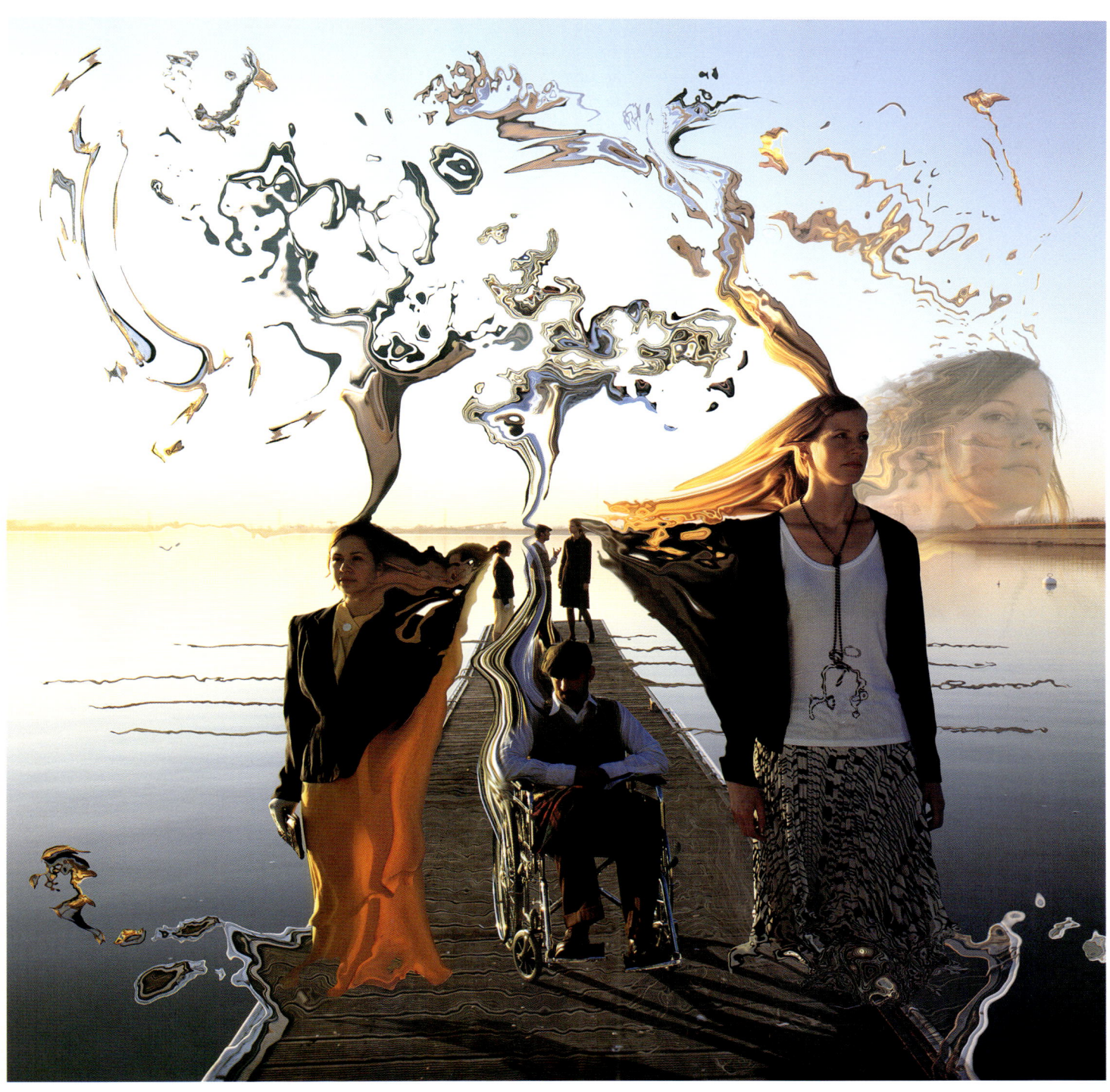

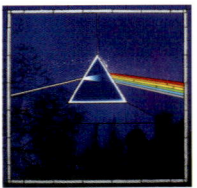

THE DARK SIDE OF THE MOON 30TH Pink Floyd's *The Dark Side Of The Moon* album was remixed from original tapes in 5.1 surround sound or Super Audio (SACD for short) to provide an even more detailed and splendid audio experience. It was the same music but not the same mix. A different beast in effect and it seemed appropriate to indicate as much on the cover by re-working the original design which was an airbrush illustration with line work for tint lay. What more fitting then than a glass rendition of the same design? A design about light (passing through a prism) represented via a medium of light, *i.e.* glass or rather a stained glass window. So simple, pure and succinct – a visual complement to the pristine surround sound provided by SACD.

The stained glass window was made in the same proportions as the original design but substituting a deep purple hue for the black background since black glass does not admit any light and might defeat the whole purpose. The stained glass window was photographed outside against a winter sun (actually in the back garden of a house belonging to one of Pink Floyd) highlighting the texture and imperfections of the glass itself. All very radiant we thought, especially in the flesh.

For reference and comparison are shown the original 1973 *The Dark Side Of The Moon* (an illustration) and the twentieth anniversary version of 1993 (a photograph).

Pink Floyd **The Dark Side Of The Moon** *CD front EMI/Sony 2003*
Design & Photos StormStudios Location Hampstead, London

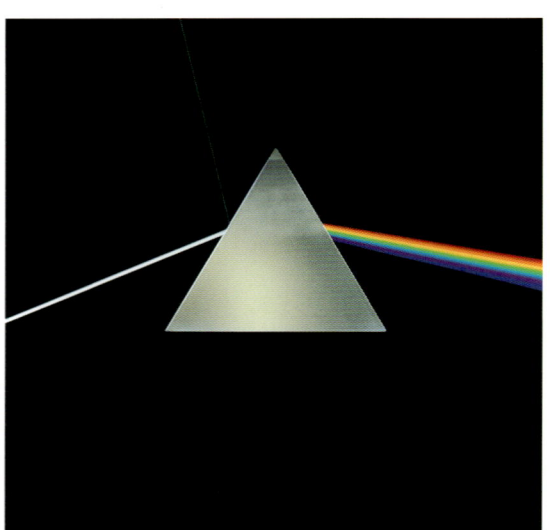

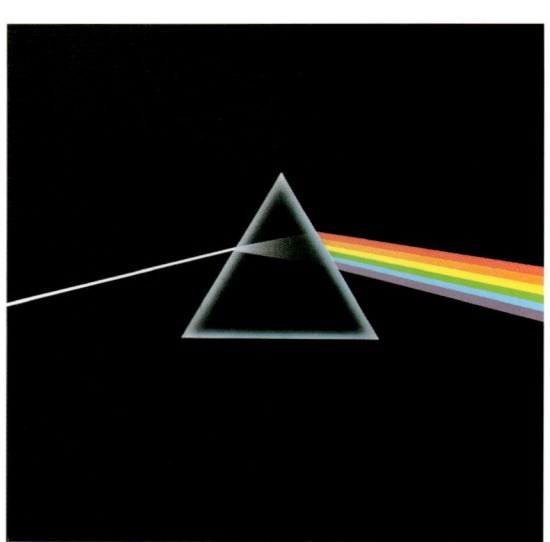

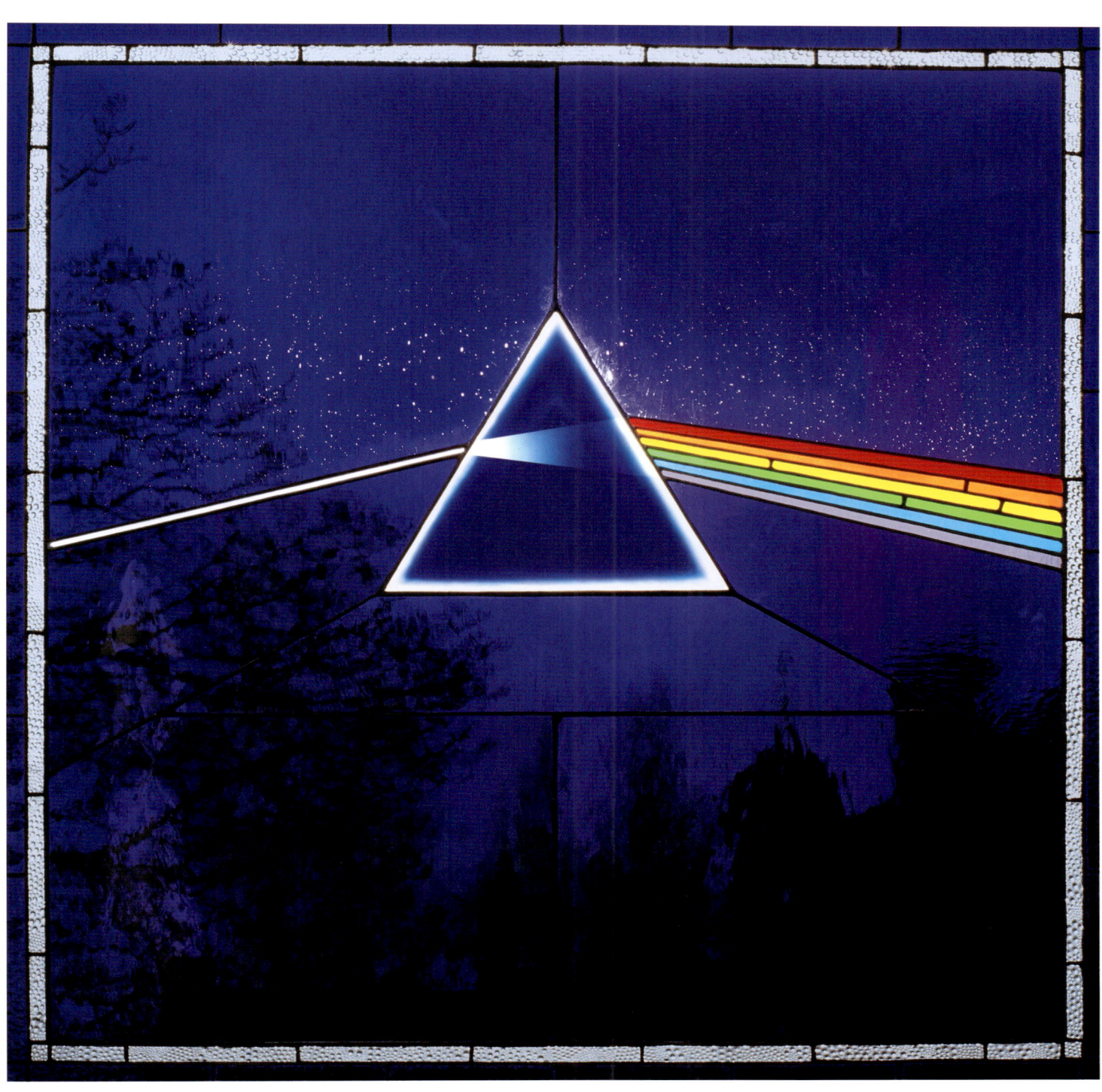

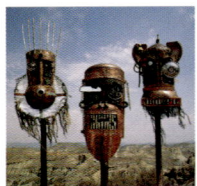

HOMELANDS Ellis, Beggs & Howard was a band from the Eighties consisting of three very different characters – Steve Ellis, white from up North, Nick Beggs, lately of Kajagoogoo, white from down south, and Austin Howard, black from London but born in Jamaica. They liked the idea of marking their ethnic diversity by calling their debut album *Homelands* – a musical homeland for whoever felt connected to, or even disconnected from, their real homeland. In cahoots with fellow designer Keith Breeden (Scritti Politti, The Mission, ABC and others) we came up with the idea that the edge of homelands, the borders between different tribal homelands, would be indicated by totems or masks representing different tribes.

We devised three such totems or masks (for the three band members) which Keith then proceeded to make from old boilers and motorbike parts – contemporary sculptures from scrap metal, suggestive of both modernity and ethnicity. A very physical and demanding exercise which Keith undertook with great relish and deftness to make three very original and particular totems which we then carted to a wild part of Spain to erect on poles and photograph by natural light, standing eerily like metal gargoyles guarding the musical homelands of Ellis, Beggs and Howard.

*Ellis, Beggs & Howard **Homelands** CD and vinyl front BMG 1988*
Design Storm Thorgerson & Keith Breeden Photos Andy Earl & Tony May Location Almeria, Spain

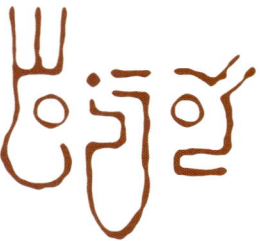

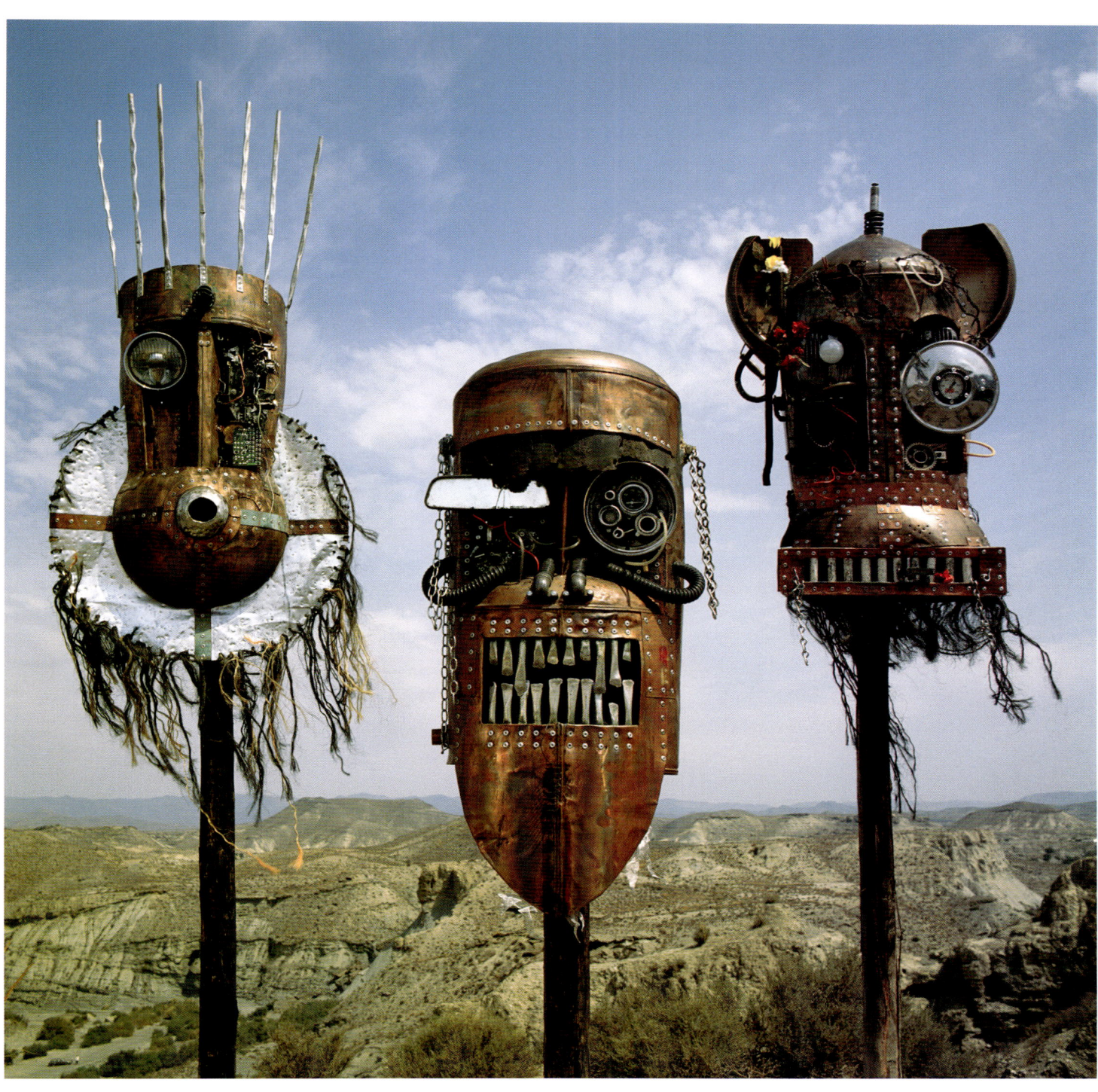

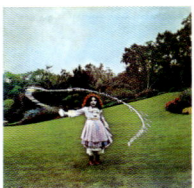

ON THE SHORE I'm not proud. If a good idea comes along I'll nab it. Good ideas, good insights, good designs, are all very useful and come from so many different sources that it is usually impossible to put your finger on exactly where they originate, but not in this case. The American artist John Blake, was at the Royal College of Art at the same time as me, and occasionally slummed it in our Hipgnosis studio. I mean by this that he was usually preoccupied with conceptual art, installations and esoteric projects, involving photographs, sculptures, recordings, texts, etc. I suspect he thought sleeve design was a bit lightweight if not too commercial and prone to be trite. He never said this, of course. He looked so like a Seventies TV sleuth called Cannon that we forgave him everything.

I was talking to him about Trees, a folk–band from the early Seventies, and about their singer Celia who had a very distinctive voice. I told him the album was called *On The Shore*, and he said, "I've got a thought, throwing water," a procedure close to my heart, for I have done thrown water, thrown paint, thrown milk both in stills and in movie because the shapes taken by flying liquid are often very dynamic.

A conversation ensued. I asked him, "What water?" "Out of a glass," he said. I asked, "Thrown by whom?" He said, "A girl", after the girl singer. But because the voice was so distinctive it was necessary to make the girl distinctive, almost magical, like in a children's story. And then we had it, an idea became an image. It would be a young girl in Victorian dress in a town garden. In this case a garden in a Hampstead park. Imagine a secret garden, wherein the ritual of throwing the water is akin to opening a portal, when she would then be 'on the shore' of some distant lagoon, or some far away planet even, before returning to the garden in Hampstead. Alternatively the water from the glass is the nearest she can get to a wave, falling on the metaphorical shore, stuck for the most part, as she is, in an urban garden.

I think the hand colouring is as much a response to the folkiness of the music, as it is to a then current infatuation of ours, evidence in UFO (below), also a black and white photograph hand coloured. This is the story of the faking of a UFO picture, because the band was called UFO and had a good sense of humour. The suburban husband throws the proverbial hubcap in the air whilst his suburban wife is taking the picture they will later misrepresent as a UFO sighting, but she's annoyed because we've caught her in the act, snapped her taking her fake photo of something she will later purport to be real. So what's fake and what's real, huh folks? UFOs right?

*Trees **On The Shore** Vinyl front CBS 1971 Design & Photos Hipgnosis & John Blake Location Hampstead, London*

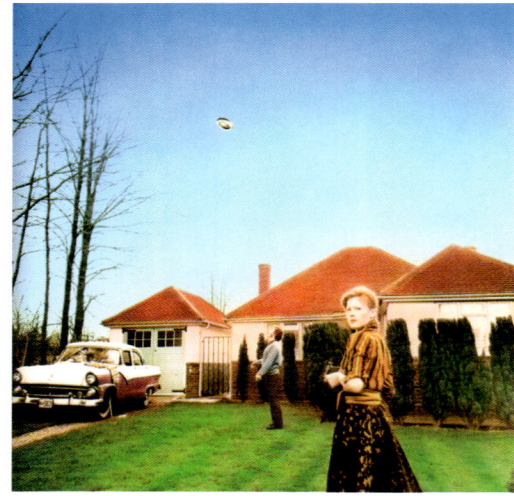

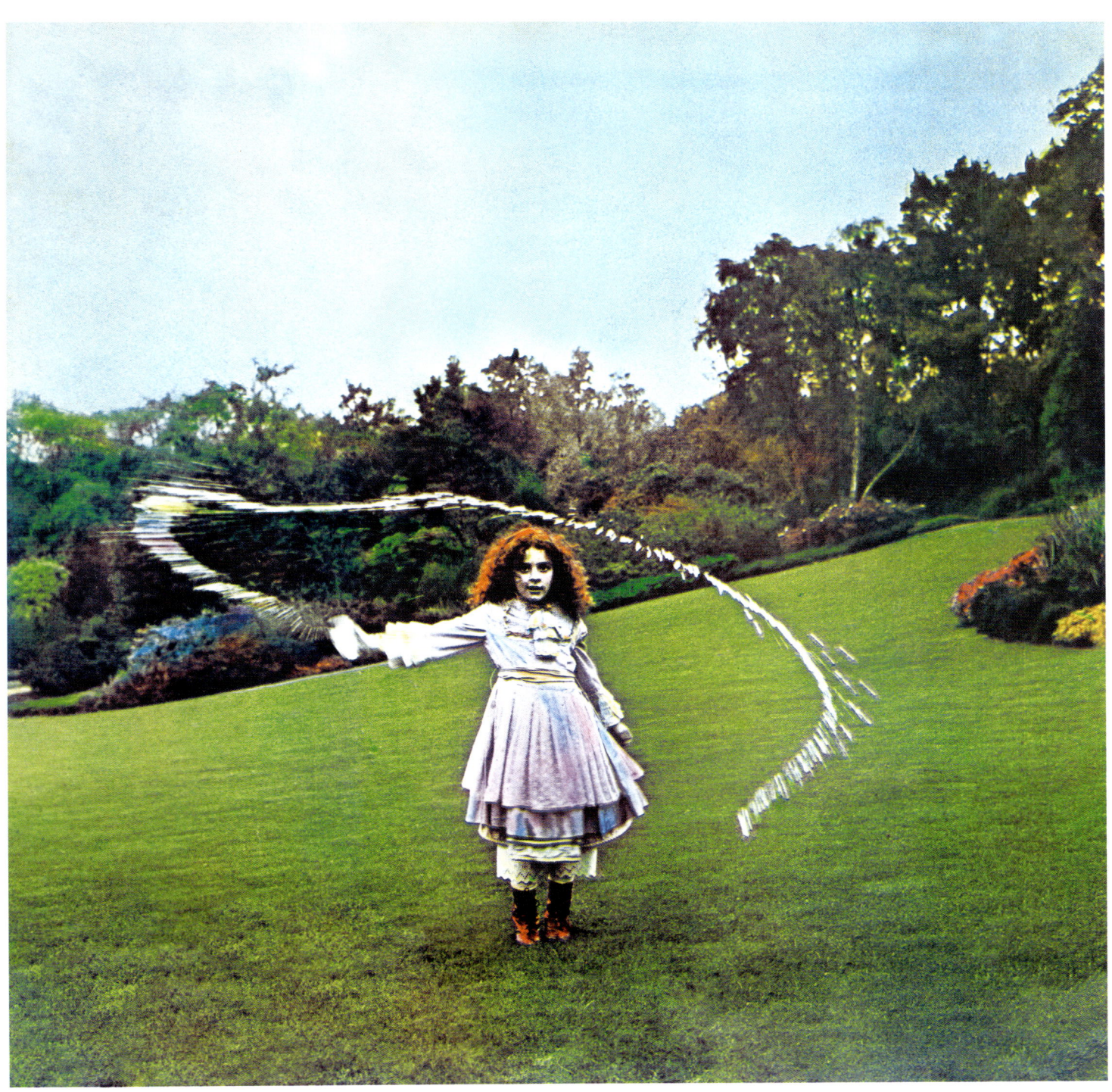

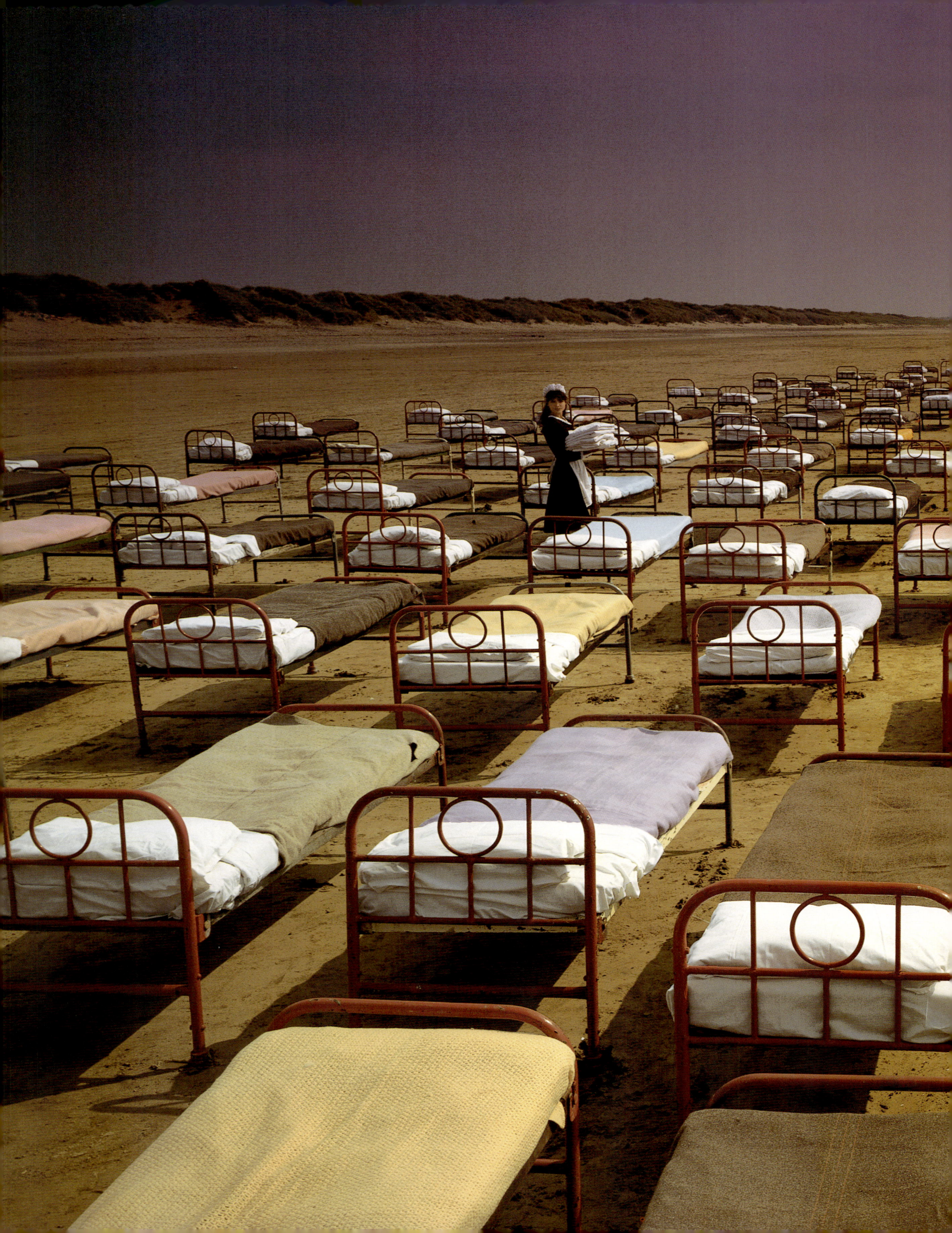

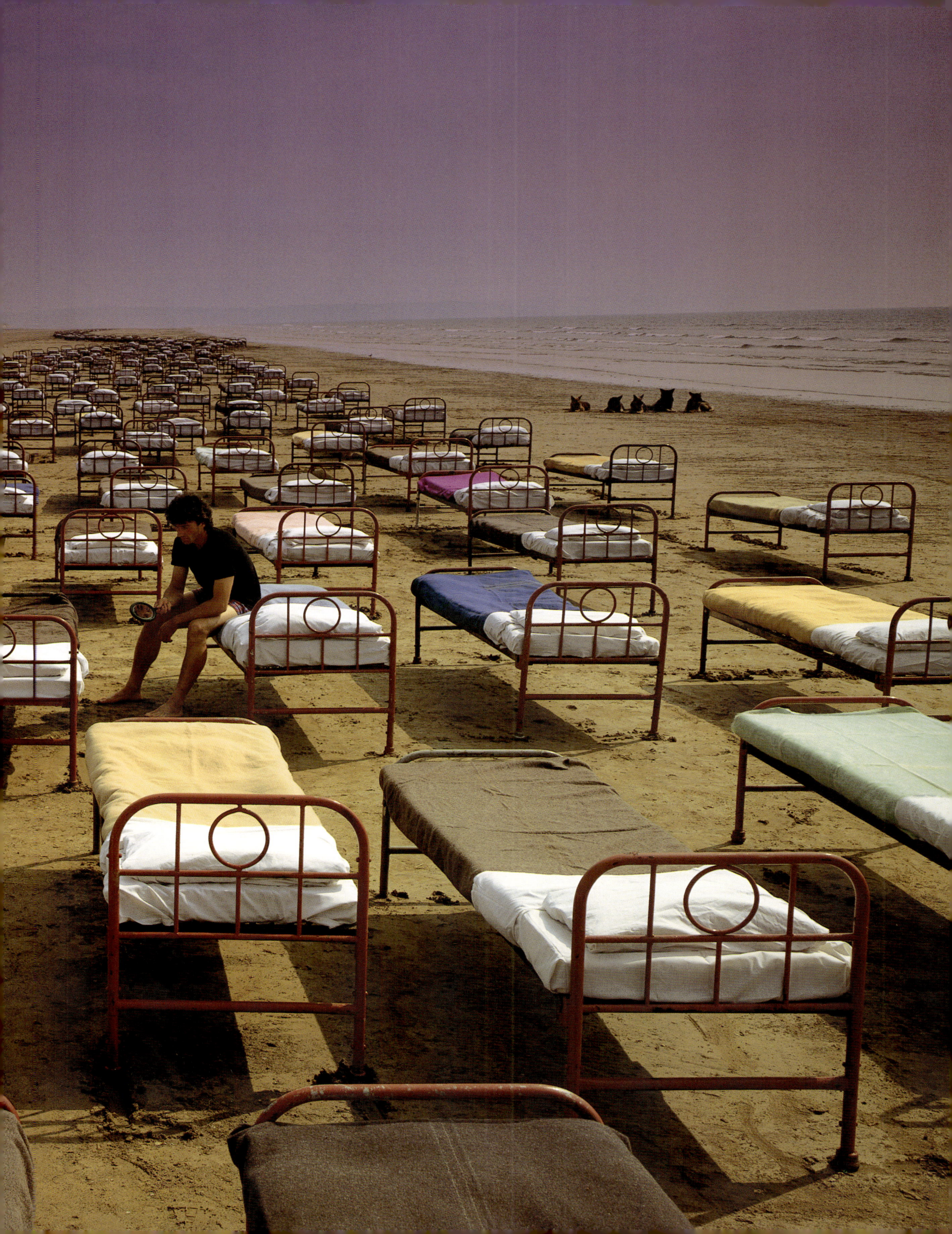

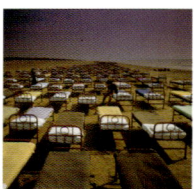

A MOMENTARY LAPSE OF REASON Like, but not like, The Mars Volta 'Televators', the design for *A Momentary Lapse Of Reason* (previous page) by Pink Floyd came initially from a line of lyric, namely 'visions of an empty bed' from the song 'Yet Another Movie'. The line prompted 'a vision of empty beds' stretching into the distance, winding away from the camera like a river, as in 'river bed'. It seemed preposterous enough to suit the album title: loads of beds sitting on a beach certainly constituted something crazy, an act of madness, a momentary lapse of reason at the very least. Considering the events that followed, the idea became even more appropriate.

In typical Floyd tradition we decided to do it for real. No computer trickery here, what you see is what you get. Seven hundred wrought iron beds on a beach, each one separately made up, using different blankets, sheets etc. The whole insane exercise took six hours using four tractors and flatbed trailers and 30 helpers. And to cap it all just as we began to shoot the weather turned ugly and it started to drizzle. We couldn't see the end of the beds and so abandoned the shoot and repeated the whole crazy thing two weeks later, which makes for two rather lengthy lapses of reason but also for a very gratifying result. The microlite in the sky and dogs on the beach are also in attendance along with the two characters and 700 hospital beds – beds of recovery since the Floyd were recovering from the departure of Roger Waters. It looked sufficiently mad enough in reality for some of it to rub off in the photograph. Who but the Floyd would be crazy enough to endorse shooting a vast number of empty hospital beds on a sea shore? And pay for it, the lovely crazy fools.

*Pink Floyd **A Momentary Lapse Of Reason** Vinyl gatefold EMI 1987*
Design Storm Thorgerson Photo Bob Dowling & Storm Thorgerson Location Saunton Sands, Devon

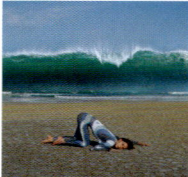

LATE SEPTEMBER Some things are truly difficult (*Transmissions* pg.49) and some are infected with bad luck (Healing Sixes pg.69) but this is one shoot where everything went well. Great locations, great weather, good model, fantastic waves, great organisation (thank you 2 Productions, Cape Town) excellent retouching care of Badger. Even the record company liked it (or is that the kiss of death?).

The idea came from something about 'keeping tabs', keeping up with the news, finger on the pulse i.e. having your ear to the ground I had also always wanted to use a very large wave or tsunami ever since *Dark Side*, when we had suggested a photographic version of the comic book hero the Silver Surfer. In our design the person with their ear to the ground had initially been aboriginal and the wave had been a wave of rock like Ayres Rock in Australia rather than a wave of water. The body painting, suggestive of depth contours on a map, came from some work Peter was doing on the CD booklet for Alan Parsons' *A Valid Path* (pgs.194-195) and suggests some unfathomable affinity with what's to come or some peculiar ritual involving the girl and the sea: does she know what's coming? Or is it about missing the obvious – she doesn't need to hear 'no distant drums' because she is about to be trashed by the tsunami. In fanciful moments I like to think of this design as Pink Floyd meets Roxy Music. Deepest Blue said they loved it, envisaging perhaps their music as about to wash over an unsuspecting public.

*Deepest Blue **Late September** CD front Ministry of Sound 2004*
Design StormStudios Location Cape Town, South Africa

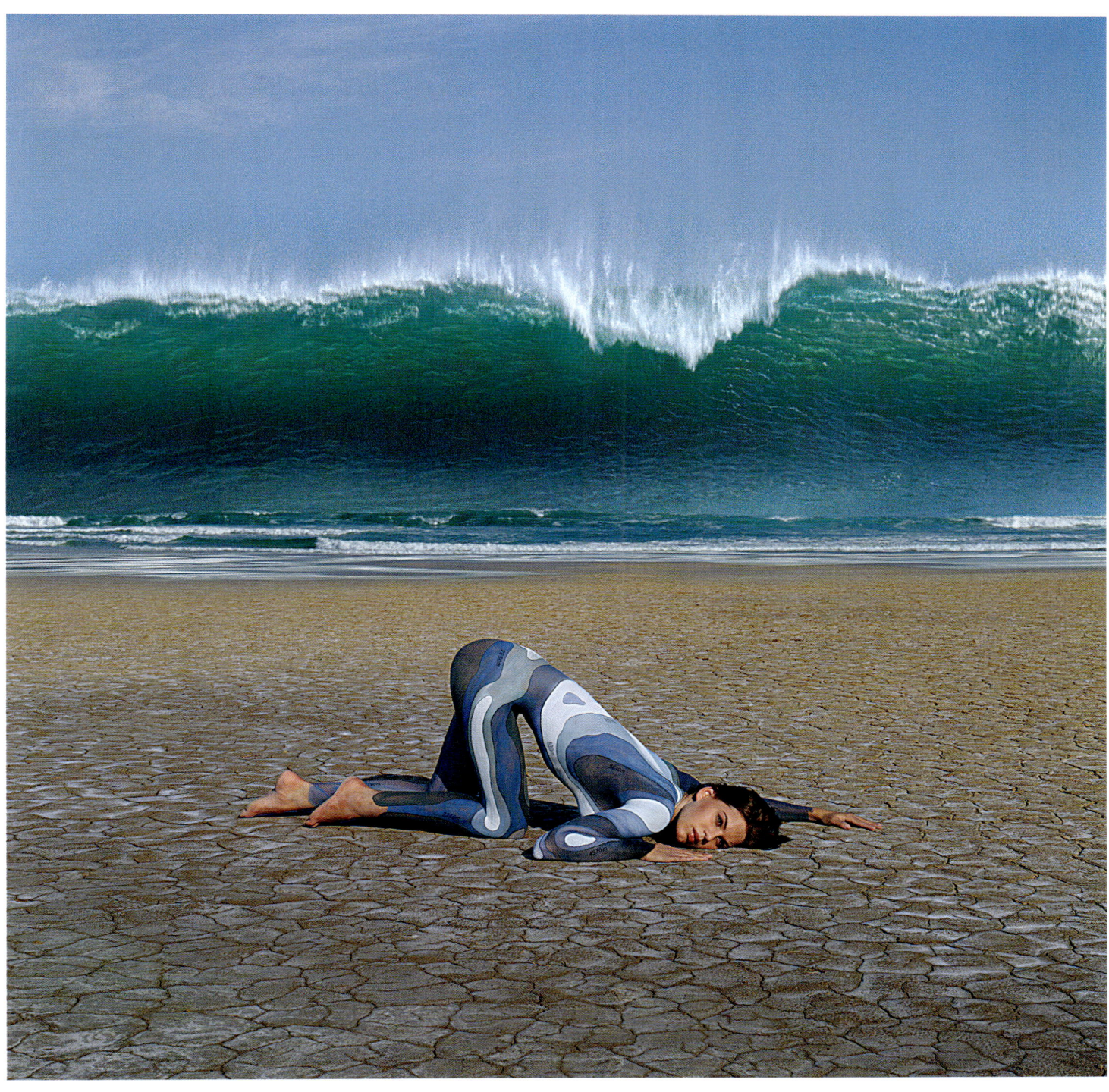

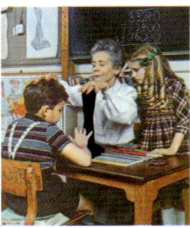

PRESENCE I was greatly impressed that Led Zeppelin, the mighty Led Zeppelin, could take this low key, off the wall, domestic semi-kitsch, partially retro design... so obscure really. Impressed and delighted because I always felt that the understatement adds to the power of the image.

A standard, bourgeois family – mum, dad and two kids – sit around a table in some strange marina (actually an indoor boat show) not to eat or commune but to examine an oddly shaped black object that seems to enthral them. Seems they don't need much else – the table is bare. Does the black object represent Led Zeppelin? All the family needs is to bask in their musical emanations.

The object (or power source) was as mysterious as Led Zeppelin. It didn't need to be physically huge because it was powerful. The family are invigorated (refuelled) by exposure to the object, one of which could sit in every home in the land becoming the new totem or religious icon revitalising our humdrum lives.

The retro quality was a response to homely kitsch photos overused by Art Directors to adorn album covers – a way of thinking and working which I found very annoying, the recycling of old tat and stifling new creation, thereby putting the likes of us out of work. The final twist or icing on the cake was to make the black object no object at all but rather an oddly shaped hole – an absence rather than a presence (Led Zeppelin were so powerful that the thought of them was enough, they didn't have to be there in the flesh). There are no shadows or moulding on the 'object' just flat black – hence it is a hole. I once demonstrated this 'illusion' to an audience in Japan and to a particular fan who had loved the cover for years, 25 years to be precise. He was fascinated to learn the significance of the black object but appalled to discover it was not an object at all, but a hole - a hole cut in the wall in the appropriate shape. I invited him to put his hand in, to prove it was a hole but he refused, shocked and shaken it seemed, by the merciless disabusing of a long held belief. Not a presence (an object) but an absence (a hole). I remembered feeling both sad and elated.

Led Zeppelin **Presence** *Vinyl front Swansong 1976 Design & Photos Hipgnosis George Hardie*

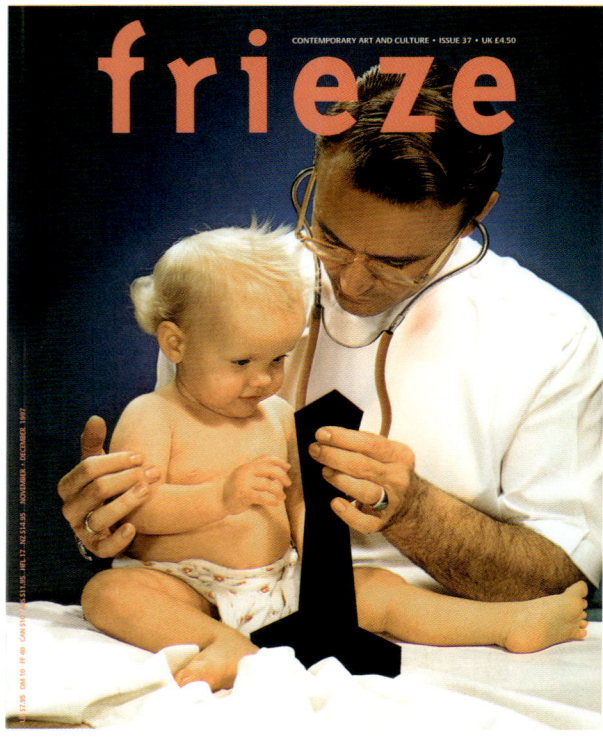

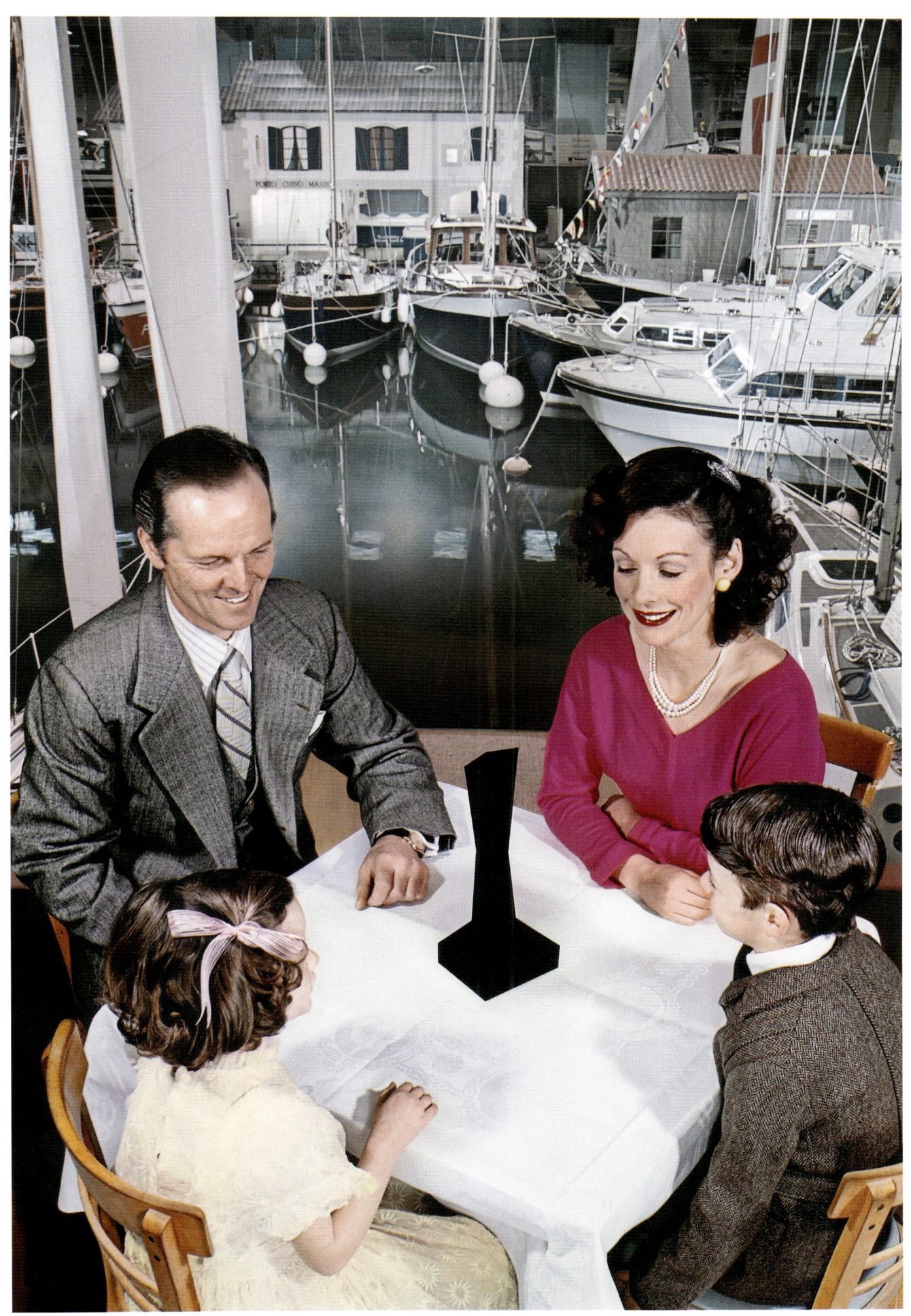

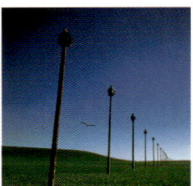

TRANSMISSIONS When I look at this picture, I think I must have been a bit crazy, because it was such a nightmare to produce. Doing it for real, my avowed philosophy, necessitated on this occasion huge wooden telegraph poles (20 of them, which in turn required locating and transporting them), bulldozers, pile drivers, and teams of rugged chaps to help erect the poles in conditions – not that you'd know looking at the end result – which were truly abysmal, comprising acres of wet slushy mud, wind and driving rain. Whichever memory I dredge up serves only to confirm a suspicion of implicit madness, be it the awkwardness and sheer weight of the poles, or the bad tempered farmer who doubled his location price the night before the shoot; be it digging holes deep enough for the poles to remain erect, or persuading luckless friends and models that they were perfectly safe sitting on top (and how they wouldn't die of exposure or vertigo no siree), and for what? All for a band with an overstated name, ecological leanings, mixed motives, lofty ideals, no financial profit, and a shitload of aggravation. Just as well I like the environment. Just as well I like the image, or I'd know for sure there was a screw loose.

And there they are sitting atop their poles, stretched out across the landscape transmitting their message skywards, mental transmissions forming a line or thread like beacons of old, receivable at a distance, the message free from ground interference, free from the business of everyday life, the messengers atop their special poles saying save our planet, save the Earth from its own suicidal tendencies. This message can only be successfully transmitted if human transmitters do it together, focussed, in concert combining the energies of lots of people at the same time. Fanciful you might say, but overwhelmingly desirable.

Gentlemen Without Weapons **Transmissions** *CD & vinyl front A&M 1988*
Design Storm Thorgerson Photos Tony May Location Cambridge

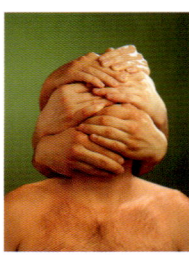

GRAPHICA OBSCURA These wrap around hands were an idea, I think, from slimline Finn, our resident black frocked artiste, who had a fondness for Arabian visuals, and I suspect this idea was some mad turban, a turban of hands, whereas I always saw it as a deranged variation of the way women wrap towels round their heads after bathing - a towel of hands. Either way what you get is what you see, no trickery here (well, just a touch) though the man under the wrapping hands sees very little. This image was used ironically to advertise an exhibition of our photographic work held in my father's home town of Drammen in Norway.

Not camera obscura, but graphica obscura.

Graphica Obscura *Exhibition poster Norway 2002 Design & Photos StormStudios*

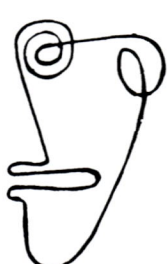

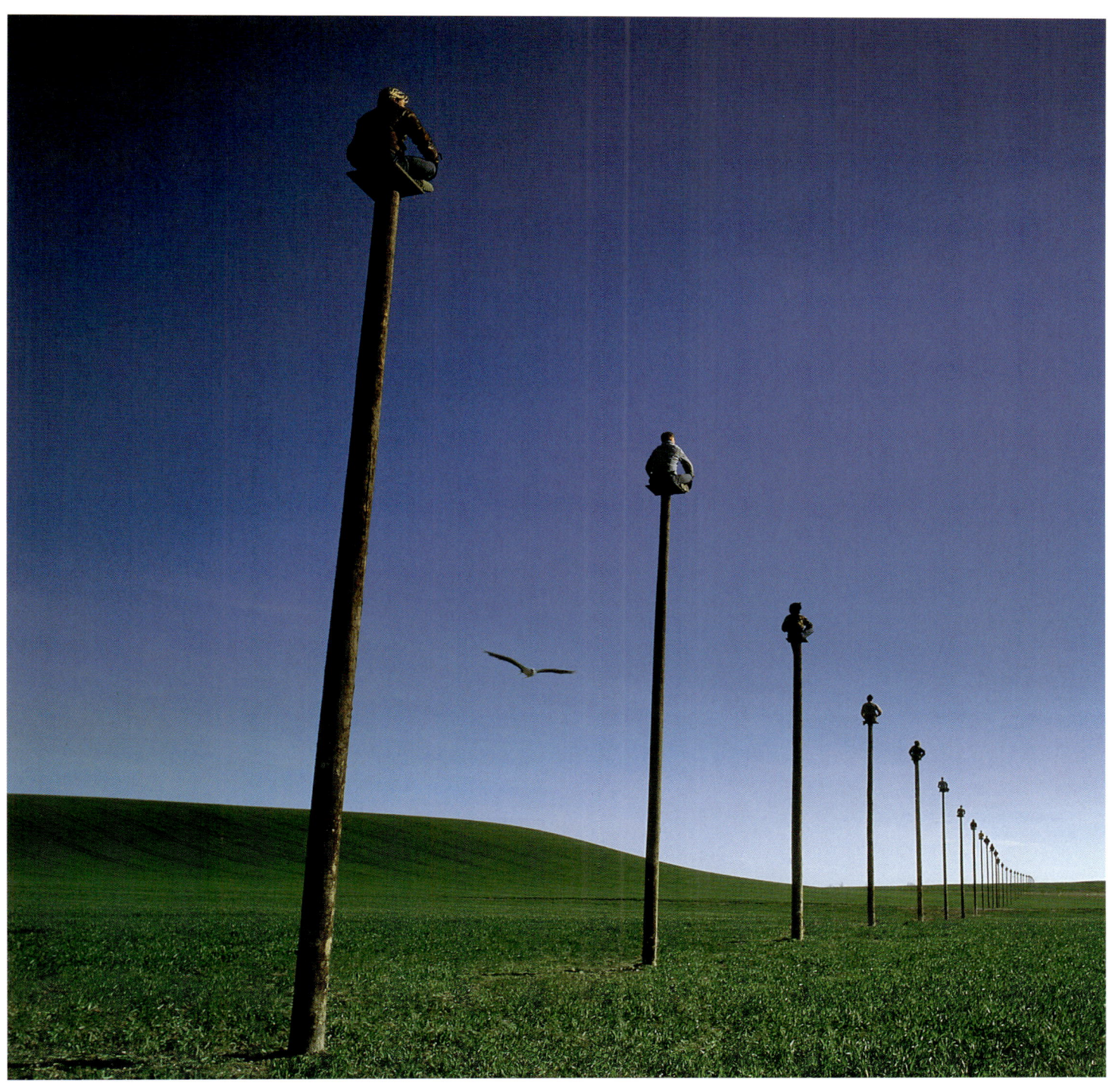

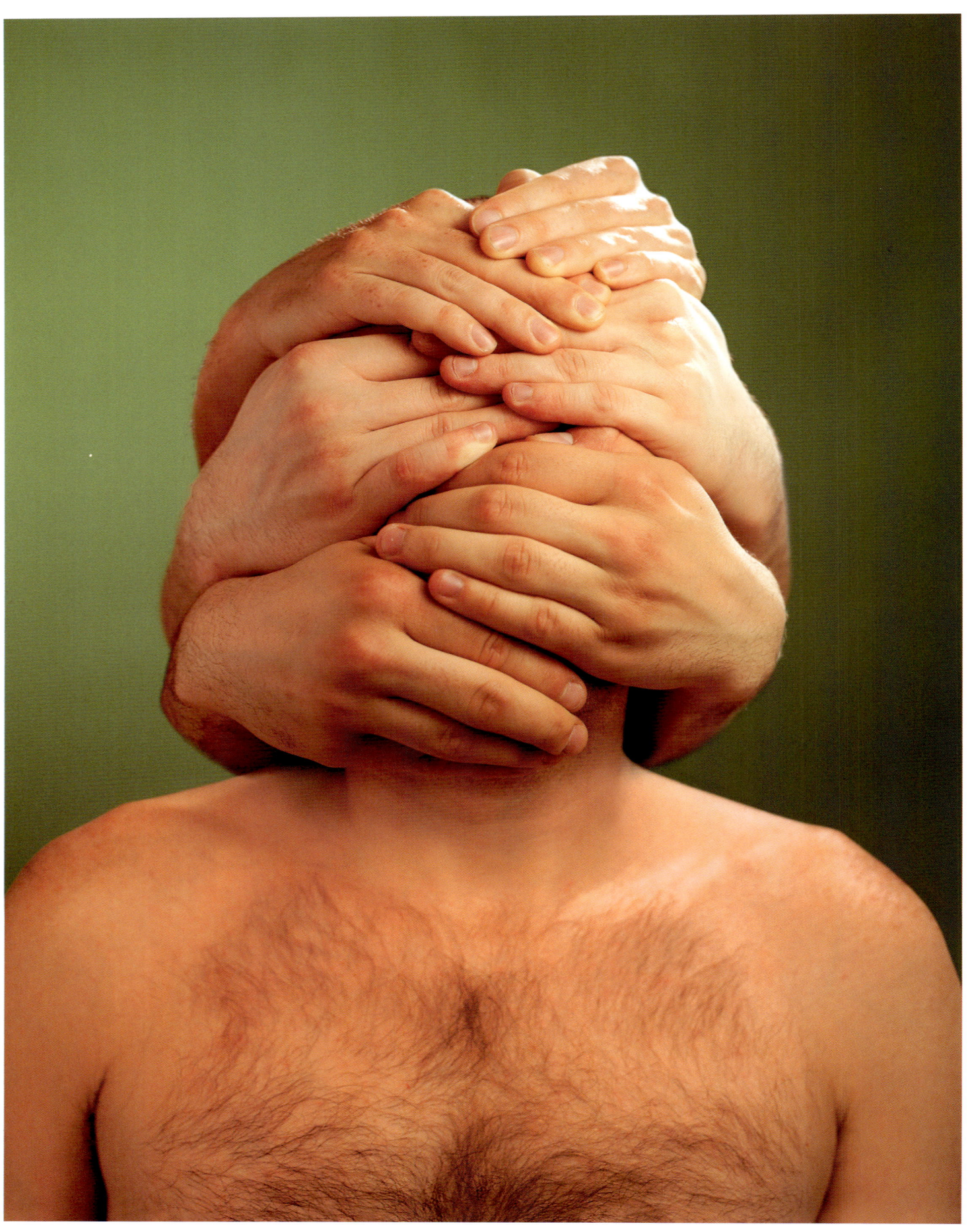

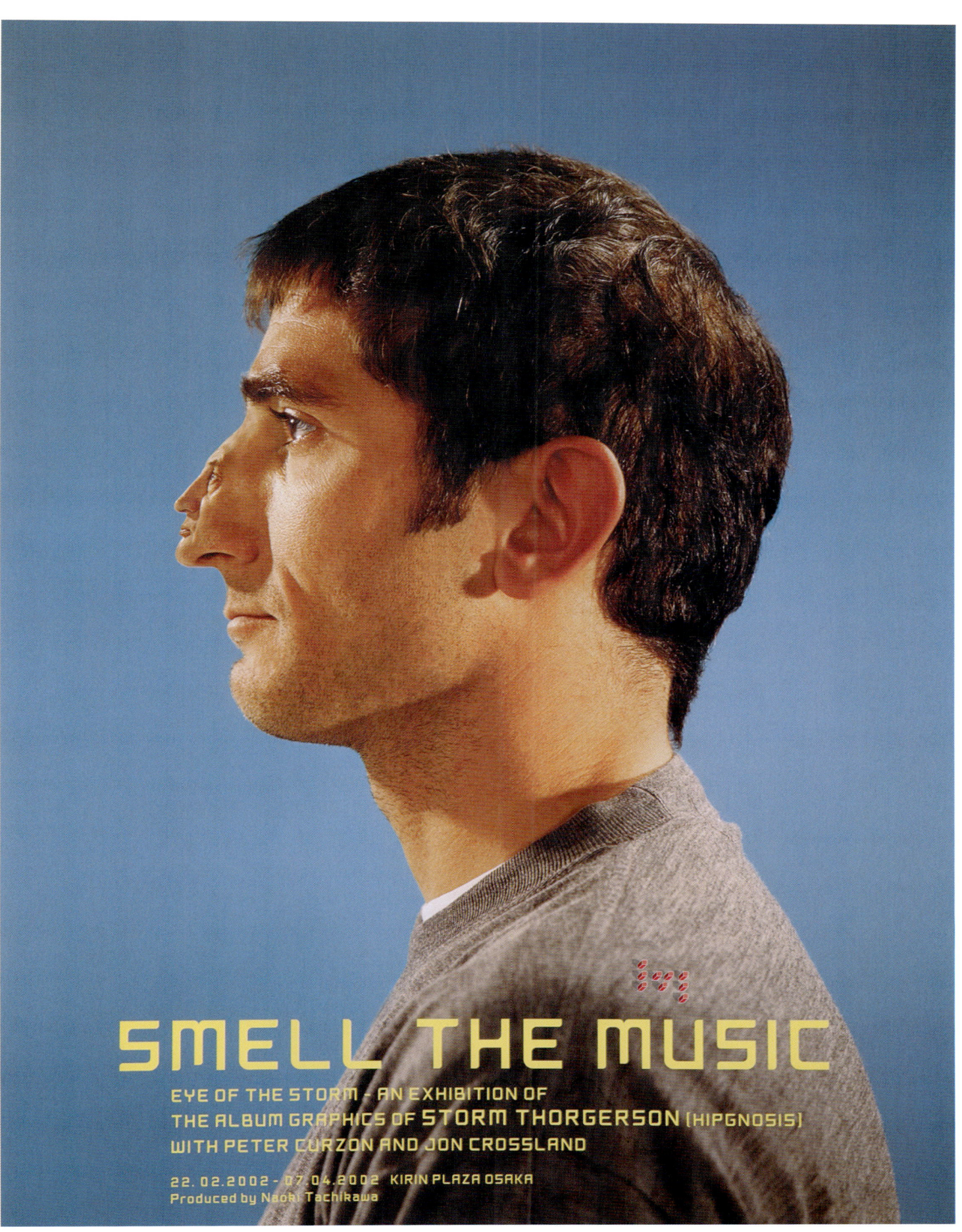

SMELL THE MUSIC

EYE OF THE STORM - AN EXHIBITION OF
THE ALBUM GRAPHICS OF STORM THORGERSON (HIPGNOSIS)
WITH PETER CURZON AND JON CROSSLAND

22.02.2002 - 07.04.2002 KIRIN PLAZA OSAKA
Produced by Naoki Tachikawa

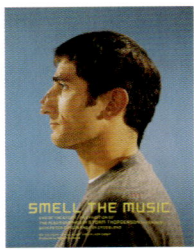

SMELL THE MUSIC This design was also used as a poster for another exhibition but in Japan, set in a department store in Tokyo. This is apparently quite a cool thing to do in Japan. I thought their very particular mindset might enjoy both the title and the insane picture of a talking nose with a face on it, or more specifically emerging from it. This deranged design was from Peter and was, I recall, a rendition of the idea of a Homunculus or voice inside one's head, being not a voice of conscience but a litttle person, a separate entity living in the brain, who is seen in our picture trying to escape its host and is taking the shortest exit route through the nose.

Smell The Music Exhibition Poster Japan 2001 Design & Photos StormStudios

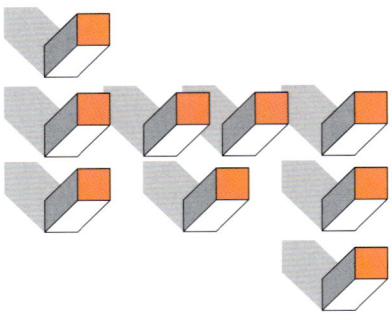

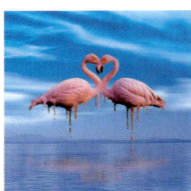

YOU AND ME We are not often prone to romanticism or sentiment but hey, there are times... 'You And Me' was a simple love song and something romantic and lyrical. We had been pursuing melting images for some time and in addition flamingoes had been a possible subject matter but we had been unable to fuse these thoughts successfully until this moment. Somewhere in my memory banks there is a trigger of Valentine's Day, represented by a heart, which then involved dripping flamingoes who were so deeply in love that they were melting together, in a heart shape. This seemed an appropriately romantic image for this romantic song, but without being too much of a cliché.

With the mercurial brilliance of Jon Crossland this idea was turned in to a great image, or so I feel. (Perhaps Jon didn't feel the same for he disappeared soon after to California to get married, so he said.) It was the long necks of the flamingo that made the entwining possible, an aspect which was verified by a visit to a local park in my part of London where there are flamingoes. Jon's artistry was to effect the retouching so that the necks caressed gracefully and also that the dripping quality added a sense of mystery and lyricism, this being no ordinary event but one of the imagination – just for you and me.

The Cranberries **You & Me** *7" single MCA 2000 Design & Photos StormStudios*

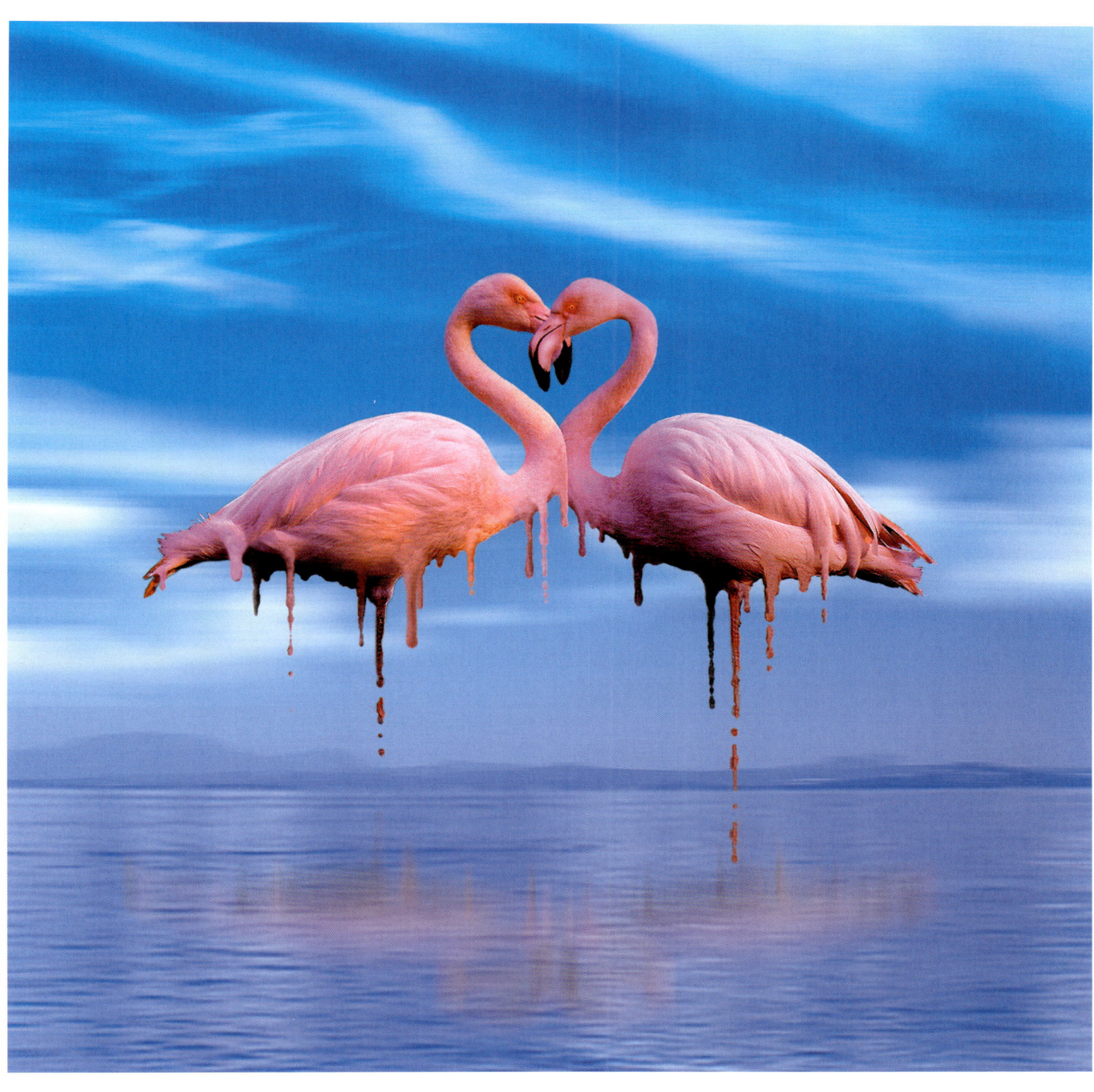

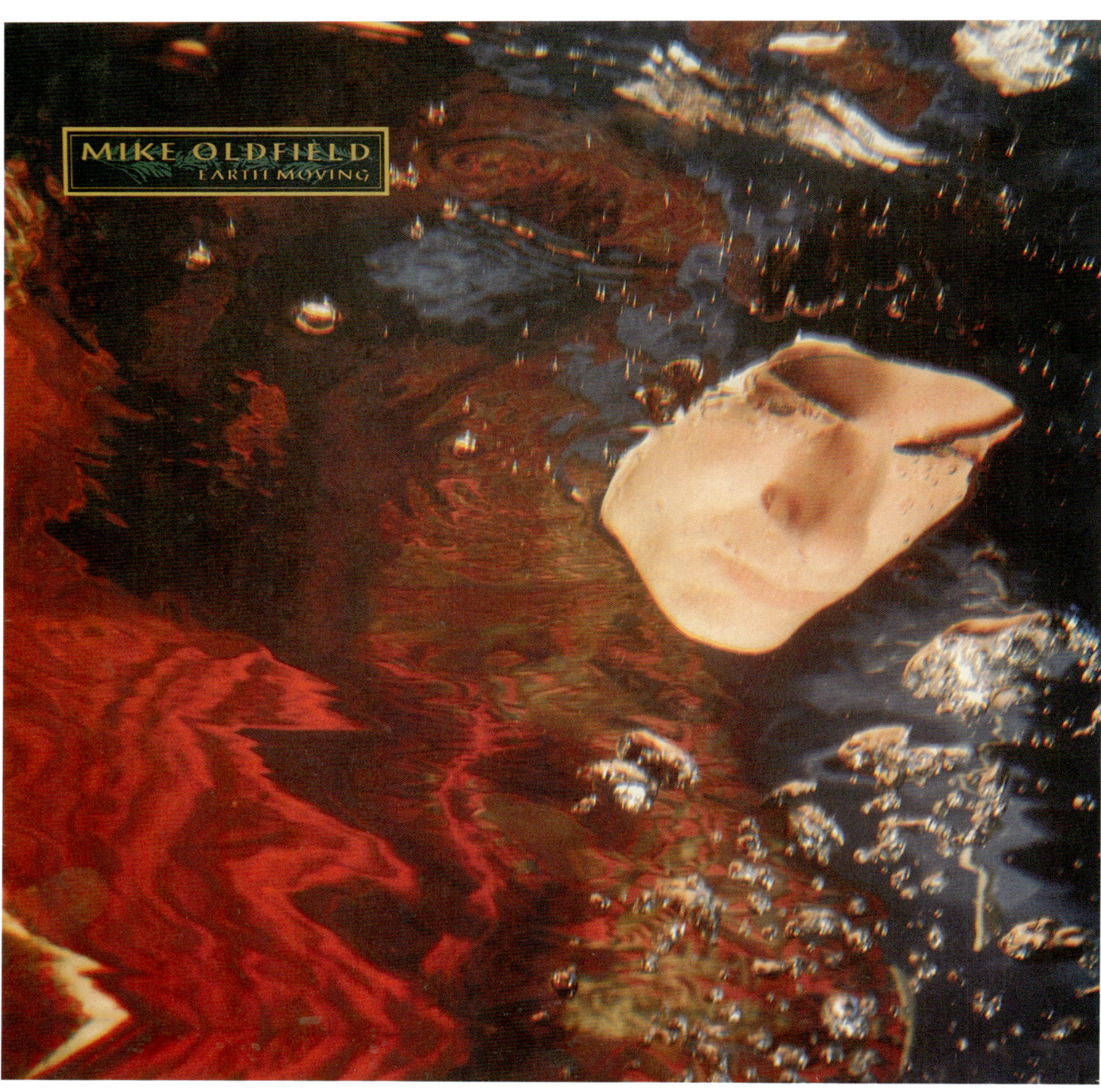

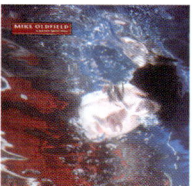

EARTH MOVING What you love most hurts you most - aint that the truth? I lurve swimming underwater be it in a swimming pool, fresh water or open sea, it's all just fab to me, but, four years ago whilst on summer holidays my ears were sloshing, they felt and sounded like my head was immersed in a bucket of water. It drove me round the twist, especially at night. No matter how much I dried my ears and jumped up and down on one leg, the sloshing continued.

When I got home Ian Dury told me to see his ear specialist, the wonderful Mr Bull, who said, "Son, you have swimmer's ear," and promptly showed me a book called *Swimmer's Ear*, would you believe? Swimmer's ear, like surfer's ear, is a condition of excessive bone growth wherein the bones of the middle ear grow to protect themselves from the cold water, forming a kind of ridge, behind which water can collect next to the ear drum, and unable to get out. The cure is simply to wear ear-plugs, de luxe, custom-made ones that is, which keep the water out and prevent the great sloshing.

The upside of swimming underwater is the beauty, the sense of floating in the void, drifting, flying above the ground, and when you look up you may see a blurry vision of the outside world, or if the angle is at a certain degree the surface of the water acts like a mirror, and reflects the ground beneath, or the side of a pool, which is what this picture is.

The redoubtable Andy Earl and I had a five feet square tank built, which we filled with water. As we looked up through the tank side, the underside of the water surface reflected the floor of the tank, upon which we laid coloured material. The cool thing about this mirror is that it is soft - you can put your head through it, literally by putting you head over the tank side and immersing in the water, which is exactly what Mike Oldfield did, the clever chap.

*Mike Oldfield **Earth Moving** Vinyl front Virgin 1986*
Design Storm Thorgerson Photos Andy Earl & Storm Thorgerson

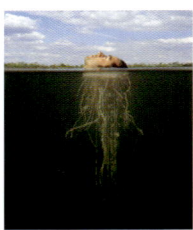

DE-LOUSED IN THE COMATORIUM Wild, eccentric, eclectic music from two of the most delightful and talented musicians ever, plus a very tight band, make up The Mars Volta. Progressive rock indie laced with jazz overtones, a soupçon of Latin American and a dash of punk – powerful and always inventive, fast and furious episodes interspersed with lyrical atmospheric passages - all this and the guys a joy to work with at the time.

Their album *De-loused In The Comatorium* is a collection of songs detailing the tragic history of a friend of theirs from school days in El Paso and Juarez, Mexican border towns. This much admired friend lapsed into a coma and drifted in and out of consciousness, alternately surfacing into the daylight of a shared reality or sinking into the murky waters of his own mind, populated by artistic demons intent on dragging him down. Our jellyfish/jellyhead, floating at the water's surface, seemed a suitable rendition, looking in part like a Portuguese Man-of-War but also half human, half nasty tentacles, making its poisonous way across the sea of consciousness. A nightmarish vision like the nightmares they imagined their friend had to endure when lapsing into coma.

*The Mars Volta **Deloused In The Comatorium** CD Album front cover*
Universal 2003 Design StormStudios Location Heathrow, London

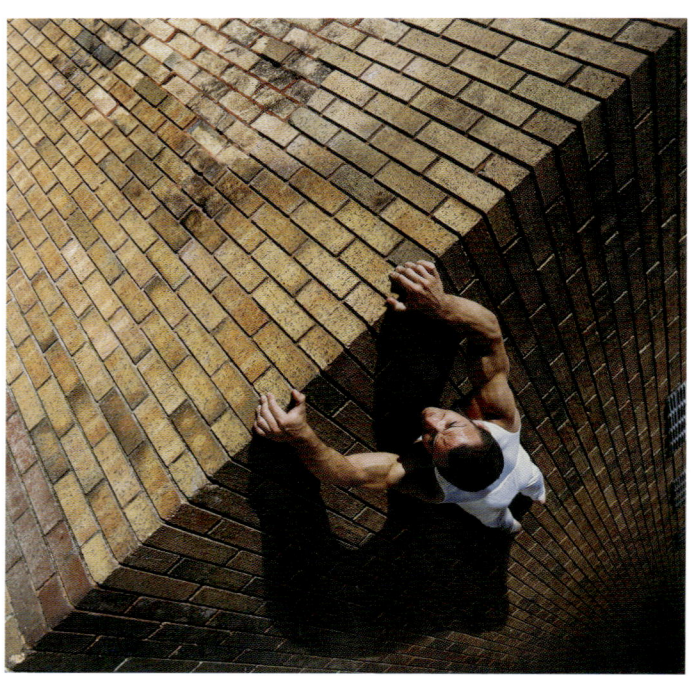

*The Mars Volta **Inertiatic esp** 10" Vinyl front cover Universal 2003 Design StormStudios*

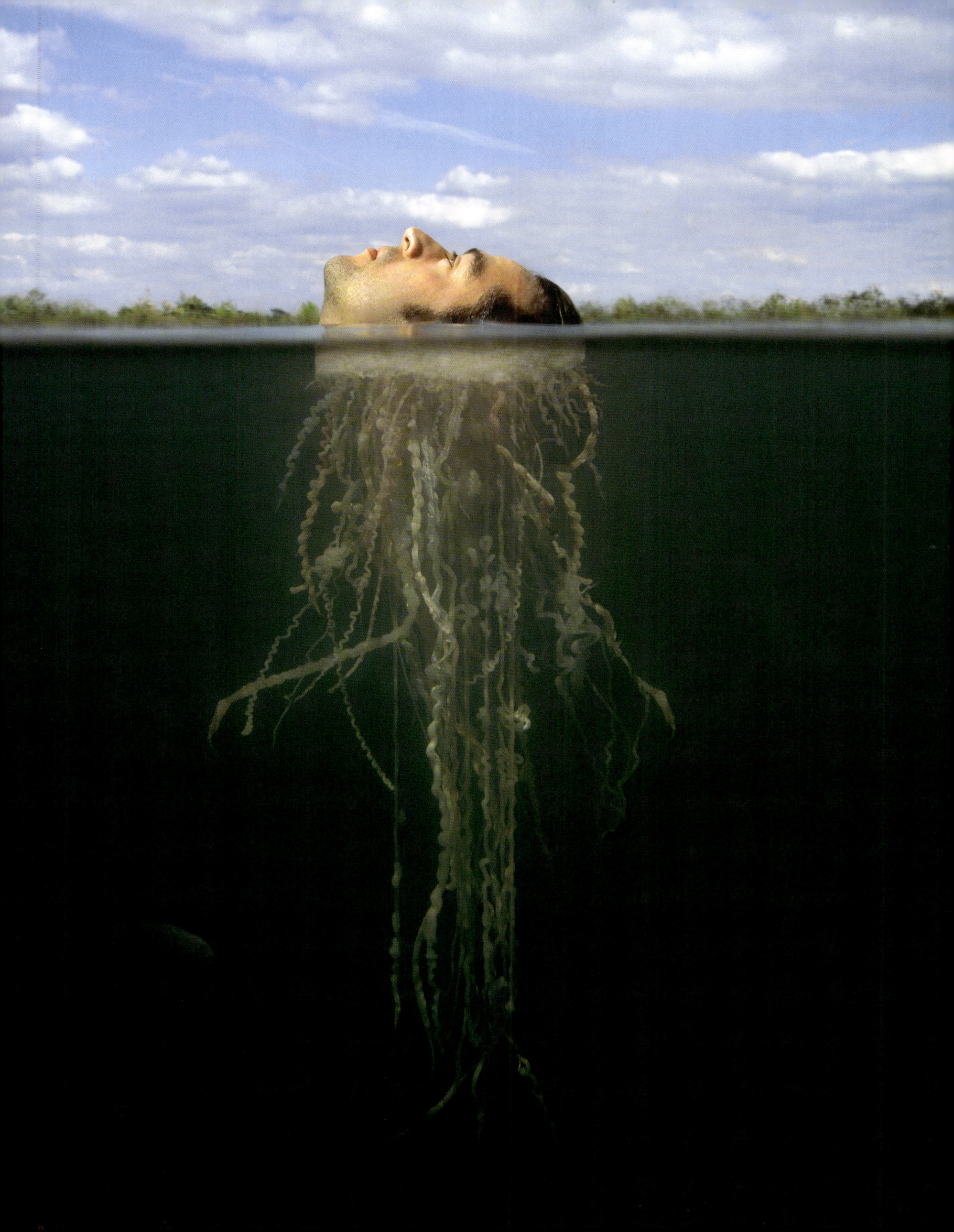

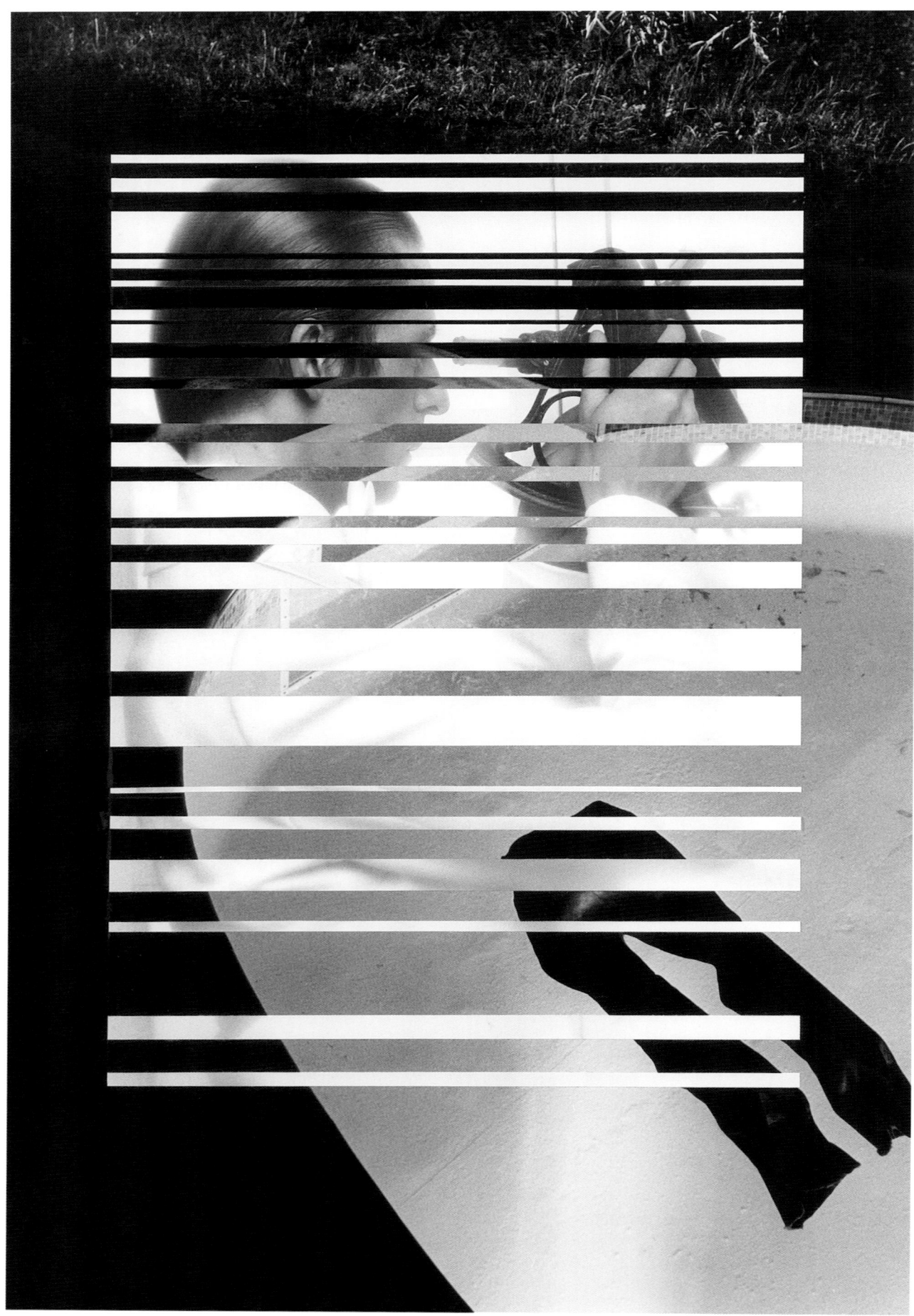

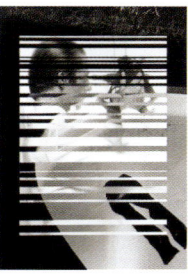

JEAN POOL What silly humour! Gene Pool – *Jean Pool* – a pair of jeans in a pool – but so useful in some ways in opening avenues to lateral and surreal thoughts and images. This one was designed for a poster for a play presented by the theatre troupe Lumiere & Son run by Hilary Westlake and David Gale whose humour can be pretty silly too, though invariably there was an edge, be it macabre cross-referenced or damnedly clever.

Where was I? – Ah yes, devining the source of these jeans in a pool, looking like a corpse, better at night underlit by pool lights, floating eerily like a scene from a Ross Macdonald thriller, which was doubly appropriate since the play featured a surreal detective. Hence our detective is dressed in a dapper white suit and is using a sextant rather than a magnifying glass. Because the play is full of dual layer and double meanings, this design attempts to incorporate the 'two pictures in one' principle, you either see the detective or the jeans in the pool. If you see both at the same time you're nothing but a smart Alec! Which of course, was the name of the detective in the play.

Lumiere & Son **Jean Pool** *Theatre Poster 1978 Design & Photos Hipgnosis*

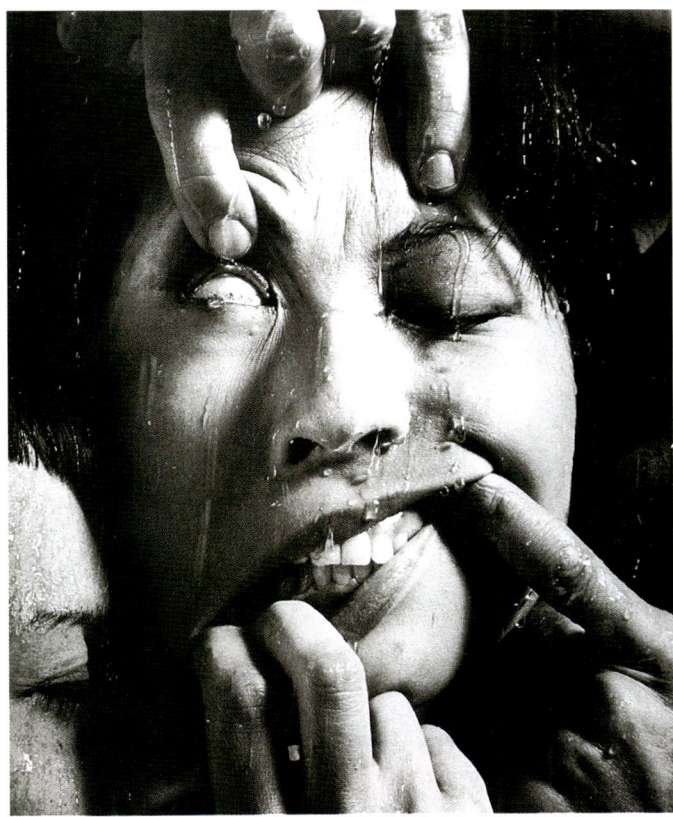

ONION LADIES Wild Perry Farrell - a name possibly derived from 'peripheral' or 'partly feral'? One 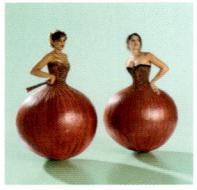 never knows - asked us to design a cover for Jane's Addiction, which seemed a bit weird, I can tell you, since he designed a pretty good cover himself, *Nothing Shocking*. So why come to us? I should've read the signs and known the trouble it would cause. Perry said he wanted something very sexual and provocative, I think, in fact, he actually said he wanted sex. Not with me I presume.

Sitting around trying to think about something sexual as part of a job is harder than you think, a bit of a turn-off actually, like thinking of your parents having sex! Anyway we tried jolly hard, submitted several designs, of which he chose two, though I had a sneaky feeling they were the wrong ones. We discussed models, locations and so forth and shot the whole damn thing only to have him reject both of them, in favour of a rather drab group picture.

What he should have had was the *Onion Ladies* you see here, which came spontaneously during our design meetings from a mixture of round things, testicles, breasts, bums and weebles, weebles? and *Alice in Wonderland*. Add to this curious mixture the idea that big girls make you cry and you get onions that are ladies. You should see my initial scribble, or maybe you shouldn't. You can see Fin's rough drawing, which was great.

My nose was so put out of joint, firstly, by Jane's Addiction's rejection and then another rejection by Deepest Blue, that I decided to shoot it for myself, and copied the drawing fairly faithfully. The key was to use red onions and clothe the woman in red and black corsets a la Moulin Rouge, which I'd just seen with Nicole Kidman, well I didn't actually go with Nicole Kidman. I have a feeling that this picture is a mild critique of female vacillation, but mostly it's a lot of fun, angry onion ladies, rolling backwards and forwards, intemperate, like the Queen of Hearts, demanding, sexy and going nowhere in a hurry. They will surely make you cry if you're a bloke. Simply photographed in the studio by crazy Rupert then simply comped together by the indefatigable Badger.

Onion Ladies *CD album front, rejected 2005 Design & Photos StormStudios*

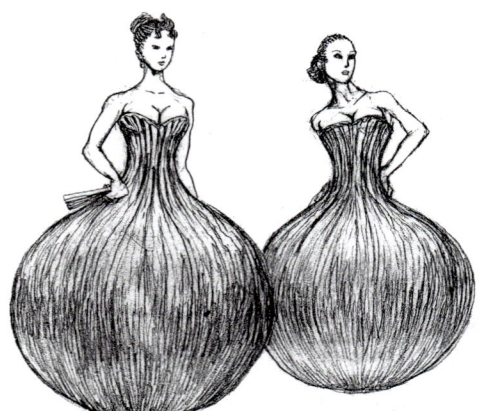

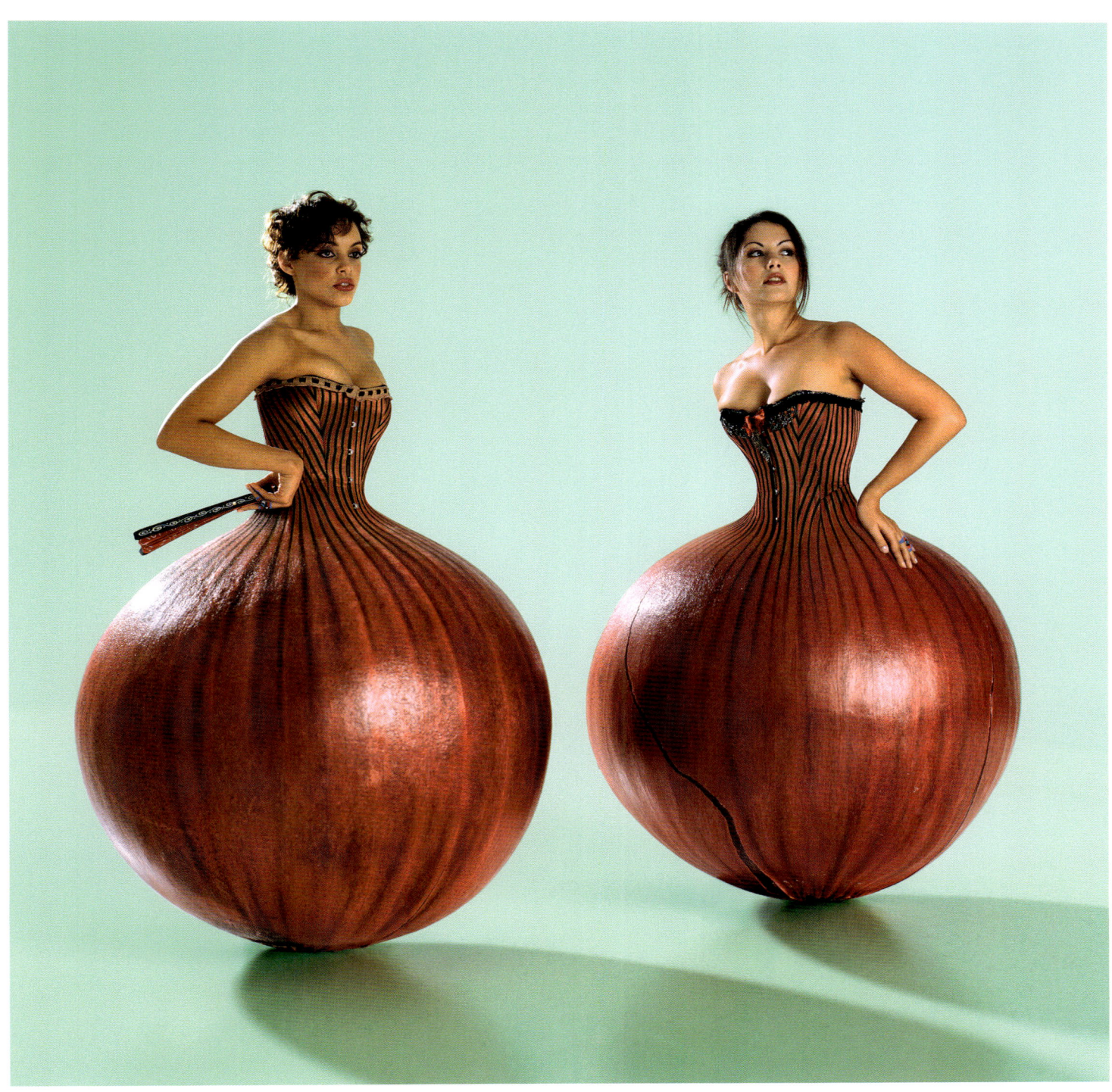

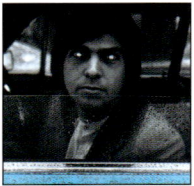

PETER GABRIEL So there I was sitting in a cab in a traffic jam in Trafalgar Square in the rain with little to do but watch the cab next to me. On the bonnet of this vehicle sat myriad drops that were being shaken by the vibrating cab. Each drop seemed to have a quality and a life of its own, held by surface tension upon the waxed metal with an exaggerated highlight in each one. I thought, "That looks cool, can I duplicate it one day?" Which is how Peter Gabriel came to be sitting, looking furtive in the front seat of my beloved Lancia Flavia which had been heavily dowsed with a garden hose, the car not Peter, I hasten to add.

I feel that what makes this shot distinctive is the hand colouring (the blue) and the fact that each individual highlight was scraped clean with a scalpel by a very patient Richard Manning. This low-key portrait approach was a credit to Peter Gabriel's modesty. He appeared similarly obscured in the next two albums namely Melt and Tear, in which the designs were more concerned with idea, mood, and evocation than with cosmetics and how good looking we made him. Don't get me wrong… he's not bad looking, is our Pete.

Sanity rather than vanity.

Peter Gabriel **Peter Gabriel 1** *Vinyl front Charisma 1977 Design & Photos Hipgnosis*

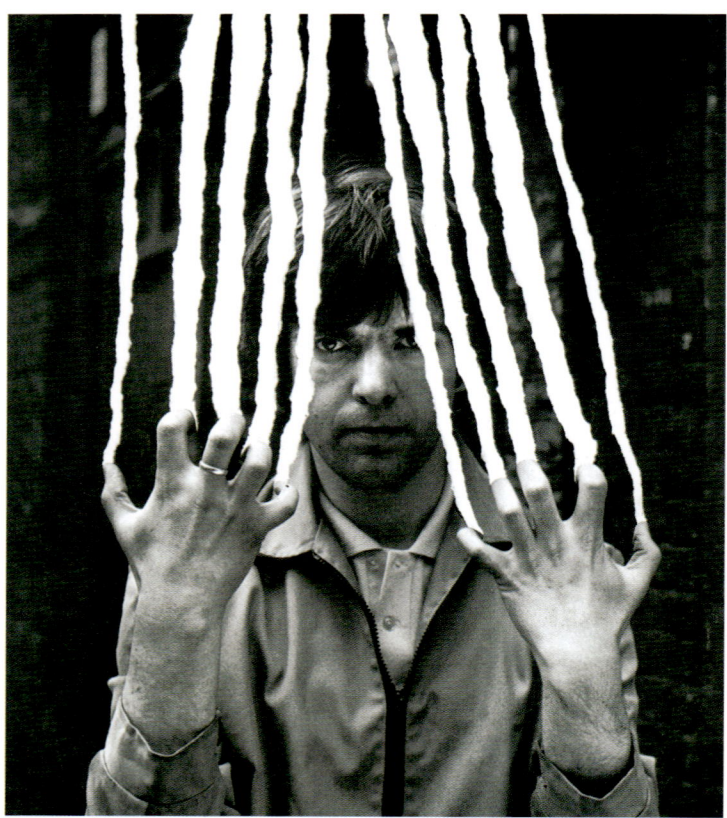

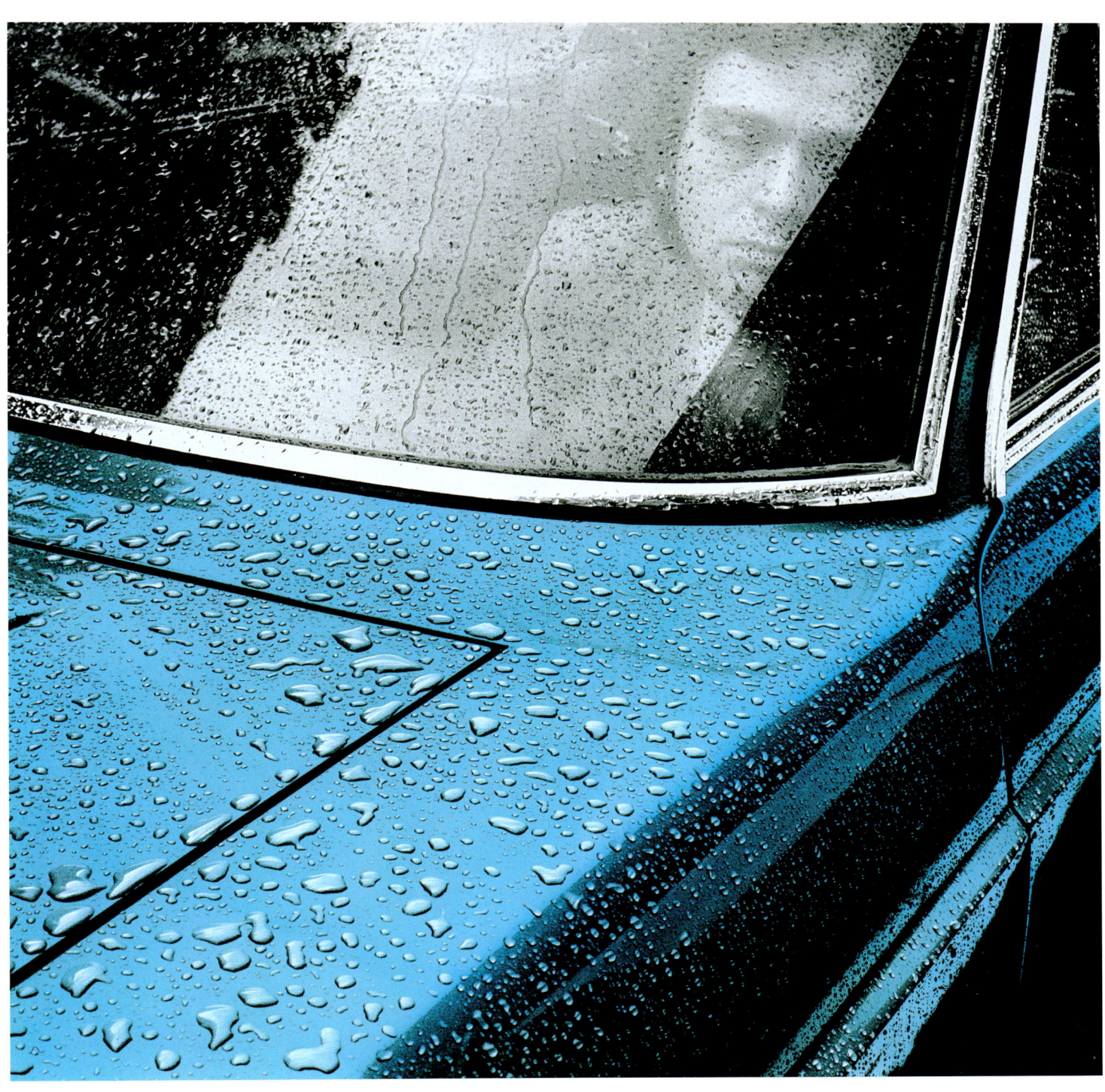

STAGES IN SLEEVE DESIGN

THE STAGES in designing an album cover, as far as **I** know them, are broadly the same, but individually always different. **N**o two bands are the same, thank **G**od, and neither are two albums from the same band. **I**n this text **I** am going to talk about *The Division Bell*, 1994, by those lovable mop tops, **P**ink **F**loyd, as **N**ick likes to call them.

1. THE BRIEF A commission to design an album cover, known euphemistically as 'getting a job' comes via the telephone, e-mail, face to face, through an intermediary (manager record company) by pigeon - in any number of ways. If there is already a relationship it is quite straightforward, as would be the case with Pink Floyd. We have to start with something because most processes, including designing an album cover, are generally linear. (Anyway if we didn't have a starting point we'd all flounder around in a sea of male confusion.) Our starting point is called The Brief and is usually made up of three elements, 1) the music, always the music, often in demo form, or trial mixes or even unmixed material, 2) the lyrics, even if incomplete or scribbled on notepaper, and 3) words of wisdom from the musician, descriptions of intent and preoccupations, musical themes, and anything else that feels remotely salient, including the stuff that doesn't. There may also be a title. This melange of music, lyrics and words from the horse's mouth, becomes our brief.

2. ROUGHS Our design process begins by delay, avoiding the issue, pretending it's not happening, and having a beer. I josh of course, but there is a grain of truth - when faced with a problem to solve, a sleeve to design, there is a great tendency to prevaricate. You know what I mean, something you've gotta do, but you put it off temporarily. More seriously, there is something fearful about approaching the blank page or canvas and trying to find something with which to fill it.

The first mark is the hardest, the first cut is the deepest, they say. We convene in the studio to discuss the brief and make notes and comments upon comments - these jottings often just consist of a random word or two, trying to pin down some theme or grand idea, often concerning a basic feeling for the music, we then go and have another beer, and re-convene the next day, to do it all again. The spectre of deadlines (as they were for Charles Dickens) compels one to action. Private thoughts are made public in these meetings, and further notes are made, and debates had as to what the music is all about, if indeed it's about anything. In the case of *The Division Bell* there were two or three themes, namely communication, or the lack of it (Keep Talking), childhood (High Hopes).and ghosts from the past (Poles Apart). Via several meetings and numerous jottings, thoughts emerge and re-occur, be they serious analysis or silly word play. Ideas begin to concretise and take shape in the form of sketches. Every now and then in the studio one of us may have an idea, an inspiration, a little 'visionette', and another scribble follows and then by a further process of nailing it down, and thinking harder, and focusing on the issue, there develops a set of clearer visual ideas.

These are then transposed into figurative illustrations, usually by Dan Abbott or Finlay Cowan, who can draw, not by me and Peter, who cannot. In the case of *The Division Bell* however, the rough was drawn by Keith Breeden, from an idea about communication. Rather than focusing on content (what's communicated) I was interested in the mechanics

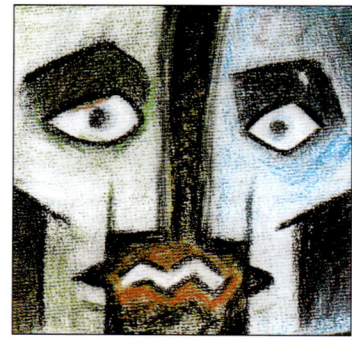 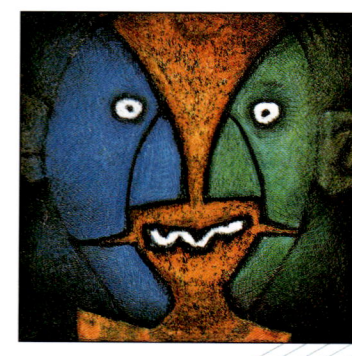 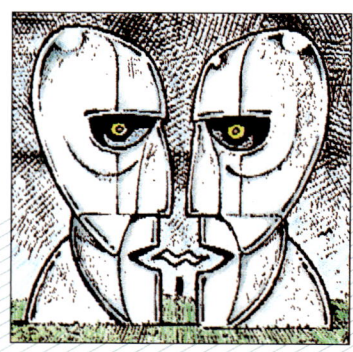

(how it's communicated)and was thinking of something unavoidable, something which was communicated with the viewer whether they liked it or not, and was thinking of how to embody one of those illusion line drawings, such as The Candlestick Illusion - is it a candlestick, or two profiles? There are several of these, minimally drawn illusions, old lady/young lady, rabbit/duck, and so on. And they involve a dialogue, i.e. a communication, between the viewer and the drawing. This dialogue is not about something specific, but about how you see something, is it this or is it that? The viewer is often sucked into this communication whether they like it or not.

I realise that this mode of thinking was an extension of the cover of *Ummagumma*, (pg.125) i.e. the physical embodiment of a two-dimensional line drawing. For *The Division Bell* it was two faces that were looking at each other or it was one face looking at the viewer? Various tests with different kinds of drawings were presented to the local population near my studio, and it invariably worked no matter what kind of drawing. I always thought the finished piece to consist of large sculptures, like Easter Island heads, and then be photographed. But the band didn't like the idea at first and took three weeks to be persuaded not realising that a photo of the large sculptures was intended - clearly a problem of communication.

3. TESTS Once a rough has been accepted and approximate budgets agreed, the project is in Go mode, and what was a drawn rough has now to be actualised as a photograph. In this case the heads were large sculptures, taken to a location, and photographed. Firstly, we might make some tests, to double check the idea before going into debt. In this instance we cut two unattractive profiles out of polystyrene and took them to the local park. They looked pretty daft as you can see but confirmed the potential for the design. The detailed shape of the sculptures was then devised by Keith Breeden, because I am not a sculptor and he is. His accurate drawings were given to the prop-house (Model Solutions), who first made maquettes, three feet high versions of clay, which looked great, and were given the green light, whereupon they embarked on the construction of the real thing - a pair of 22 feet high sculptures.

4. SHOOT In reference to the themes of childhood and spectres from the past, it was decided to shoot near Cambridge, in fact it was was the band who suggested Ely Cathedral. We found a friendly farmer, who rented us a field nearby, in which we could erect the statues and leave them for a couple of weeks - very necessary because of

doubts about the weather, for it was January at the time. The full scale statues were eventually completed and looked fantastic, but weighed a fucking ton. They were put on a flatbed lorry, driven to the location, carried by an army of helpers into a field, and erected with scaffolding, ropes etc. Mostly so they would stand secure and not crush some unfortunate farmhand. It was all in all a Herculean effort and I'm jolly glad I didn't do it myself, but issued instructions poncily from off to one side. But I have to say the crew from Model Solutions were brilliant, and all their sterling efforts were justified because when you stepped back to see the statues on location they looked majestic, and it then comes home to you that a) it is all worthwhile and b) the realisation of a little idea on paper, (look at the first rough), is working and therefore quite a relief really. The statues, like sentinels guarding the Cathedral, stayed in position for two weeks whilst we photographed them in every conceivable weather, occasionally changing the line of communication between the profiles and experimenting with filters and so on.

5. EDITING This stage could as easily be called selection and it is quite simple and painstaking, but profoundly important - and involves a review of the film material you have taken. Since film is one of the less costly elements of the whole procedure, there can be quite a lot of it, and it is of great importance to select the best material. You might in the end be looking for just one shot out of several hundred. In some ways this is a very tedious process and I find it quite stressful, don't want to make a mistake, but you're looking at one similar shot after another for a couple of hours if not a couple of days. Mind you, better to have something to choose from than nothing, a lot of crap film or incorrectly exposed material, is even more worrying (I once did a photo session of The Pretty Things and forgot to adjust the flash setting back to manual, due to the ingestion of forbidden substances, and there were no exposures at all. No pictures to look at, not one. I never touched the stuff again, I swear).

6. ARTWORK Having selected our favourite shots, there may be some computer work to do, but in this case, very little, a little cleaning and tidying up but not much. Removal of the posts to which communicating lights were attached also the stays that held the eyes and the odd bit of scaffolding and that was it, cover done. All that remained was to insert it into the artwork of the CD booklet, which is a separate and lengthy process, involving text, graphics, layout, pagination, cropping, re-cropping etc etc extra photos etc, all of which is another story.

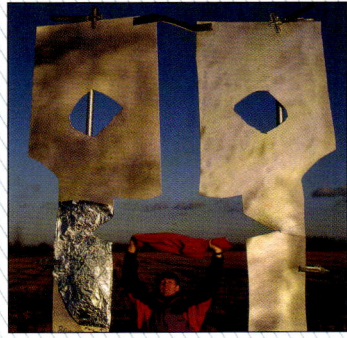 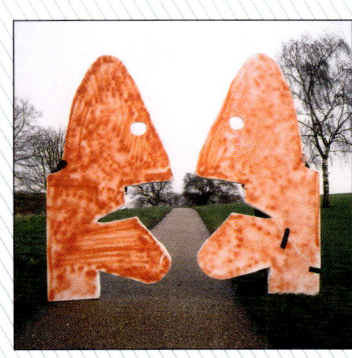 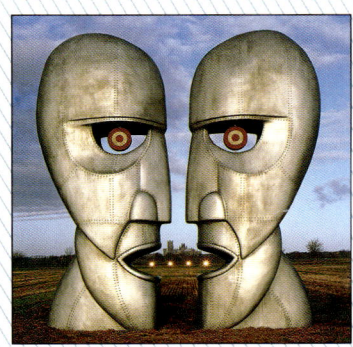

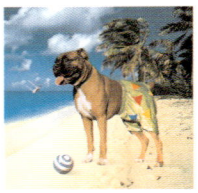

MR LOVEPANTS Raconteur, humourist, art teacher, rock'n'roller and bon vivant Ian Dury employed us to design an album called *Different Strokes* but he wasn't very enamoured with any of our suggestions and dealt with this disappointment by telling us he'd changed the title to *Mr. Lovepants* at the last moment. "What do you think?" he asked with a big grin. I said, through gritted teeth, that I thought it was "great" whilst cursing under my breath that my ideas were now redundant. I left shortly after.

As I walked down his front steps it struck me, literally between the eyes, that *Mr. Lovepants* was not human but a dog, a dog who panted heavily, namely a boxer who wore pants or boxer shorts. Ho ho, job done. The shorts had to be anatomically designed as one might imagine, a boxer being 'well hung' as they say. Custom made shorts had to be worn on the beach in Bermuda, of course, as in Bermuda shorts and decorated with triangles as in Bermuda Triangle of course. All this word association was right up Mr Dury's street. The hard part was getting a suitably leery picture of the dog, lascivious, with panting tongue extended. And despite 'Nubi', care of the Galer family, being keen and available, it took seven attempts to achieve the necessary result. Can't teach an old dog new tricks, it seems.

*Ian Dury & The Blockheads **Mr Lovepants** CD album front*
Ronnie Harris Records 1999 Design & Photos StormStudios

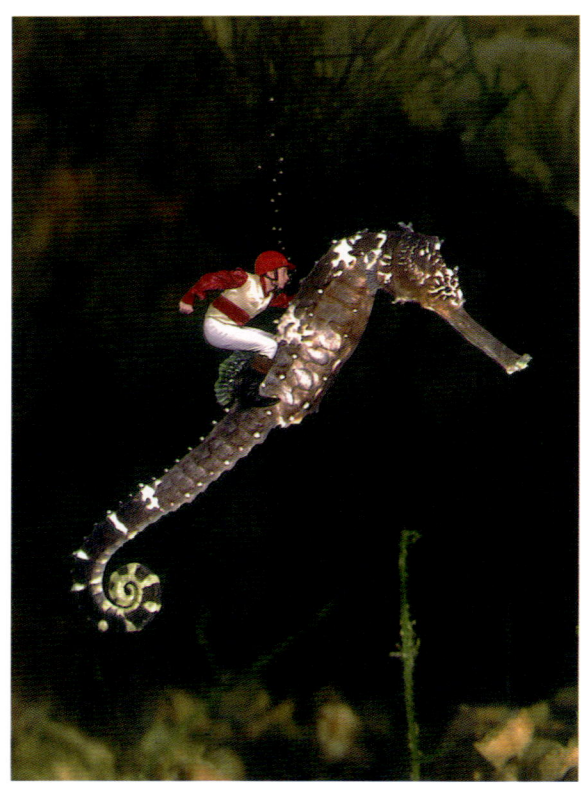

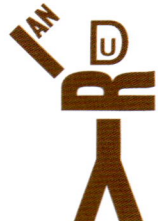

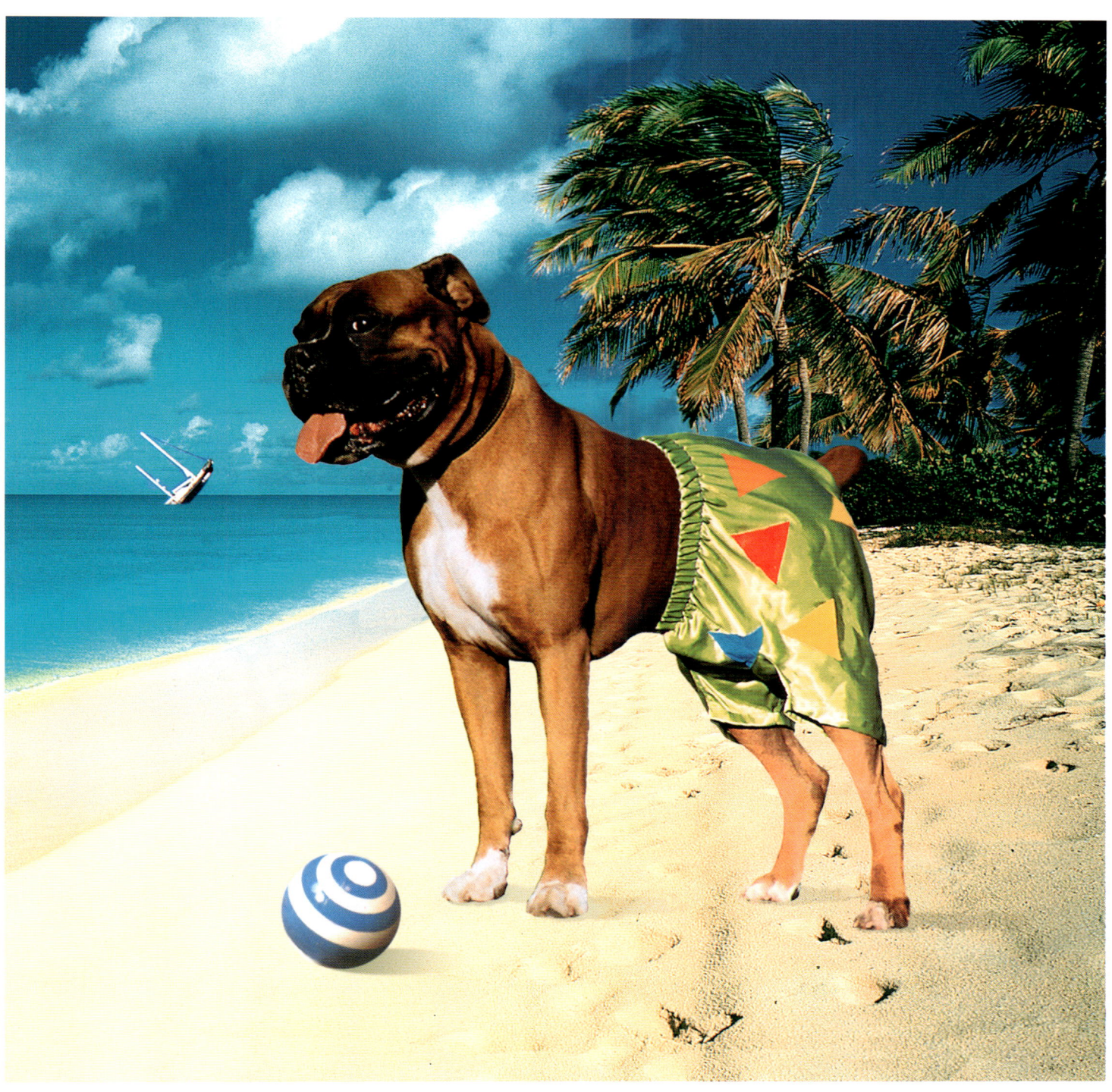

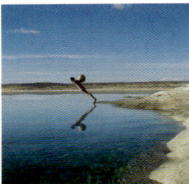

HEALING SIXES Here's an escapade if ever there was…working for mad-cap Kevin Shirley and his new proteges, Healing Sixes, who didn't have a record deal yet, but still wanted a cover from us. Their music – hard rock with introspection – had moments of depression, especially the lyrics, which seemed more self-deprecating than necessary, bordering at times on the misogynistic. For some reason I remember addiction being part of the story, but I'm not sure why. The singer was gloomy and self-critical, at least the persona was.

Addiction is a complex issue. Via my uneducated analysis, I determined that a core ingredient was lack of self-esteem – you have to think badly of yourself in order to abuse your body to such an extent, to think little of yourself to the degree that you will put your mind and your health at risk. I searched for an idea about destruction of self-image, which is why the man is falling into the water.

Like 'Sparks Are Gonna Fly' (pg. 183), this picture is concerned with what is going to happen next, not what is happening now. In this case, his reflection in the water i.e. his image, is about to be shattered by his falling. What causes him to do this? Well it's probably too complex to be identified, and is instead represented by a round wooden ball, known as the Great Ball of Worry, pressing down on his back - the weight of the world on his shoulders, so to speak.

This job depended on finding a great location, namely Lake Powell in Utah, and calm, unwindy conditions, such that the water was flat and the reflection clear. Despite getting up at 4am every morning for five days, it was unbelievably windy all the time. This was the most tiring job I have ever done, looking in vain at the crack of dawn for a windless patch of water. Every day, shagged out and anxious, anxious at time slipping away, as well as the budget.

And to think we took the Great Ball of Worry with us all the way from London to Utah. How worrying is that?

*Healing Sixes **Healing Sixes** CD album front Corazon 2002*
Design & Photos StormStudiosLocation LakePowell, Utah, USA

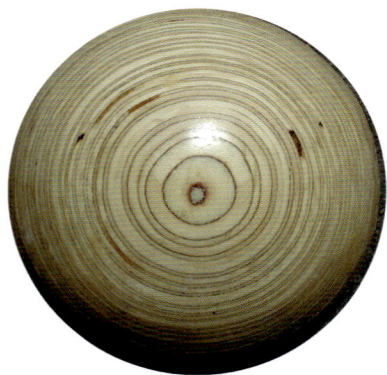

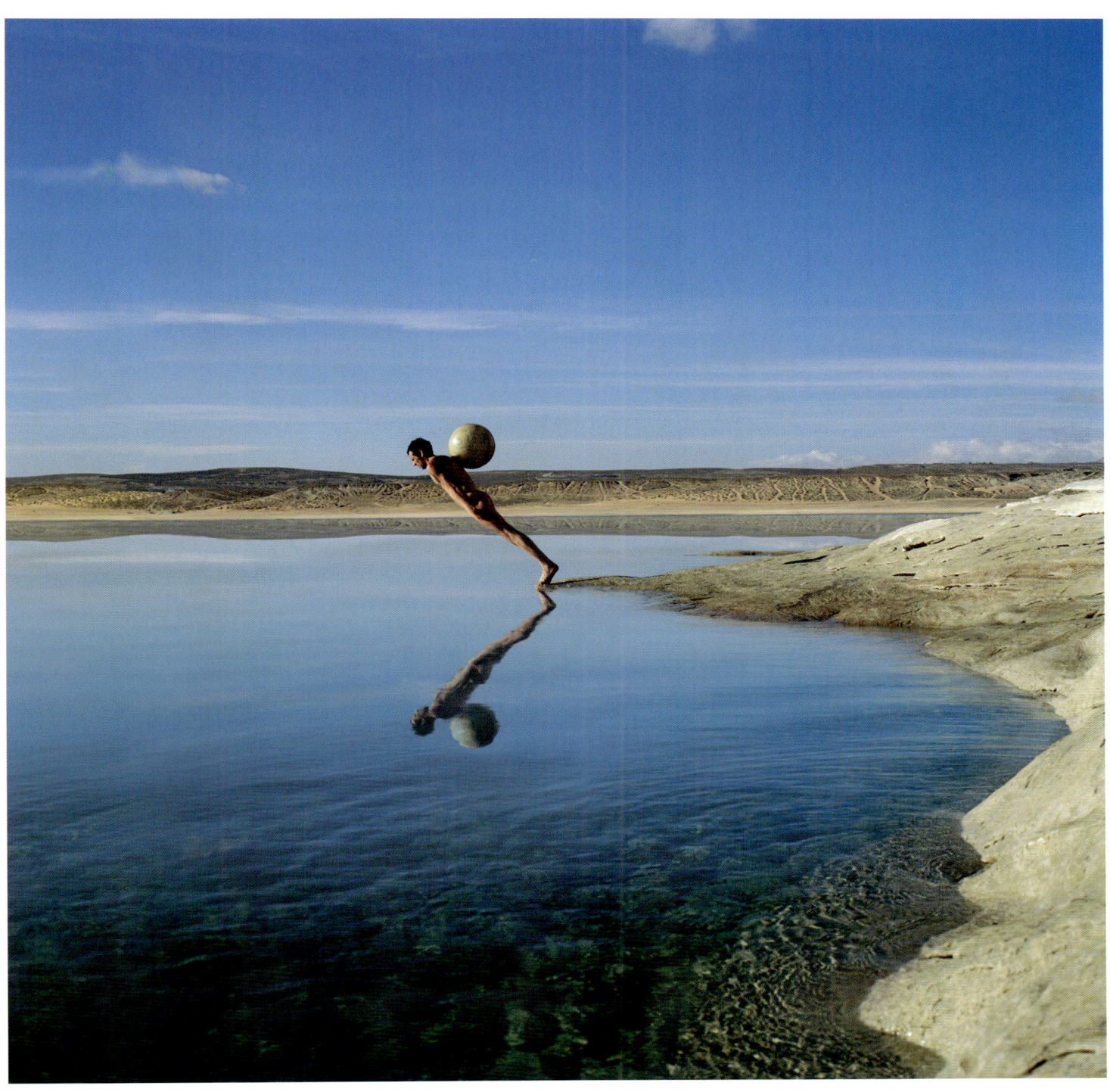

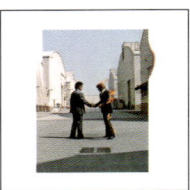

WISH YOU WERE HERE It was very difficult to design this cover following the phenomenal success of *The Dark Side Of The Moon*. After prolonged conversations with all of the band, especially with Roger, it seemed that 'absence' was a recurring theme, especially absence of commitment – either to relationships or to work. There in the flesh but not in the spirit. At this moment in time, the band was beginning to drift apart and Roger was getting divorced. I racked my brains for good ideas as to how to represent 'absence' whilst being present. I went through the motions, until perchance we stumbled upon the notion of traces ie: shadows, footsteps, things that indicate presence but are in themselves insubstantial or not very present. These ideas became intermingled with empty gestures, maybe a handshake where people, especially in America, grip your hand warmly but don't mean too much. From there to absent emotions and thence to people who were absent for fear of being hurt, or burnt, and from that to a person on fire.

I clearly remember the conversation with illustrator George Hardie, then the fourth unofficial member of Hipgnosis, in which I said hurt people were afraid of being hurt or burnt again and so held themselves back and became kind of absent and George said, "Being burnt! A man on fire!" and I said "Yes, a real man on real fire". And there you have it - men enacting an empty gesture whilst on fire, paying no particular attention to the flames as it is a metaphor and therefore not real, although of course it is real. Therein lies the conundrum and part of the appeal, I suspect. Real but not real, not surreal or hyperreal but unreally real or really unreal.

This idea was brilliantly photographed by Po and Peter in a vacant film lot in Hollywood, vacant as in absent. Nothing real in films, now is there?

Pink Floyd **Wish You Were Here** *Vinyl front EMI /Columbia 1975*
Design & Photos Hipgnosis Location Burbank, Los Angeles

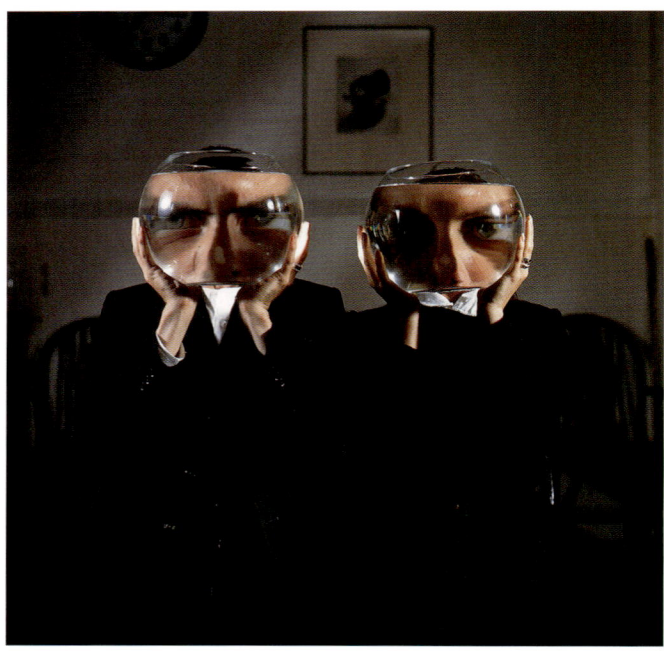

"We're just two lost souls swimming in a fish bowl, year after year."

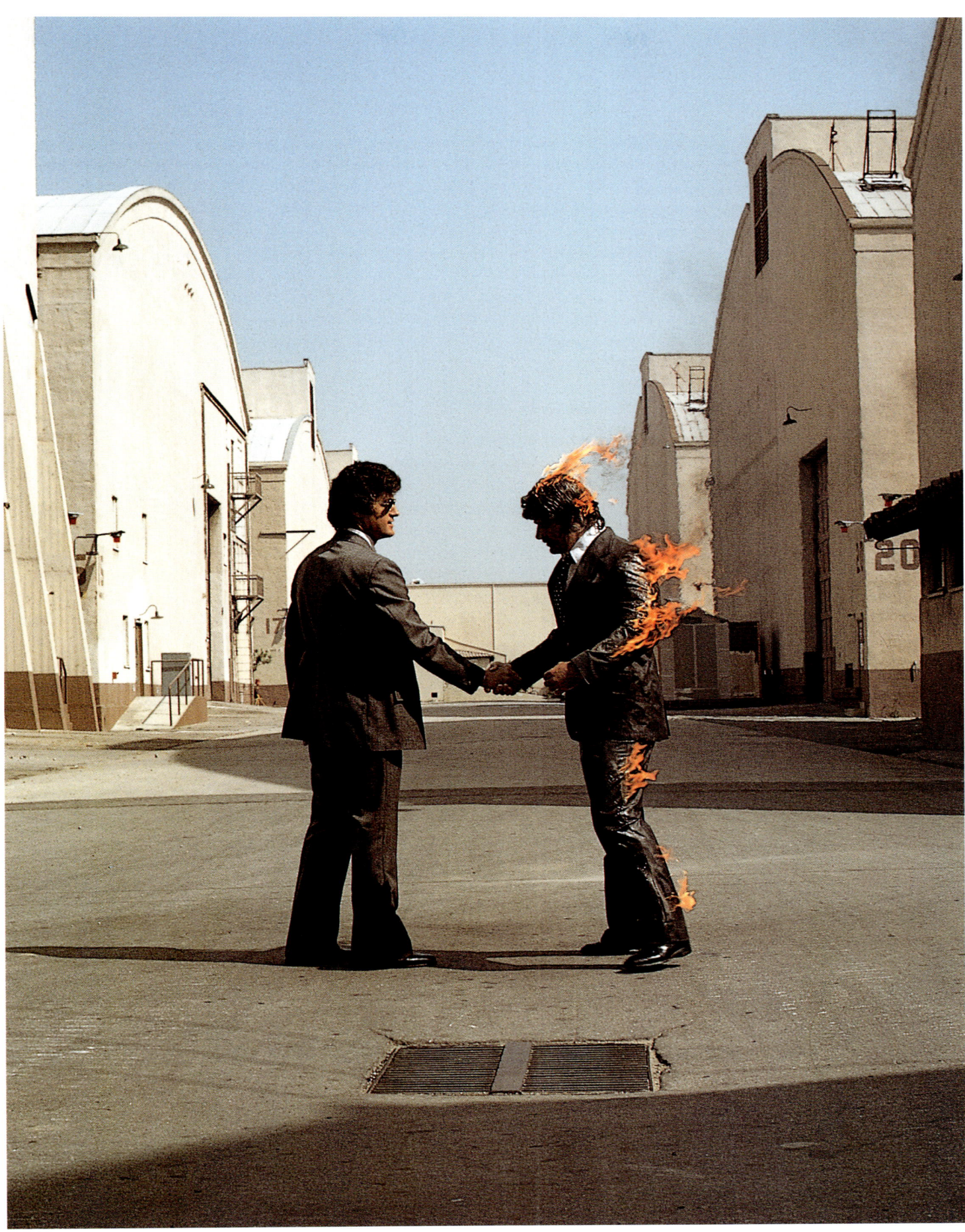

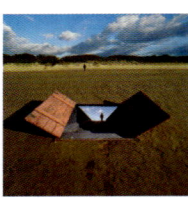

COME AGAIN We are not often inclined to do fantasy, preferring instead to mess around with reality (just a bit). I mean, you can't really have a trap door in a beach, now can you? Or stairs going down to the sky except in fantasy land? Or unless you have ingested a large amount of pharmaceutical psychotropics, and heaven knows we wouldn't want that. However, the elements in our picture are real enough and the trapdoor was custom-made and transported to a likely beach where we dug a hole in the sand and embedded the door. We installed a couple of steps which were then computer-joined to some stone steps in a back alley in West Hampstead, London. The same figure is seen at the top of the stairs (or is it the bottom?) as is seen walking away towards the dunes. I have no idea what it all means but like much surreal fantasy it simply felt engaging. Up? Down? Where do the stairs lead? Down into the earth or up into the sky? To darkness or to the light? Is it positive or is it negative? Is the figure coming or going? Are things real or false?

Is this a crock of shit or not?

The footprints, I think, are a neat touch.

Thornley **Come Again** *CD front Road Runner Records 2004*
Design & Photos StormStudios Location Burnham Beach, Weston-super-Mare, Somerset

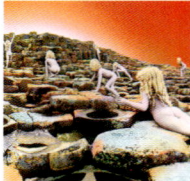

HOUSES OF THE HOLY When Peter Grant, the infamous but sadly departed manager of Led Zeppelin, first rang us at the Hipgnosis studio, I happened to be in a frivolous mood and was pretending to be Groucho Marx, imitating his voice, badly I might add. Mr Grant was not amused. From that point on, Po handled the communications with Led Zeppelin, which was just as well. He also tended to take the photographs whilst I tended to do the designs, though this was not an inflexible arrangement.

Jimmy Page had liked a cover we'd done previously for Wishbone Ash called *Argus*, and asked us to come up with some ideas. Good grief, how do you come up with ideas for the biggest band in the known universe? Gods of rock surrounded as much by myth as by statistics. We were flattered, thrilled, and fairly scared, I'd say. I remember that one of the first ideas involved flying to Peru and photographing the Nazca plain where there are huge markings in the earth, decipherable only from the air, attesting to the idea that aliens had previously visited our planet, obviously a big enough idea for Zeppelin, but somewhat expensive.

They decided instead to go with an idea I'd had from reading *Childhood's End*, by Arthur C. Clarke, in which kids from the future were imagined to coalesce spiritually in mass mutation and leave the Earth as a tower of flaming energy. Yup, that should be big enough for Zeppelin. Our variant was to have blonde and blue-eyed kids (*Midwich Cuckoos*) clambering across the rocks in some magical location, climbing towards a fiery dawn.

The location chosen was the Giant's Causeway, in Northern Ireland, whose hexagonal, basalt rocks seemed the perfect setting, natural but magical. Unfortunately the weather was not so magical, it was grey and flat. Po was undaunted, and took the picture in black and white, which was then painstakingly hand-coloured bit by bit, inch by inch, and the sky made a vivid orange, in an effort to make it dramatic and inflamed. In retrospect I sometimes feel this design is a tad garish, if not kitsch, in its colouration, but mostly it works a treat, though they didn't think so in Oklahoma and Spain, where the cover was banned.

Led Zeppelin **Houses Of The Holy** *Vinyl gatefold Swansong 1973*
Design & Photos Hipgnosis Location Giant's Causeway, Northern Ireland

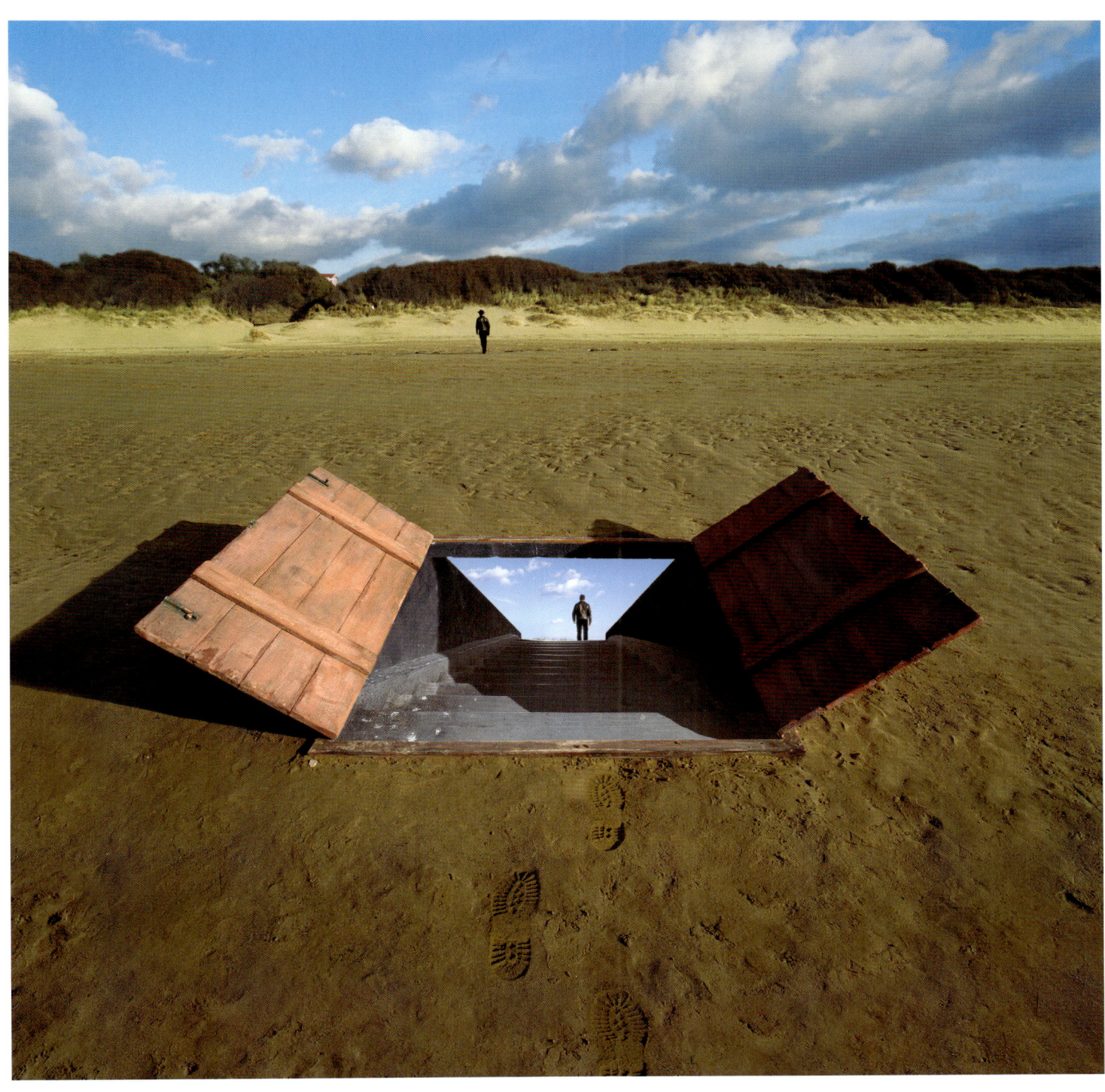

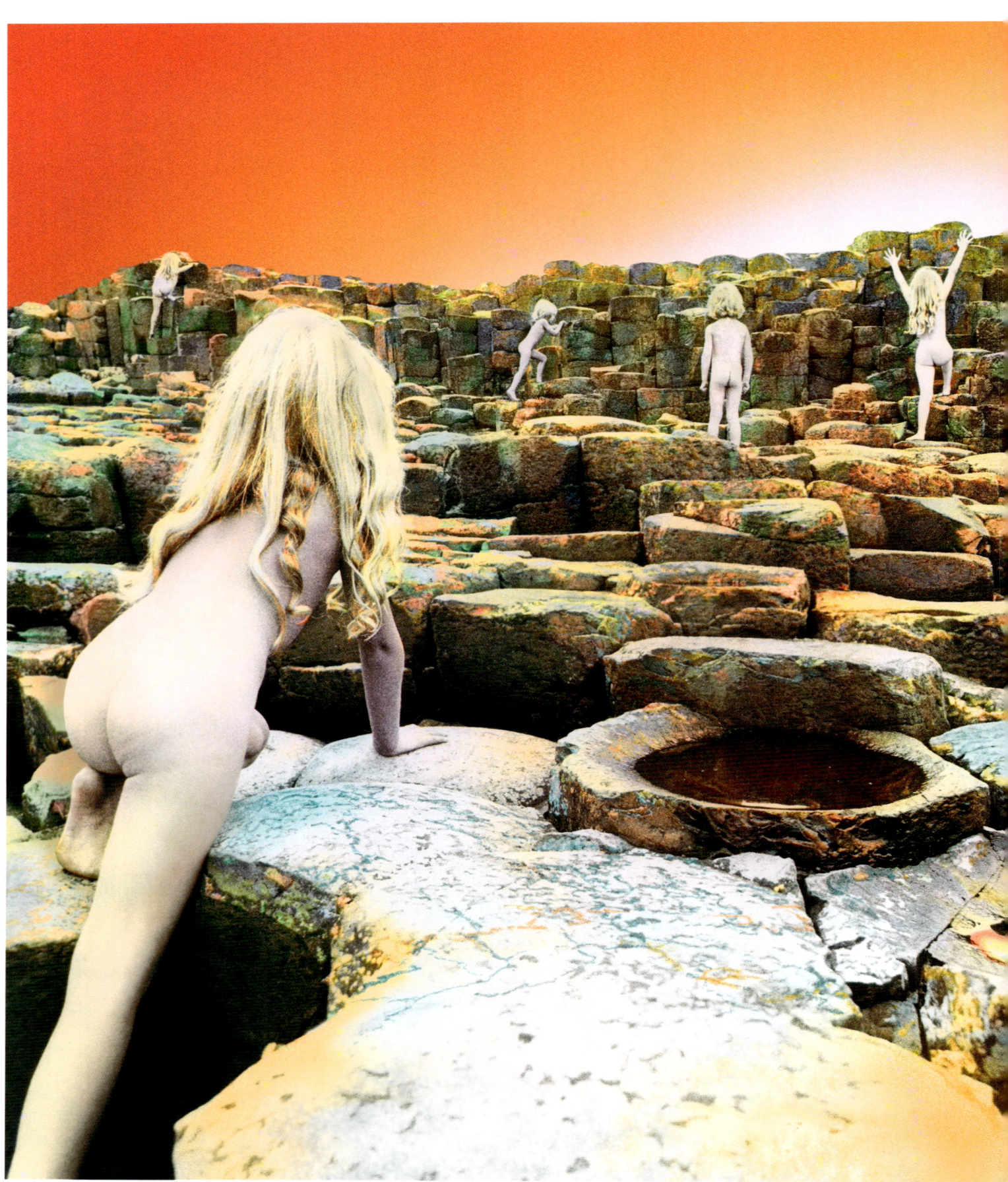

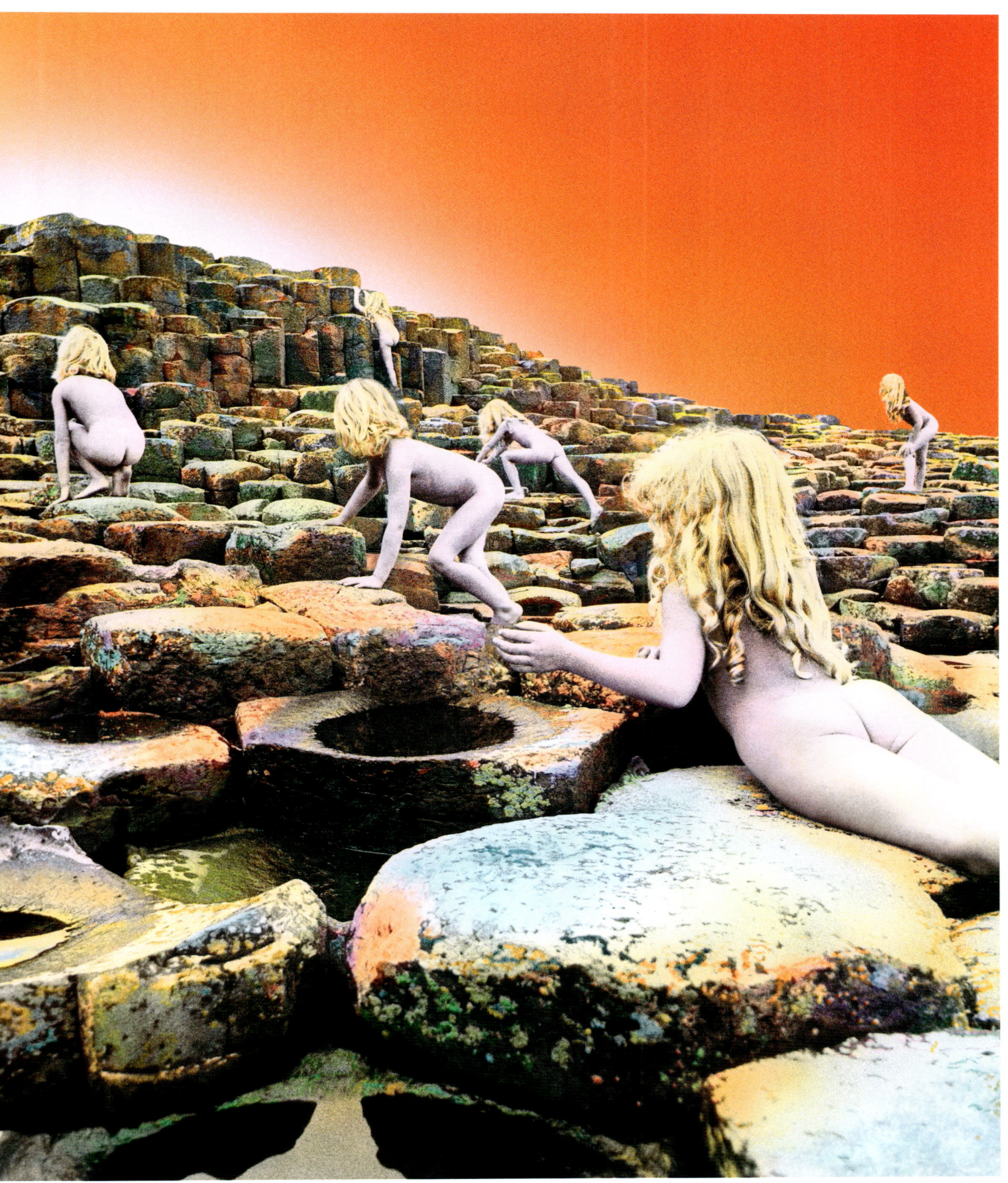

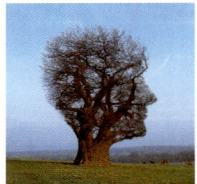

TREE OF HALF LIFE The majority of our images are specific, specific to particular music. All are original as much as one can ever be, and most are strictly custom, but this one is not. Tree of Half Life was originally designed for a song called 'Hurt' by Catherine Wheel, which had a line about a boyhood memory of being in a tree, voluntarily hiding from somebody, but being lonely and in pain. There was sadness, a tree and a memory, hence we presented a leafless tree, its branches redolent of brain cells (neurons etc) and made into the shape of a head or profile.

There was also something about the spirit of youth, a childhood remembered, and in a similar way the spirit of the tree could be represented by the tree taking on a human shape temporarily. I envisaged the tree was communicating with me, talking to me by fleetingly adapting a shape that I would recognise, namely a human profile. But no sooner had it shown itself than it withdrew and resumed its normal outline. In order to experience or see the spirit of the forest, you have to be alert and catch it quickly because it is only there for a moment. It is too risky to be exposed for long.

This image was adopted by the Floyd as a t-shirt and as a frontispiece in a book because they liked it and it felt Floyd-like. As a Sony executive once said to me, "It's a cover of an album never made". Unashamedly I love this picture, it's feels so wistful and dreamlike. Sometimes I am surprised I ever did it.

I met a man who said he'd seen this tree, from a train. When I am asked how this image was done, I say helicopter topiary. You believe me don't you? As much as you might believe in talking trees.

*Pink Floyd **Tree Of Half Life** T-Shirt / Frontispiece 1997*
Design & Photos StormStudios Location Richmond, Surrey

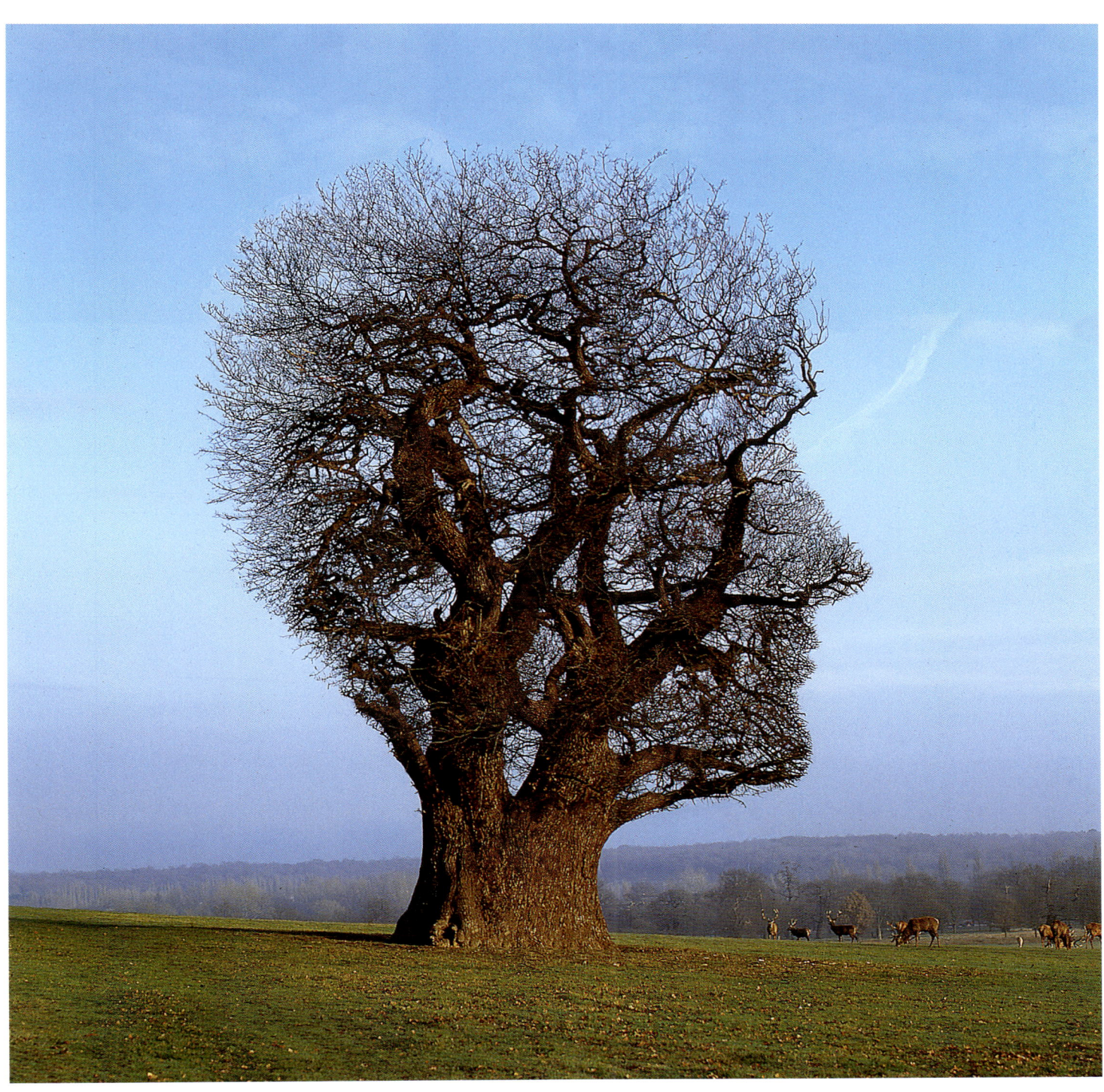

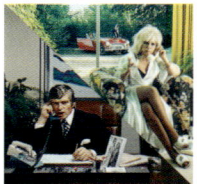 **HOW DARE YOU** One of the more fruitful relationships was with 10cc who penned one of the most succesful singles of all time, 'I'm Not In love', and with whom we worked on several occasions (see *Deceptive Bends* pg.175). 10cc were particularly fond of word associations, cross-references, puns and all manner of connections, either within their own work or to the rest of culture. So we already had an idea for this album, even before we knew what was on it, namely, 'connections', and what better at connecting than telephones, whether to another number or another person. Just to show how connected this all was, it turned out there was a song on the album called 'Don't Hang Up', which we didn't know until after.

We took our design cue from telephone conversations in old movies, which were often represented by a split screen, usually dividing the frame diagonally. In our 'film' the business man is at work, whilst his neglected wife is at home, toting the gin and smoking a ciggy, looking forlorn and dishevelled. We added another layer of connection, a story of the 'other couple', in the background or on his desk.

Rather than making it in the fashion of an old movie (in which 10cc were not interested this time round, though later they of course recorded *Original Soundtrack*), we made it in the style of middle-class naffness, epitomised at the time, by Sanderson Fabrics, whose catch-phrase was 'Very so and so, Very Sanderson'. So we went around for weeks saying 'Very 10cc, very Sanderson,' which we thought was well funny, but it doesn't look so funny now in print.

What was funnier was the inside spread - a picture of a crowded party, full of people talking not to each other, but into telephones. It was totally chaotic, since it was done for real, before the days of the mobile, such that twisted cords and bulky telephones were everywhere. We also designed great inner sleeves with George Hardie, but that's another connection.

Oh for the heady days of vinyl!

10cc **How Dare You** *Vinyl front Phonogram 1975 Design & Photos Hipgnosis*

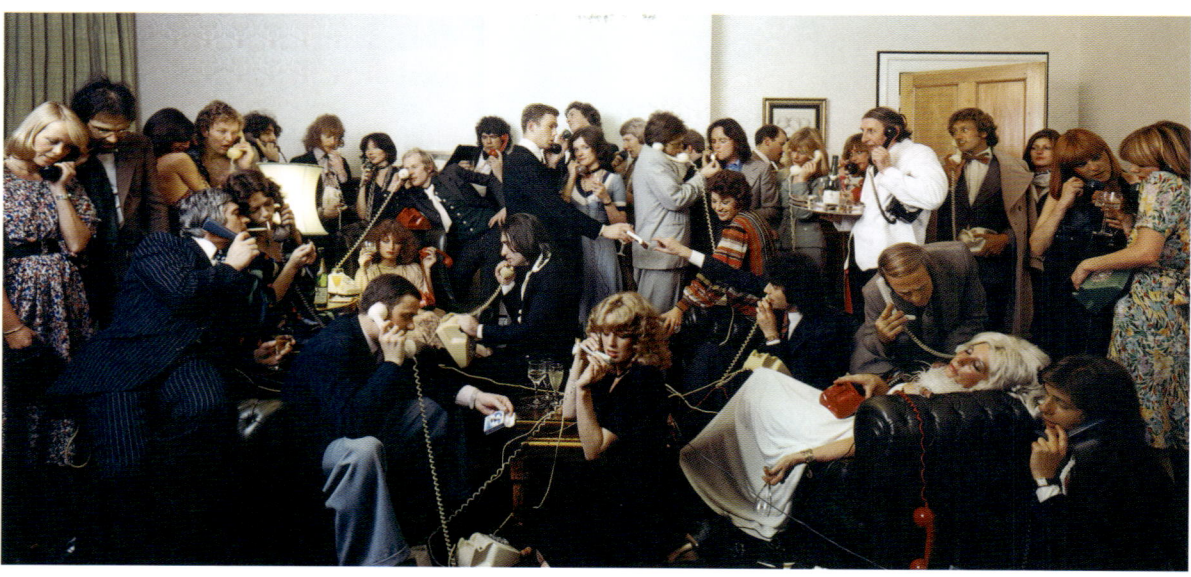

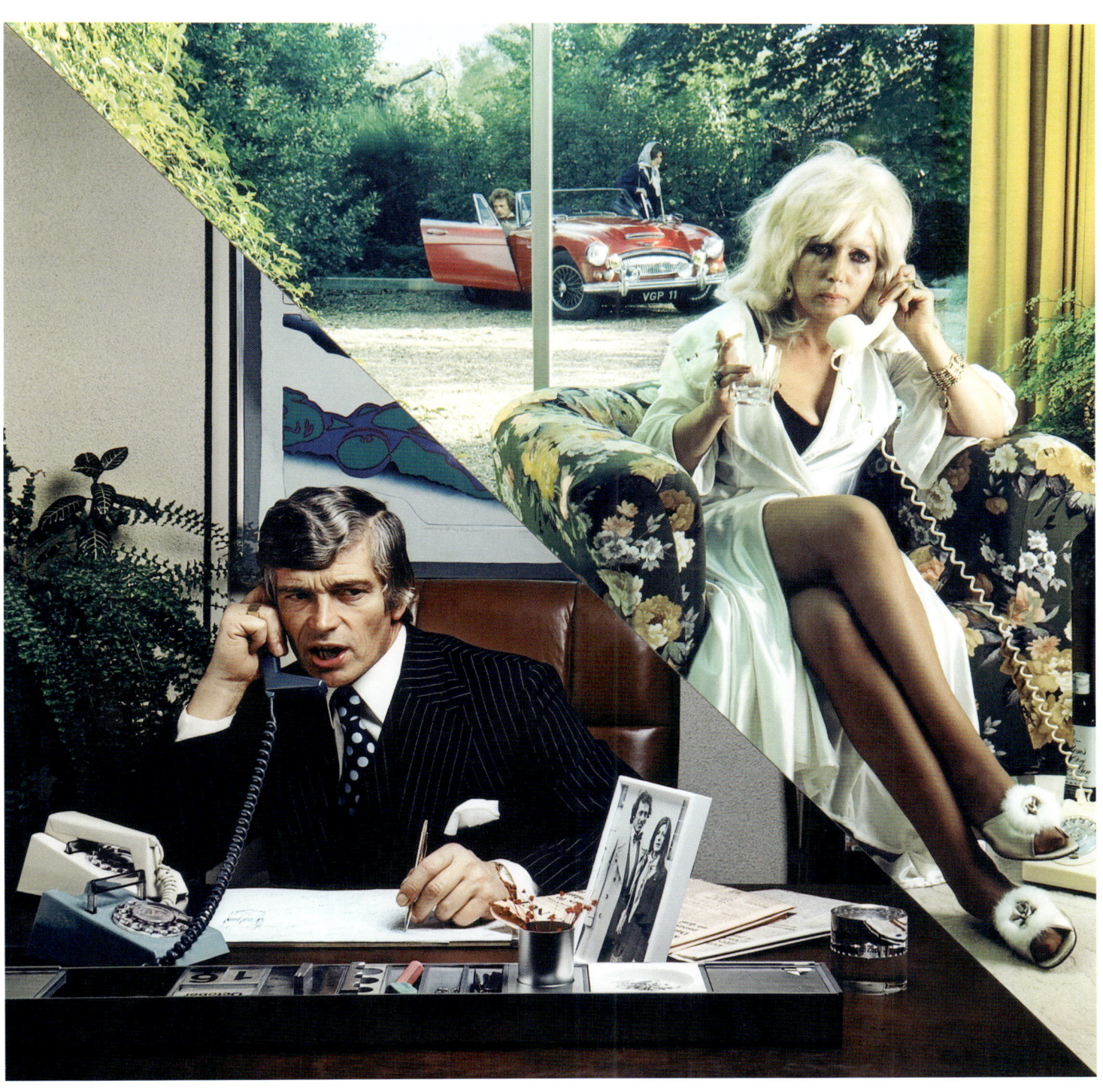

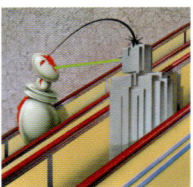

TECHNICAL ECSTASY Here is a design taken unequivocally from the title. More often than not I glean ideas, and hence images, from a compote of music, lyric, and descriptions from the musicians, but not in this case. I don't think I heard the music, I'm sorry to confess, but the title was so evocative and promising that it wasn't necessary. One immediately experiences a contrast in the title: ecstasy, being a very human thing and technical being not so human. The question seemed to be, 'How would one experience ecstasy in technical terms?' or rather, to turn this around, 'How would technical (non-human) beings experience human-like ecstasy?'

Not to beat around the bush, ecstasy would need to involve an exchange of fluids. Technical beings, or robots, might therefore exchange fluids of a lubricating nature. I imagined that these robots might not have the complexity of humans, and rather than a host of subtle ways of indicating strong feelings might be rather direct – squirting fluid or radiating a beam of light or electricity at each other as they passed on the stairs or, on this case, on an escalator – love at first sight, strangers in the night, etc. These robots have no shame and share their technical ecstasy for all to see.

Stylistically speaking, it was decided that our robots could not be manufactured, for budgetary reasons, but might have to be drawn, this allowed of course for imaginative flair, as it was less subject to scientific or technical limitations. The greater problem was how to display the escalator without a violent clashing of styles, so we ended up photographing the escalator and then reducing its detail via re-touching to lend it a more illustrative quality, thus to mesh better with the illustrated robots. The end result is more graphic than photographic, in line with the shameless ecstasy of robots.

*Black Sabbath **Technical Ecstasy** Vinyl front Phonogram 1976*
Design & Photos Hipgnosis & George Hardie

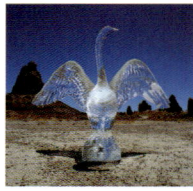

AUGUST EVERYWHERE This commission came out of the blue, the Californian blue and involved a new artist called Jordan Zadorozny, from Canada, who thankfully called him and his band Blinker The Star, though I never knew why. Is it because a star blinks? or is it twinks, or rather twinkles? His debut album was originally called *Heaven For Now*, and the irrepressible Jon Crossland and myself recalled that the swan is a symbol for the muse, i.e. Blinker's creativity and quite heavenly in its elegance. It was Jon who suggested it be made of ice, because it wouldn't last long – heavenly for a limited period only. One place it wouldn't last long would be a desert, and of all deserts it would be Death Valley, one of the hottest places on Earth, especially around 4pm in the afternoon, when the heat suddenly rises another 10 or 20 degrees and smacks you in the face like a boxing glove.

Simple then eh? Take an ice swan to Death Valley and photograph it, but not of course as simple as we thought. We found Gus, an ice-sculptor, over 60 but ever charming and resourceful, but even he couldn't prevent the ice truck from leaking, and couldn't prevent punctures, and couldn't envisage how rapidly the swan would melt, especially above its neck. The virtue of doing it for real was that the incandescent quality of the light bouncing around inside the ice swan was sustained, and would not have been nearly as good if we'd done it as a comp in the computer.

The major thing I remember was the poignancy - how the beautiful swan melted in font of our eyes, drop by inexorable drop, each drop greedily swallowed by the dry desert floor until the neck snapped, and the swan 'died' as it were, right in front of us, its memory frozen in the camera for some degree of permanence, something so cruelly denied it by the heat of the sun. A beautiful thing.

*Blinker the Star **August Everywhere** CD front A&M 2001*
Design & Photos StormStudios Location Death Valley, California

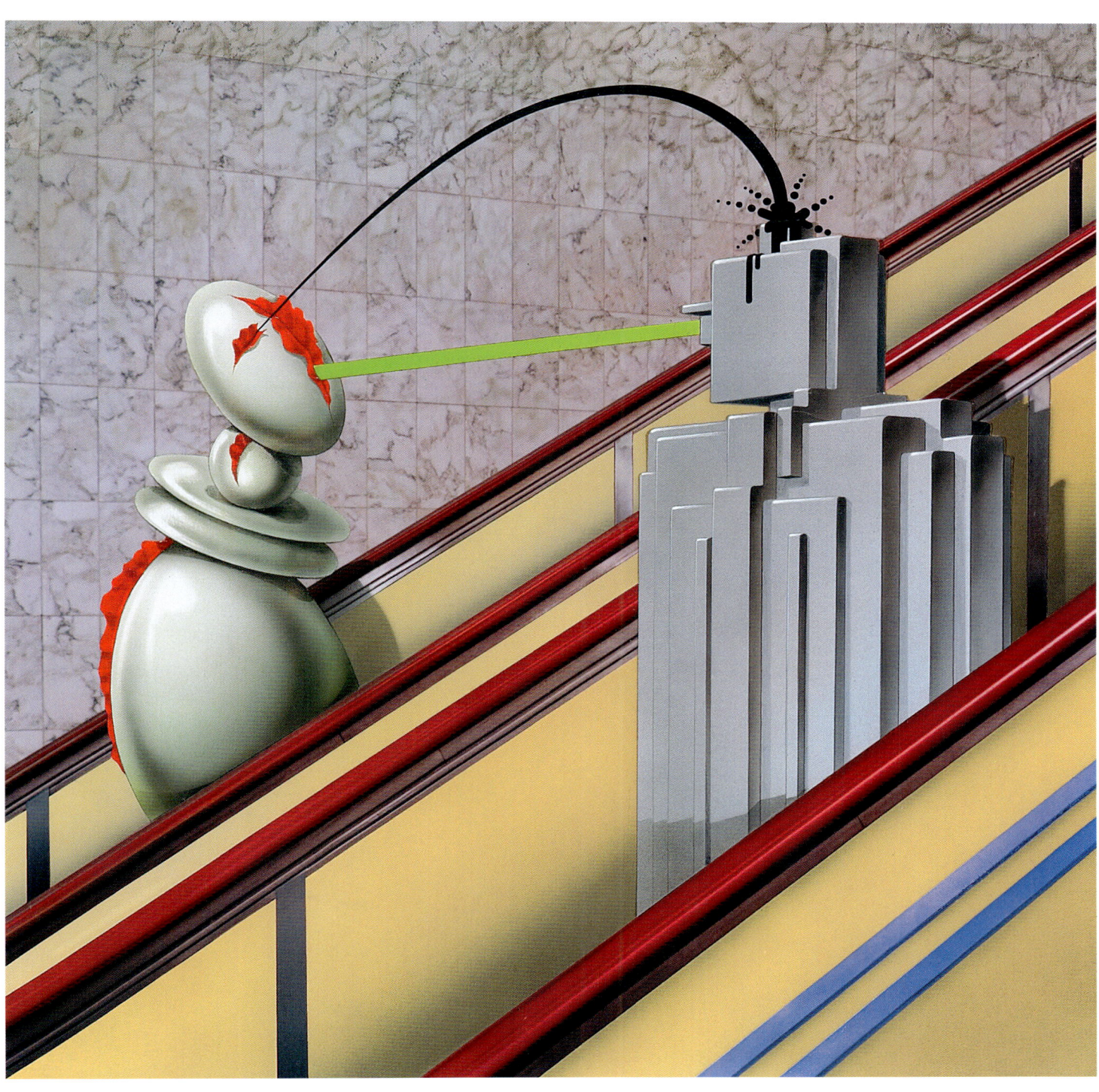

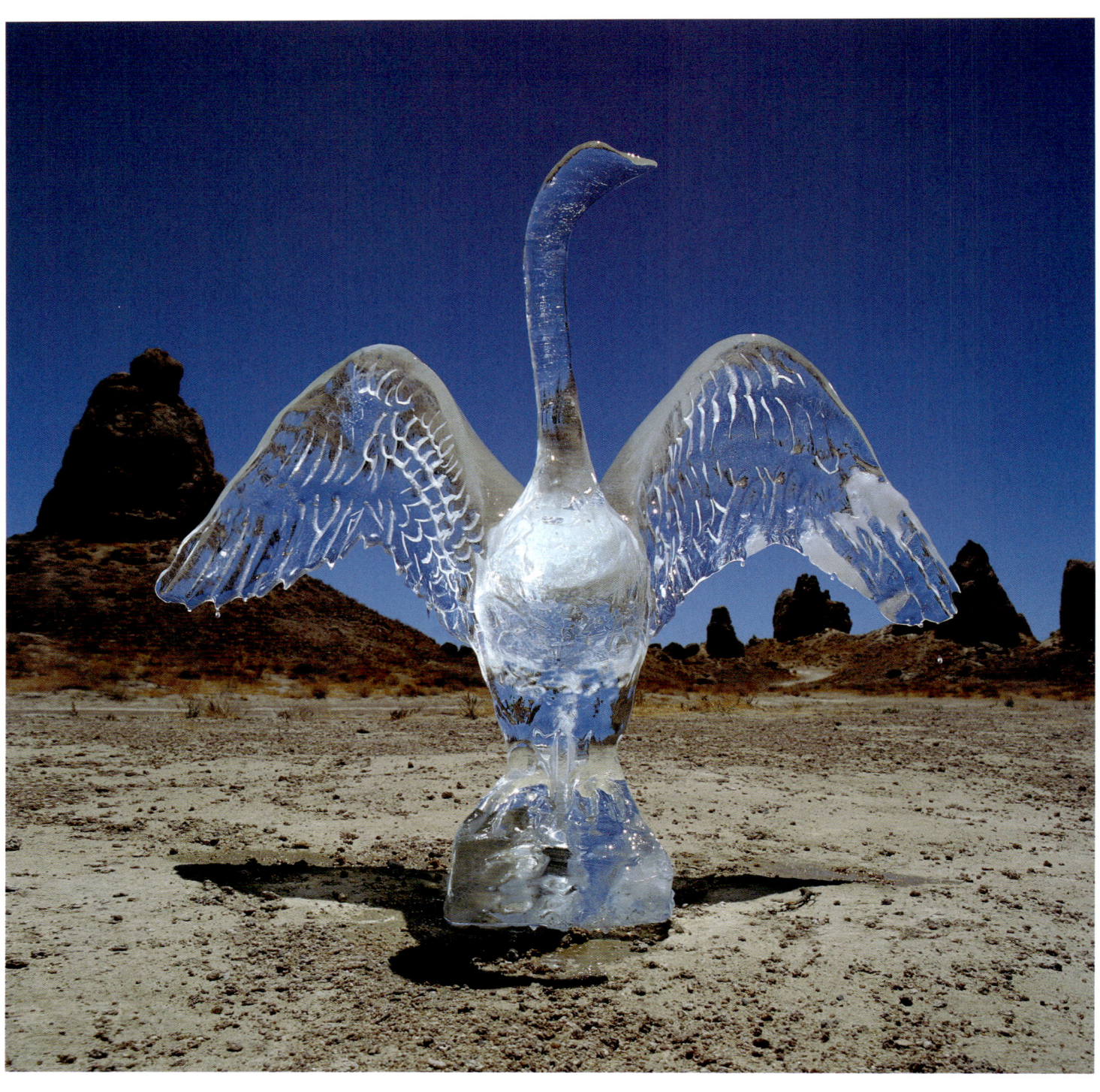

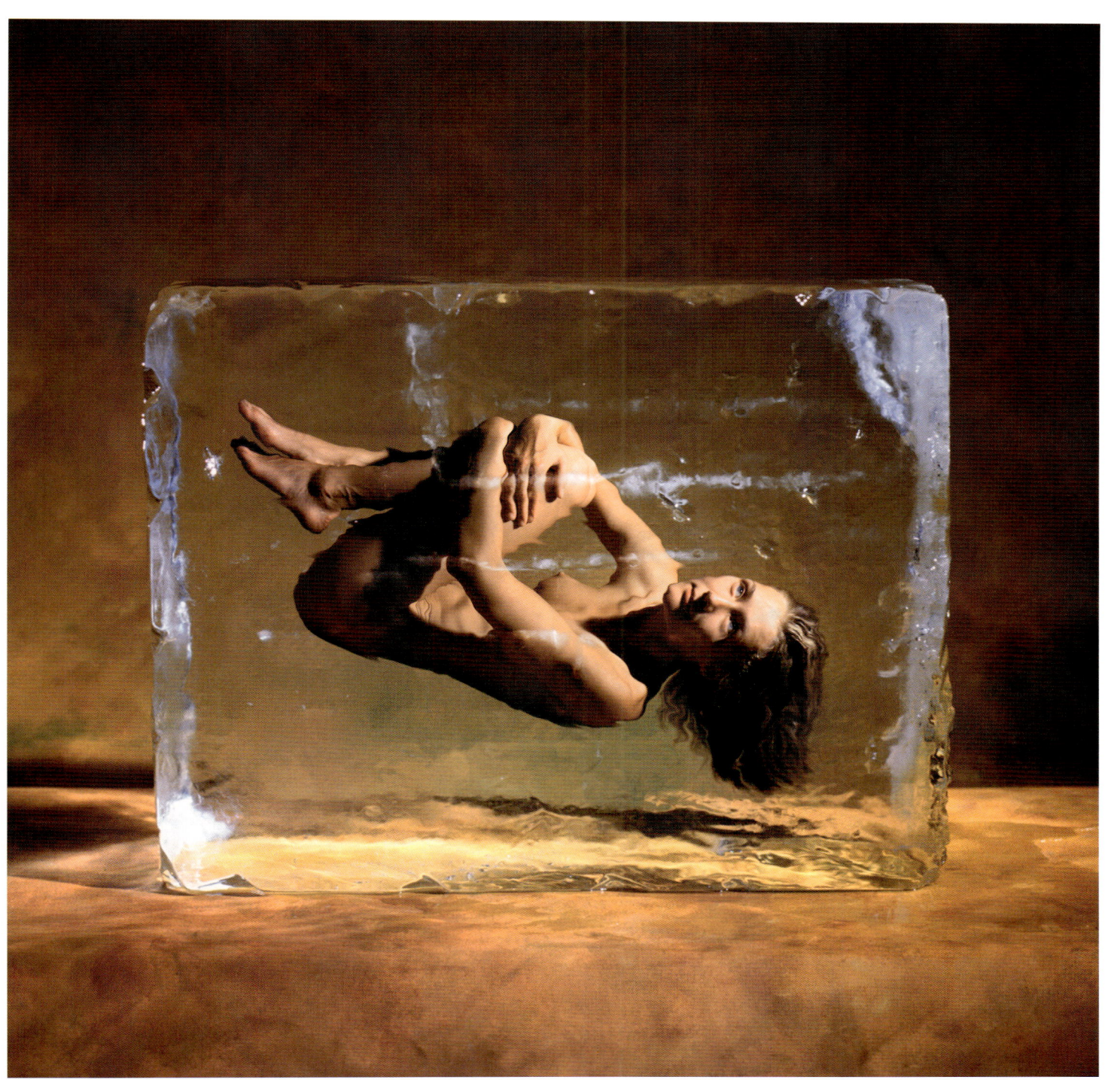

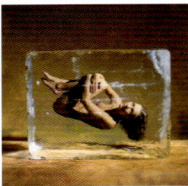

JUDY 'Judy Staring At The Sun' to give the full title, was a design based largely on the lyrics. 'Judy' was a single release by Catherine Wheel in 1995, and the song concerned an aquaintance of theirs who succumbed, unfortunately, to the temptations of heroin. She became isolated and detached through her addiction. The lyric referred to her ability to stare directly at the sun without blinking. I took this to be a metaphor for her emotional detachment; she was entombed, as it were, in a heroin world, protected, not only from the sun, but also from the vicissitudes of daily life - I surmise that this is why heroin is so addictive, it's not just a physiological thing, but also a psychological thing because it makes one immune to emotional pain - you kinda just don't care any more...you are untouchable.

Our Judy is equally untouchable and therefore entombed in a block of ice. Partly so that we clearly see she's entombed and partly because ice was a good vehicle for the coldness of her detachment. People on heroin don't give a shit, they are 'removed', cool, sometimes coldly indifferent, icy.

There are two qualities I like about this image, one of which is the hovering quality, as if the nude is floating, and the other is the open eyes, she's not frightened by her 'incarceration', in fact she doesn't mind it. There are some details I also enjoy - the rippled body contour, the striations on the front of the block of ice, the cold nipple, and the overall and contrasting warmth of the brown, set against the icy block.

Although it is our avowed philosophy, generally speaking, to do things for real, this image is not for real but 'comped' in the computer. So dear listeners, do not attempt this at home on your younger sibling.

Thank you.

*Catherine Wheel **Judy Staring At The Sun** Single front Mercury 1995 CD*
Design & Photos StormStudios

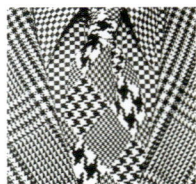

LET YOUR FINGERS DO THE TALKING As a designer I suppose one might discover, develop and refine a personal style so that one could be said to design in this or that style. It is the style that marks you out. Or you could alternatively be a tart and ransack the world around you, purloining ideas and thoughts, any way you can get your bloody hands on them. I'm afraid I am of the latter variety, and ideas come from the great cosmic soup milling about my lower brain which is informed by upbringing, culture, fashion, history, other peoples' ideas, etc. Every now and then, instead of the preferred oddness, intrigue, narrative, surreality, contrariness, fantasy and so forth, it is the observations of daily life that generate an image, such as Pete Gabriel (pg. 63) or Ashra (pg. 21) or Billy Karloff (pg. 85). I had seen someone wearing a checked jacket and a checked shirt. I had seen someone else wearing a checked tie with a checked shirt and was visually non-plussed, it was like a walking optical crossed with bad taste, wherein the wearer suffered from some minor eye defect and hadn't realised that his clothes were clashing violently We acquired a set of checked jackets, checked ties and checked shirts, and found the most virulent combination.

I photographed it in our beloved but grotty Denmark Street studios in about half an hour, didn't need any special lighting, and certainly no colour. Cheap and cheerful, and very snazzy. Smart dresser, huh? (The finished cover was printed in four different colours and made an even snazzier set, although I regret to say that I don't think it helped Mr Karloff and his fortunes much).

*Billy Karloff & The Extremes **Let Your Fingers Do The Talking***
Vinyl front WEA 1980 Design & Photos Hipgnosis

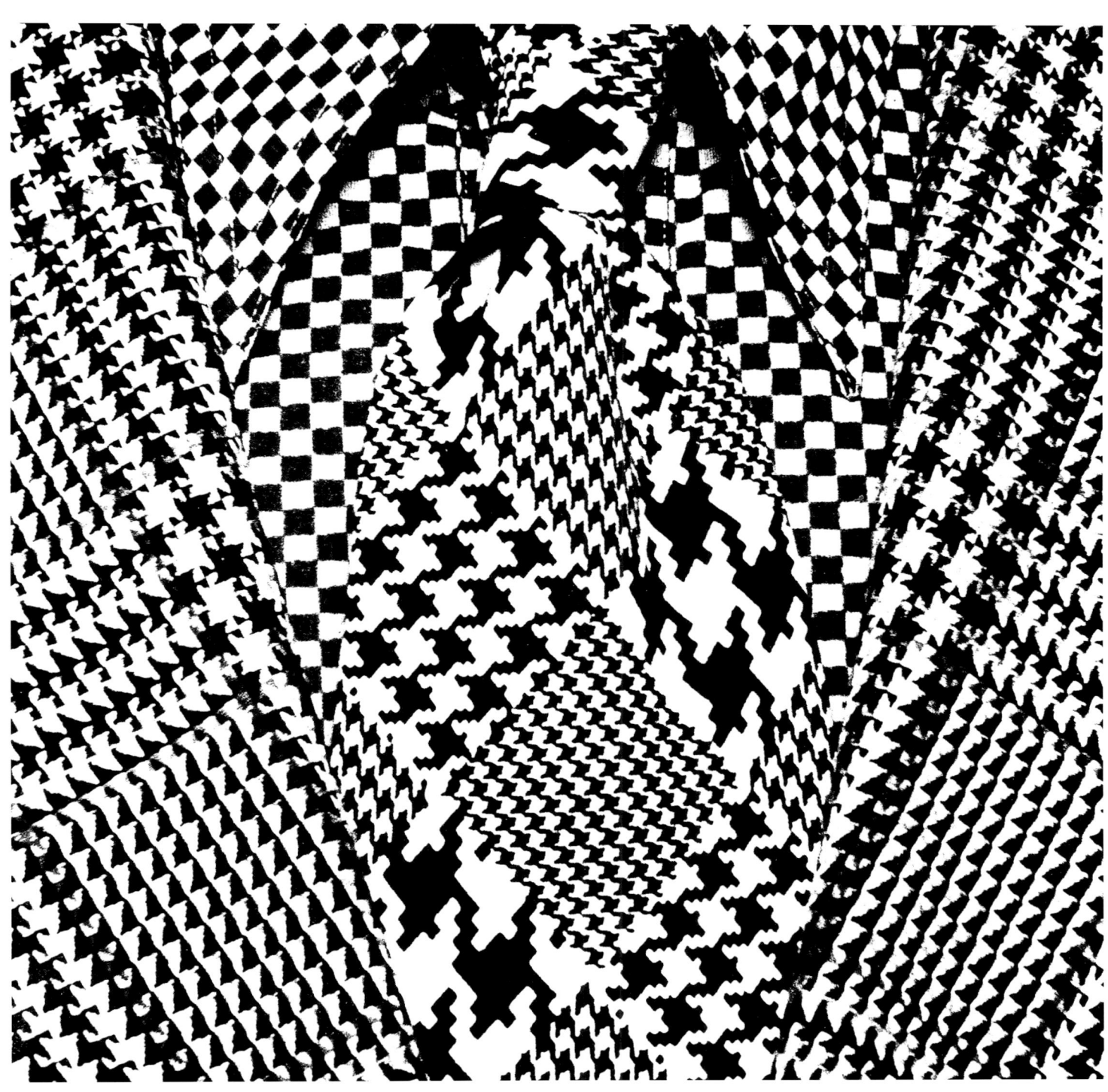

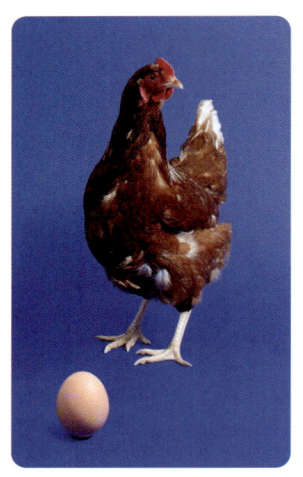

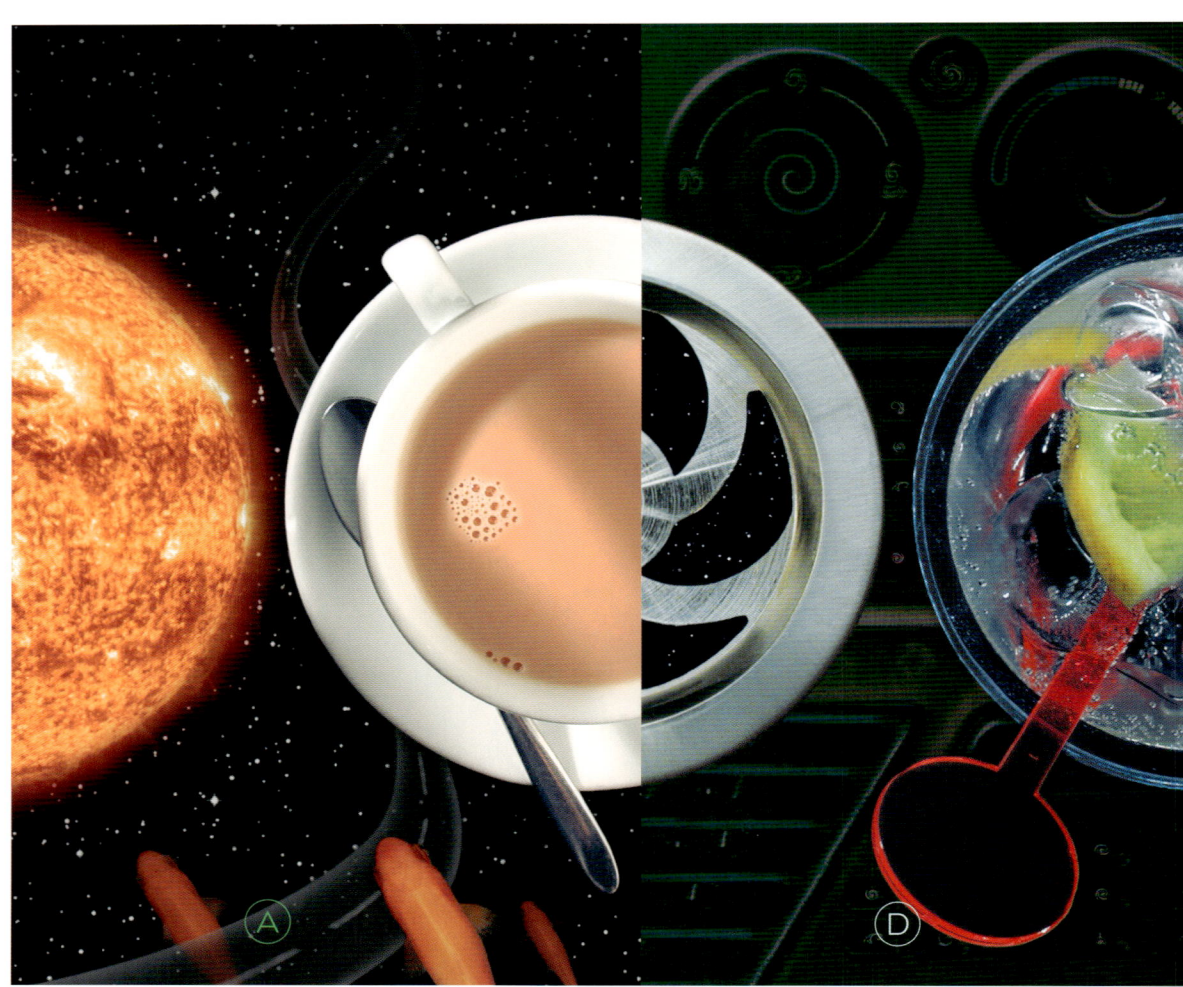

DOUGLAS ADAMS

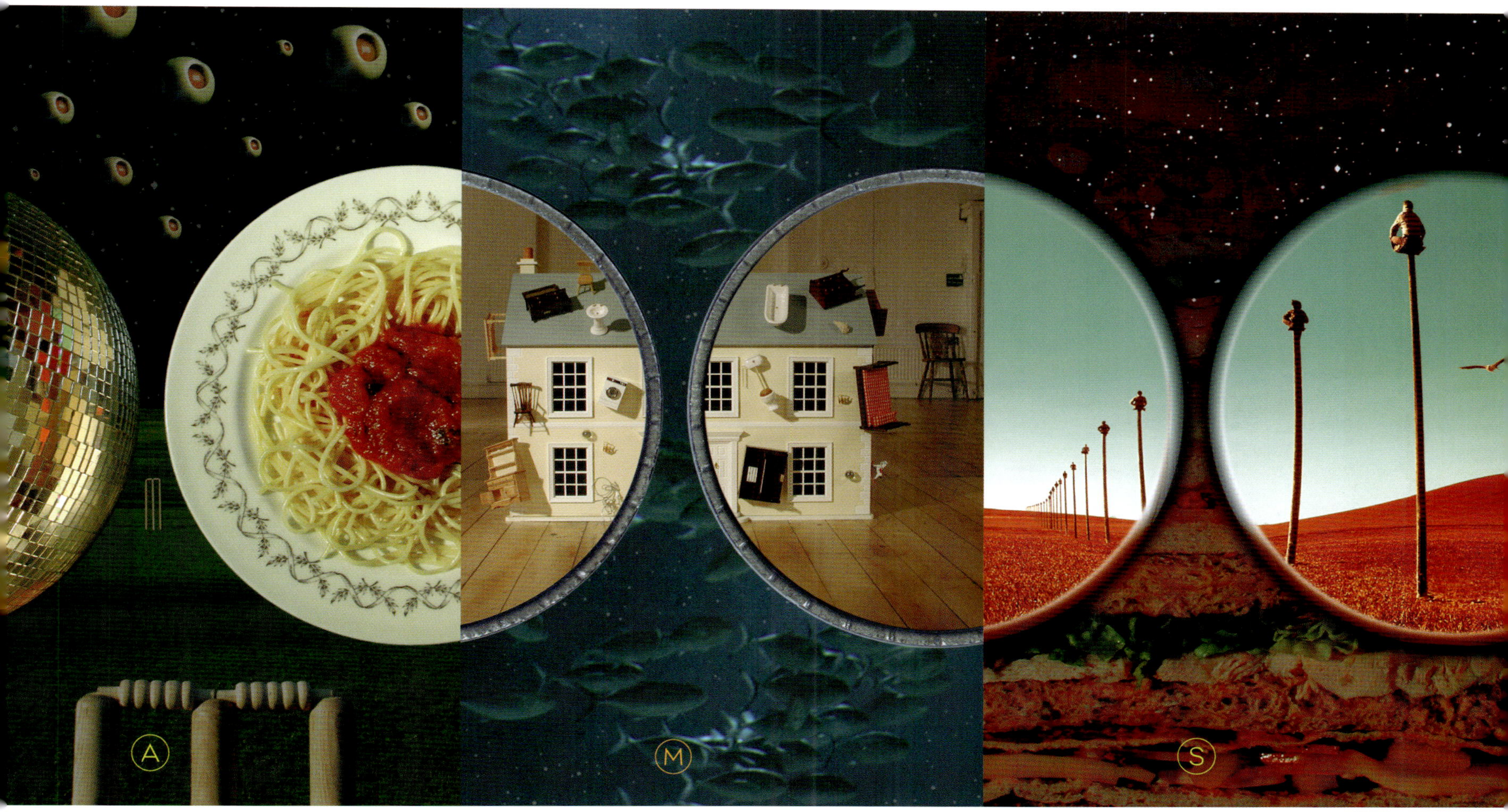

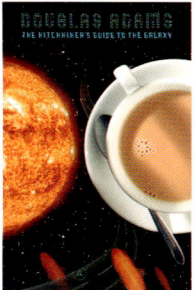

THE HITCHHIKER'S GUIDE TO THE GALAXY Book publishers, as opposed to record companies, are inclined to change book cover designs quite happily and without qualm, though I remain unconvinced of either the purpose or the ethics. The late Douglas Adams asked me to re-design his *Hitchhikers'* trilogy which was in true Adams style actually a quartet. Since the publisher also wanted an omnibus edition there was a total of five books.

Five books huh? Five letters in his surname each one writ large on the spine would look cool on a bookshelf when placed in the correct order, reading ADAMS, visible from some feet away. If the spines were to be connected so then should the fronts such that if placed face out, say in a shop window, they would in effect constitute one long design in place of one small single design. Furthermore the book contents were clearly related being the same trilogy... er... quartet... quintet. Douglas himself loved the principle so that settled that. In order that each cover was separate, but connected, we needed a graphic not figurative thread, not a theme but part shapes which when placed adjacent formed a whole shape or graphic that superceded the visual contents, which in turn were specfic and different for each book. Hence bisected circles which, as you can see, make complete circles when joined side by side, a bit like binoculars or telescopes through which one might view something distant – like the galaxy perhaps.

Douglas Adams **The Hitchhiker's Guide To The Galaxy** *Book jackets Picador 2000*
Design and photos StormStudios

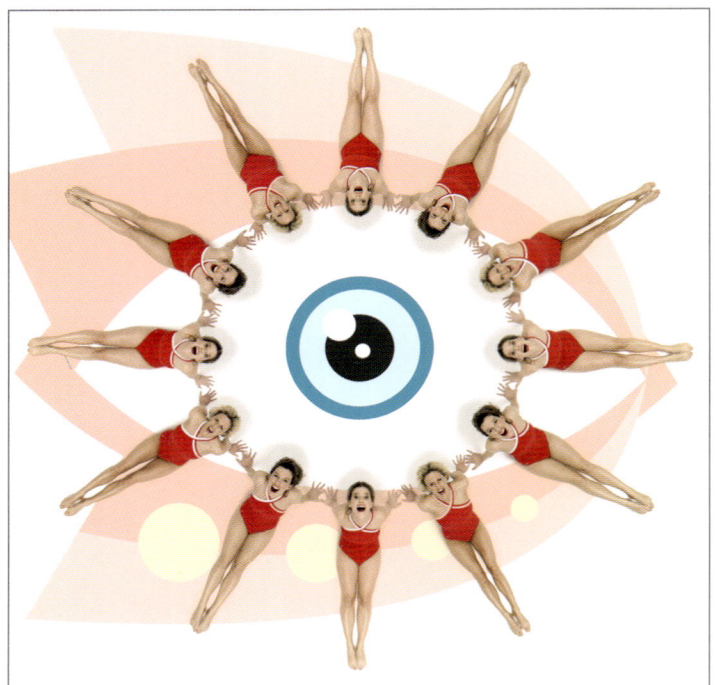

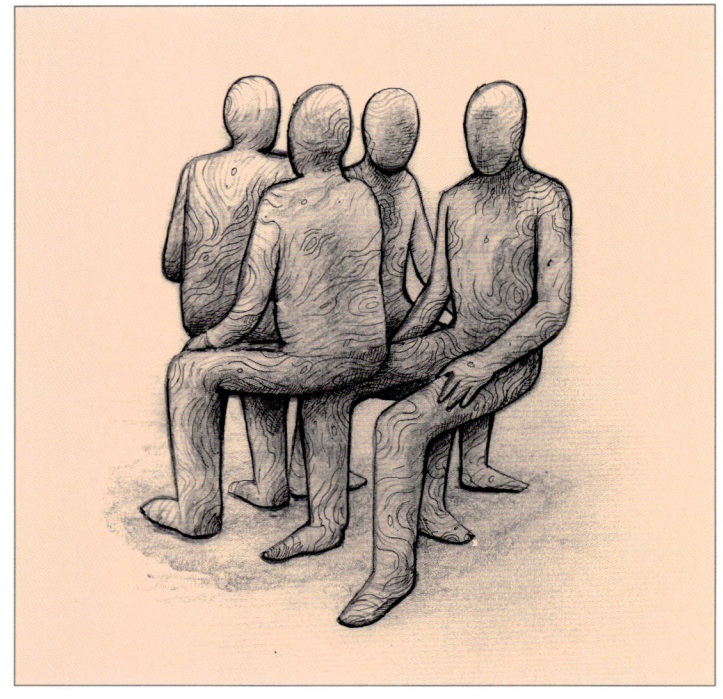

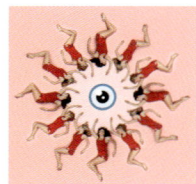

SUPERMASSIVE BLACK HOLE The world of music graphic design is quite changeable, you know, subject to circumstance, misadventure, budgets, company politics and the whims of musicians. Topsy turvy nothing… Some ideas are too fruitful to discard easily, whilst others are too readily jettisoned. Some designs linger to re-emerge years later in some renewed fashion, and some die a quick death unless salvaged temporarily in a magazine, website or book… just like this design for a Muse single called *Supermassive Black Hole* released in the summer of 2006.

Due to release schedules, frantic business, indecision, interrupted communication lines and any combination of the above, this design started as one thing but soon became another, then another. It began life as four men carved from wood sitting on each others laps, became four flesh and blood corporate men sitting on each other's laps to suggest both conspiracy and financial collusion – 'in each other's pockets' as it were, and then changed to four women because the song was about women rather than politics and then became more intimate - women in lingerie, not suits. Then the circles became more (black) hole-like, then, via Busby Berkeley, into patterns of girls in circles, then via black holes again into black pupils and the seductive depth of eyes by which time the plot was lost and the band had gone off the idea.

In retrospect I was not that surprised nor upset, all parties behaved reasonably… it was simply one of those things… some ideas just don't make it… but we like this design, and this is our book… so here it is, but without super massive petulance, just a moderate amount.

*Muse **Supermassive Black Hole** CD Single unused Warners 2006*
Design & Photos StormStudios

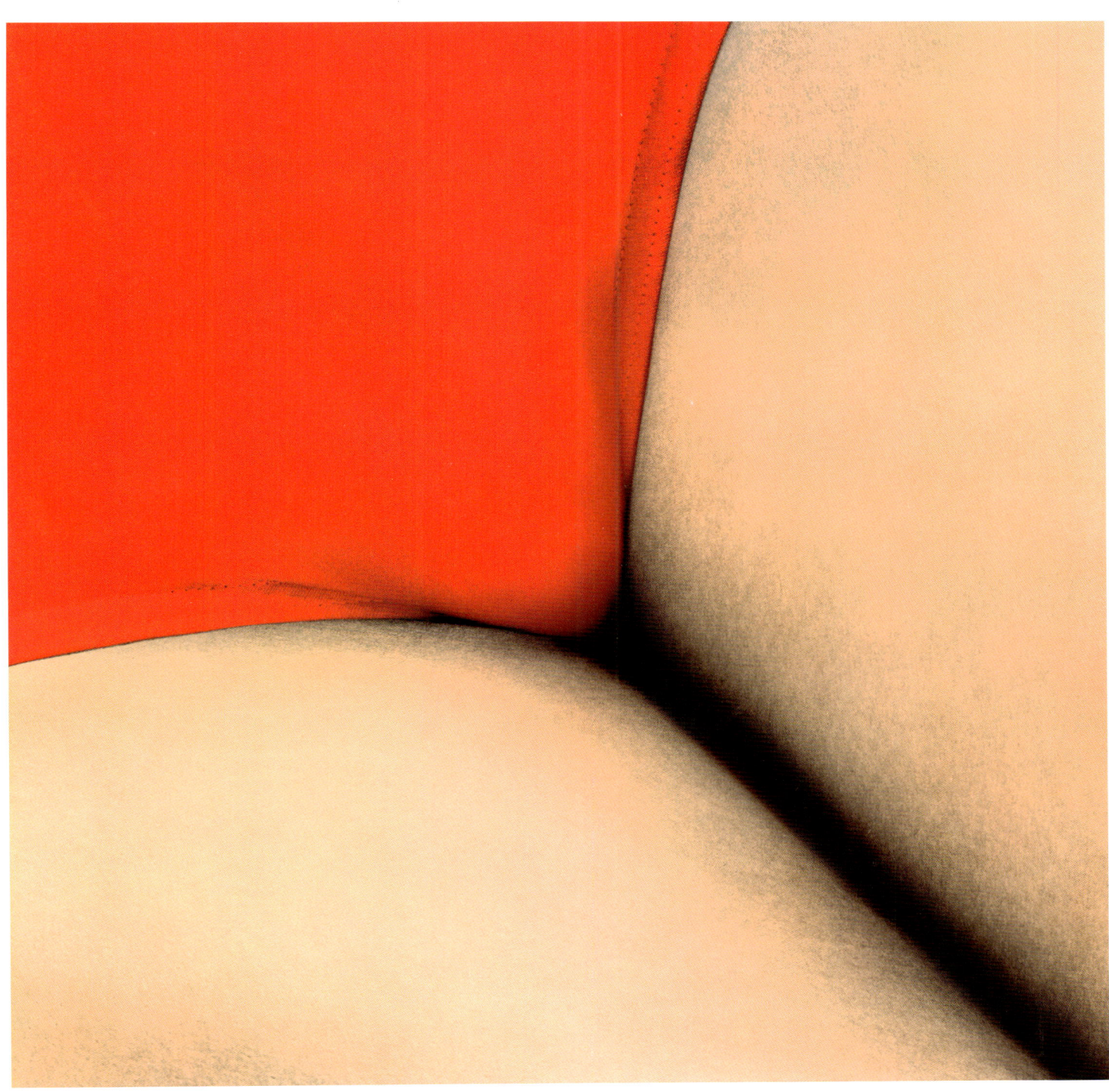

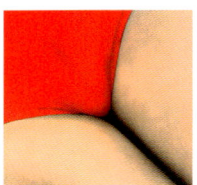

JUMP ON IT Hard rock bands, or musicians in general, are often a delightful mix of the sophisticated and the unsophisticated, or is it just plain crude? Montrose, a Seventies rock band from Canada chose a rather unsubtle title, *Jump On It*, but had the good sense to ask us extremely subtle chaps at Hipgnosis to design their album cover. In an effort to capture this contrariness we devised an image of something erotic but executed in a clinical fashion, something curvaceous, but done geometrically, something hot but composed with a degree of detachment, warm but cold. And this contrary approach has resurfaced at other times (*Correlations*, pg. 21 and 'Like A Satellite', pg. 147).

This very formal picture of a female crotch in a bright red bathing suit is very symmetrical, great emphasis is put upon the diagonal, and the symmetry of the V is enhanced by the bright colour of the costume. It's all very simple really, although the content of the picture is of course all very complex. Such is life, huh? Deep but trivial, straightforward yet convoluted, down but up.

This image is photographed from above (girl lying on the floor) in our studio in sunny Denmark Street using a Hasselblad and flashlight with black and white film. The resulting print was made sepia and then hand coloured, in an effort to add warmth-the human touch enhancing the cold medium of photography.

*Montrose **Jump On It** Vinyl front Warner Bros. 1976 Design & Photos Hipgnosis*

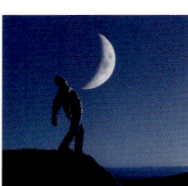

SPLINTER This highly graphic design is an amalgam of something observed in nature, a natural event, and an interpretation of the title. I imagined that the splinter of the title might be the splinter that broke a heart, the heart of a lover betrayed, which I am sure was probably the subject of one or two of the songs. And the thing that I saw in nature occurred one night on my way home when I saw a very bright moon, positioned low and symmetrical above the street where I live, seeming unnaturally close, unnaturally large between the roofs. The idea also involves an echo of a Canadian TV show called *The Kids In The Hall*, where large close up fingers are seen to squash someone's head at a distance, with a voice over gleefully saying, "I'm crushing your head"! This also works on the principal of spatial association. So I envisaged the splinter as a sharp moon (a crescent moon), about to pierce the heart of a lover like a scimitar, although only spatially speaking of course, seeming both angular and poetic like the music. And what more appropriate weapon with which to pierce (or splinter) the heart of a lover than the moon, more usually the lover's greatest ally. Ah the irony of love!

*Offspring **Splinter** CD booklet Sony 2003 Design and photos StormStudios Location wiltshire UK*

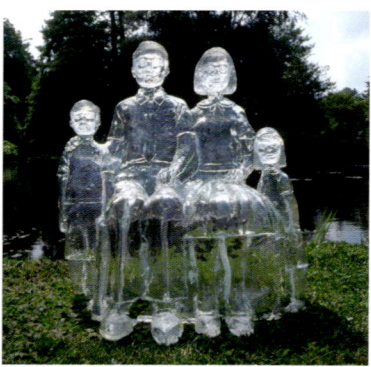

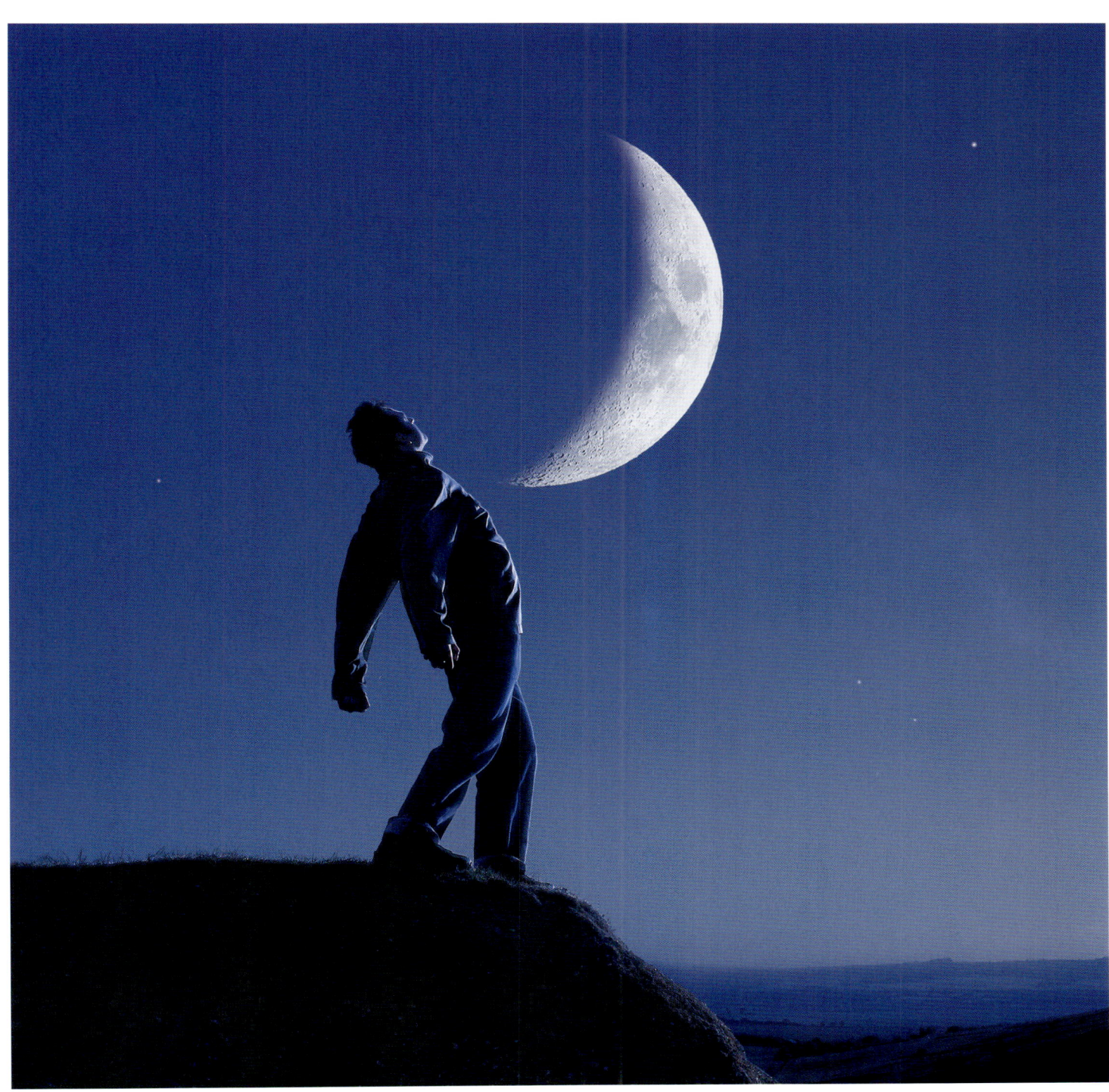

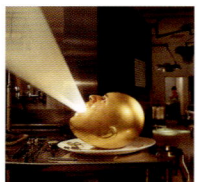

DELOUSED IN THE COMATORIUM This album, from the intrepid musical explorers The Mars Volta, renegades from At The Drive In, contained a set of songs about their close friend, artistic mentor and wild man Julio, who as a result of numerous misadventures and over indulgences, spent much time in hospital, slipping in and out of a coma. This accounts for the hospital setting for our design. The Mars Volta imagined that their friend, in his unconscious state, was being pulled down by his artistic demons or imaginary figures called Tremulants, from whose clutches he was continually trying to escape. When successful he surfaced briefly into consciousness. The light from his mouth is the cry for help, a shaft of daylight piercing his hospital gloom. His head is bobbing (or rolling) in and out of consciousness, and was therefore represented by an egg-shaped sculpture of bronze which could literally roll backwards and forwards, and was clean edged and very 'deloused', but with a real skin face... scary huh?

PS This album had two interchangeable front covers depending which way the booklet was packed in the jewel box, see pg. 57.

*The Mars Volta **Deloused In The Comatorium** CD Universal 2003*
Design & Photos StormStudios Location West Middx Hospital, West London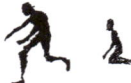

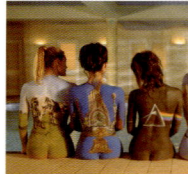

BACK CATALOGUE EMI, Pink Floyd's record company, requested an image to promote a back catalogue campaign, meaning a spate of advertising to promote the sale of all Pink Floyd's previous albums, in case anybody had forgot. We sat around discussing how to re-display, dredge-up, show again, and re-use images that had perhaps had their day, done the rounds. Me, personally, from my totally unbiased position as designer, loves them to death, but wasn't too sure that the unsuspecting public would need to see them again. Finlay Cowan made a bad joke and said self-consciously, why don't we put the cover images on the backs of beautiful girls, back catalogue, ho ho. Not only was this joke a tad unsubtle, it may also be open to a sexist critique. I was going to say that's why the record company might have reservations, but they loved it.

I have to say despite being sensitive about the use of nudes, I greatly enjoyed this photo-shoot. It took place in a private indoor swimming pool in sunny Putney, South-West London. Kim, our friendly model from *Shine On* box set, had secured the services of five of her friends, who behaved with both great dignity and great humour, despite spending most of the day totally naked. It took six hours to paint the backs, a Herculean effort from Phyllis Cohen and stoic patience from the models who had to spend most of the day flat on their tummies. During this time Tony May, the photographer and I lit the set and decided from what position to take the picture.

The photography took about another three hours. I had always imagined that the girls would have to be sitting down on something like the side of a swimming pool, where they might be bathing, in order to best show their backs. I think that because of the wonderfully friendly atmosphere, it emerged that they should chat and talk amongst themselves in a relaxed naturalistic manner which is how we arrived at this particular pose, and it is precisely this atmosphere that I most admire.

I had thought my wife and her friends would be the sternest critics but in fact they agreed that though there was a question of sexism, it was still a very likable picture and I think they found it not too offensive. So relaxed was the event and so used does one get to the nudity that one was unaware of it, lest you be a bloke returning from the loo on the far side of the pool, which I did midway through the session, forgetting their nudity, and was confronted suddenly by a row of magnificent breasts, and was temporarily distracted and nearly fell in the pool.

*Pink Floyd **Back Catalogue** Ad Campaign EMI 1996*
Design & Photos StormStudios Location Putney, London

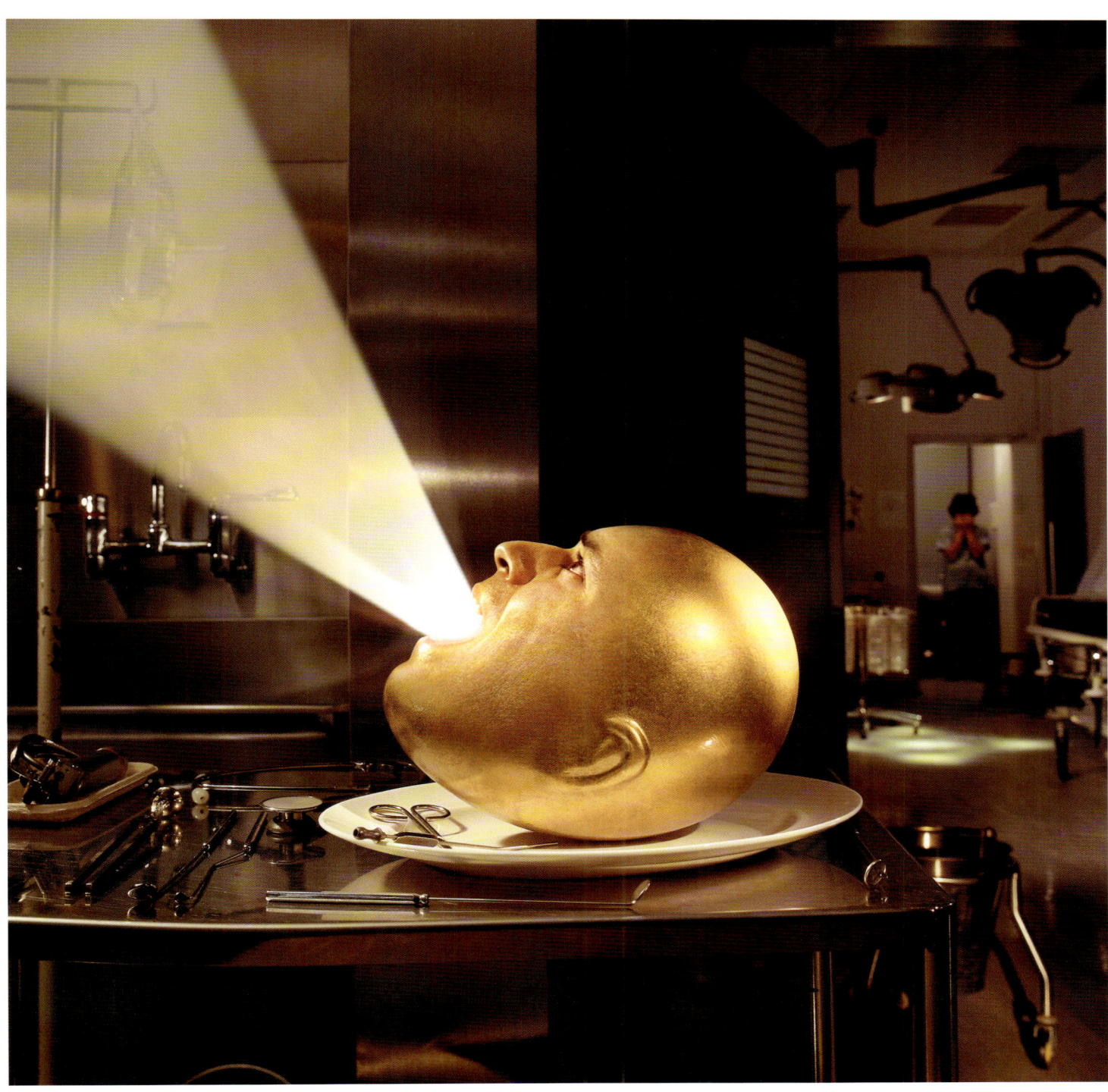

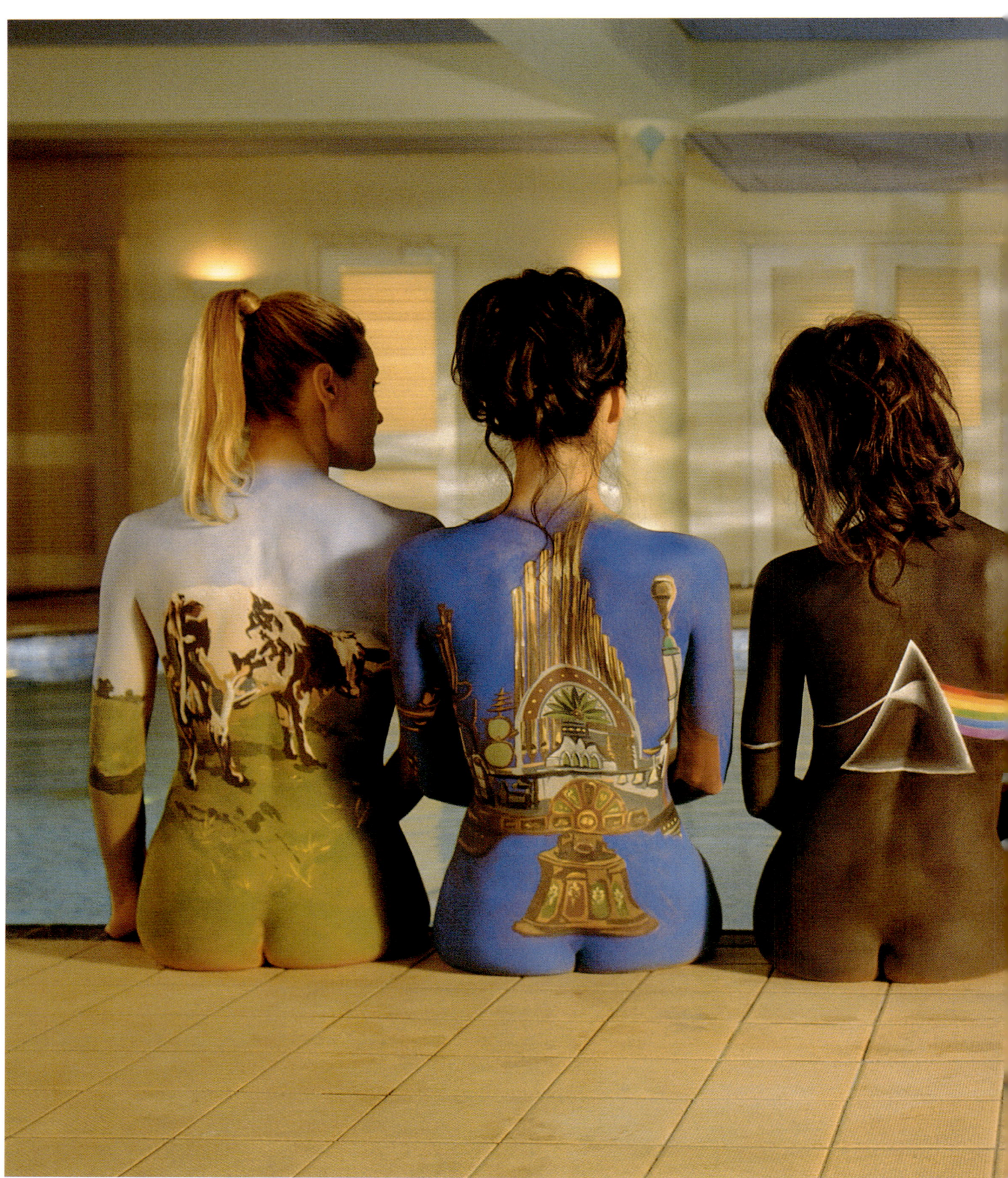

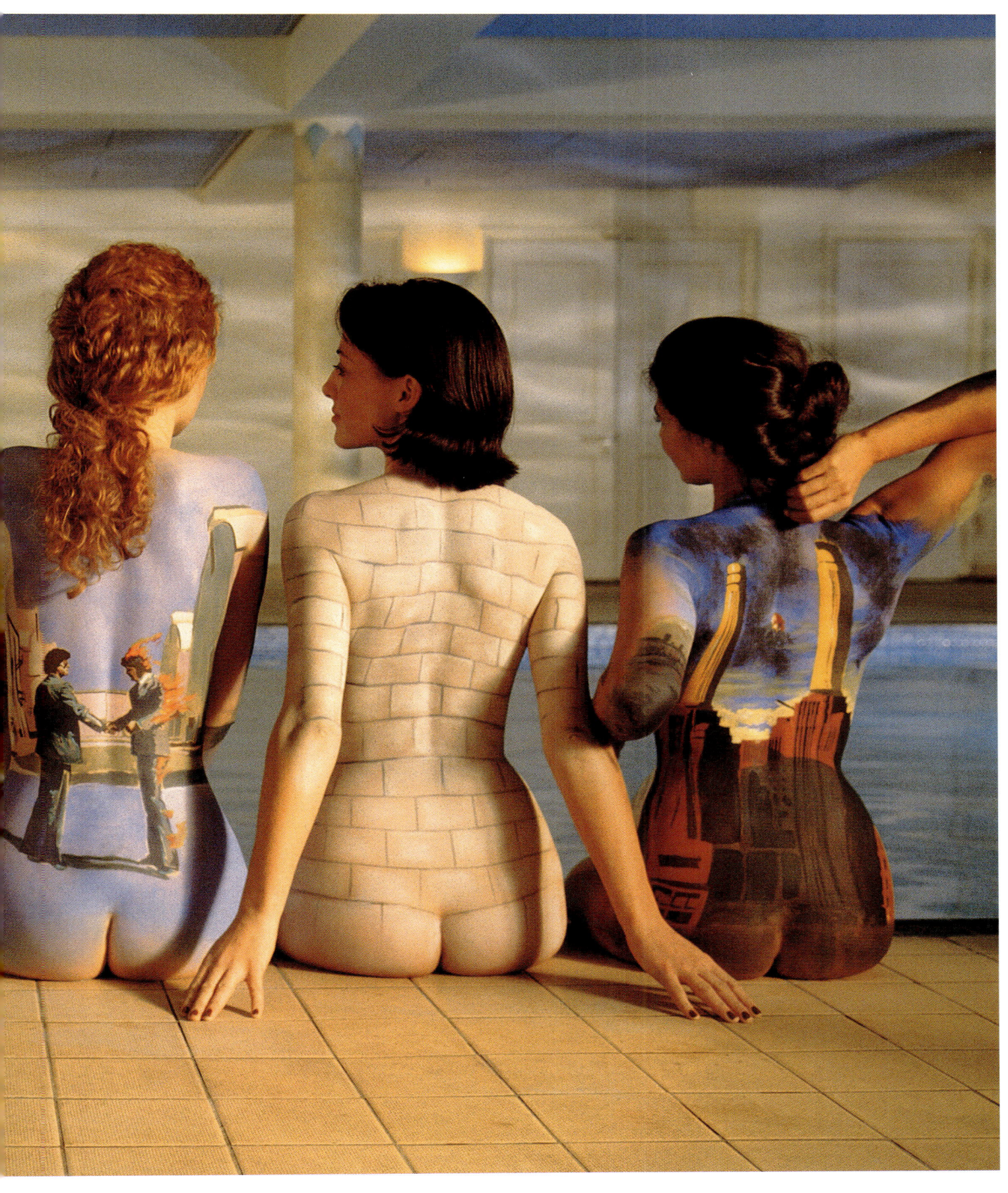

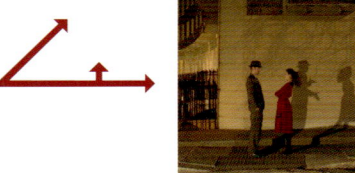

RAPT. DEPT. Much as I love photography, since it makes a relatively faithful recording of our occasionally grandiose ideas, be they large sculptures, flying pigs, or myriad gym balls, there are also aspects that disagree with me, such as its coldness and its lack of hands on. However, there is one overriding thing that one can both like and dislike, namely its 'frozen moment' quality. As much as one might treasure the moment caught, the unexpected moment, or the moment of fleeting beauty (fluttering bird, leaping ballet dancer) one might also wish to have extension, time to tell a story, be durational. This of course has been tried in many ways, such as time-lapse or long eposures or multiple pictures. But this is the first time I have ever come across duration expressed in a single shot in quite this way.

So it's hats off to Larry, or rather to Danny for devising this anti-photograph photograph. The story it tells is a before and after scenario, or more precisely, this moment and the next. 'This moment' is displayed in the usual way, by showing two lovers in quarrel, starkly lit by street-light, but their shadows, however, tell a different story, that of the moment after when the woman walks away in disgust and the man is left wondering what the hell is going on. A scenario of everyday life in many a city street, across the world I bet, from Rangoon to Runcorn, from Delhi to Dartford, a lovers' tiff is the same.

What I thought was so effective was that this little story was told in one picture, no multiple exposure, no time lapse, no picture sequence here – it's very economical, an everyday story in one shot. The inset on this page employs a similar technique, but tells a different story – the story of what's in one's mind. The hunched figure of the paranoid imagines paranoically that even his own shadow pursues him with evil intent, a kind of humourous twist on Nosferatu. There is no escape, your shadow's always with you. The idea of independent shadows, comes I guess from Peter Pan... Peter Pan meets Nosferatu, childrens' fiction meets gothic horror, which is like the inside of Dan's head. There's a thought.

Yourcodenameis:milo **Rapt. Dept.** *CD single Fiction 2005*
Design & Photos StormStudios Location Mornington Crescent, London

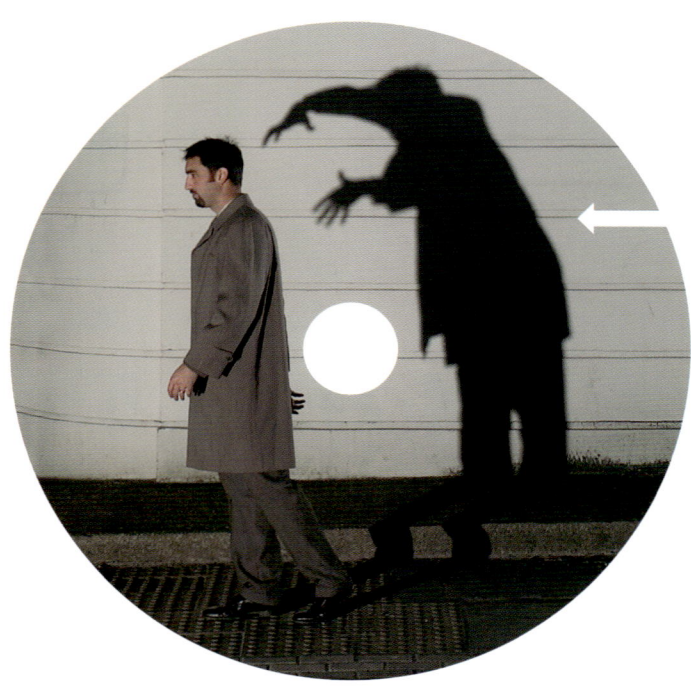

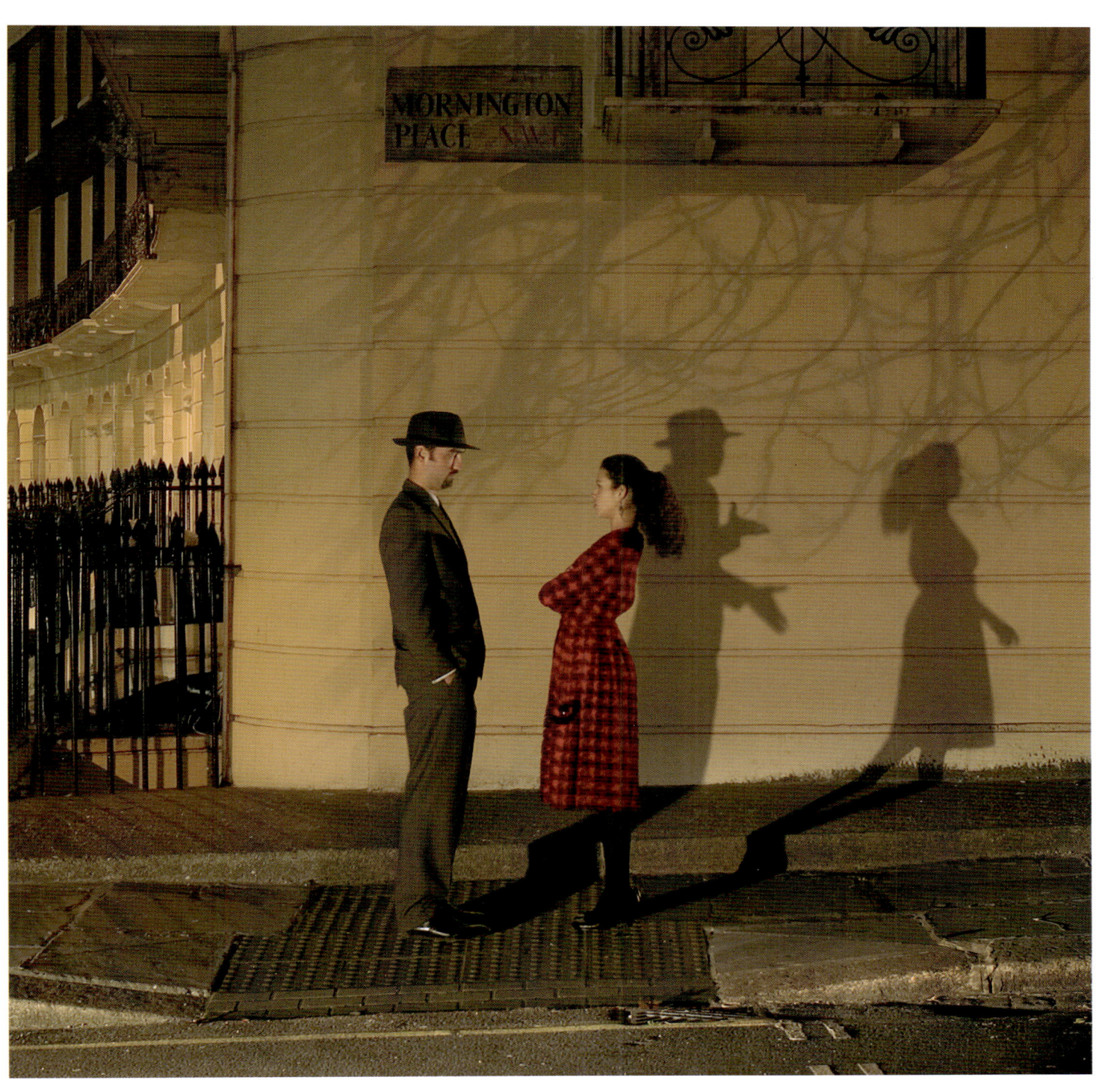

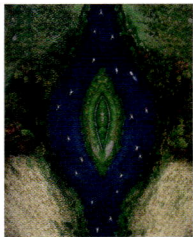

TWIN RIVERS I tend to think that re-visits are a good idea, but I'm not sure about this instance. I was re-visited in the Nineties by Wishbone Ash, with whom I'd worked in the mid-Seventies. They were having a box-set compiled by Repertoire, whose motto was 'Look to the future through the past', they were German, Repertoire, not Wishbone Ash that is. The fortunes of Wishbone Ash were not the greatest (possibly because we did a set of covers for them), and they never sustained their earlier promise (voted New Band of the Year, in *Melody Maker* circa, 1972). However their spirit was commendable and despite changing fortunes, they soldiered on, mainly thanks to the efforts of Andy Powell, one half of their twin guitar ensemble. The title *Twin Rivers*, for their box-set, seemed most appropriate, for they had continued a long and windy path like a river, and were still flowing.

I imagined a river dividing into two branches, forming twin rivers in which swimmers were seen to be progressing upstream, ploughing the furrows of their creativity, so to speak. The two rivers represented two guitars, the figures in the water represented the different members in the band, and the femininity of the whole image, represented their music or creativity, which has often been portrayed as a feminine trait. That the aerial view of the twin rivers might resemble something else, something possibly sexual, seemed like a good idea to me. What is rock 'n' roll without sex? I ask you, and what is wrong with being a tad suggestive on a rock 'n' roll album cover?

The rough design was approved, but then everything went downhill. The shoot was immensely difficult, and for once doing it for real was a bad idea because this was November, and the river was extremely cold, the swimmers nearly died of hypothermia, and the helicopter, from which the shot was taken (300 feet above a small stream in Berkshire), was damned expensive. The computer re-touching was painstaking and quite complex. And to cap it all, the shot was rejected by Andy Powell out of hand. He was very angry and accused me of trying to insult the band, cause offence to women, and endanger his career. He claimed the image was disgusting, and looked like a vagina.

My reaction was equally unqualified, I told him, never mind vaginas, I thought he was a prick, insomuch as vaginas are rarely green and blue, or have trees around them, or swimmers in them. I thought he had lost it or indeed had suffered some traumatic childhood experience. Despite my protestations, he or was it his wife, remained obdurate, and the image languished unused until appearing in *Eye Of The Storm*, 1999, and again here, because I like it even if they don't.

*Wishbone Ash **Twin Rivers** CD album front, unpublished Repetoire 1999*
Design Storm Thorgerson Photos Tony May Location Berkshire UK

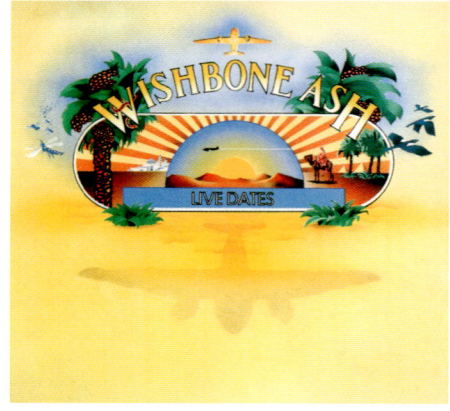

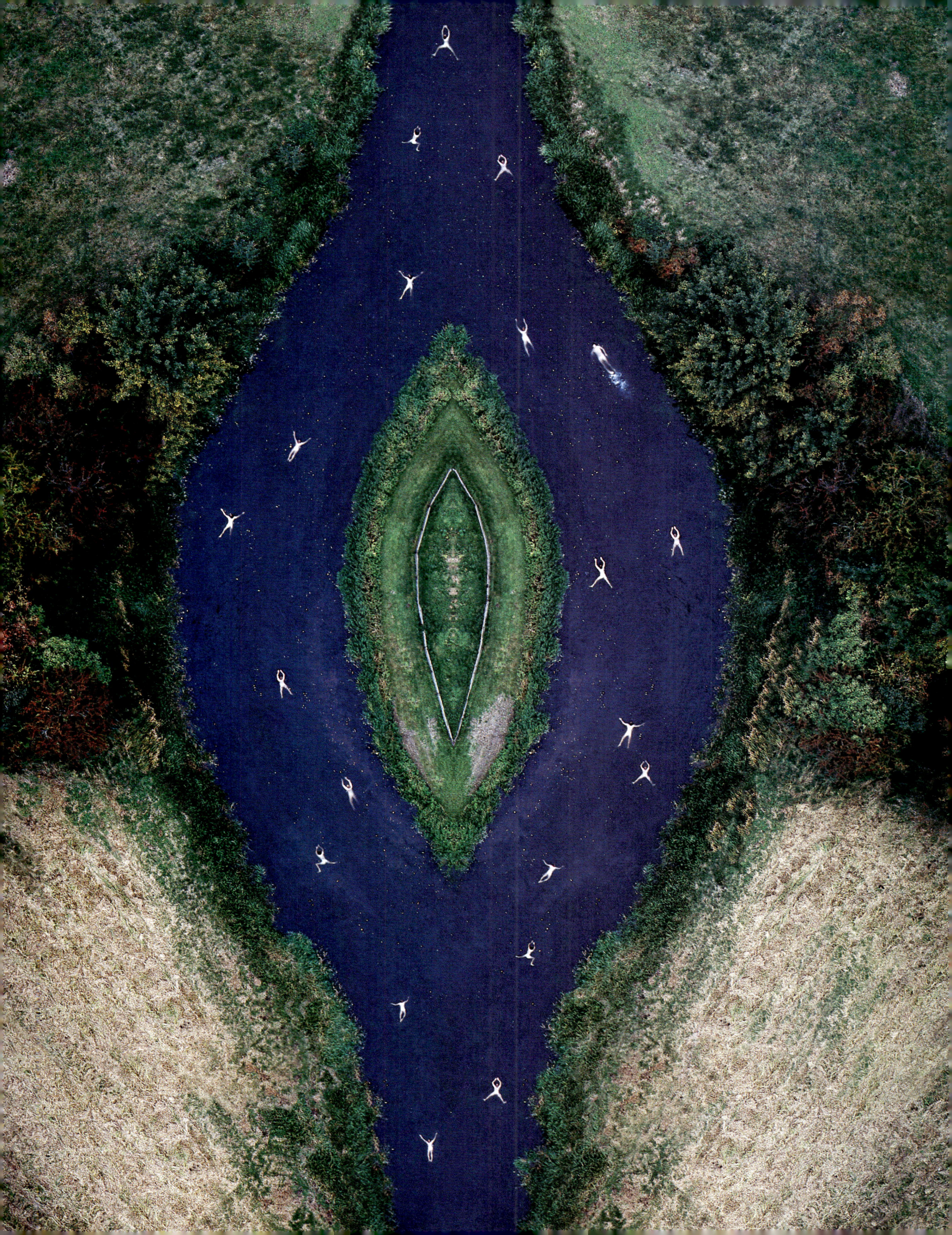

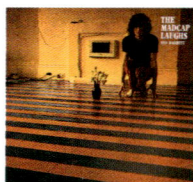

THE MADCAP LAUGHS This is the cover of the first solo album by Syd Barrett and was taken in his flat in Earl's Court, where I think he'd painted the floor especially for the occasion. He crouched down by the fire place and I took a 35mm pic quite quickly. Something in his tousled hair and haunted eyes, something in his cat-like position spoke volumes for how he was.

At the time of writing this, Syd has just passed away. So to speak volumes I cannot.

I loved him dearly but couldn't cope.

*Syd Barrett **The Madcap Laughs** Vinyl front Harvest 1970*
Design & Photos Hipgnosis Location Earls Court London

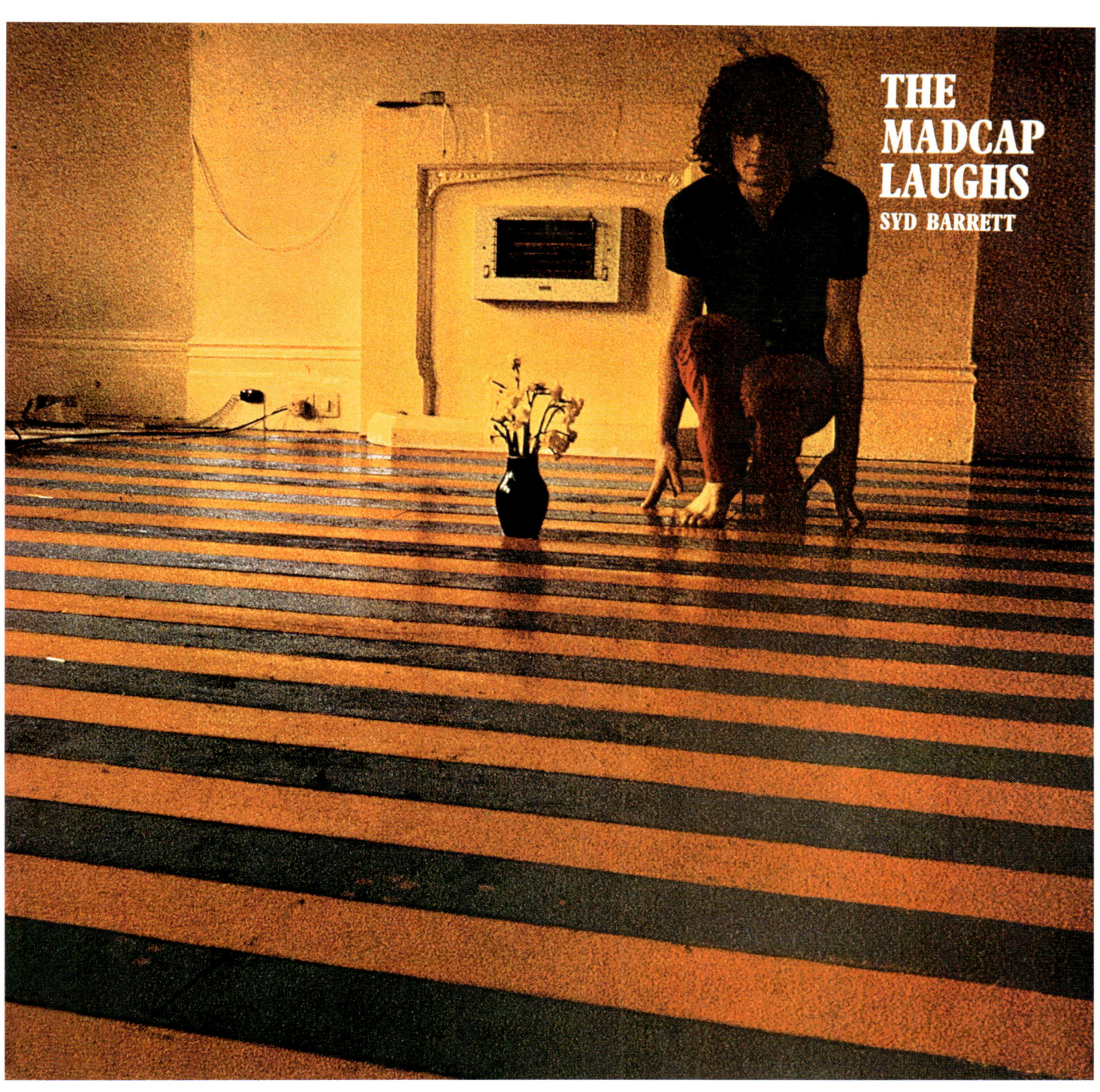

THE
MADCAP
LAUGHS
SYD BARRETT

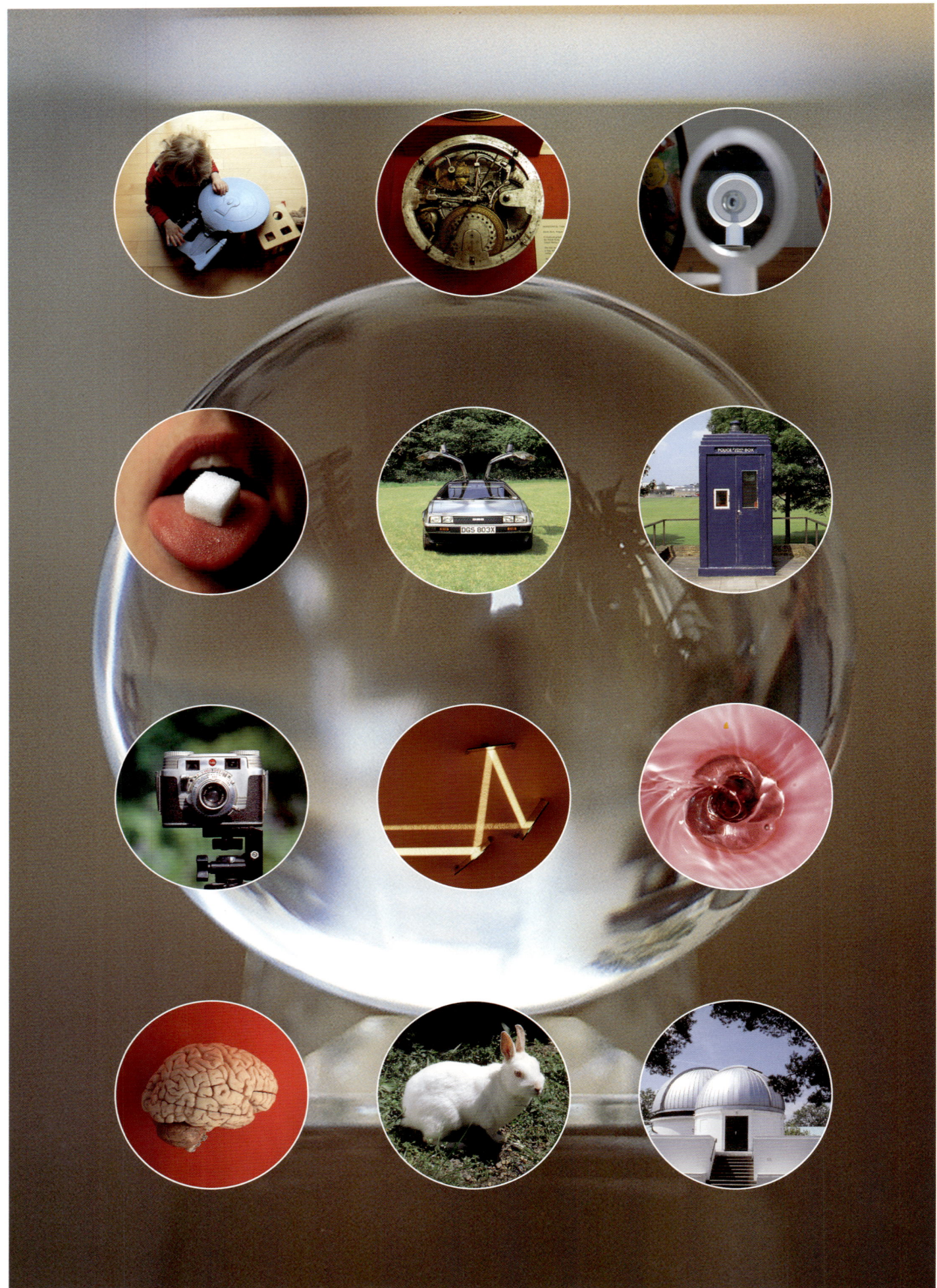

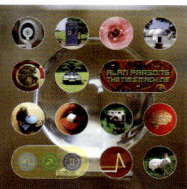

TIME MACHINE In the choppy waters of popular music the great height of Alan Parsons may allow him an overview, a vantage point from which he can perceive the follies of others and remain seemingly calm himself, his head above water, as it were. I never know whether he is 6' 4'' or 18' 10'', all I know is he towers over me. When he makes a record, (as producer extraordinaire, songwriter, etc) he has a preponderance to select, and pursue an idea or story, including Edgar Allen Poe, pyramids, Gaudi, Big Brother, the idea of flight amongst others. One imagines he likes something thematically substantial with which to wrestle (not his sumo neighbour of course) and in this instance he chose time, a notoriously elusive subject for a theoretical physicist let alone a rock musician, which is probably why he called it *Time Machine*, which is slightly easier to get a grip on.

In the face of such complexity a simple solution seemed attractive, but what is a time machine? What does it look like? And how can we design one that would avoid being a copy of a previous attempt or appear too obscure to recognise? We started to think of time machines in a more general fashion, ones which already exist, and then put them in some relevant and attractive configuration.

The basic ingredient of the design is circular because measurements of time are usually arranged around a circle, and for us mere mortals to register time, we must describe it in terms of cycles, 60 seconds in a minute, 60 minutes in an hour, 24 hours in a day etc. Even so time is damned elusive, how for example do you find time? How do you keep it? Let alone be in time, on time, or out of time? All in all it seemed timely to display our different time machines in an array of twelve (hours of the day) circles, each circle containing a different kind of time machine, framed against a defocused background that suggests it is unclear what time really is. This background depicts the ultimate time machine; a crystal ball.

I hope the viewer, that's you out there that is, enjoy locating and naming all the different time machines, and your time starts now.

*Alan Parsons **Time Machine** CD front Miramar 1999 Design & Photos StormStudios*

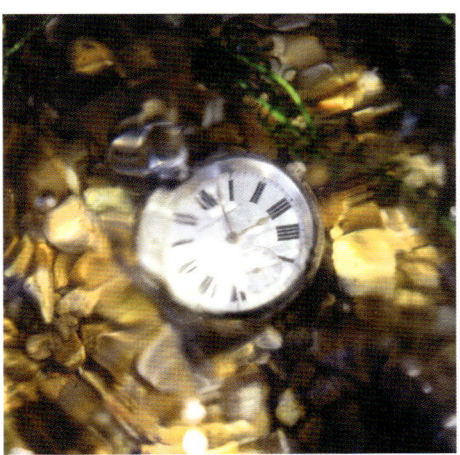

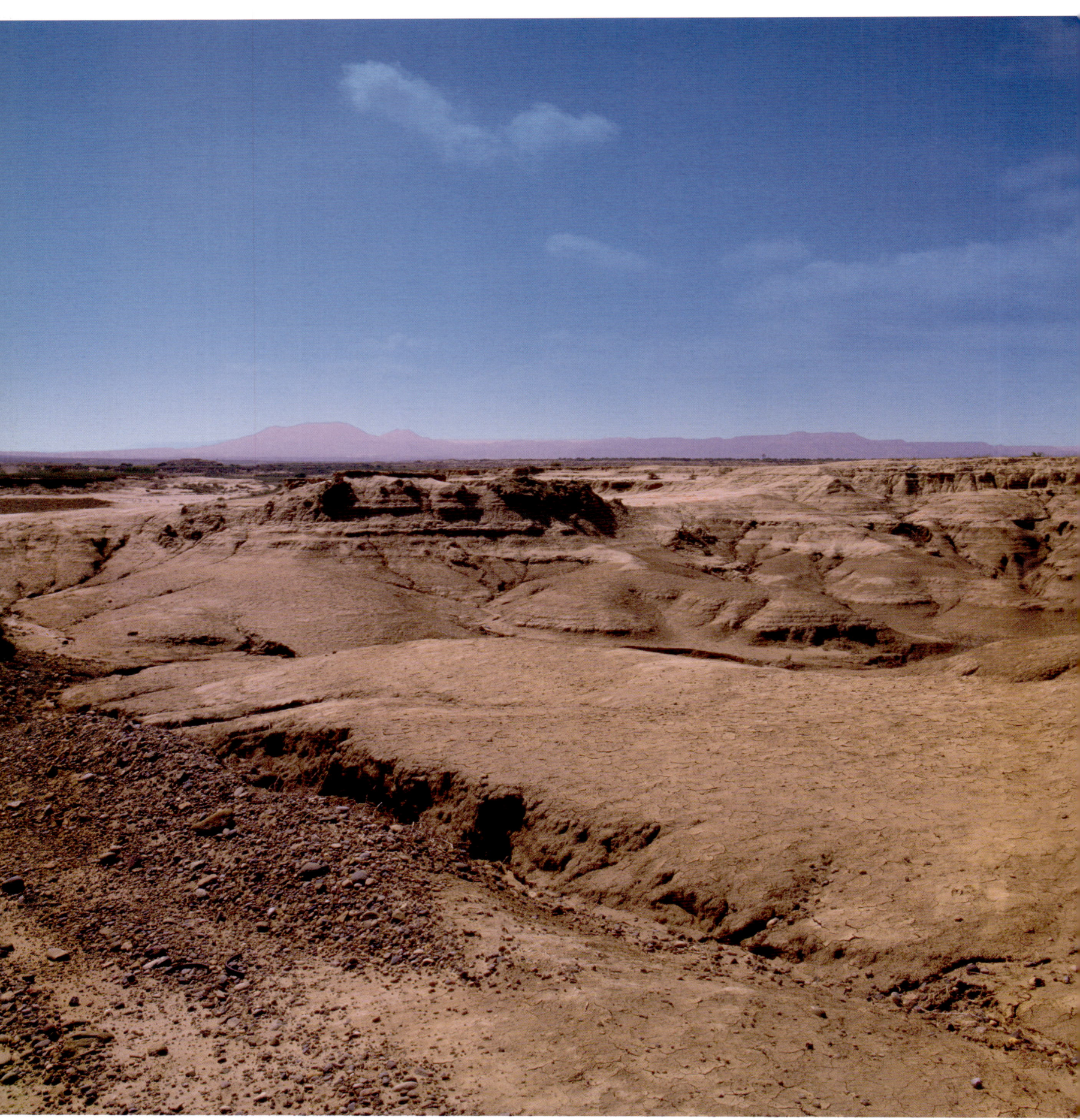

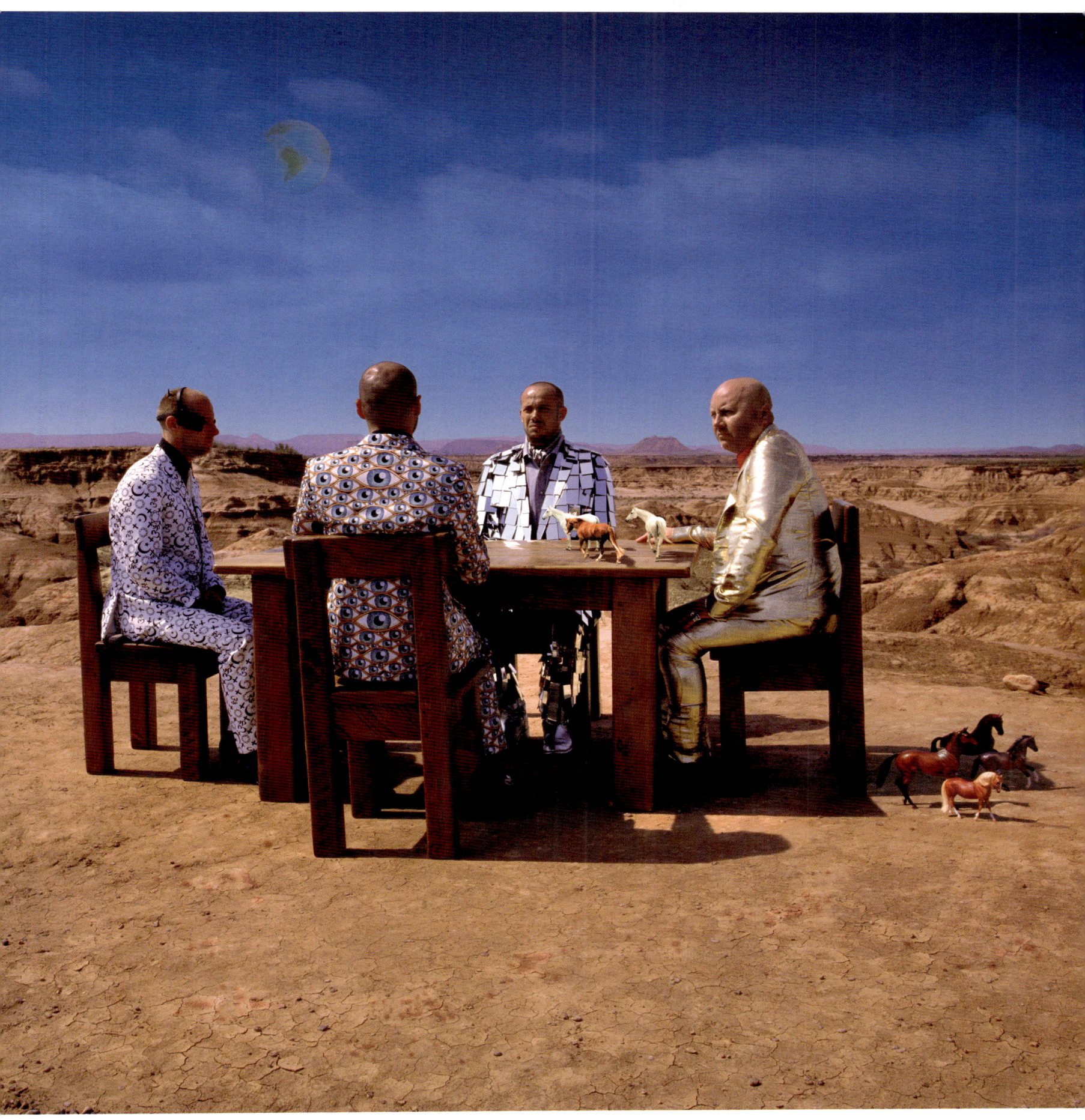

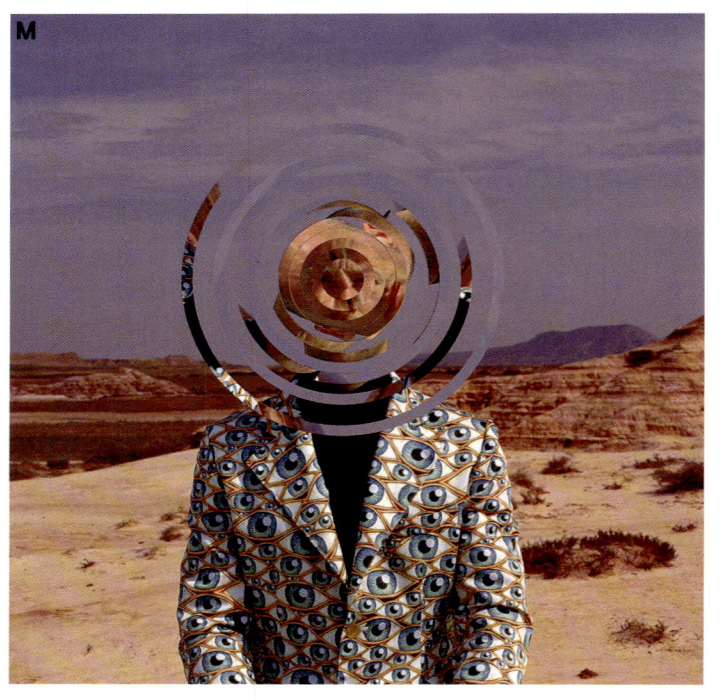
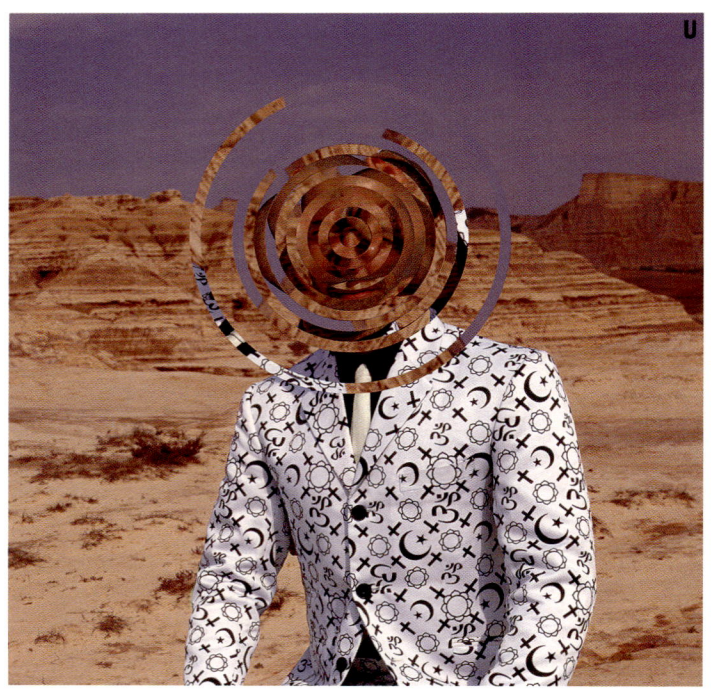
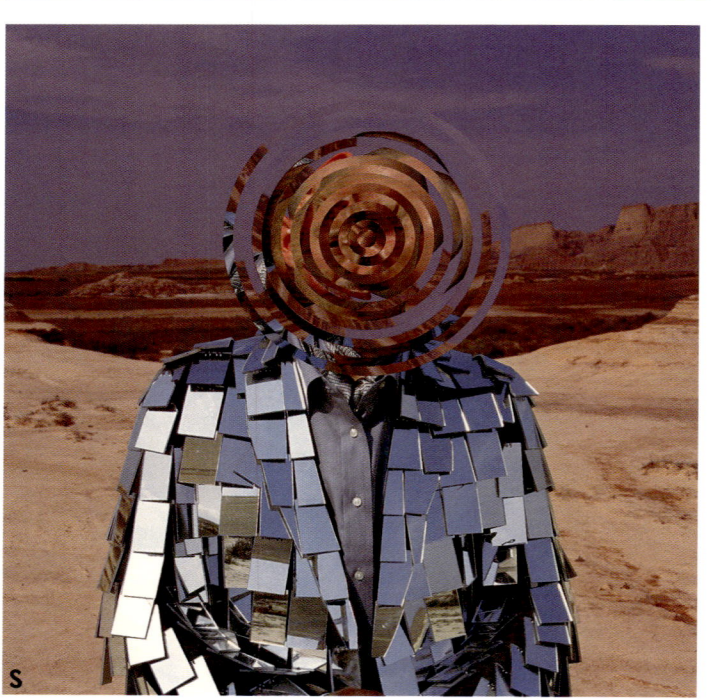
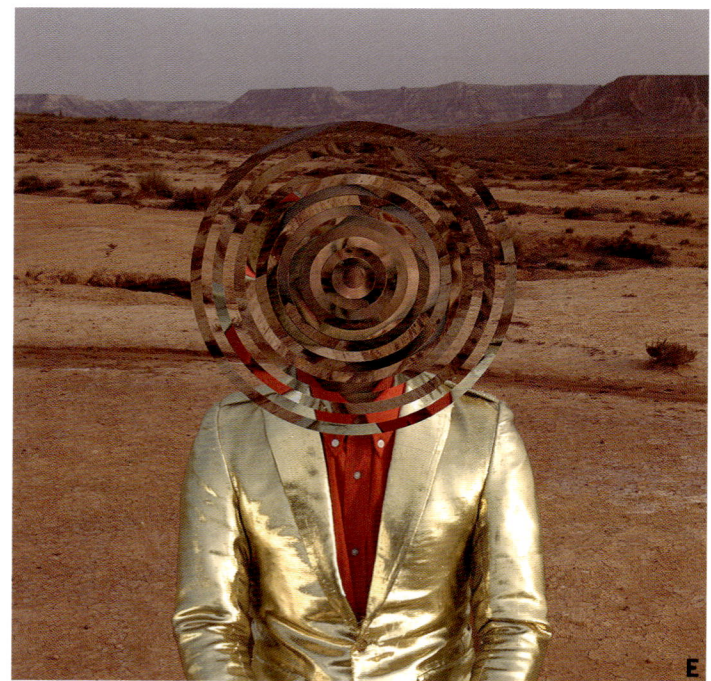

106

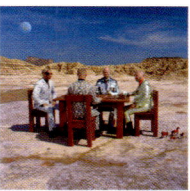

BLACK HOLES & REVELATIONS Matt Bellamy of Muse was quite preoccupied, apparently with conspiracy theories, at the time of making this album. When we heard the demos, however there were two or three tracks, which sounded to us like galloping horses, one being a song called 'Knights Of Cydonia'. Also in the music were rising crescendos, powerful riffs, feelings of open landscapes and epic vistas, even biblical overtones. Horses and conspiracy... biblical... gotta be the Four Horsemen of the Apocalypse, conspiring to end the world.

In the medieval version, the four horsemen were representative of War, Plague, Pestilence and Famine. But Muse are contemporary not medieval, for heaven's sake, so what is a contemporary version? What are the four worst or most apocalyptic characteristics of mankind today?

I imagined that the four modern horsemen of the Apocalypse would meet round a table in a conspiratorial manner, but since they are metaphor and not literal, this table setting is not ordinary, not a hotel, or a boardroom, anymore than the horsemen are real or their horses. For me the setting had to be other-worldly, the horses had to be magical, or very small (because the ills of mankind had gotten bigger and bigger), and the horseman should wear contemprary suits, symbolising their modern day dreadful qualities.

After much racking of brains we decided, in our infinite wisdom you understand, that the roots of all evil were as follows: Paranoia, Intolerance, Narcissism and Greed. It looked to us as though those megalomaniacs who waged wars in the last hundred years, if not before, exhibited one or more of these qualities in spades. In our picture Mr Greed is wearing a suit of gold obviously and might be trying to negotiate a new deal for his horses, since he has more than anybody else. Mr Paranoia has eyes in the back of his suit. Mr Narcissism wears, of course, a suit of mirrors, and Mr Intolerance has a blinkered perspective, his suit decorated with the symbols of the major religions of our time.

This perambulating explanation doesn't really matter much, it's simply the route by which I arrived at the image. Basically, four evil-looking, bald-headed bastards, sitting at a rustic table in the middle of a lunar landscape, arguing about something, with unnaturally little horses on the table. In the sky, barely seen, hangs the Earth, telling you that the Earth may be the subject of their deliberations, but not the location.

*Muse **Black Holes & Revelations** CD front Warners 2006*
Design & Photography The Men Of Mystery Location Bardenas, Spain

PS For those interested in numerology the number four is important to this cover. Clearly there are four Horsemen of the Apocalypse (not any more or any less), there are four letters in the word Muse and four words in the title *Black Holes And Revelations*, etc. This is studio album number four, there are four legs to a table and to a chair (not to mention a horse, of course), and of particular note to fans (also a four letter word) there were three members of Muse but are there about to be four?

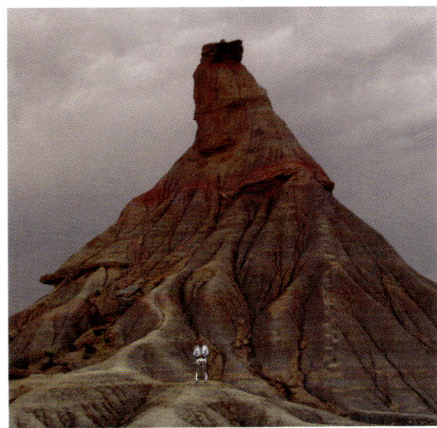

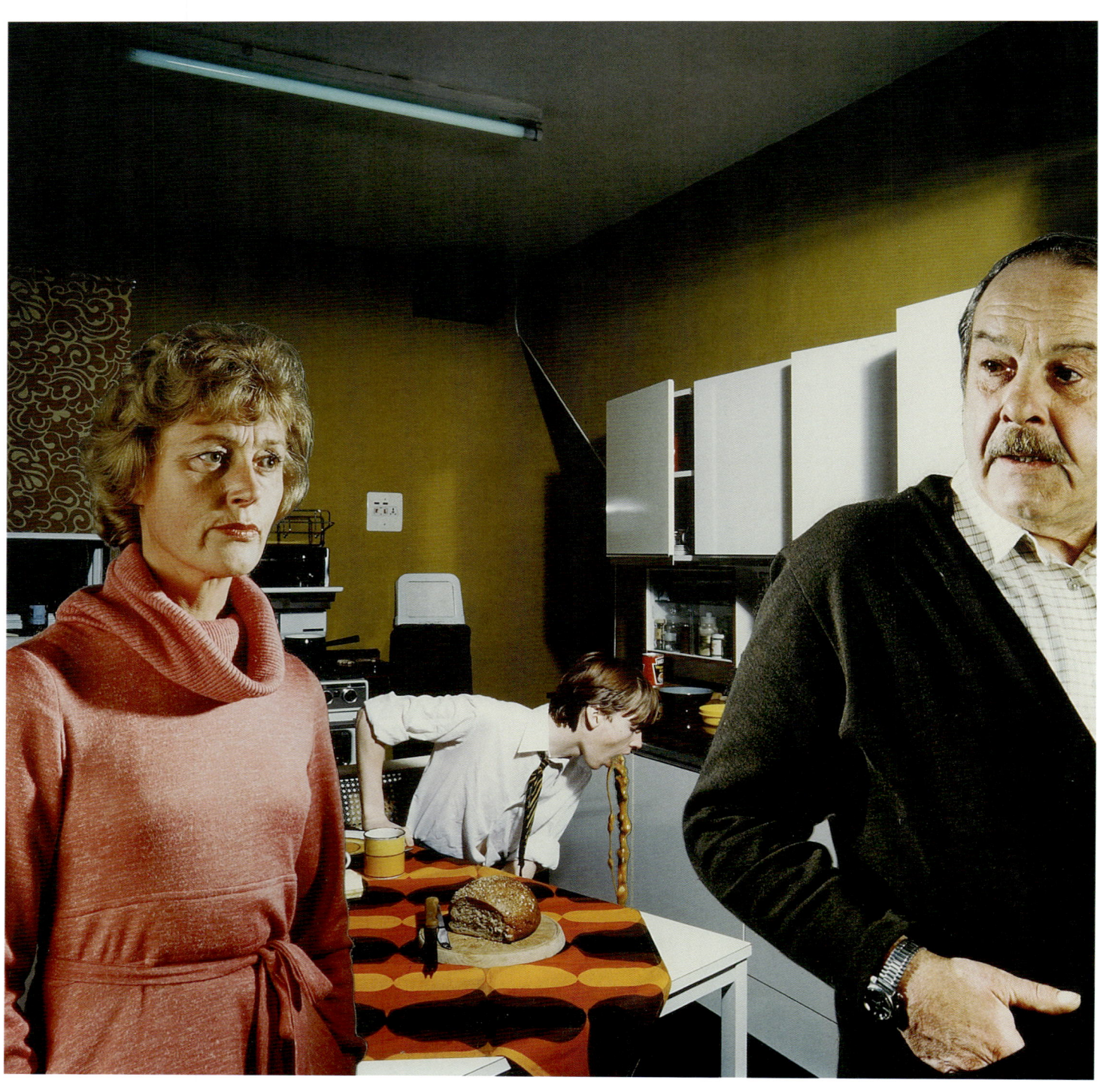

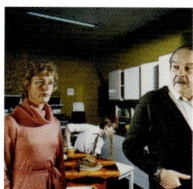

DEFIANT POSE Defiant Pose The punk phenomenon of 1976 in London was very funny, energetic, hugely exciting and largely hormonal. A prerequisite of such movements is the expulsion of what went before. I remember Johnny Rotten wore a t-shirt which proclaimed 'I hate Pink Floyd'. No wonder we at Hipgnosis felt a bit paranoid and thought our days of working for the music business might be numbered. Yer Pistols, Clash, Sham 69, Undertones, etc, were hardly likely to employ us. In fact our only contribution, visually speaking, was this image for The Cortinas, called 'Defiant Pose', and XTC's *Go 2* album on pg. 179.

In retrospect, we were far too interested in graphical qualities, ideas and meanings. One imagines the punk ethic would be 'fuck ideas'. However the simple idea that one's parents might make you sick was not too complicated, nor too involved for The Cortinas, or at least their management in the form of fast talking Miles Copeland, later manager of The Police, who knew us through the likes of Wishbone Ash, Renaissance and Al Stewart, all a far cry from punk.

My idea was quite simply to show a teenager throwing up at the sight of his parents arguing. It struck me that the first rebellion is not against society nor previous musical heroes, but against one's parents. Young Jimmy can't stand his parents, they make him sick so he vomits in their presence, ejecting a stream of green and brown lumpy fluid (ox-tail soup). The manner of the comping/simple cut-outs, stuck down with cow gum, also reflected the punk ethic of being unfussy, cheap, and affordable by teenagers; no over-production here. I have always liked this image as I have thought it succinct and revolting, mind you, what do I know? Disqualified, in a way from punkdom, owing to my middle-class roots, but on the other hand parents can be very aggravating, whatever their class.

The Cortinas **Defiant Pose** *Single Step Forward Records 1977 Design & Photos Hipgnosis*

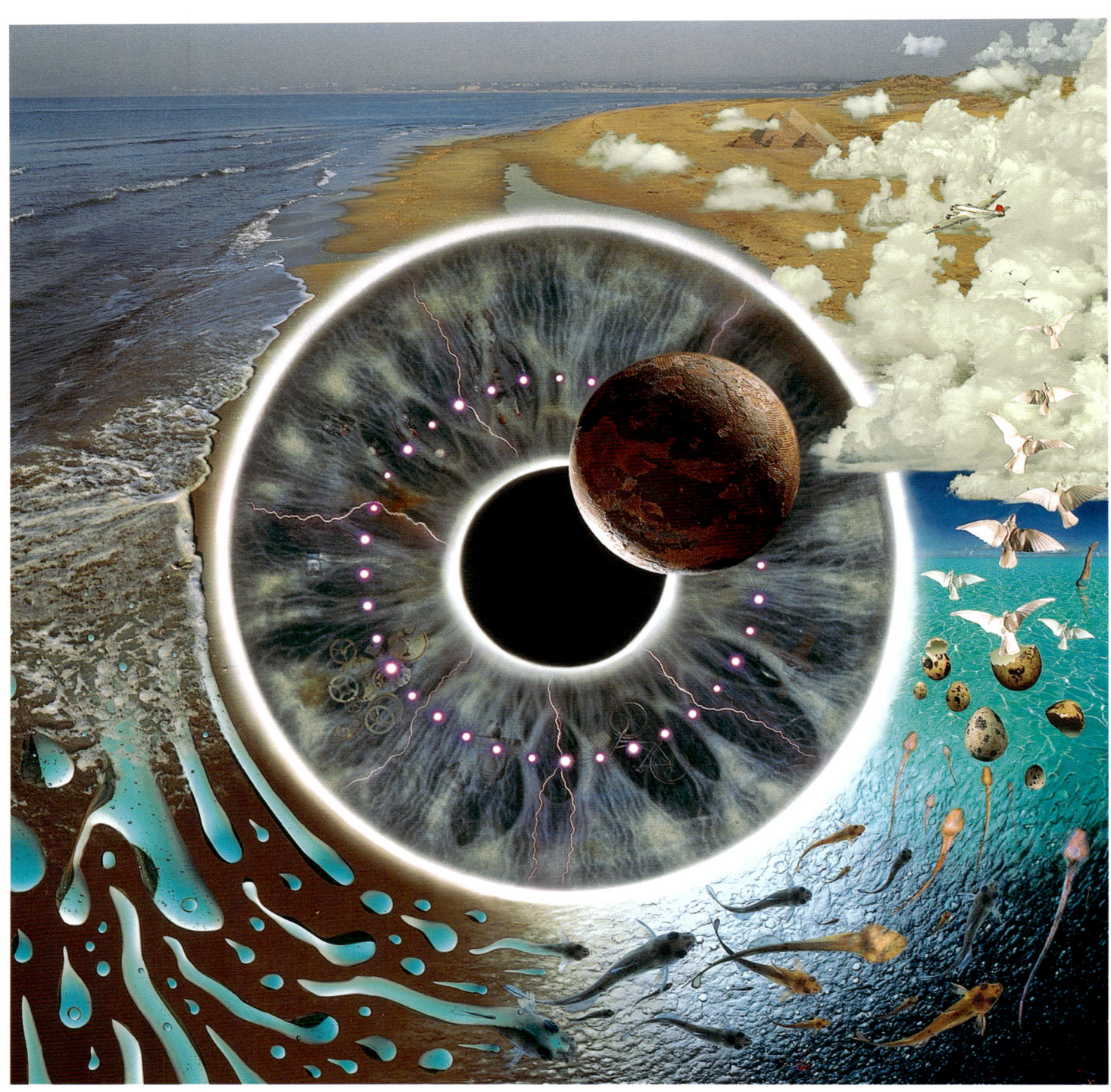

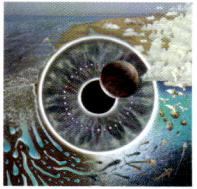

PULSE Much as I'm fond of books I regret that we cannot show you here the pulsing red light which was a feature of the package for Pink Floyd's *Pulse* CD - a double live album of *The Division Bell* shows at Earls Court London 1994. I wanted the cover to be 'live' like the music, so I suggested to the band that the package contain a pulsing red light - a small LED which flashed approx 70 times a minute like a human pulse, like the heartbeat at the beginning of *The Dark Side Of The Moon*, which was on the album. It was, I agree, a preposterous idea but I made a mock up, put it in the bottom of a dark bag and showed it to the band in a surreptitious manner - "'Ere guv'nor look what's in my bag", and opened it slightly to reveal the little red light flashing in the interior gloom. They said, "Great, we'll have it", much to the consternation of the record company who envisaged mega production problems.

But to their credit they surmounted the problems, outsourced it successfully and produced a million or two packages containing a chip, a capacitor, a battery and L.E.D. and housed it all in the spine of the slipcase. The little red light flashed merrily away in the spine, saying, "Hello I'm here in your collection, you can find me in the dark or use me as an anti-theft device in the car". It continued to pulse for a year or two and the American version even had a replaceable battery. A gimmick to be sure but a real cute one and very appropriate for the title *Pulse* and for it being a live album.

You can't see it here, as I said, but you can of course see the cover design. This was based on standing close to a fan at a Floyd show and seeing their wide eyed response to the lights, the films, the lasers and sundry effects, the whole kit and caboodle as it were reflected in their iris along with their delight and understanding of the many references and images conjured by the music. Thus what we designed was in part literal and in part imaginitive - a big close up of an eye with the Floyd lightshow 'reflected' in it plus various images referring to some of the songs and to albums from which other songs came. Along with Jon Crossland this idea developed as we drew more roughs, amending and embellishing on the way, realising that the circularity of the iris also echoed Floyd history, the band playing again early material as well as very recent material, coming the full circle as it were - recycle and rebirth which accounted for some of the elements outside the iris.

Finally, came the thought that this visual cornucopia could only be accomplished by computer, presenting the old via the new, the Floyd continuing to use technology creatively as they always had - 'still first in space', as David liked to say. Approximately forty different photos all prepared and shot to order and then 'comped' to fit Jon's drawn template and then meshed seamlessly. It took fucking ages.

So I ask you....whaddya think... was it worth it?

*Pink Floyd **Pulse** CD special package EMI 1995 Design and photos StormStudios*

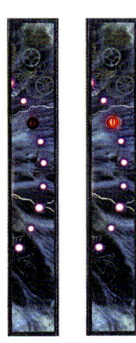

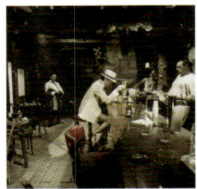

IN THROUGH THE OUT DOOR I find I've written about this image three or four times in the past but it's a design I still love dearly, even to this day. Thus, I'll say what I said before. The image tells the story of a lonely man in a dingy bar in some dreary town. The place is sparse save for a few lost souls – a failed sales rep with his jacket off, a jilted blonde in the corner, a nonchalant bartender. The joint is run down, dead on its knees. The lean, white suited guy in the middle could be a private detective on the skids, or a sleazy lawyer, a man on the run perhaps, not so much from the law as from his own past. He is burning something – a calling card or a note telling him that he's too late, he's missed the boat. The whole atmosphere is jaded, dusty, from the past, sad even: a fragment from a tale untold, a frame from a 1940s movie.

That's part of what was intended anyway. I hope some of this comes across because Peter Christopherson, Aubrey 'Po' Powell and myself, as the design team Hipgnosis, worked jolly hard to get this shot. Po styled it on actual New Orleans bars which he researched thoroughly, and then had recreated in a studio in West London. Peter lit the bar set exquisitely with just the right atmosphere, and I directed action and arranged composition through the lens. The sepia quality was meant to evoke a non-specific past, and to allow the brushstroke across the middle to be better rendered in colour and so make it more visible. This selfsame brushstroke was like a lick of fresh paint across a faded surface, a new look to an old scene, which was what Led Zeppelin told us about their album. They also told us that the music returned to some of their old blues type roots, which was why the bar was modelled on one from New Orleans.

That's what they said but, being Led Zeppelin, matters didn't stop there. While it's a simple enough shot to look at – just a portrait of a man in a bar – it somehow grew in proportion and became six view points of the same man in the bar, seen by the six other characters. Six different versions of the same image generated six different covers, and on the back of each cover was the opposite view, from the opposite side of the bar (by now the bar set was more than just a set: it was in fact a whole bar). Things didn't end there. The liner bag was printed in invisible colour ink, that is black ink which released colour when water (or spittle) was added, like some children's colouring books from the past. Finally this entire six version cover plus magic colour liner was then sold to the public in a brown paper bag through which you could see nothing. This ordinary looking but expensive device was in response to jibes that Led Zeppelin didn't really need a cover design at all, certainly not a detailed nor flashy one, since they would sell even in a 'brown paper bag'. Being Zeppelin they did both. As Robert Plant agreed later, it was very over the top, but then rock 'n' roll is over the top. "All power to pomp," he added cryptically.

*Led Zepplin **In Through The Out Door** Vinyl front Swansong 1976*
Design & Photography Hipgnosis

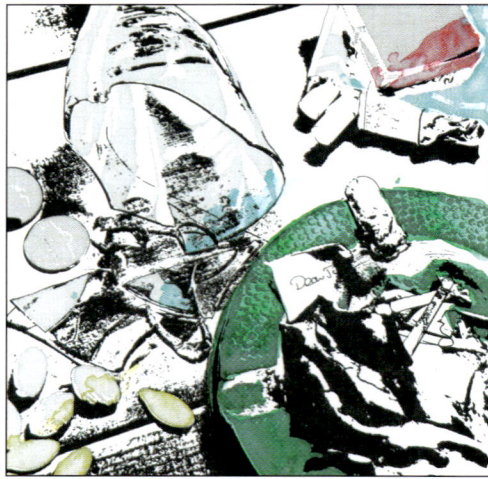

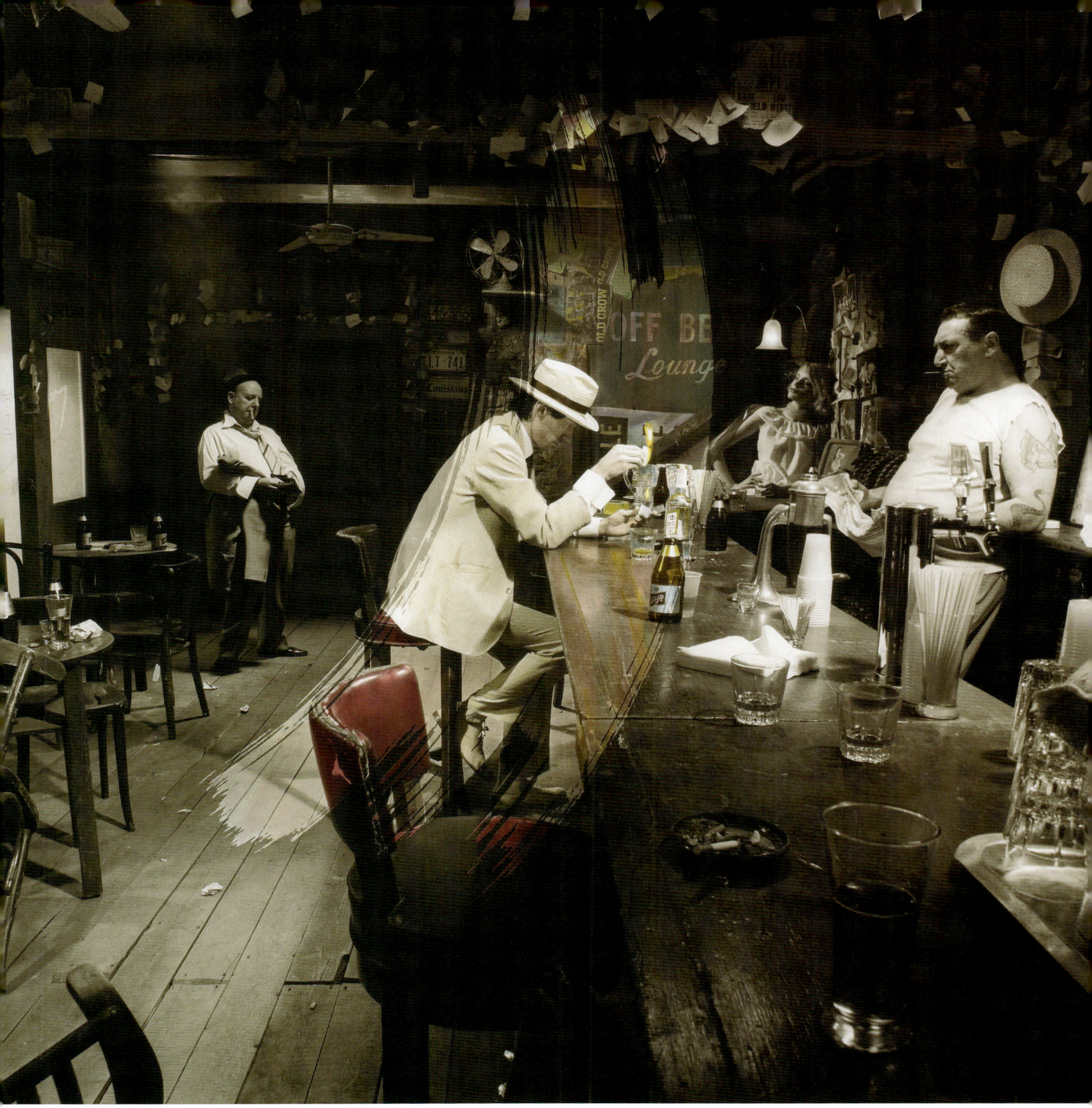

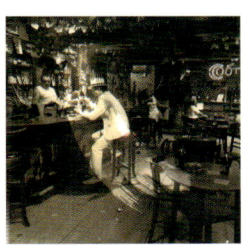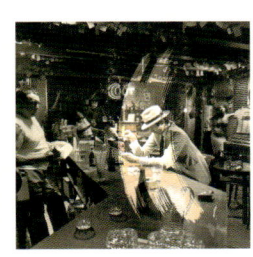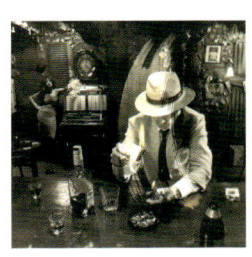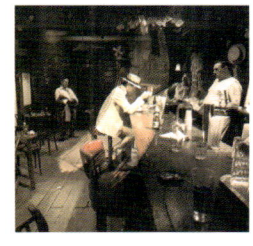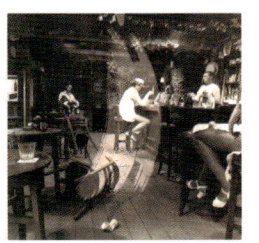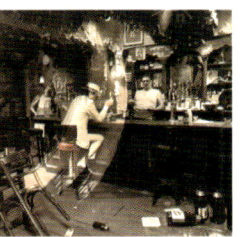

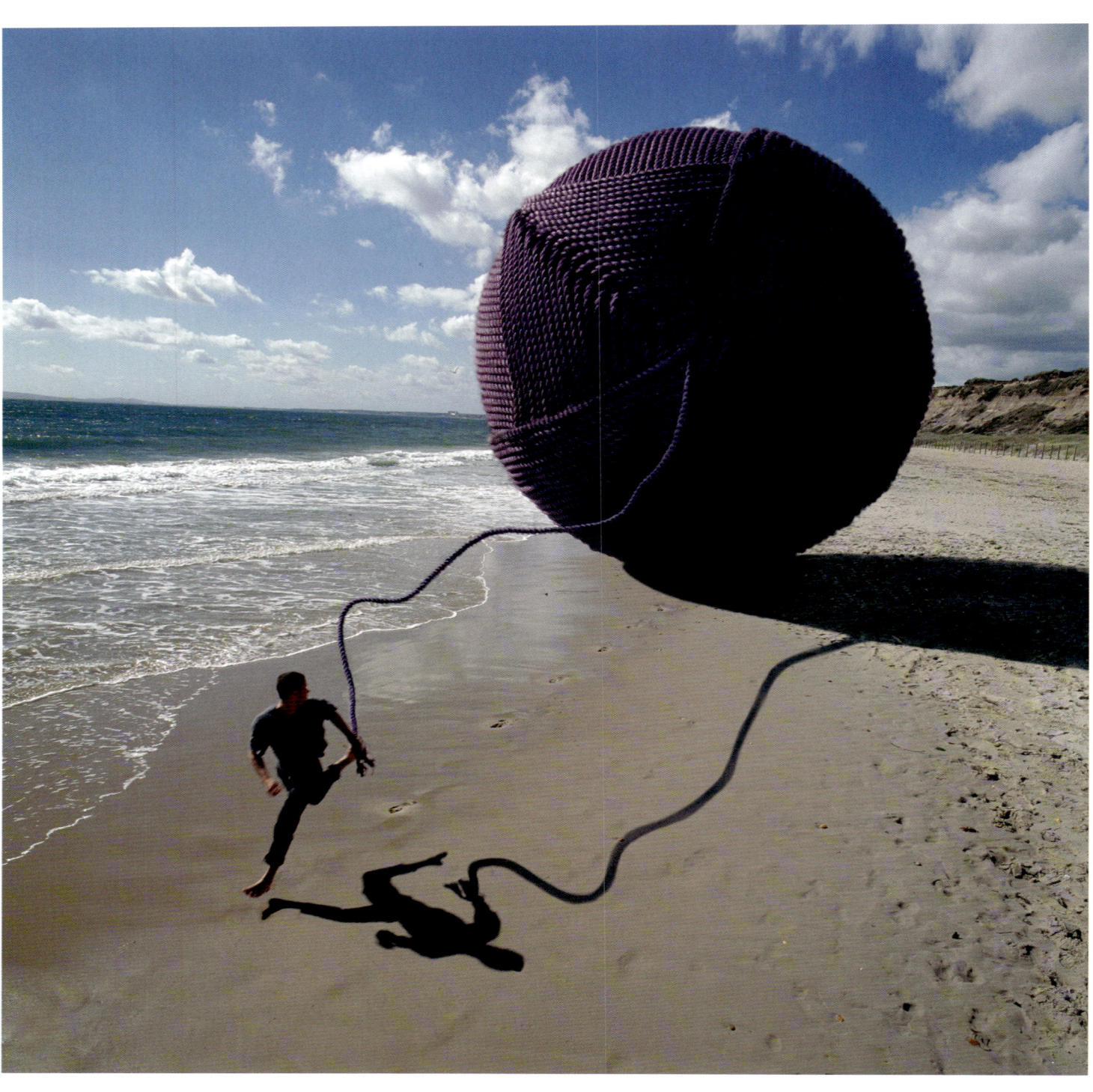

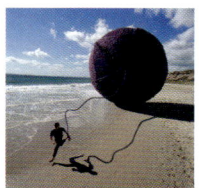

SLIP STITCH AND PASS The most impressive thing about the band Phish was going to see them live and discovering first hand that they did not have a set list. No set list? Horrors! How do they know what to play? Well, like the best jazz combos, as I have imagined, they play what comes to mind – once someone starts a song, say the pianist for example, then the rest follow easily. They told me later that they once did an entire set of Beach Boy variations using only percussion and none of their own songs, not something they ever anticipated. The second impressive thing about Phish is the degree of improvisation in their concerts, and improvisation is what I was trying to represent in this design.

I thought of improvisation as a large ball of string (a melody as yet unravelled) and the improvisation as the unravelling, wherein each musician took the melody, ran with it for a while and then passed it on to the next musician, somewhat like a relay runner passing the baton. A little fanciful you might say, but not quite as fanciful as trying to construct a giant ball of string. Giant, because, after all, how long is an improvisation until finished, how long is a piece of string? The most fanciful part of all of this is that a giant ball would require giant string, namely rope, the kind of rope that ties a ship to a dock, which made the ball fucking heavy and a complete nightmare to transport and carry down rocks and onto a beach, it seeming relevant to put Phish near the sea.

*Phish **Slip Stitch And Pass** CD front Elektra 1997*
Design & Photos StormStudios Location Hergeistpoint Beach, Bournemouth

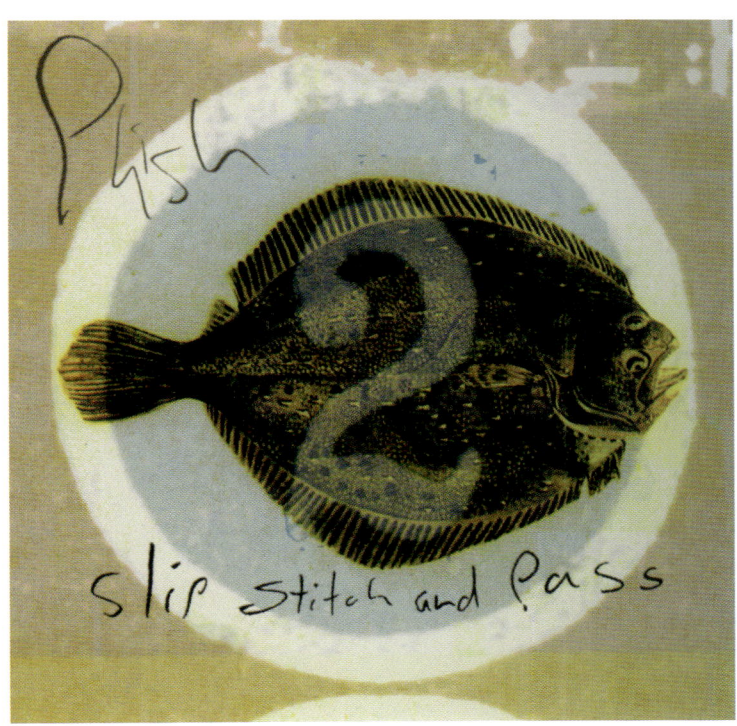

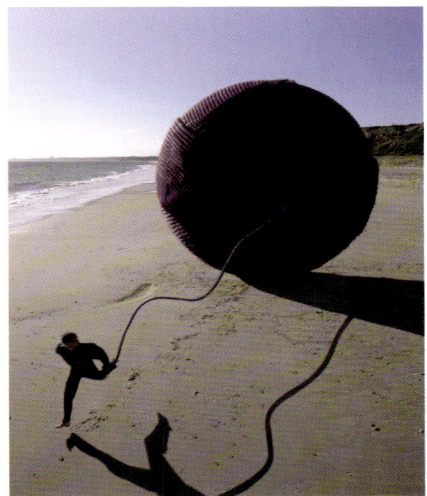

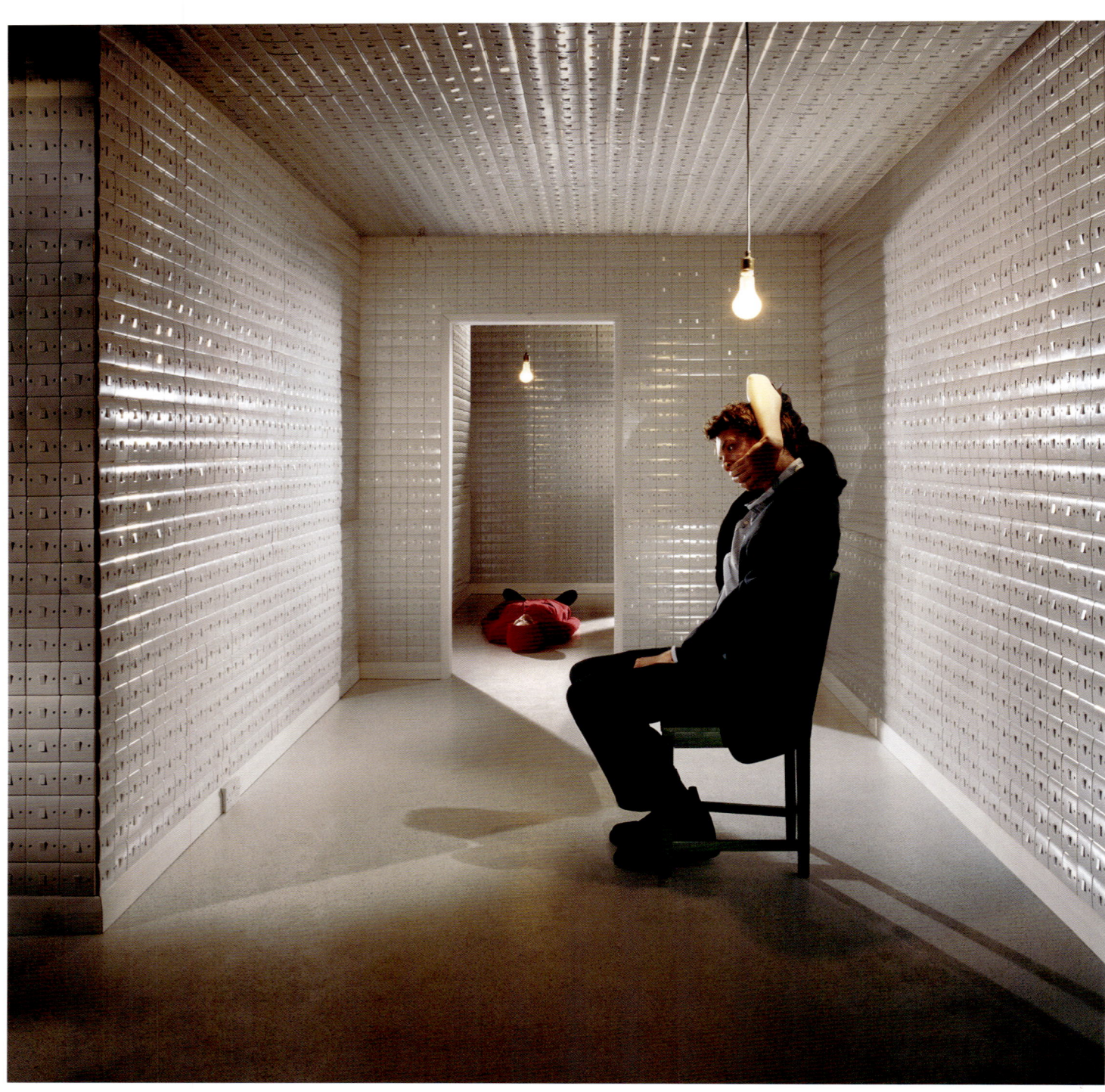

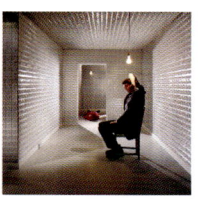

IGNOTO I hope when they come to read this they don't mind me saying, what a nice bunch of guys they are, that's YCNI:Milo - Yourcodenameis:Milo. There were five of them and they hailed from Newcastle, which is where I was in fact from the ages of five to eight if not at boarding school (and thereby hangs a tale). After long and vociferous discussions in the pub, a sort of nascent idea emerged. In a later meeting, with producer Flood now in attendance, this idea would come to signify 'conflict'. It became a key word, describing the way the band worked, how their songs were composed, and also the subject of some of those songs. This idea of conflict seemed also to fit the sound, which contained basic rock ingredients, but also a range of more subtle references and melodies.

One of the songs was about interconnecting plane flights and the difficulties that can beset anyone trying to make connections in a big airport. Another song was about the on/off nature of young relationships, another considered the bureaucratic labyrinth one can confront as a young person, trying to get ahead in a capitalist society. The song saw a young person branded as disadvantaged in some way or another, obstructed at every turn, disoriented, bumping into walls whether real or metaphorical.

Hmm... conflict, contradiction, something that is and is not, something that is not really possible, but looks as though it is. Freedom and restraint, what a creative cornucopia! And it generated three images 'Rapt' (pg. 97), '17' (pg. 186-187) and the switch room opposite.

On-off, off-on, like a light switch. Since there are so many off-ons in life, there would have to be a plethora of switches to manage, or as Peter suggested, a room made entirely of light switches all then designed to turn on one little light bulb. So conflicted by choice is our protagonist that he is gagging himself in frustration. The switch room also resembles a padded cell, a cell to contain the madness of a person in conflict or of a person in a rock group. You'll note that the red figure appears in all the three pictures, by way of continuity in a conflict-ridden universe, in the conflicting world of YCNI:M.

yourcodenameis:milo **Ignoto** *CD front Fiction 2005*
Design & Photos StormStudios

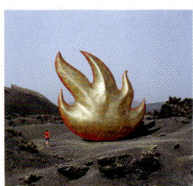

AUDIOSLAVE Ideas spawn further ideas. We had been working on a *Live At Pompeii* DVD and volcanoes were much in our minds. The sultry rock music of Audioslave seemed to suit the brooding power of volcanoes, not that we knew what to do with them at first. Eventually we imagined a volcanic landscape with a graphic flame Peter was working on 'plonked' in the middle of it. An eternal flame symbolising how two deceased bands, Soundgarden and Rage Against The Machine lived on in the reincarnation called Audioslave. This shape that looked like a hand or flame was turned into a large sculpture made of beaten bronze, like a sounding brass. The little figure is paying homage to the sculpture and acting as both a size and a reference point. A pilgrimage to the mystic sounding brass set in the volcanic wasteland of Lanzarote – paying homage to an eternal flame (Audioslave) as any slave to sound should. A design that seemed to resonate well with the music and atmosphere but containing a graphic focal point – a spiritual flame of remembrance, as well as a neat contradiction in terms – flames always flicker but this sculpture is frozen. Frozen movement sitting majestically in a primeval landscape... and what a landscape... if you ever get the chance to visit, take it. A truly extraordinary place.

Audioslave **Audioslave** *CD front Epic 2002*
Design & Photos StormStudios Location Lanzarote, Canary Islands

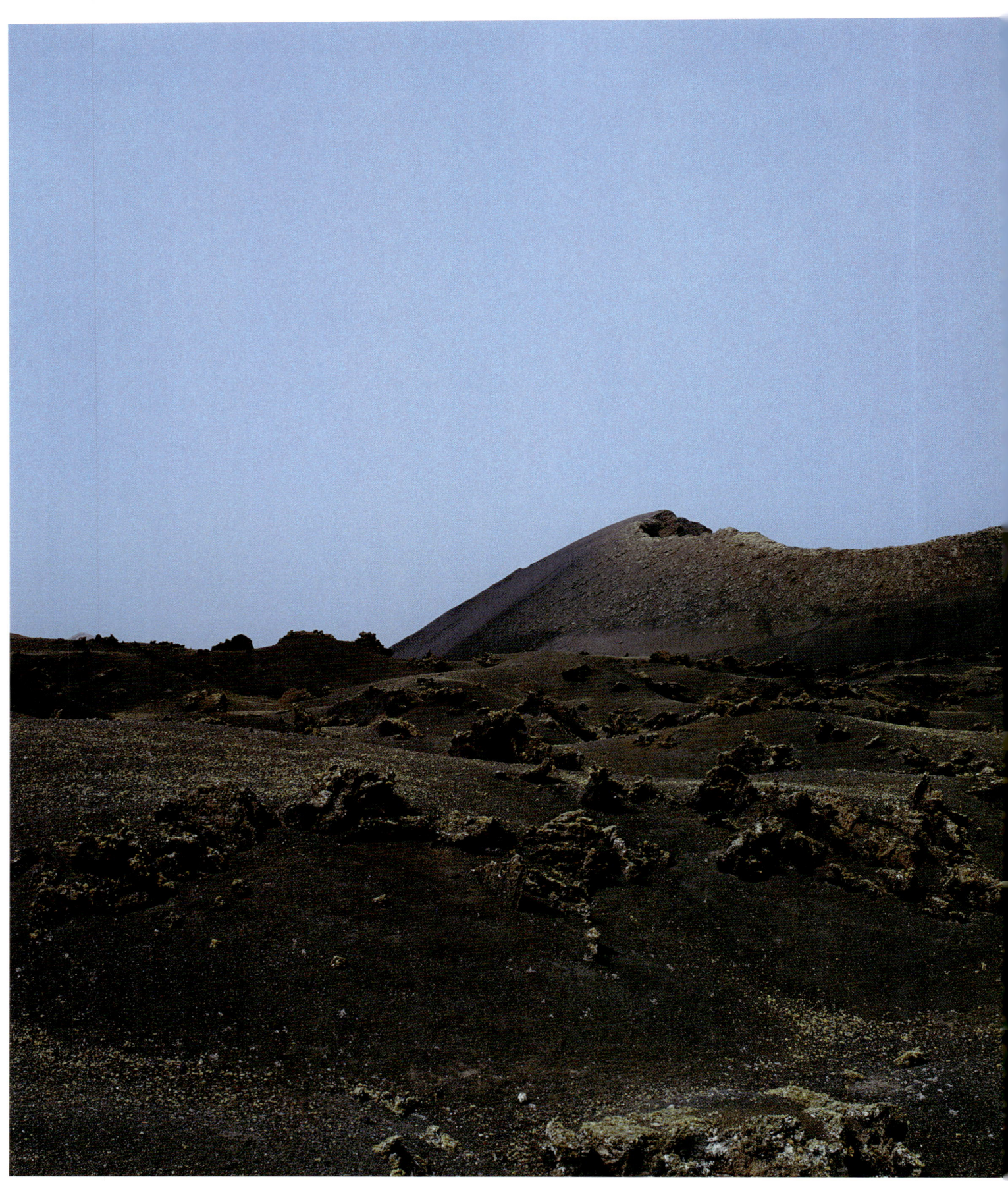

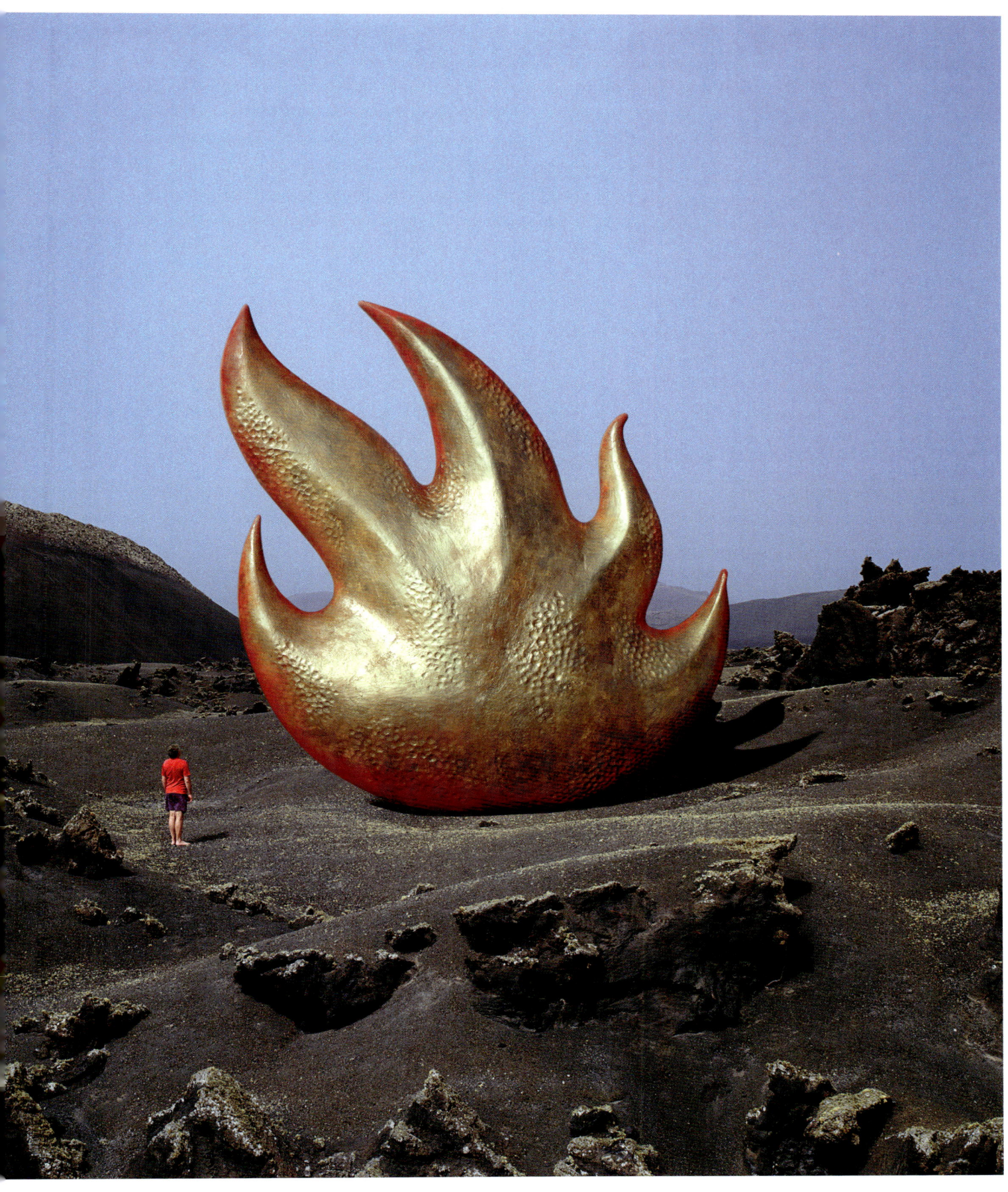

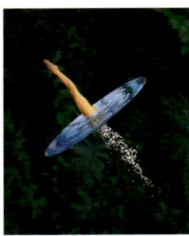

BROKEN CHINA Richard Wright, noted keyboard player from popular rock'n'roll ensemble Pink Floyd, made a solo album in 1996. Apart from his hallmark lyricism and keyboard swashes, the theme of the album dealt thematically with an emotional breakdown, occasioned by some unstated trauma followed by subsequent attempts at recovery. In essence there was a time before and a time after the breakdown - the former characterised by a wholeness and the latter by a broken quality. We imagined a human figure that was half natural and half fractured, yet comprising one and the same person.

This design was an adaptation of an uncompleted earlier idea about a magic disc through which one could pass as if through a time gate, from one zone to another. For Rick's record we saw a woman divided by a disc of water, being whole and natural as she dived in, legs of flesh and bone, but fractured as she came though the other side, the upper body now made of broken china. It seemed an elegant and lyrical way of suggesting a breakdown, in sympathy with the music, and appropriate in that the fractured half was literally made of pieces of broken china like a cracked jug (the back cover was the reverse, broken china legs and flesh or mended upper body to indicate the recovery). Also appropriate was that the trauma was in fact represented by a disc of water, not something heavy and dark but something more lyrical and liquid like the music.

*Richard Wright **Broken China** CD front EMI 1995*
Design & Photos StormStudios

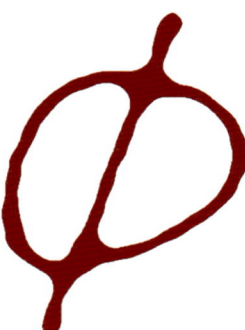

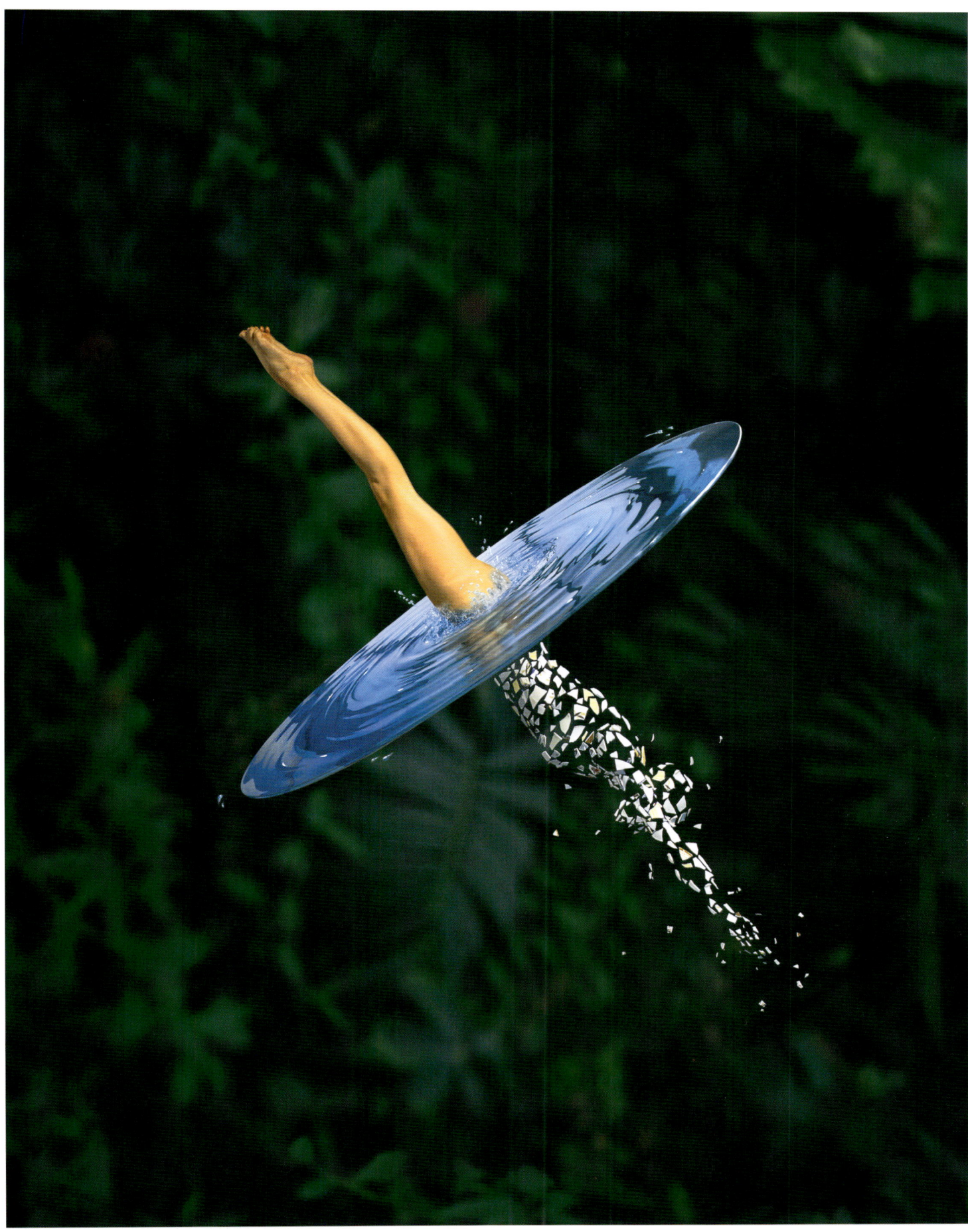

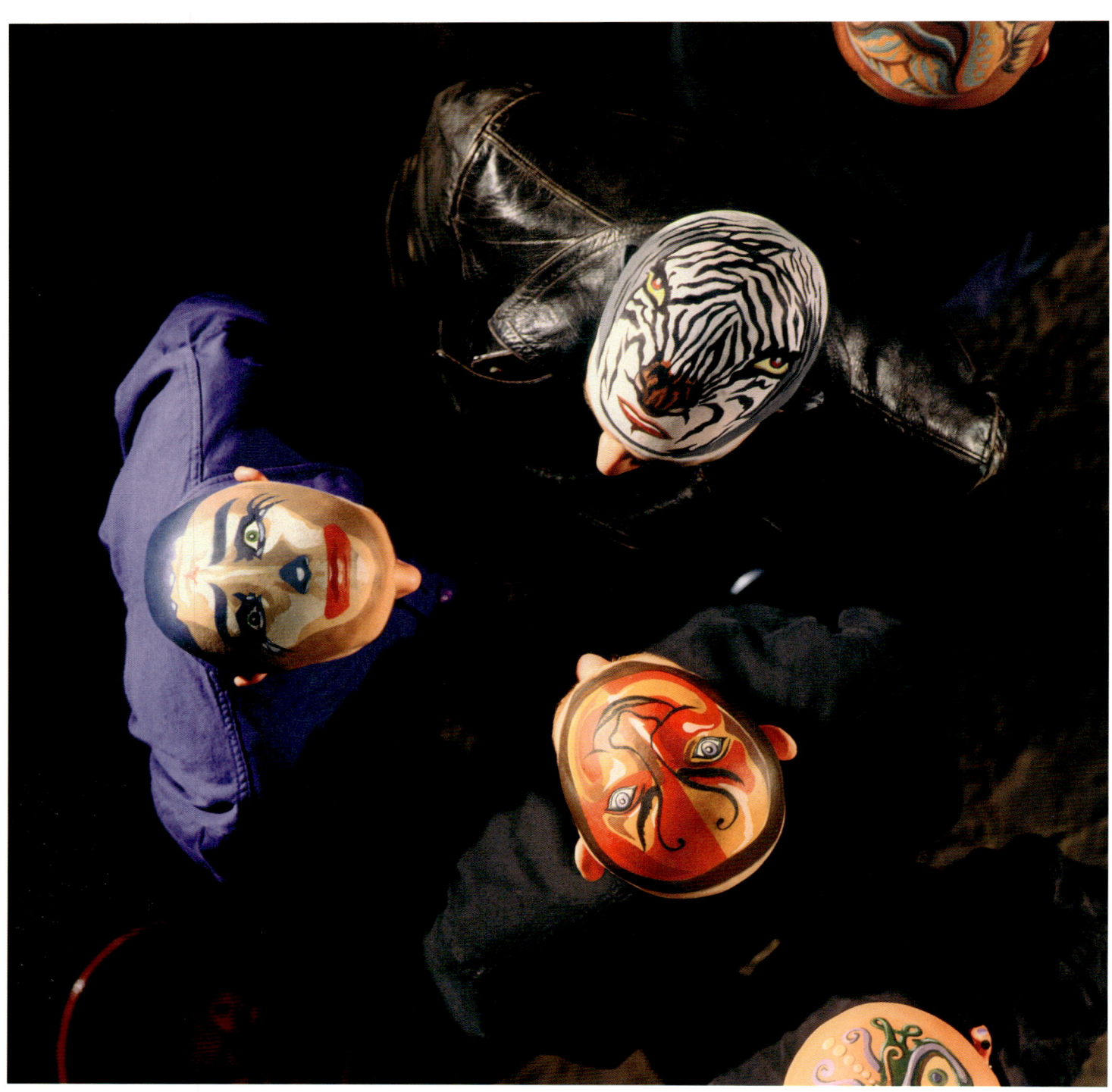

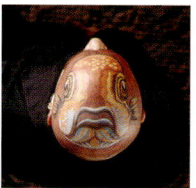

RAGGA Couples and coupledom, not to mention coupling, kinda weird in some ways – monogamy, staying together, not straying. Magpies do it apparently, but not walruses, lobsters maybe? Ragga and the Jack Magic Orchestra featured an Icelandic couple called Ragnhildur Gísladottír and Jakob Magnusson (relatively unpronounceable for us Britishers) of which the woman was a delight and the man was a stickler, who needed desperately to know every detail before it was enacted. A procedure which can drive designers to distraction. I don't obviously begrudge a client wanting to know what's going on or how it's going to look, but in every detail? More like a lawyer than a musician, more anal than creative. Apart from being a touch disrespectful, such insistence tends to prolong the work, making it more arduous rather than more effective. But then again 'who am I to disagree' as the great Annie Lennox said.

Ragga explained that their esoteric music often painted pictures or told stories and this prompted the realisation of a long held view about pictures in the head, a view that there is something magical about pictures in the head, something mystical even about how a word like 'ship' could conjure an image of a ship, masts and sails wind and sea and so forth in one's head, though the word is either just a simple sound, or marks on a piece of paper.

And there you have it, pictures in the head or rather pictures on the head, literally painted upon the pates of bald people (you try painting a picture on a full head of hair OK?). This is in theory a simple shoot – hire a studio with appropriate ceiling gantry, locate several bald people, hire a body painter to execute designs on heads and decide content of said designs. This last item turned out to be the most difficult because it required detailed communing with the great coupledom, though it was at least agreed that painted faces were the best bet. What you see is again what you get, but it's not what the bald heads see because they are looking straight ahead, not up at us the viewer. This involves a slight trompe l'oeil wherein the face looking up 'shares' the nose of the real face looking forwards and so ironically, the characters are all looking at you, the viewer, but not at each other.

I particularly like the face of a fish....well I would, I'm a Pisces.

*Ragga **Ragga & The Jack Magic Orchestra** CD front EMI 1997 Design & Photos StormStudios*

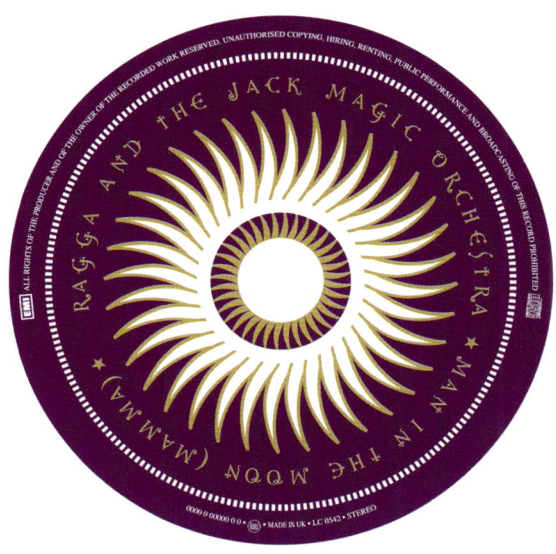

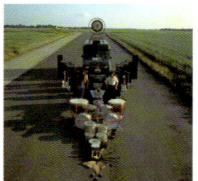

UMMAGUMMA This was a second design for Pink Floyd after *A Saucerful Of Secrets* and was an attempt to represent the many different layers in their music. No ephemeral pop band this, therefore no surface trivia, instead wheels within wheels, layers beneath layers, tunes replete with meaning and all this for heavens sake in the same music. It was progressive in the best sense of the word involving structure and improvisation, craziness and order, catchy verse and chorus or long, extended pieces, screaming guitars or orchestration. Much of which, of course was to come to fruition later.

In conversation with my then girlfriend, Libby, about how to represent layers, she mentioned infinite regression drawings, line drawings of receding squares, like a lift shaft or opposing mirrors, and I thought 'Great, let's do an infinite regression, but as a photograph, not as an illustration, not a mirror but a picture on a wall, and the picture on a wall is a picture of the room in which the same picture is hanging! This becomes a picture within a picture, which in turn of course is a picture within a picture within a picture, endlessly receding. Physically it's like a window, but metaphorically it's an endless set of pictures, an endless set of layers, going back and back, regressing infinitely.

And that's what we went with. And fittingly took the photograph in my girlfriend's house, looking out into the garden on your right, or looking into the picture within a picture within a picture on your left. It always felt to me that you could step so easily into the next picture or into the next room as if through a window, so compelling was the sense of receding, so effective the depth in the music.

The artwork was rather amateurishly executed, with Stanley knife and ruler, and suffered from my lack of control (so a brain surgeon I was not). But none of this incompetence seems to detract from the finished piece. The rotation of the group members was, I feel, the icing on the proverbial cake, though I am not always sure how much it is detected. I am more often asked about the *GiGi* cover, which is a false trail or red herring, a theme for the Floyd, that was extended big time in *Atom Heart Mother* (see pg.188).

With the benefit of hindsight I can now say that I think this image, along with *Elegy* (pg.13), was a turning point for me.

Pink Floyd **Ummagumma** *Vinyl gatefold front EMI 1969*
Design and photos Hipgnosis Location Shelford Cambridge

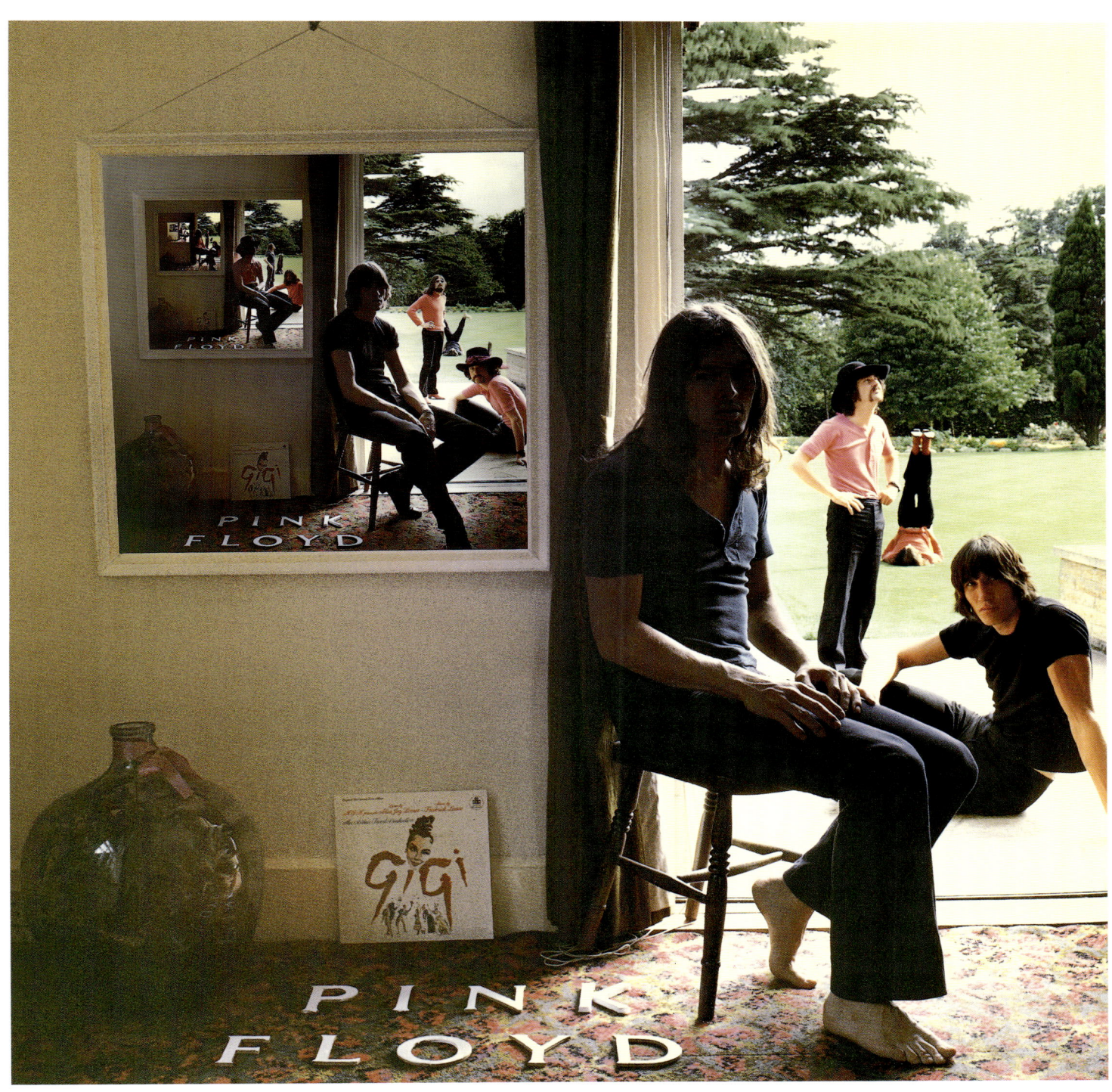

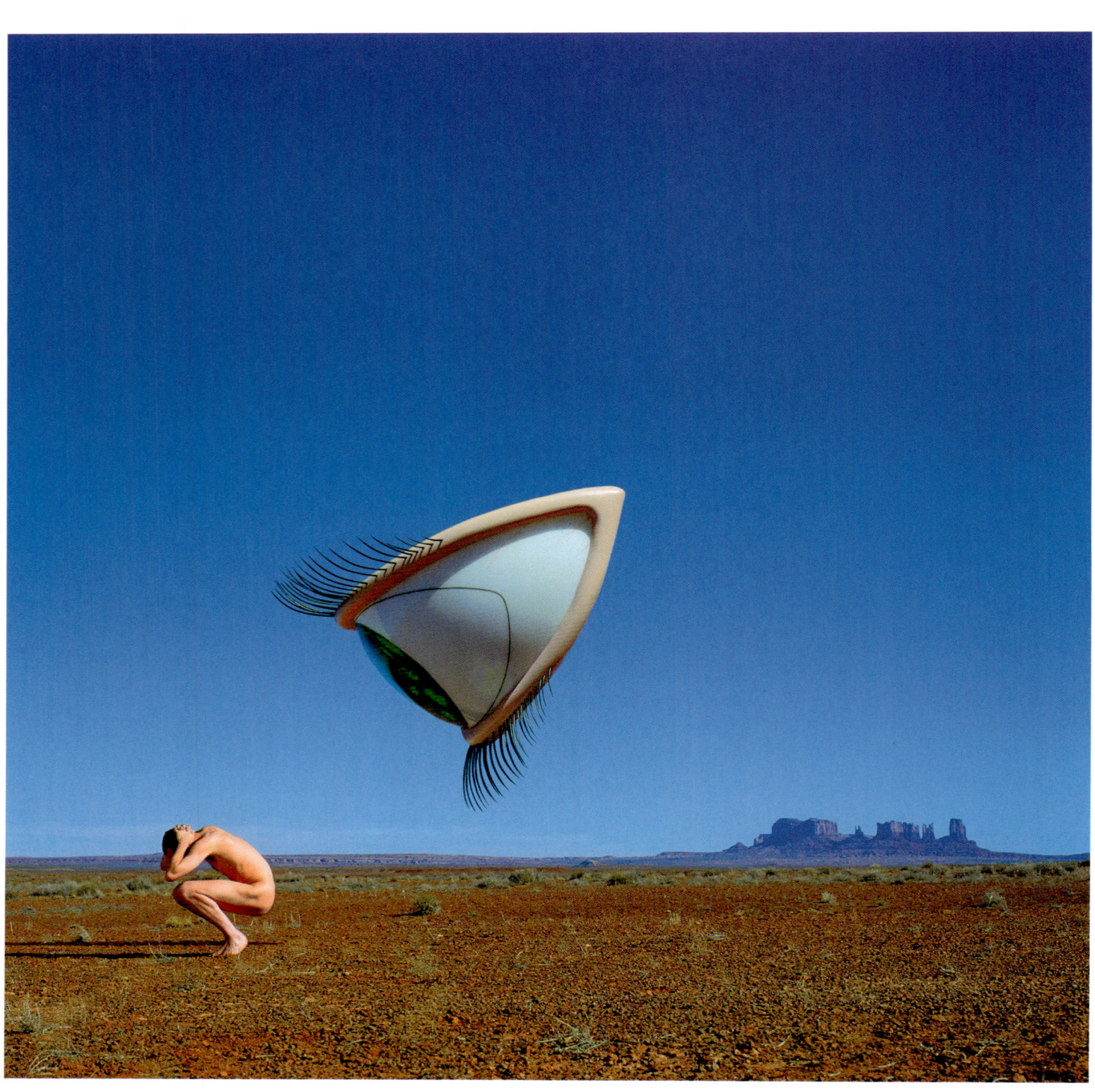

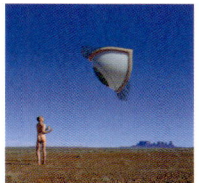

BURY THE HATCHET They were three minor miracles about *Bury The Hatchet*. First I was both surprised and heartened that The Cranberries, who come from Limerick in Ireland, chose this design at all. I was similarly taken aback by Led Zeppelin's choice of *Presence* (pg.47), because at first sight these designs were not obviously appropriate. The Cranberries had previously used pictures of themselves, often on a sofa. Our image was clearly a departure, not a sofa in sight.

The second miracle arose after we had decided that red earth was paramount, to contrast with a blue sky, which had to be empty, *i.e.* cloudless in order to echo the empty landscape in turn to emphasize that the All Seeing Eye can get you anywhere. Wherever you try and run, you cannot escape. We decided that Australia was too far away, Namibia too dangerous, so it had to be Monument Valley in Arizona. We went in November in the wild hope that the weather would be good. When we arrived in neighbouring Flagstaff, it was fucking snowing, and by the next morning there were icicles hanging off the trees outside our hotel. I was crestfallen, wondering how I could ever explain to The Cranberries that this costly exercise was sabotaged by bad weather! In a desert? As we drove North from Flagstaff, down from the hills, the weather changed abruptly, and we arrived in Monument Valley to blue skies and clear vistas. It was a miracle. A second miracle. (Whatever else one may say about America the landscapes are fucking phenomenal, and Monument Valley is certainly one of the best).

We drove around looking for the perfect spot, and we found several, particularly the one you see. It was very like the rough I'd shown the band, including the distant peaks. There was not a soul or a tree for miles. The floating, inquisitive eye had cornered its victim even in the wide open spaces of America's south west. It so happened that this area is sacred Navajo ground, the preserve for centuries of proud Navajo Indians. As we were filming a naked white man, pursued by the evil eye of Agammotto, suddenly out of nowhere roared a truck, screeched to a halt and out jumped an Indian with long black hair and a face like a granite slab. The male model was hurriedly putting on his pants as we struggled to get the eye model back into our jeep. A heavy hand landed on my shoulder and a deep voice said, "You are trespassing, I confiscate your film and equipment." GULP.

Photoshoot torpedoed. What could I tell The Cranberries? Then the Indian laughed heartily, said he was only joking, got out his mobile and swapped e-mail addresses with the crew, another effing miracle. It goes to show how the idea of government surveillance, that there is always someone watching you, be it third party or one's own conscience, was truer than we thought. Even in the empty tracts of the Arizona desert, we were being watched.

But we got away with it. I guess it was the luck of the Irish.

*The Cranberries **Bury The Hatchet** CD front MCA 1999*
Design & Photos StormStudios Location Monument Valley, Arizona

WHAT WE DO AND WHO GIVES A SHIT!

I DESIGN ALBUM COVERS for my sins, and it is by and large a very satisfying occupation, though not without some stress and disappointment. I have much help in designing these album covers, couldn't do it on my own, but, whomsoever's involved, the objectives remain the same - we wish to **represent the music**, unless for some perverse reason the musicians tell us otherwise. I guess the cow for *Atom Heart Mother*, see pg.188, might be a rare example of that, but usually representing the music visually is the primary if not sole objective. There will of course be some parties who will view the purpose as commercial, the aim of an album cover, they maintain, is to help advertise and promote sales of the product. I have never shared this view, not just because it is crass, but mostly because it is unproven. There is no reliable information to support such an assertion. The old sales maxim is 'sex sells', but the biggest selling albums rarely have sex on their covers.

When visually representing the music, we secondly wish to be 'good' - interesting, intriguing, well-designed, odd, surreal, funny, well executed, evocative, efficient. effective, eye catching or any combination of the above . So we aim to be **a) good**, in the same way we presume that the musicians do, and **b) custom** - invented for the specific project and not 'off the shelf' - not an image intended or used for something else - any more than the music is off the shelf and not the work of the artist in question, unless of course the idea is off our own shelf in which case it becomes custom by specific adaptation and by singular appropriation and existing as so and so's cover and nothing else and **c) original**, in so much as the images are wrought by our good selves and not purloined from another source. I can only recall consciously utilising an existing image once in my time, but this word 'original' is difficult, for as Picasso says, nothing is original - "all art is theft." In addition, there is, of course, the complex issue of being 'like' something else, 'influenced by', 'inspired by,' 'after so and so', 'paying homage to', 'in the style of', 'ripping off' etc, much of which might be unconscious. We have, however, tried our level best to be original, insomuch as one can ever be, as original as the musicians with whom we work also wish to be.

These aims and objectives look pompous when written down but are, in all honesty folks, what we aspire to, and seem ordinary to us. For example, what is the point, really, of nabbing someone else's design and passing it off as your own? Far from having little or no direct benefit, it's always likely you'll be found out, and then what?

I am sometimes asked to describe precisely what I do... I hang around musicians is what I do, though I believe that's the cynical definition of a drummer. I sit around dreaming up visual ideas which try their best to embody the ideas and feelings in the music. These ideas (images/designs), usually take the form of installations, sometimes inside and more frequently outside, when they could be called 'extallations', and are composed of happenings or events, which have to be staged, and could involve sculptures, people, animals, props, land art etc. Such extallations are contrived, made on purpose, though they may be the result of a spontaneous thought.

Alternatively it might be the case that an everyday observation, some small ordinary event, which when isolated, framed in the camera and re-presented to the viewer, can take on a different and worthwhile quality.

For the most part these ideas are derived from the brain soup which is in turn informed by one's culture, one's surroundings, education, experiences and so on. Lateral thinking is quite helpful, as are puns, double entendres, words or sayings that sound odd, juxtapositions, contradictions, incongruities, are all good fodder, and help provide in turn for qualities in the images, qualities like weird, surreal, odd, or intriguing. It feels good to involve the viewer in some degree of dialogue, by seducing or grabbing the interest through subverting expectations, presenting ambiguity, something which may be possible but may not be. Occasionally fantasy, more usually distorted reality - reality with a twist. We like illusions, jokes, improbabilities, incongruities, etc etc, and hope the viewer likes them too.

These ideas are usually performed for real because they tend to look better that way and they give us a thrill at the time, and they don't cheat or sell the customer short. 'Doing it for real' usually imbues the idea and the event, with greater force than trying to fake it in the computer - what you see is what you get, although not always of course. The camera never lies, but words might. 'Doing it for real' also avoids complications of delicate retouching going wrong, but most particularly it confirms whether the idea has any 'legs'. For example, The Cranberries (pg. 140) looked so exciting in front of our eyes, that we felt the photo would have to work a bit. But the photo is a copy and not the real thing, regrettably.

The staging of events - the constructing of installations - is then presented formally. That is, we favour shooting square-on, front-on, without resorting to funny angles, time-lapse, selective focus etc etc. If the ideas work in the staging, they rarely need embellishing in the photography, well at least not much. On the other hand, the lighting is very carefully considered. I am, I suppose, more interested in the idea than in the photography. But then a great idea is no good badly dressed, so we engage good photographers and the best equipment to render our ideas in the best possible light... and cross our fingers.

But then, who gives a shit? Who cares about album covers? Not many people, I suppose, covers being minuscule in the grand scheme of things. Not farmers, unless we pay to go on their land, not fisherman, nor brain surgeons, not politicians, or shopkeepers, lest they be record shopkeepers, nor vintners greatly concerned with things downstairs, nor clergy overly concerned with things upstairs, nor the police or criminals too busy chasing their tails but we care like crazy, as do the musicians with whom we work and to some extent, their fans. I dearly hope the fans like them half as much as we do.

Oh, and my mother who likes them a lot.

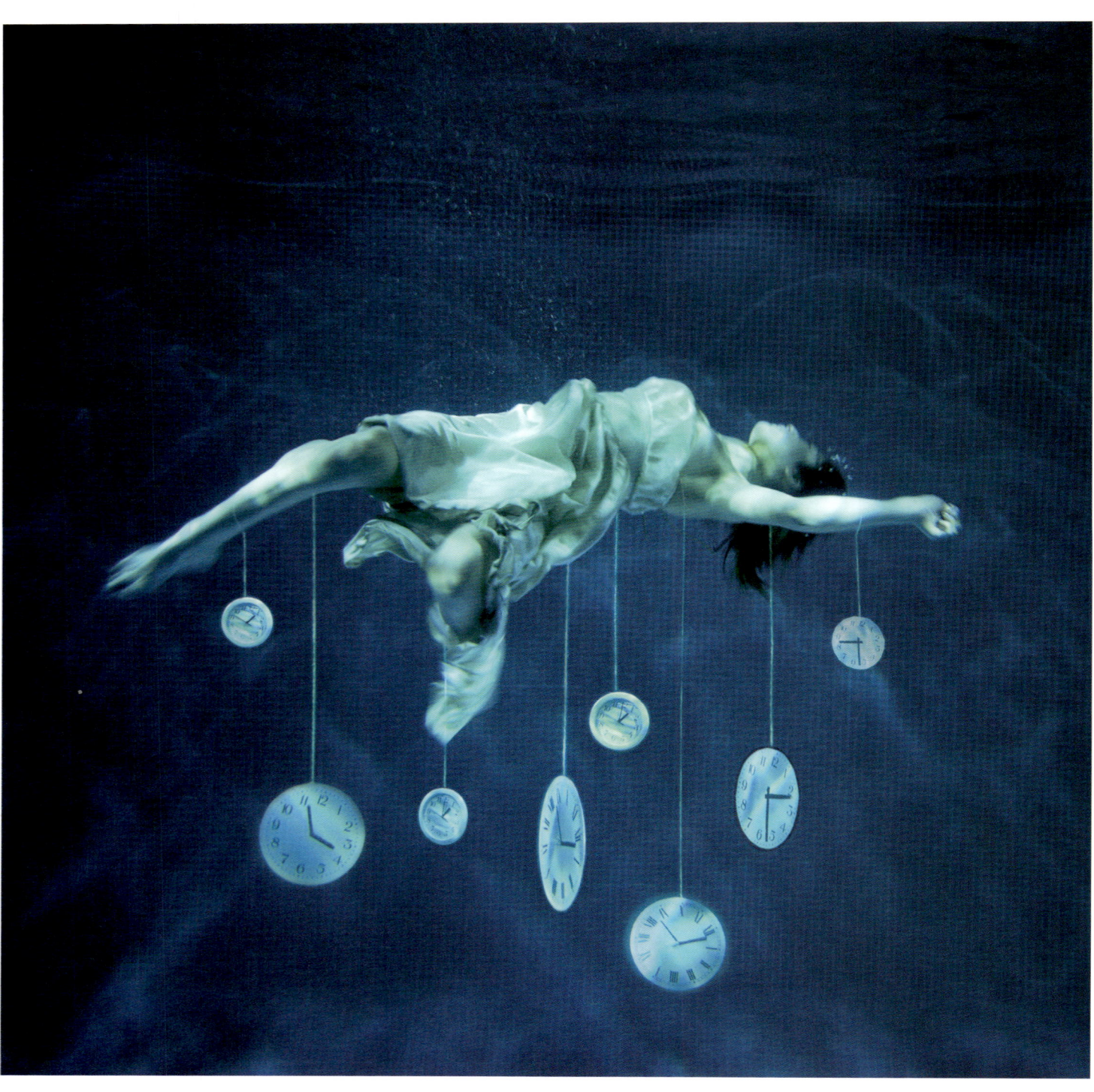

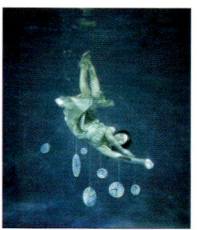

SETSUGEKKA Yumi Matsutoya is a Japanese singer/songwriter, a female Cliff Richard, but considerably more diverse and a good deal more sexy (no offence Sir Cliff), quite western in her production and her sound, but very Japanese in her approach and her lyrics. It seems 'Setsugekka' means 'moon, flowers, snow' and the lyrics were about the memory of a holiday in an alpine resort, a holiday revisited, in which the singer recalls a forgotten love - like a memory of a memory, or an echo, kind of sad and nostalgic, though ambiguous and inscrutable. The sadness seemed to be as much about the weight of memories in general as the loss of a particular love, recalling the good times but with a sense of deep regret.

I therefore envisaged a girl sinking under the weight of her own memories and being dragged down through water by time *i.e.* by clocks, which I thought at first to be a clumsy metaphor but on completing the image felt that they worked fine - elegiac rather than prosaic. The major difficulty was in keeping the clocks disentangled and encouraging the model not to give up through exhaustion, I kept trying to tell her to adopt an elegant shape, very difficult underwater, but she was great and survived to tell the tale, although I don't suppose she is keen to remember all this too clearly - some memories are best forgotten, but some images are best to keep.

*Yumi Matsutoya **Setsugekka** CD single Toshiba EMI 2003 Design & Photos StormStudios Location Shepherd's Bush*

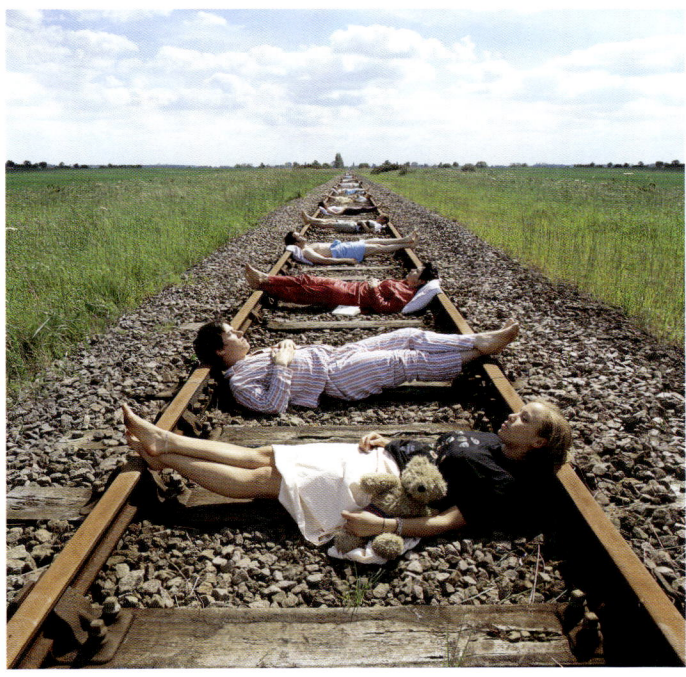

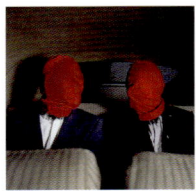

FRANCES THE MUTE What is there to say about The Mars Volta? An extraordinary coupling: exotic, extravagant, improvising, unrestrained but as tight as a drum when they need to be – a heady mix of styles woven together at a frenetic pace but interspersed with unexpected longeurs. Spun around a story for a film never made for which this, their record, is the soundtrack. One of the aspects of the story was addiction and although it had specific references it also had universal connotations, one of which interested me greatly, namely the idea that the addicted party thinks he's alright and is in control, thinks he knows where he's headed even though still addicted and therefore probably doesn't have a fucking clue.

I imagined car drivers navigating their way through town, *i.e.* through life, thinking they are steering a safe path but in fact having no idea where they are going... drivers wearing custom hoods - not hoods to hide their identity but nicely made velvet accessories that simply and surreally prevent them from seeing or having any idea of where they were driving.

Since this is a general malaise and not a local event, all the drivers in town are similarly hooded and in our picture they can be seen passing each other as if in normal traffic, blithely unaware it would seem of impending collisions. No secret society here, no evil to be prosecuted. But inhabitants in a world of velvet delusion. Soiled suits and old American cars added a slight retro feeling in this attempt to be timeless in relation to the perils of addiction in general, be it to gambling or to noble causes or even to nicotine... and so say all of us.

The Mars Volta **Frances The Mute** *CD front Universal 2004*
Design & Photos StormStudios Location Stewartby, Bedfordshire

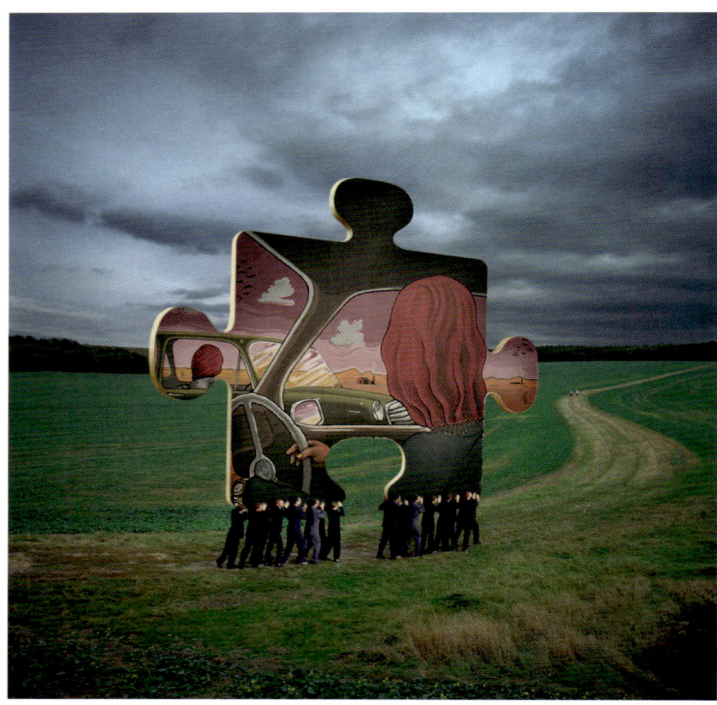

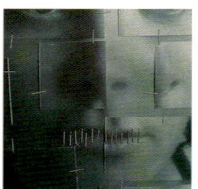

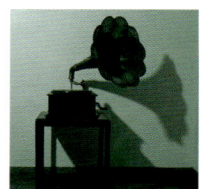

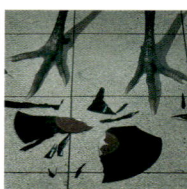

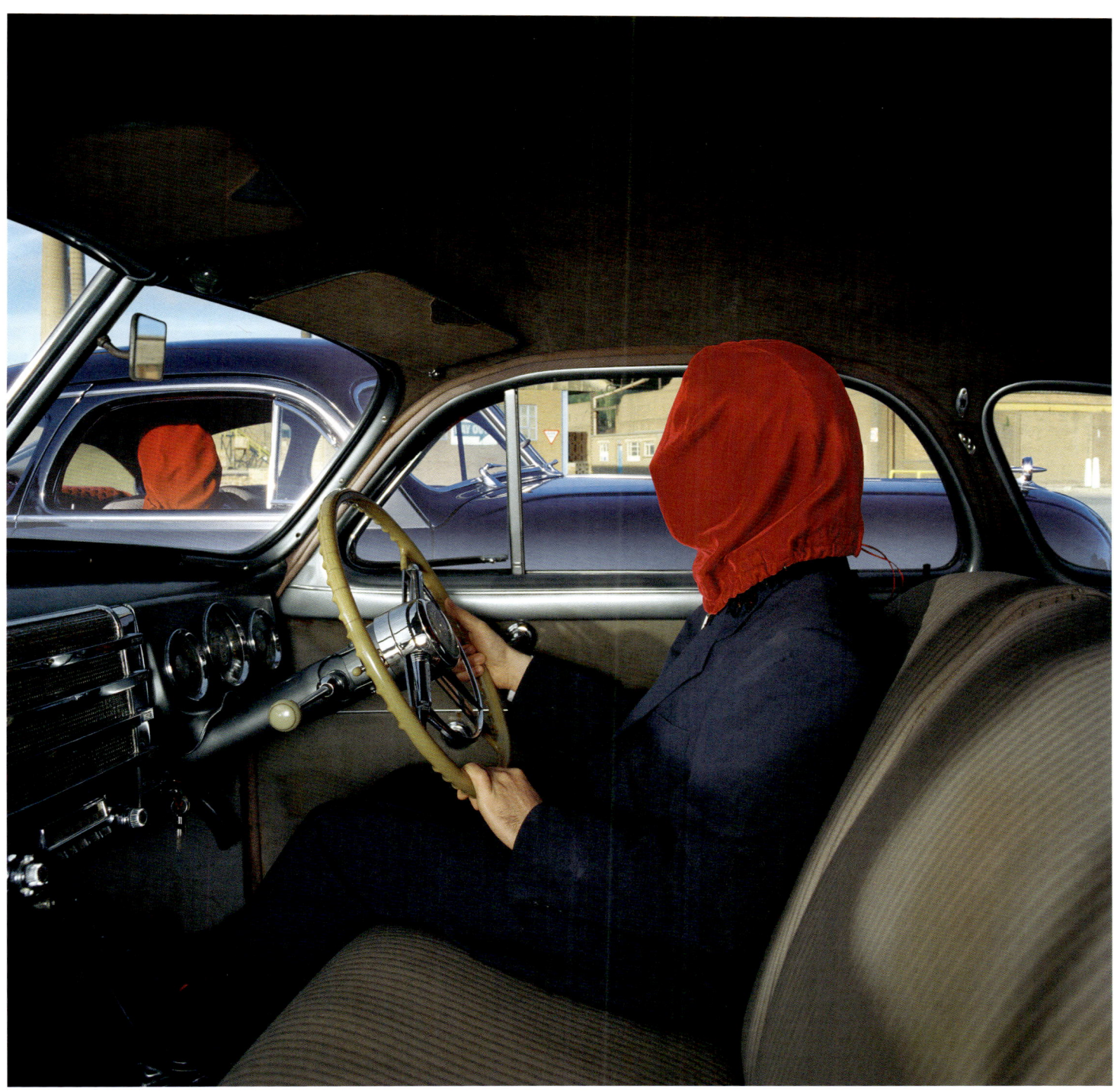

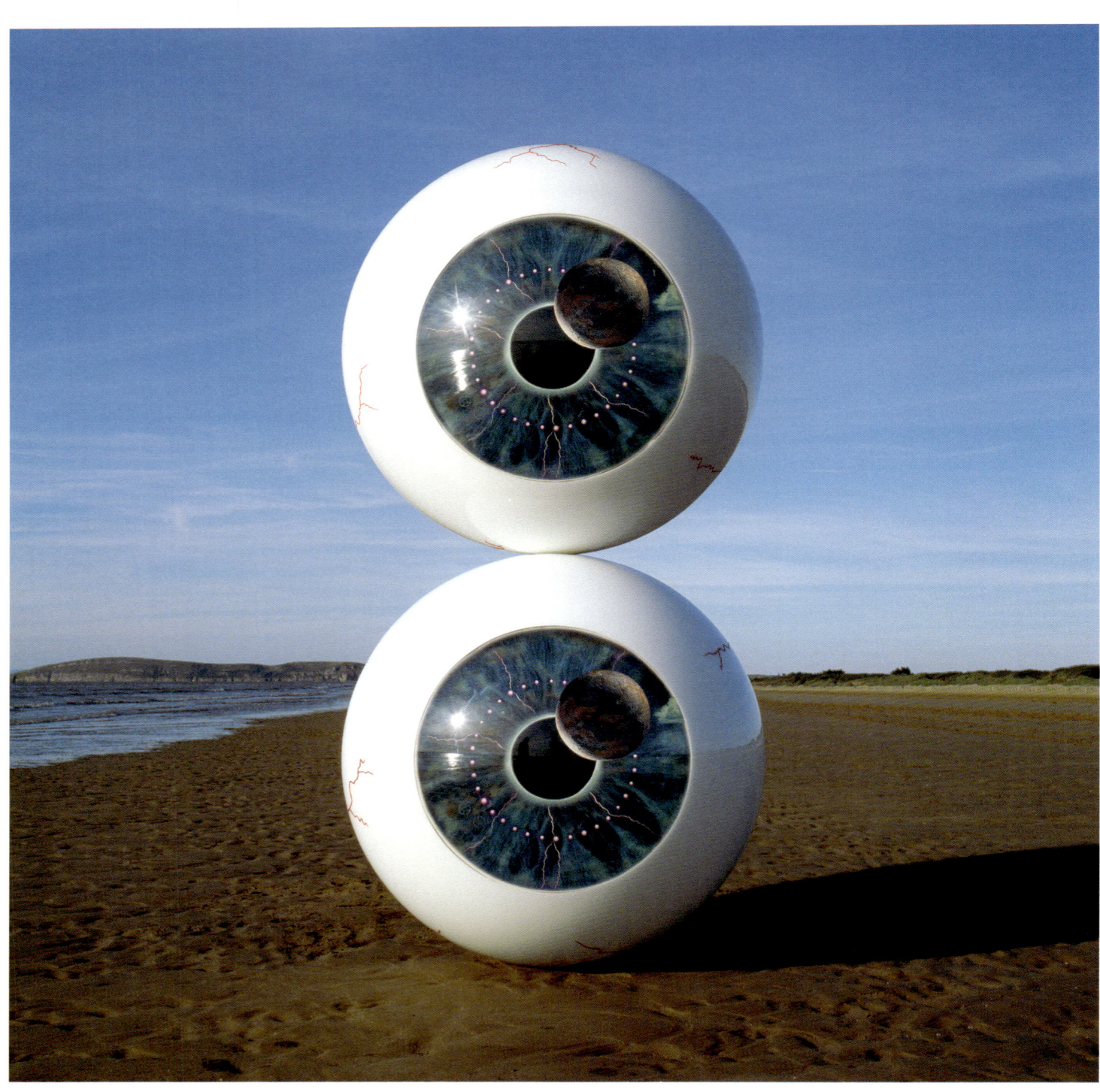

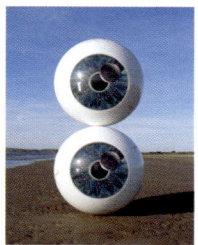

PULSE At the time of writing DVD's are all the rage, as the hardware comes down in price, no doubt. *Pulse* DVD is apparently out-selling the top audio CD in both England and Italy, would you believe that? Must be the cover, si? This was a project that had been going on for some years due in part to the intrinsic complexity of a DVD, due in part to the reluctance to complete what could be the last Floyd project, and due in part to preoccupation with other matters. So the cover was prepared in summer 2003 but not published until 2006.

Pulse DVD mainly features a recording of Pink Floyd's concert at Earl's Court in 1994. The sound had been remixed to 5.1 surround sound and the film was re-edited and generally cleaned up, though it's original aspect ratio was maintained. It seemed logical to design a cover that was referential to the audio CD of the same name, but not too obviously. The two major features of the DVD would be the visual side and that there would be two discs, the concert being too long to fit on one.

An eye was the basis for the original design (see pg 111). If we made a glass eye and used the original eye as the iris, wouldn't that be appropriate? And then if we made the glass eye a sculpture, *i.e.* a huge glass eye, and then made two of them for the two discs of DVD, wouldn't that be appropriate? And then we could balance one eye upon the other, locate the finely balanced sculpture in a wide open and atmospheric terrain to reflect the breadth of the 5.1 sound, wouldn't that be even more appropriate?

Pink Floyd **Pulse** *DVD package EMI 2006 Design and photos StormStudios*

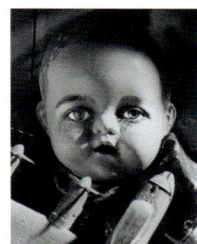

NIGHTFALL David Gale is a boyhood friend, raconteur, humourist, natty dresser, playwright and performance artist. For a time he ran a fringe theatre company called Lumiere & Son with the lovely Hilary Westlake. Together they put on a variety of bizarre productions, including *Nightfall*. Part of the story of *Nightfall* involved a squadron of nightfighters, passing over East Anglia and dropping dolls not bombs, across the country-side, hence the doll in our picture, with a World War II fighter plane leaning against it as if they were toys in the attic, revealed late at night by the light from a chink in the attic door.

But all is not as it seems, which it never was, of course, in the plays of Lumiere & Son. I thought that a scary possibility would be to use a Victorian doll, but replace its glass eyes with human eyes, as if there were lingering intelligence in this doll, instead of an empty head. This was shot in the studio with black and white film, as were the other posters for Lumiere & Son pg. 58 and 59, chosen I'm afraid for economic reasons, rather than for artistic ones, but in hindsight I feel they gain rather than lose from this restriction.

The Dogs poster was derived from the title, and the play is a bizarre detective story so our sleuth is seen in customary trilby and mac trudging along the side streets in the French quarter at night, his faithful dog in the foreground, mouth empty and agape, whilst the sleuth carries instead the newspaper in his mouth.

Lumiere & Son **Nightfall** *Poster 1978 Design & Photos Hipgnosis*

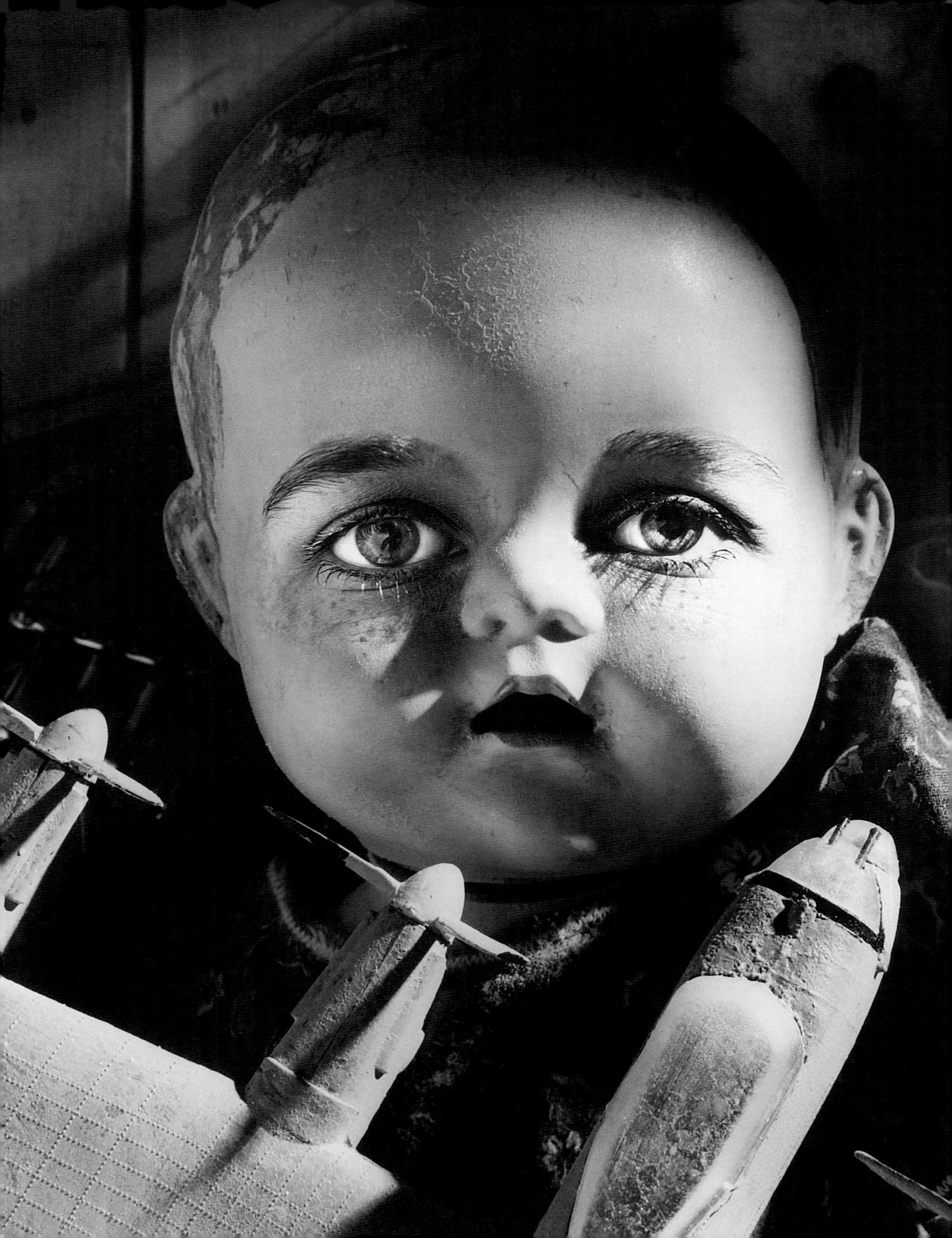

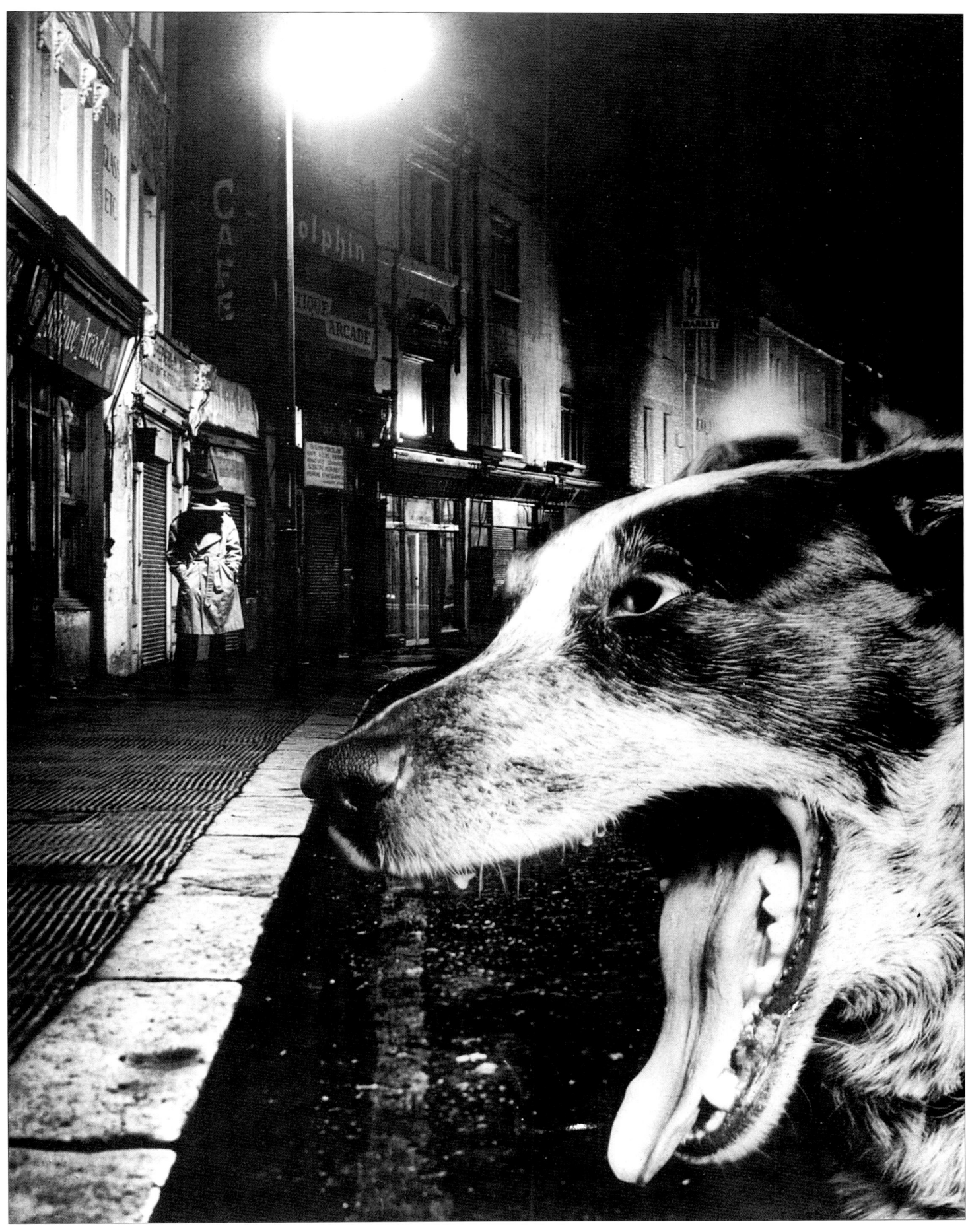

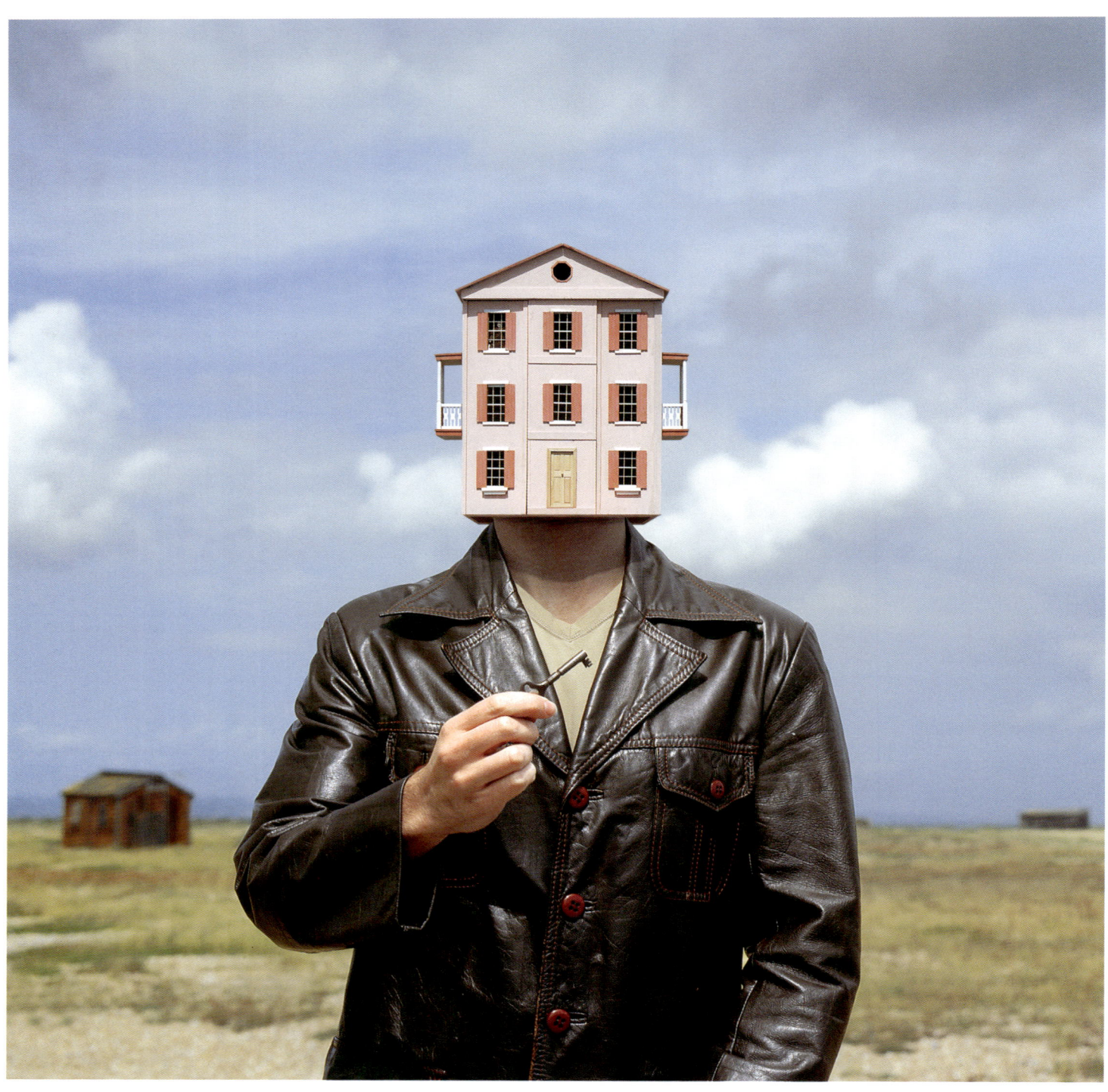

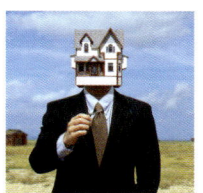

ETHNIX Ethnix are from Israel and both the albums on which we worked seemed concerned with war, the first more directly so. It appeared that Ethnix were as questioning and as critical of their own country as of others. I thought hard about war although I have no direct experience and felt that narcissism was a crucial aspect – love of thyself blinding you to the sufferings of others. I imagined a Narcissus figure not besotted by his own image reflected in the pond but by the agents of war, namely guns, resulting in quite a peculiar image, even for me. And I thought of it! (see inset)

The second album, opposite, focused more on the plight of soldiers particularly in relation to leaving and then returning home afterwards. How do they handle the emotional side which is on occasions more

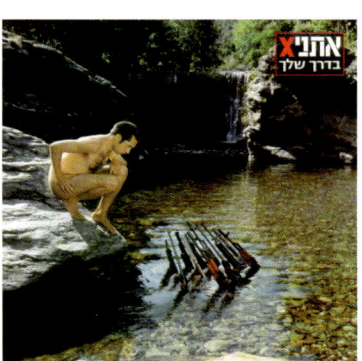

difficult when coming back? "Home is where your heart is", they say, but is it more a question of what's in your mind - are the problems mostly in your head? Is your home where your head is or vica versa? Your head is your house and the key is not in your mind but in your hand, see opposite. No corny surrealism here but a real house on someone's real head, but not a normal house, more one of make believe *i.e.* a dolls house, neatly perched on the shoulders of our model standing amongst wooden shacks equally doll like but no less real in one of our favourite locations, namely Dungeness.

*Ethnix **Thirteen** CD front Sultan 2001 Design & Photos StormStudios
Location Dungeness, south coast UK*

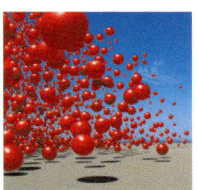

WAKE UP AND SMELL THE COFFEE Sad really, but The Cranberries self-combusted like many before them. Though I personally wonder why this is, from The Beatles down implosion seems a recurring nightmare for rock 'n' roll bands. You'd think they'd be happy enough making music and earning money whilst the rest of us slave away 'in quiet desperation' as the Floyd said. The latter also imploded, well nearly. Just prior to The Cranberries' implosion, came the *Wake Up And Smell The Coffee* album, which was, they told me, an affirmation of an earlier approach, a return to simpler, fresher styles. I imagined the little granules of coffee floating through the air, up the stairs, floating into one's bedroom, settling noisily in the folds of your nostrils, friendly pleasant, aromatic and saying WAKE UP! and let's get on with the day.

Instead of coffee granules, I imagined small, floating, red particles, red like actual cranberries, trying in their droves to get into the bedroom, under the door and through the window, to wake one up. Rarely do little things appease my rampant ego, so the little red particles soon got transmuted into large gym balls, hundreds of them, too big and too many for a bedroom but still coloured vivid red. Thus the idea shifted to the outside, somewhere flat like a beach, where the gym balls could bounce, heading inexorably towards the bed in which the horrified recipient (he who is to be woken) is reclining.

To fulfil our philosophy of doing it for real, this is precisely what we did. We purchased 200 bright red gym balls, each three feet in diameter, constructed a tower with a sloping pen at the top, put all the inflated balls in the pen, and when the cameras were ready pulled back the barrier and the balls tumbled to the ground and bounced several times in wild profusion towards and past the guy in bed. IT LOOKED FANTASTIC in the flesh and for the 10 seconds it lasted before the balls disappeared down the beach. Brilliant when it happened but rather brief, a bit like sex with men, huh? Not that I'd know. It took half an hour to recover the balls before putting them back in the pen at the top of the tower and doing it all again…and again, until the wonderful Hothouse crew were too shagged out to do it anymore.

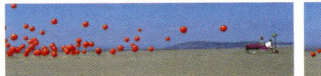 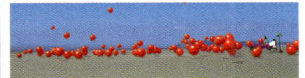

*The Cranberries **Wake Up And Smell The Coffee** CD front MCA 2001
Design & Photos StormStudios Location Burnham Beach, Weston Super Mare*

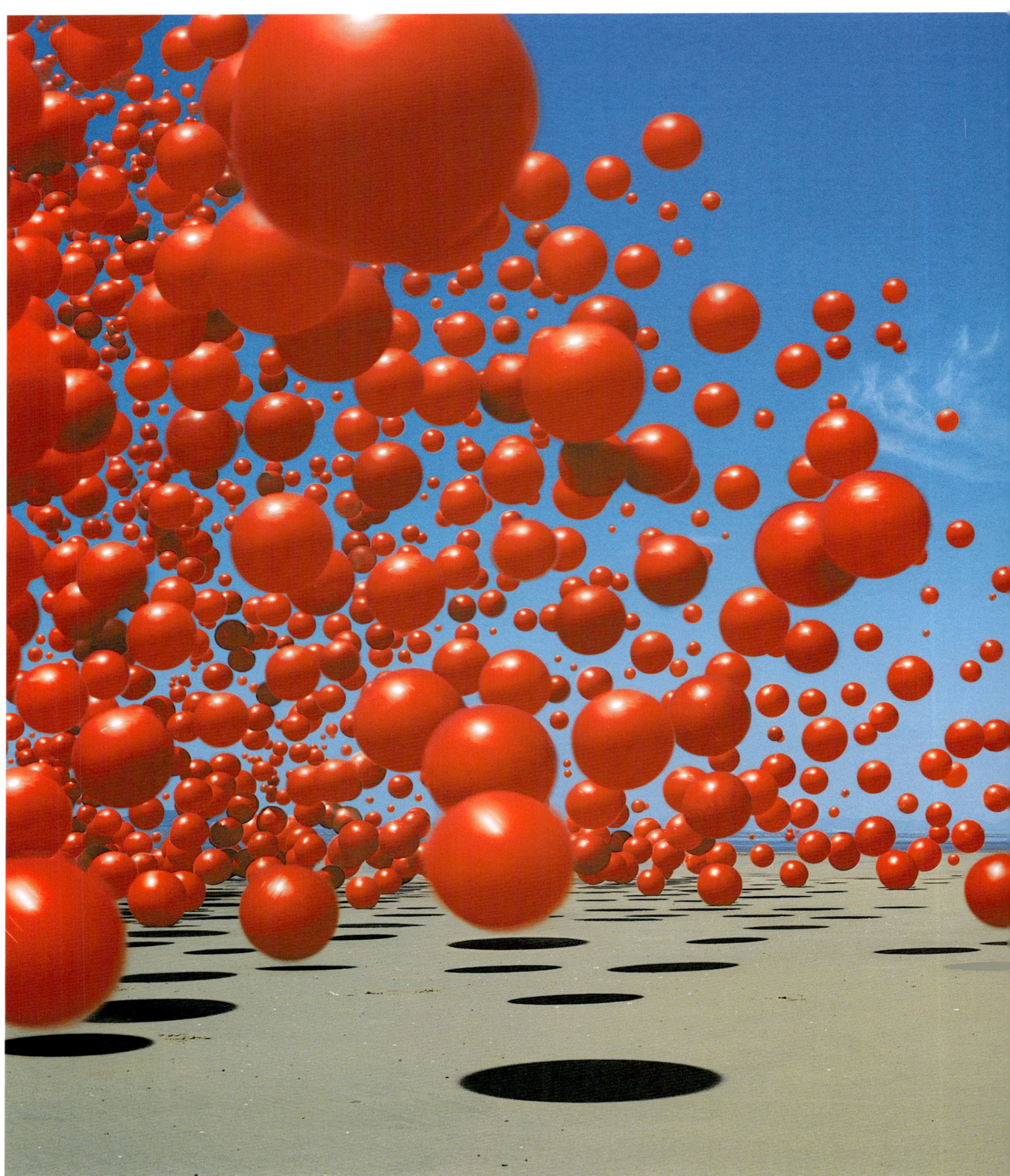

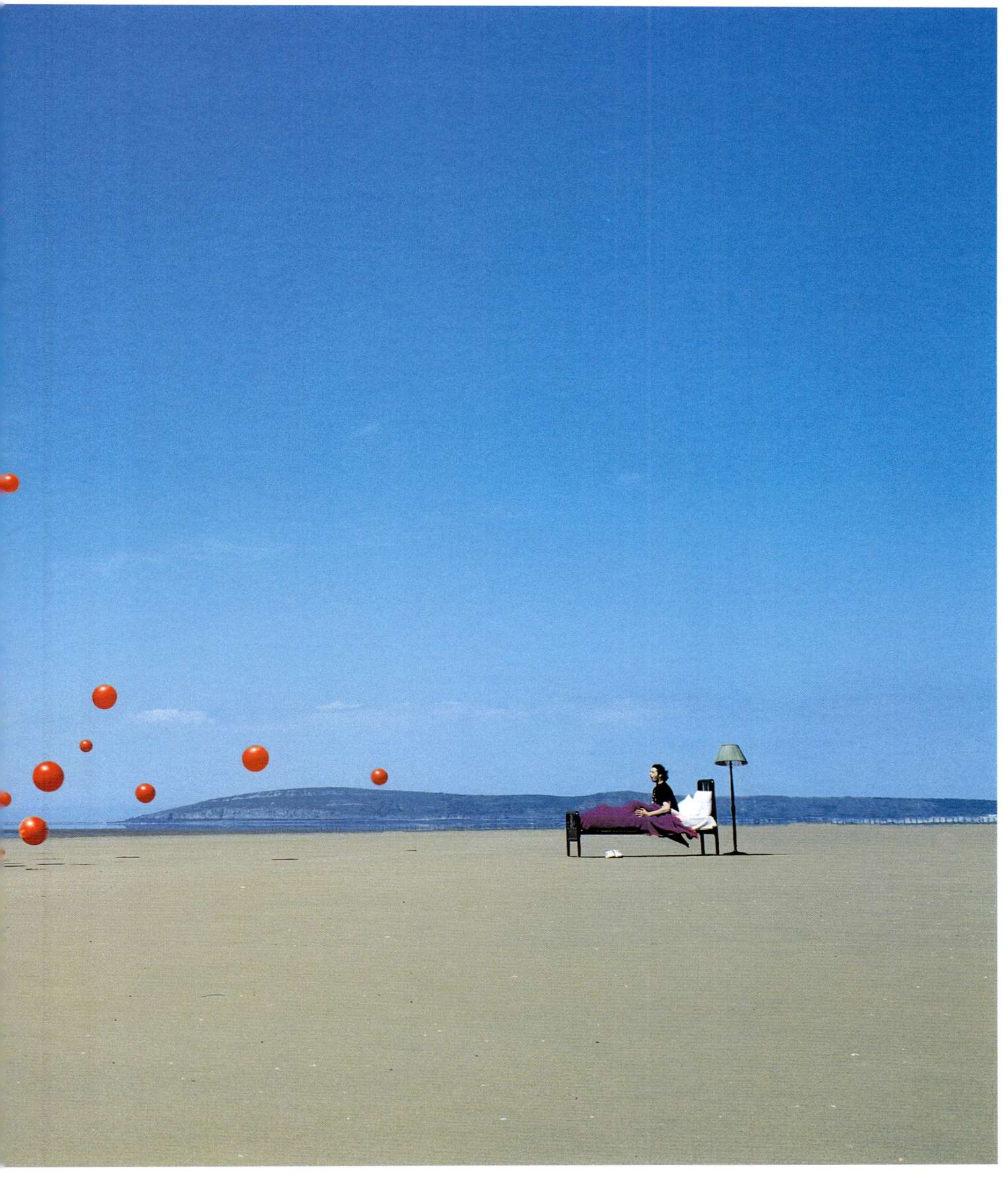

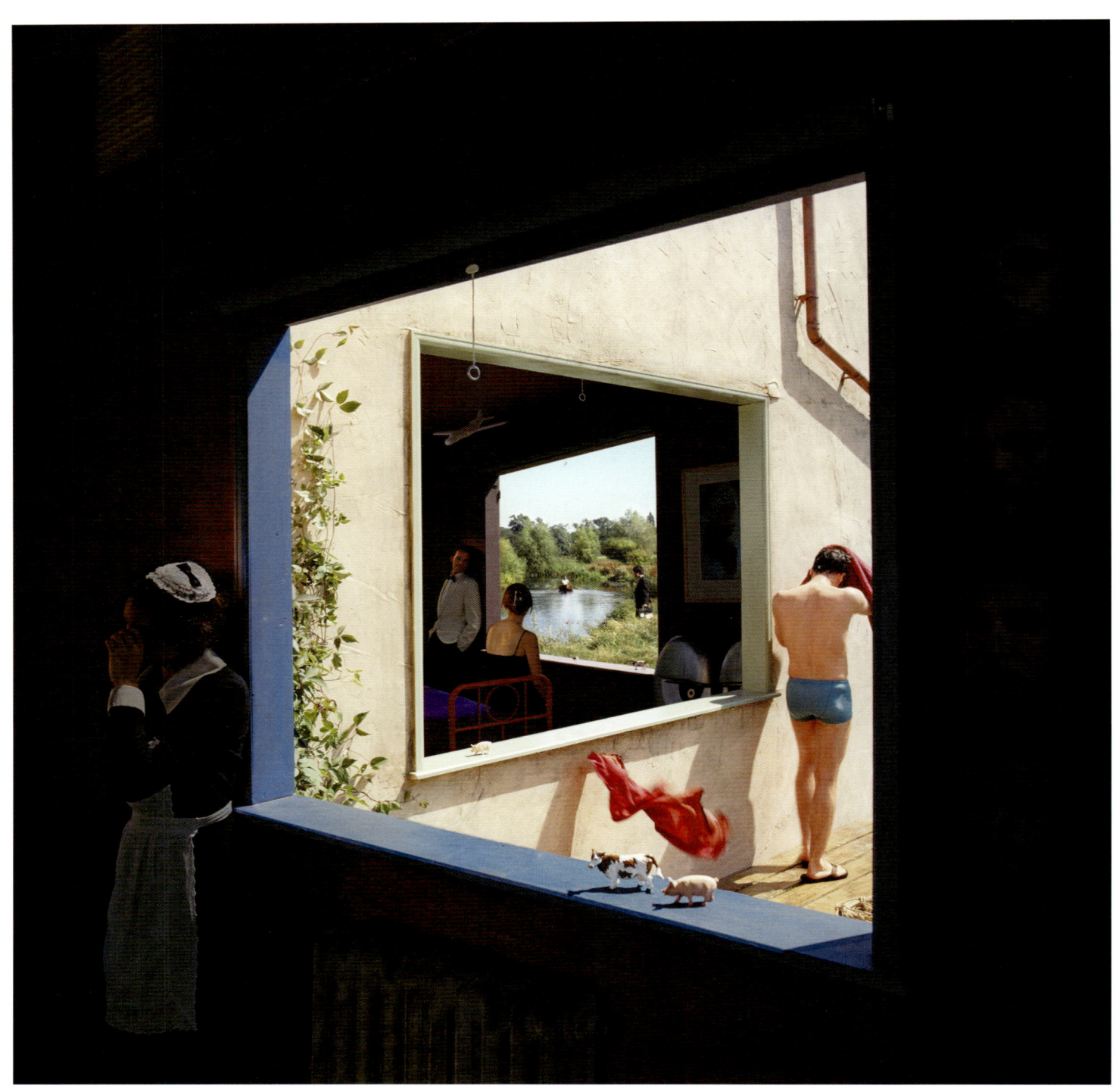

ECHOES

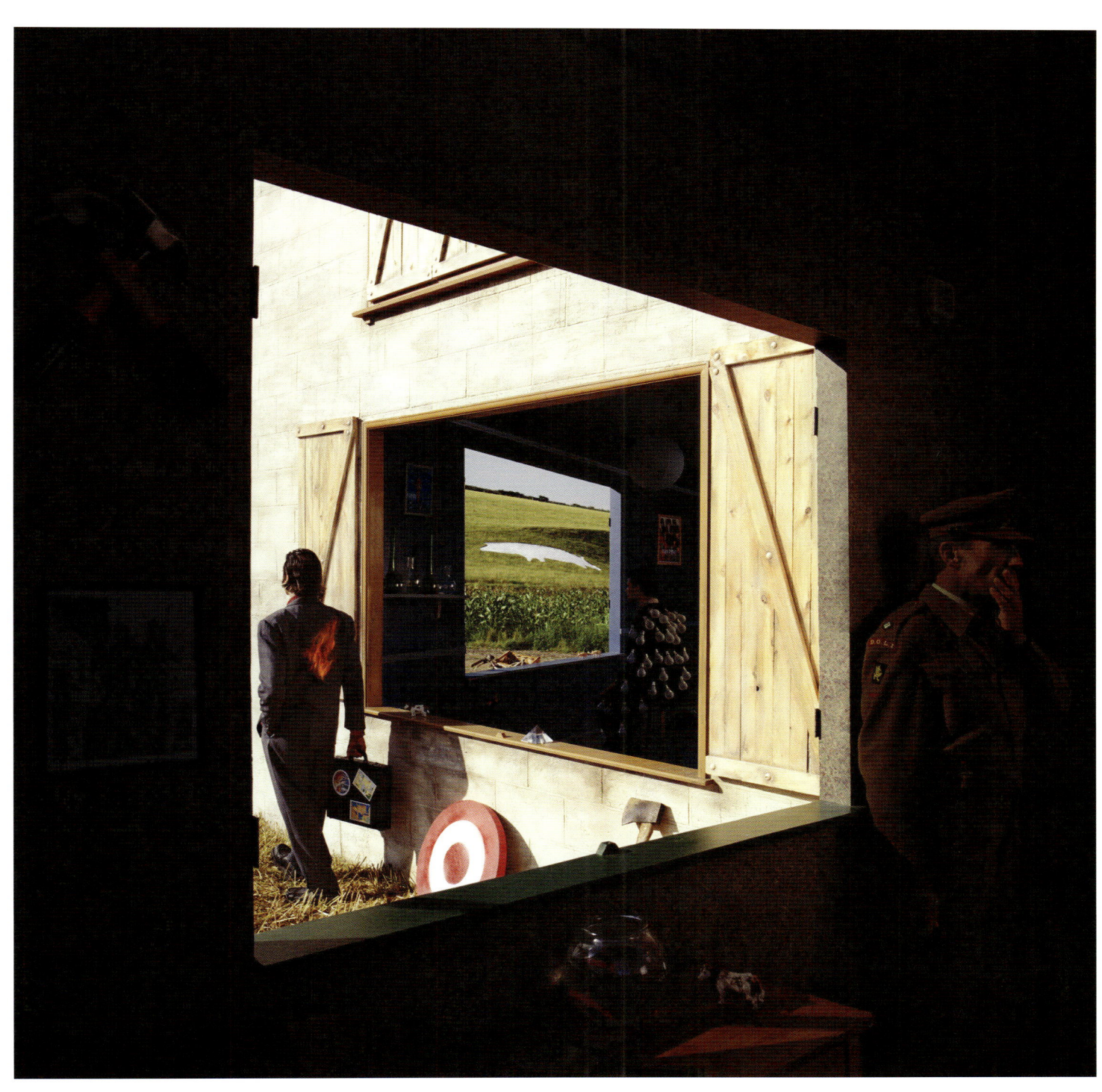

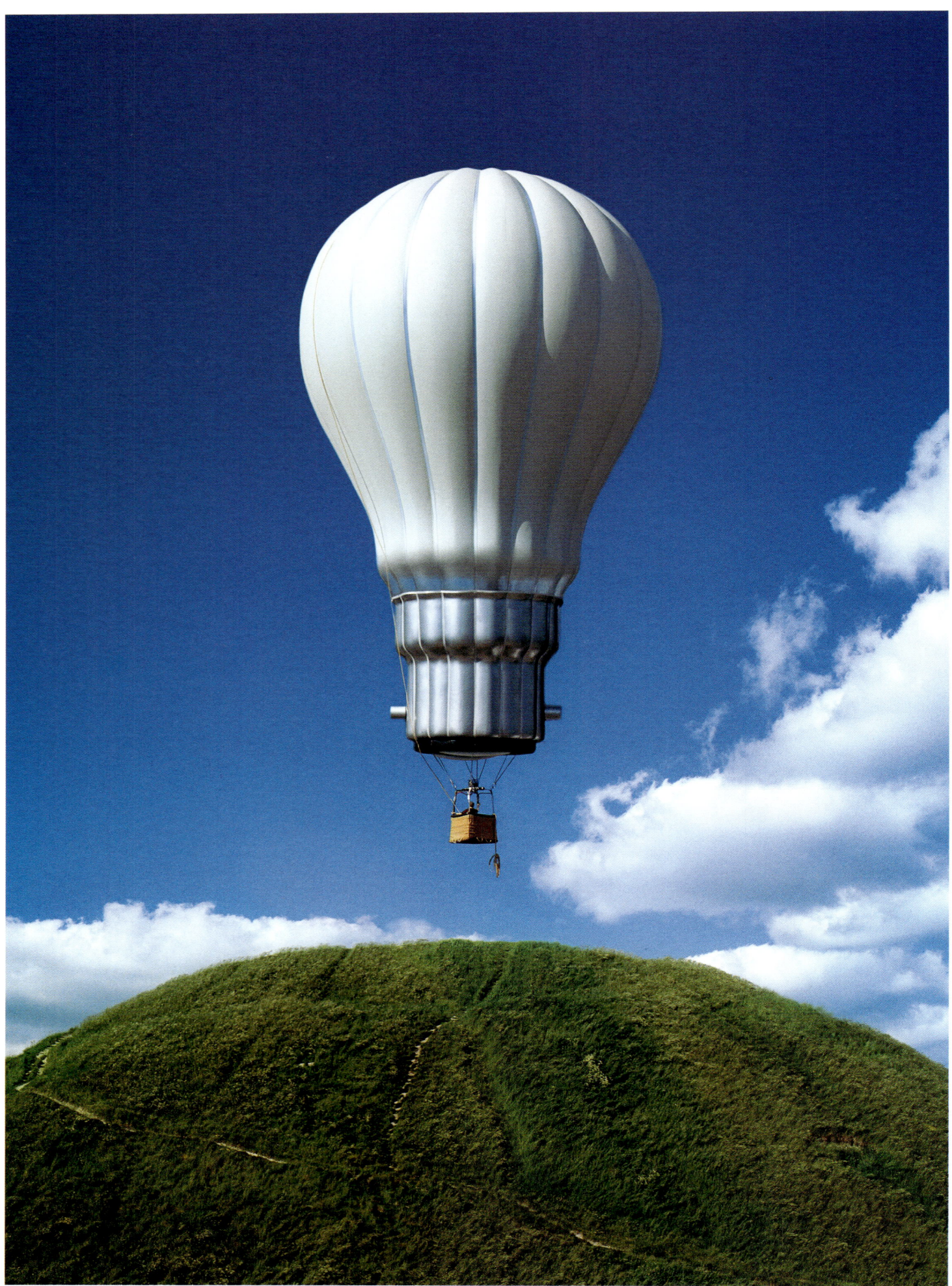

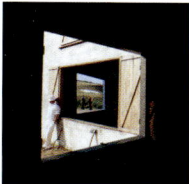

ECHOES *Echoes* or the Best of Pink Floyd was a curious distillation of Pink Floyd's favourites, few of which were actually singles, which tend to be the basic ingredient of 'best of' albums. Well, the Floyd were never ordinary and neither was this selection. It was decided for the most part by the band, though not without some minor disputation, I hear. It was fitting, if not the most innovative of ideas, to design something referential, something that contained numerous items from the covers of past albums from which the songs were taken. These items were then placed in a particular setting, which in itself referred to an extension of *Ummagumma* (pg.125) although it later on transpired ironically that no songs were taken from that album.

What you see is what you get – a receding view going back through real windows, not pictures on a wall, positioned at the corners of apartments that looked out across each other, such that one could see out through the rear window, across a courtyard, through another window to another interior and out another window, into the distant countryside. Rather than flat window to flat window, they were set at an angle, providing a more dynamic shape, a trapezium, as opposed to a front-on square or rectangle. The perspectives echo each other and recede to a view containing yet another reference. Further references are found in the first room and in the second room and in the courtyard between. I imagined optimistically that the Pink Floyd fan would have some pleasure in locating, recognising, and naming the references, the objects, pictures, people etc which refer directly to the previous covers.

I thought that the exterior set was a novel idea – instead of shooting in a studio and pretending that the outside parts were actually outside by drenching them in light, we did the reverse by taking the room set to the exterior location, thereby the outside parts really were outside. When you looked through the windows to the river, it was a real river, not a backdrop nor a collage, because that's where we put the set (the river being our beloved Cam in Grantchester). A rower from *Momentary Lapse* is rowing along the river, and there are plenty of other clues to find if you have the time (which you will because the record is quite long).

Because there were two albums we photographed two different sets in two different locations, based on the same principle, the same size sets but differently decorated and furnished. True to form, the first location was blissfully sunny, and the second was a bloody downpour. No wonder they make films in Hollywood where it is always sunny. But then you'd have to live in LA wouldn't you?

*Pink Floyd **Echoes** CD & vinyl album front EMI 2001*
Design & Photos StormStudios Location Grantchester, Cambs. & Singleton, Sussex

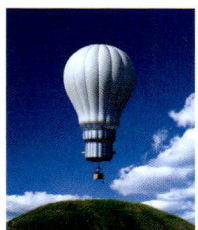

ON AIR Alan Parsons, of The Alan Parsons Project, of *The Dark Side Of The Moon* engineering fame and unreasonable tallness fame, was inclined to select ideas around which to weave an album. In the past subjects included surveillance, Gaudi, pyramids, Asimov robots, not to mention Edgar Allen Poe. In this case his *On Air* album was about the idea of flight or man's desire to fly. It was, Alan said, as much about the idea of flight as about flying itself or about the machines that fly us.

I took the visual notion of an idea, namely that of a light bulb above a head and reworked it as a bulb shaped hot air balloon above a human head shaped hillock. It is not uncommon to see air balloons of different shapes rather than only the stereotypic pear shape, so ours is light bulb shaped of course and is photographed at the same time and in the same lighting conditions as the hill over which it is gracefully flying. The idea of flight whilst flying.

*Alan Parsons **On Air** CD front North Shore 1996*
Design & Photos StormStudios Location Wiltshire

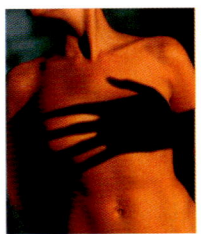

LIKE A SATELLITE Apparently his love reached out 'like a satellite', according to the lyrics of the song, performed by those likeable lads, Thunder. It was a man-woman thing, but I wanted it to be a bit threatening for a hard-travelling, hard-drinking, hard-talking outfit like Thunder. But what reaches out has also to be insubstantial, like the radio-waves from a satellite and therefore this image consists of a shadow and not a real hand.

The shadow is reaching out to the woman, or rather, across her body, and felt to me like a potential violation, but not, because it's only a shadow. Suggestive rather than actual.

*Thunder **Like A Satellite** CD Single EMI 1993*
Design Storm Thorgerson & Peter Curzon Photos Tony May & Storm Thorgerson

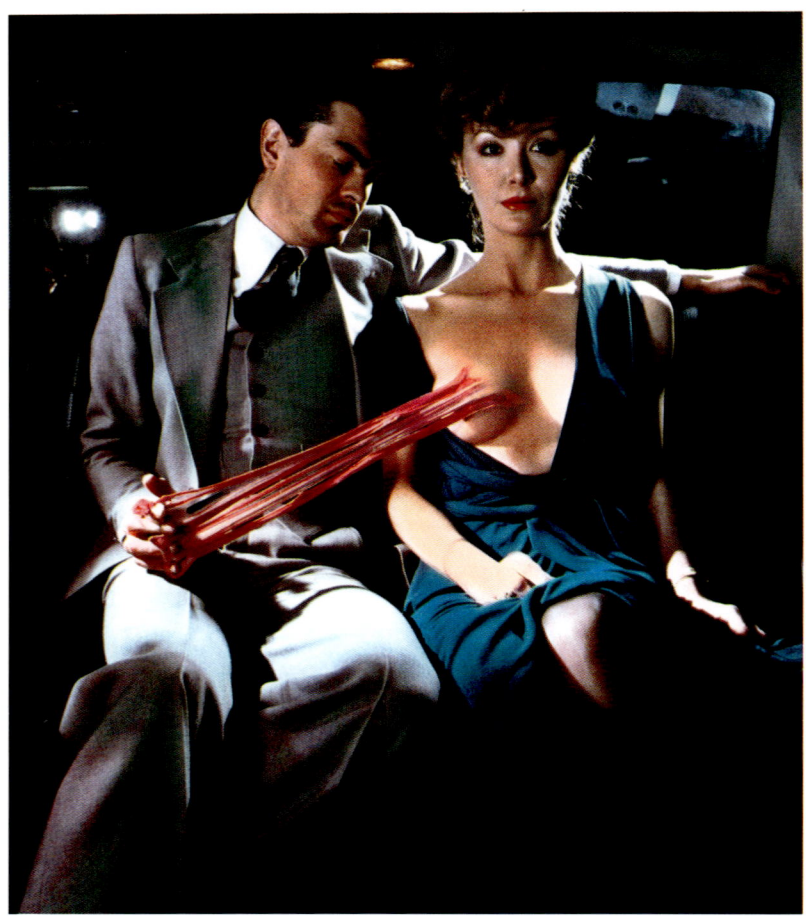

*Scorpions **Love Drive** Vinyl front EMI 1979 Design & Photo Hipgnosis*

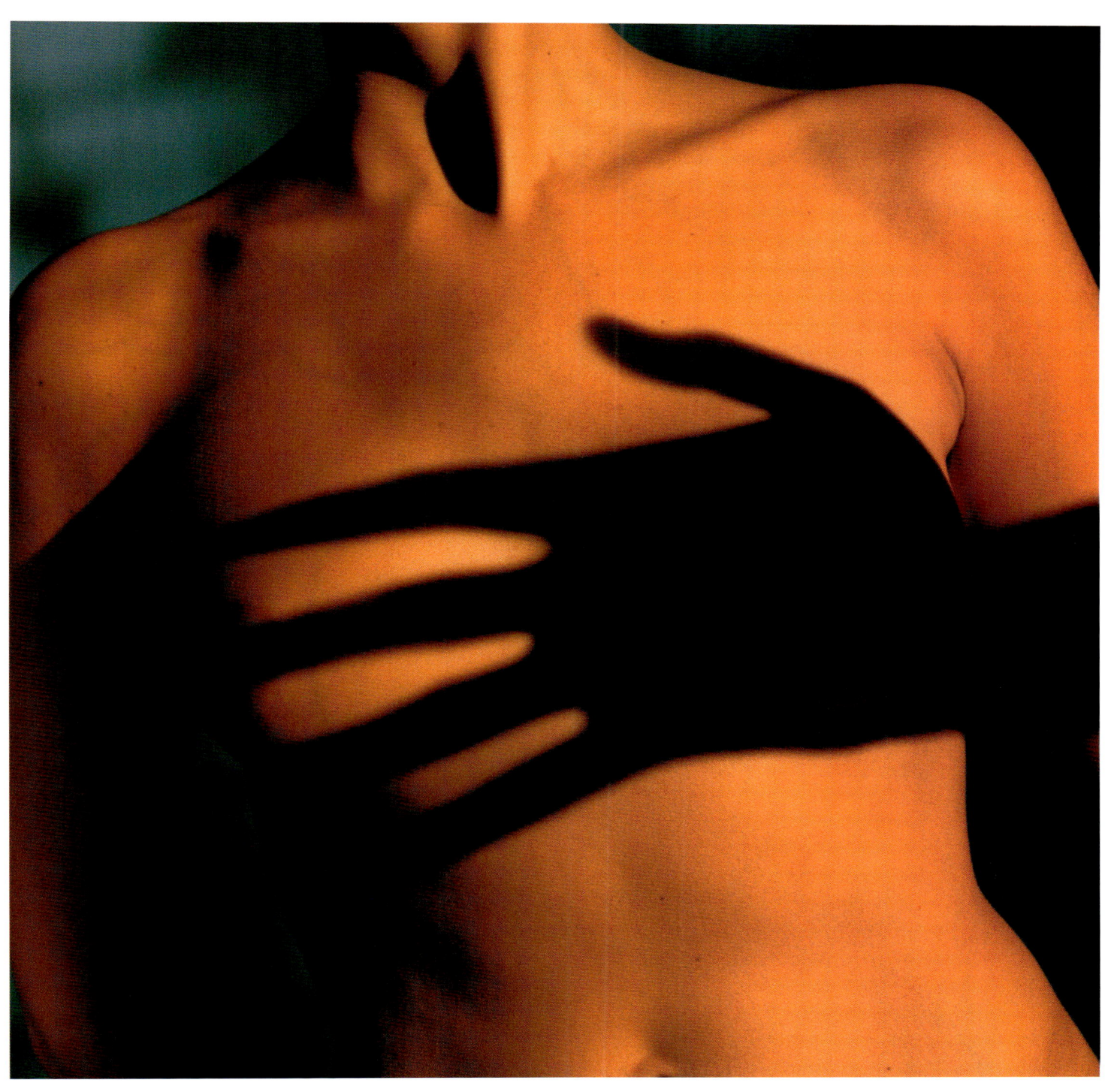

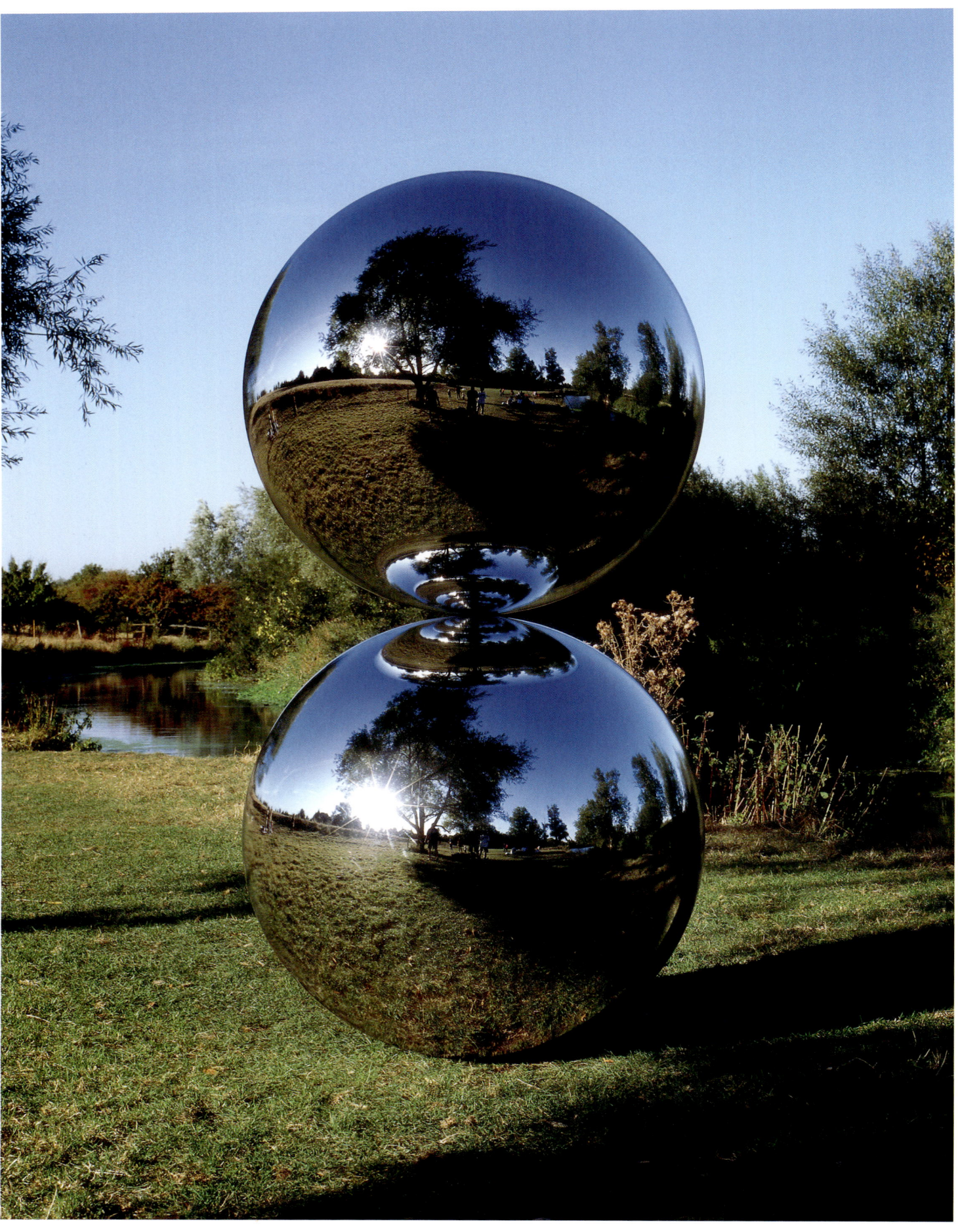

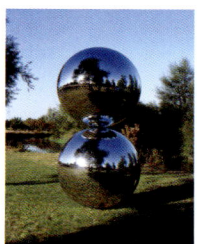

INTERSTELLAR Work begets work. It is one of the principal reasons to continue working, especially in the face of the other reasons going sour. Interstellar was designed for an exhibition of Pink Floyd of the same name, mounted in Paris in October 2003 at the Cité de la Musique and is derived from an admixture of *Pulse* DVD (pg. 134) and a visit to the Tate Modern, London to experience the eerie reflective sculptures of Anish Kapoor. *Pulse* DVD is itself an admixture of a development of *Pulse* CD (pg.110), and an obsession with eyes to which one is both continually drawn, being in the visual arts, and is continually repulsed, because it's a cliché, nestling alongside such favourites as Sunsets and Hearts.

The two glass eyeballs of *Pulse* DVD were transmuted via Kapoor into two perfect mirror balls, one on top of another, finely balanced, but comfortable, each ball, being a planet or star, and it's what goes on in between, as in 'interstellar', which is paramount. It is the secret of Pink Floyd, or so I like to think, foolish me. Between the balls, between the stars is an endless repetition, an infinite repeat of images, without end, like receding fractals, layer upon layer, wheels within wheels, etc, etc. The balls were made of perfect perspex hemispheres, which are electroplated with a perfect mirror, which means that there are no unwelcome defects or distortions. In the bright sunshine of a glorious summers day in Grantchester, by our beloved river Cam, they looked resplendent, reflecting in every detail, the leafy surroundings, so bright and shiny, they were like a magnet to children, who clustered round, finding their elongated faces in the fish-eye reflection.

The area between the spheres is reminiscent of *Ummagumma* (pg. 125) though much more difficult to define, easier to see the depths of reflection, showing the trees, clouds, river, grass, and my good self and crazy Rupert if you look hard. I find this piece very tranquil and calm... the calm before the storm, would that be?

Pink Floyd **Interstellar** *Poster Cité de la Musique 2003*
Design & Photos StormStudios Location Grantchester, Cambs.

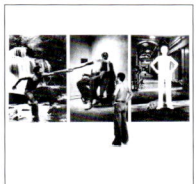

LAMB LIES DOWN ON BROADWAY I never fully understood why Genesis and Pink Floyd were always regarded as the bastions of Britishness, being described invariably as very 'English'. I suppose this might be more true of Genesis, who met, I believe, at an English public school, and spent more time forming a band and playing music than doing their studies, the naughty boys. I think Genesis displayed great enterprise in enacting changes of artistic direction, sometimes by choice and sometimes by necessity (departing personnel). *Lamb Lies Down On Broadway* was a change in artistic direction and was a sort of story to music, a music soundtrack to an unmade film. Not really an opera but similar in scope. The songs detailed the story of a central character, Rael, who has several adventures (the songs) in physical and metaphorical pursuit of self realisation, if I remember it correctly.

This change of musical direction was accompanied by a change of visual direction, which was unfortunate for the previous cover designer, but fortunate for us at Hipgnosis. We conceived of a story board or a comic strip, but made of photographs rather than of illustrations, the more usual form, alluding to the set of adventures of the central character. A major part of this involved the character stepping outside the comic strip and taking a detached view, looking back at this life, a step considered necessary in the process of self-realisation. Thus the main character is seen literally stepping out of the picture, leaving a man-shaped white hole in his wake. He stands outside staring back at the frames of the story which involve him.

All the imagery is photographed in black and white negative, and the resulting prints are reassembled, adjusted in size, comped together and recopied to provide a single flat artwork. This is a monstrously difficult and painstaking process before the era of computers, but no less worth it. (Thanks to master retoucher Terry Day.)

I like the guy holding the divider between frames four and five, or is that two and three? As if it were something solid: what is a two dimensional divider on the page to us is a three dimensional post to him.

Genesis **Lamb Lies Down On Broadway** *Vinyl gatefold Charisma 1974*
Design & Photos Hipgnosis Locations Roundhouse, Chalk Farm, London, Hipgnosis Studio & Wales

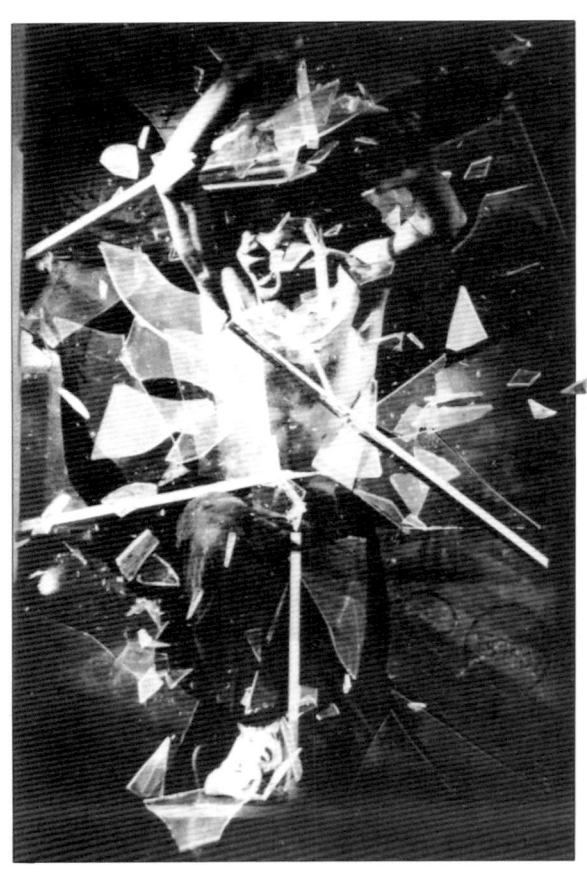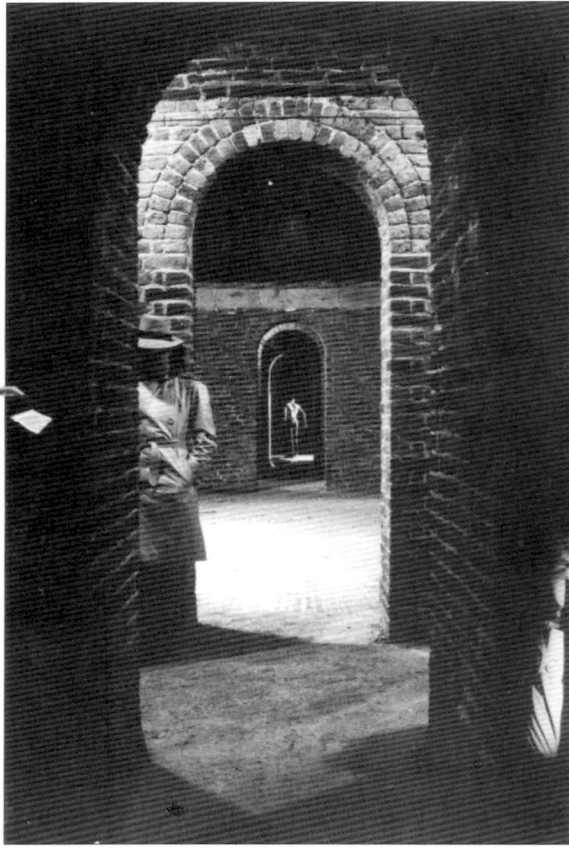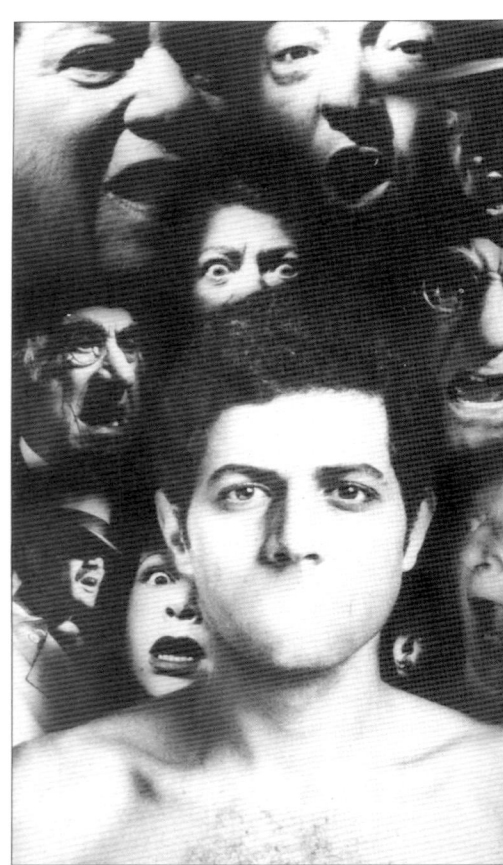

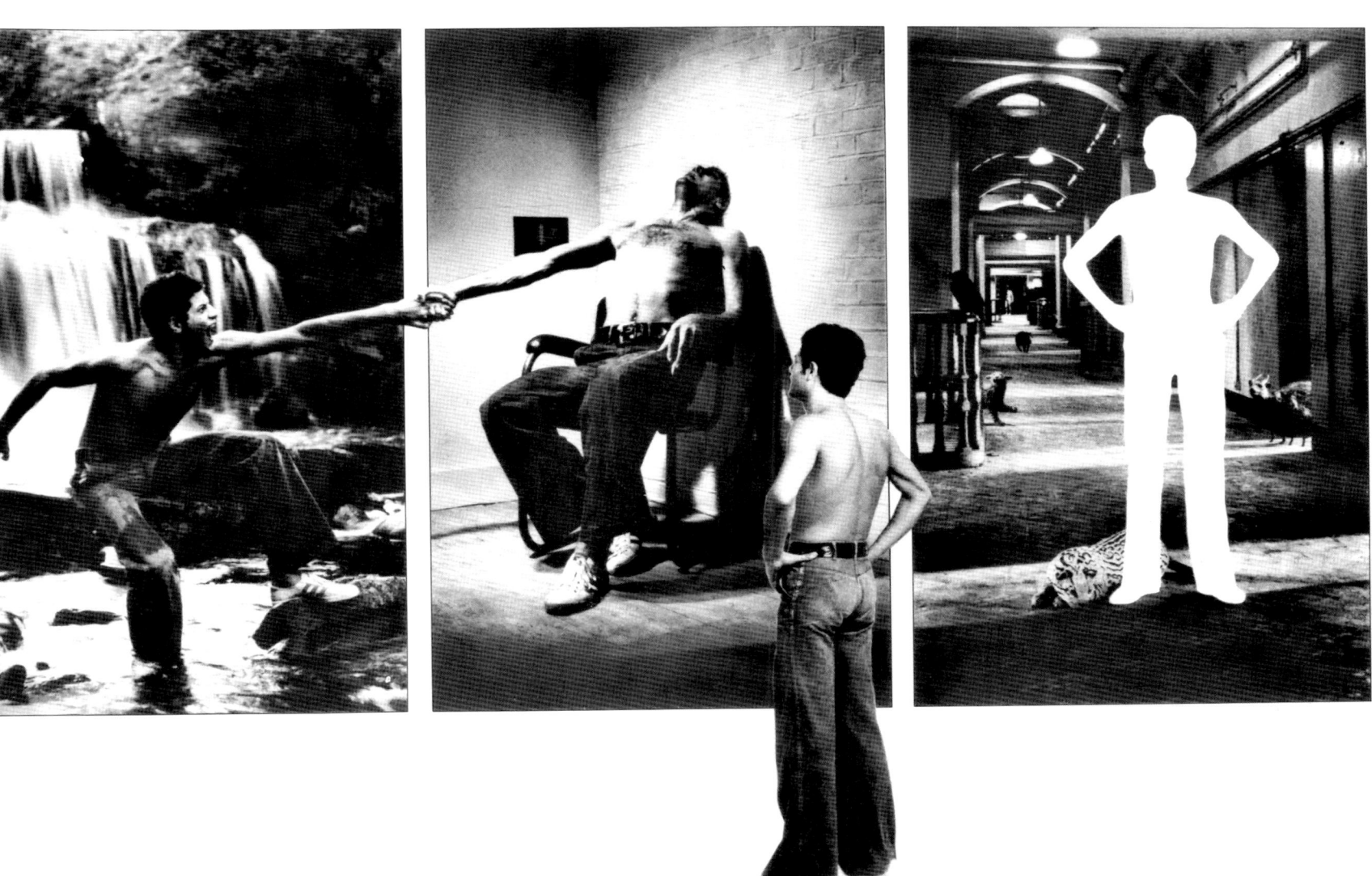

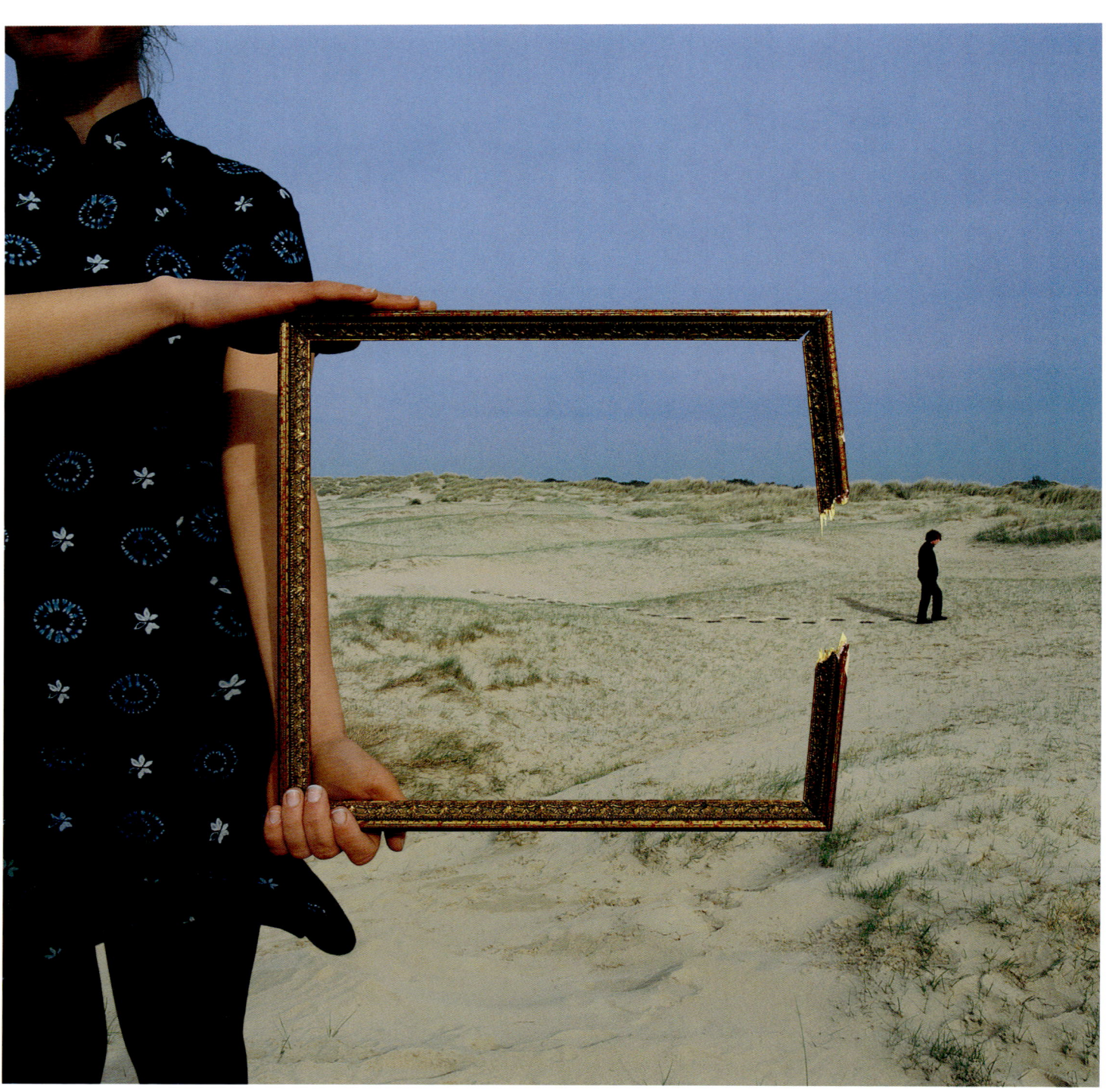

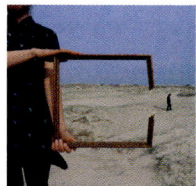

IS IT A SIN Deepest Blue, consisting of Joel Edwards from sunny Hertfordshire and Matt Schwartz from sunny Israel, came together briefly to make an album and then disappeared, if not in flames then quite speedily, subsequently to reappear, I'm sure, in different incarnations. During their brief encounter they made three or four singles, one of which was 'Is It A Sin'. Although on the surface it was a typical pop song about love won and lost, the lyrics asked 'was it a sin' to be with someone else so soon after a break-up?, turning the usual pedestrian pop fare slightly on its head. So a different approach to the break-up of boy and girl was needed. We wanted to suggest that one of the parties was now 'out of the picture', that is, had left the frame, walking from the edge of a cosy picture of togetherness into the real world of loneliness. It seemed a novel but poetic way of showing boy-leaves-girl. The sadness of separation seemed heightened both by the wintry sun slanting across the dunes, and by the sharp edges of the broken frame.

*Deepest Blue **Is It A Sin** CD single Ministry of Sound 2004*
Design & Photos StormStudios Location Camber Sands, Sussex

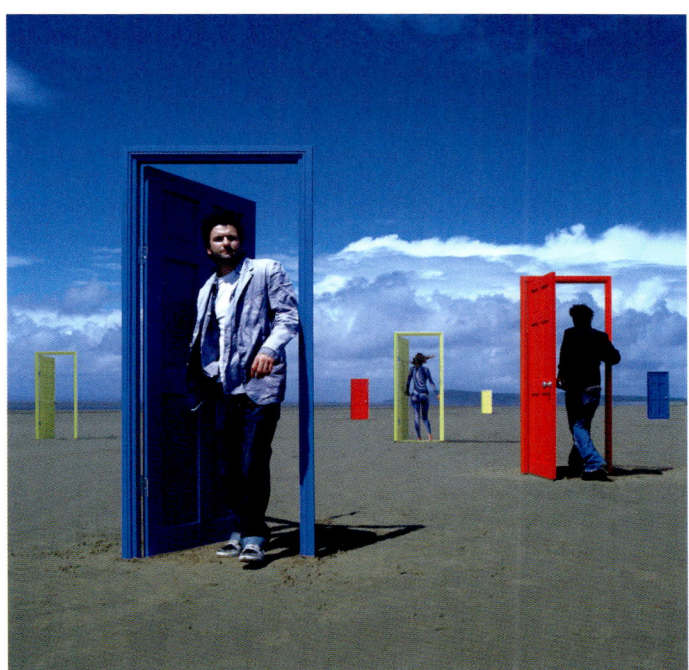

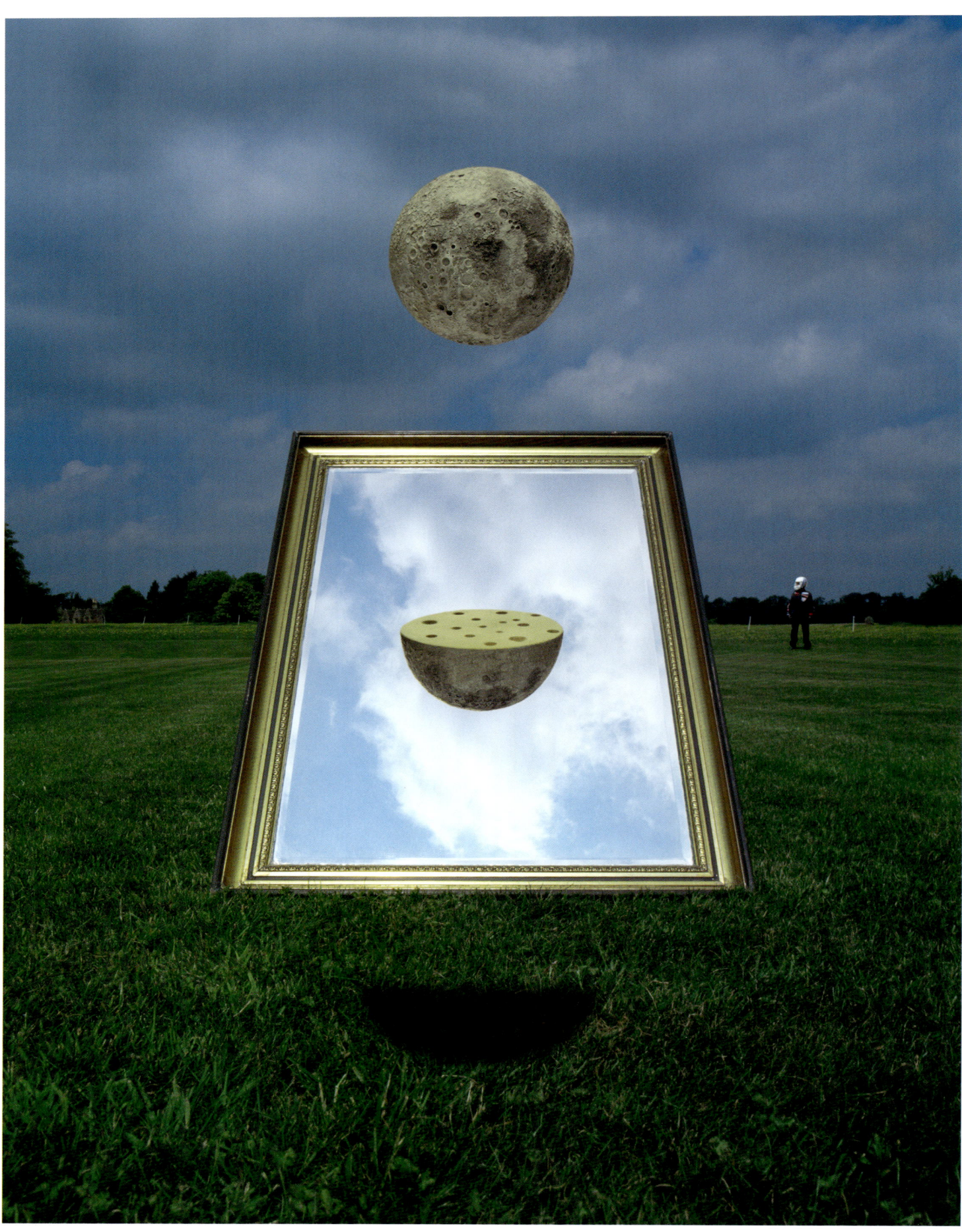

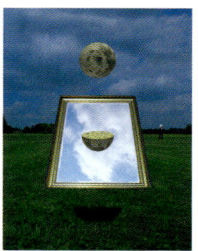

INSIDE OUT The image of a mirror at an angle such that it reflects the underside of something above it, which we the viewer can see only from the front, is a further exploration of the very nature of things, visually speaking. It came about as a result of asking questions about perspective, angle, from where do you see things? Does the light have any dramatic effect on what you see? And what does something look like from behind if all you can see is the front? This theme was first explored for *Interstellar*, an exhibition of Pink Floyd, held at the Cité de la Musique, Paris, Autumn 2003. But was ousted at that time by the Mirror Balls, see pg.148.

Nick Mason's book on Pink Floyd was called *Inside Out* and offered a suitable occasion to re-present this idea, along with some others, including the contortionist lady turning herself 'inside out', her body painted from head to toe with Floyd imagery. We thought that this latter idea was more obvious and would be preferred by the publisher, which it duly was. But then a strange turn of events occurred... the two ideas were submitted to the marketing department who selected the more serious but more arty idea of the mirror. Marketing department choose art cover instead of marketing department *trashes* art, which is more usually the case. What a turnaround, things turning inside out!

The idea was adapted for Nick's book by including a car racing figure in the background, could be Nick, by making the hovering object a moon (to see the dark side naturally) and by taking the photograph in Nick's country gaff outside in the garden but inside band territory. Outside and in, inside but out.

Nick Mason **Inside Out** *Book Cover Weidenfeld & Nicolson 2004*
Design & Photos StormStudios Location Bath, Wiltshire

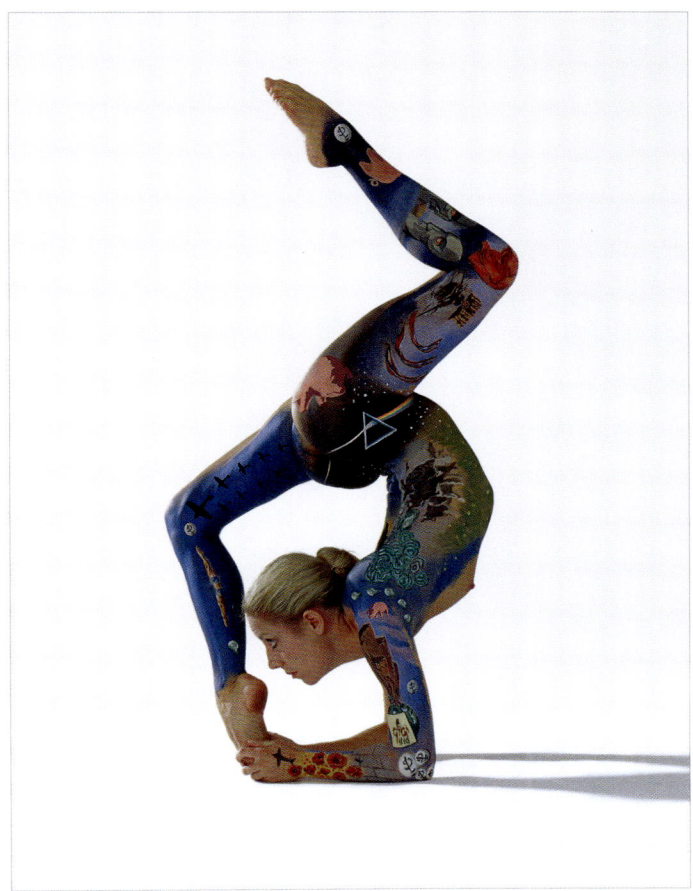

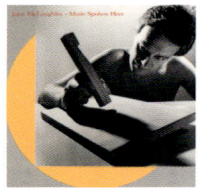

MUSIC SPOKEN HERE John McLaughlin is not only a man of diverse talent but is rather well preserved and smartly dressed. Having produced music in several different genres, he was keen to stress that his work was not easily compartmentalised. The title of his 1981 album was *Music Spoken Here*, not any kind of music, but his kind of music, music of many shades, but always played with deep feeling and great expertise.

I am rarely inclined to suggest a picture of the artist on the grounds that portraiture is not my forte, and that portraits may tell you about the musician, but not about the music. In this instance, I decided otherwise, and suggested to John that it might be fun to represent his elusive aesthetic by showing him trying to fit a square peg into a round hole. A studied procedure which might reflect his committed approach, not so much a purist as an aesthete, involved in some Zen-like game, showing his powers of concentration. A black and white approach seemed preferable in order to accentuate his no-frills attitude.

The back cover continued this black and white approach and constituted another studied portrait, showing this time John's power of concentration as he endeavoured to measure the length of a piece of string. How long is a piece of string? is as we all know and a notoriously complex question to answer – one of life's great conundrums. It is therefore encouraging to see John tackle this problem with such purpose.

John McLaughlin **Music Spoken Here** *Vinyl front Warner Bros 1982*
Design & Photos STD, AAP & Assorted Images

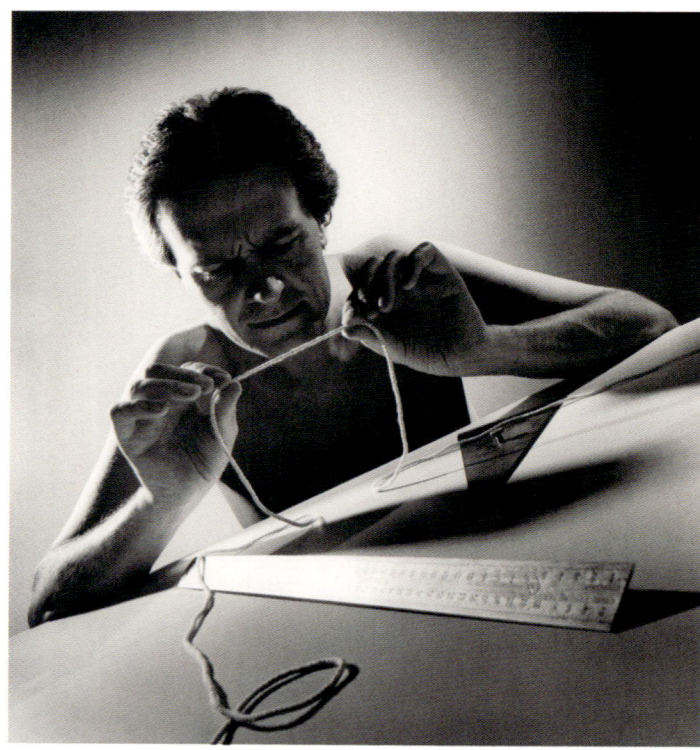

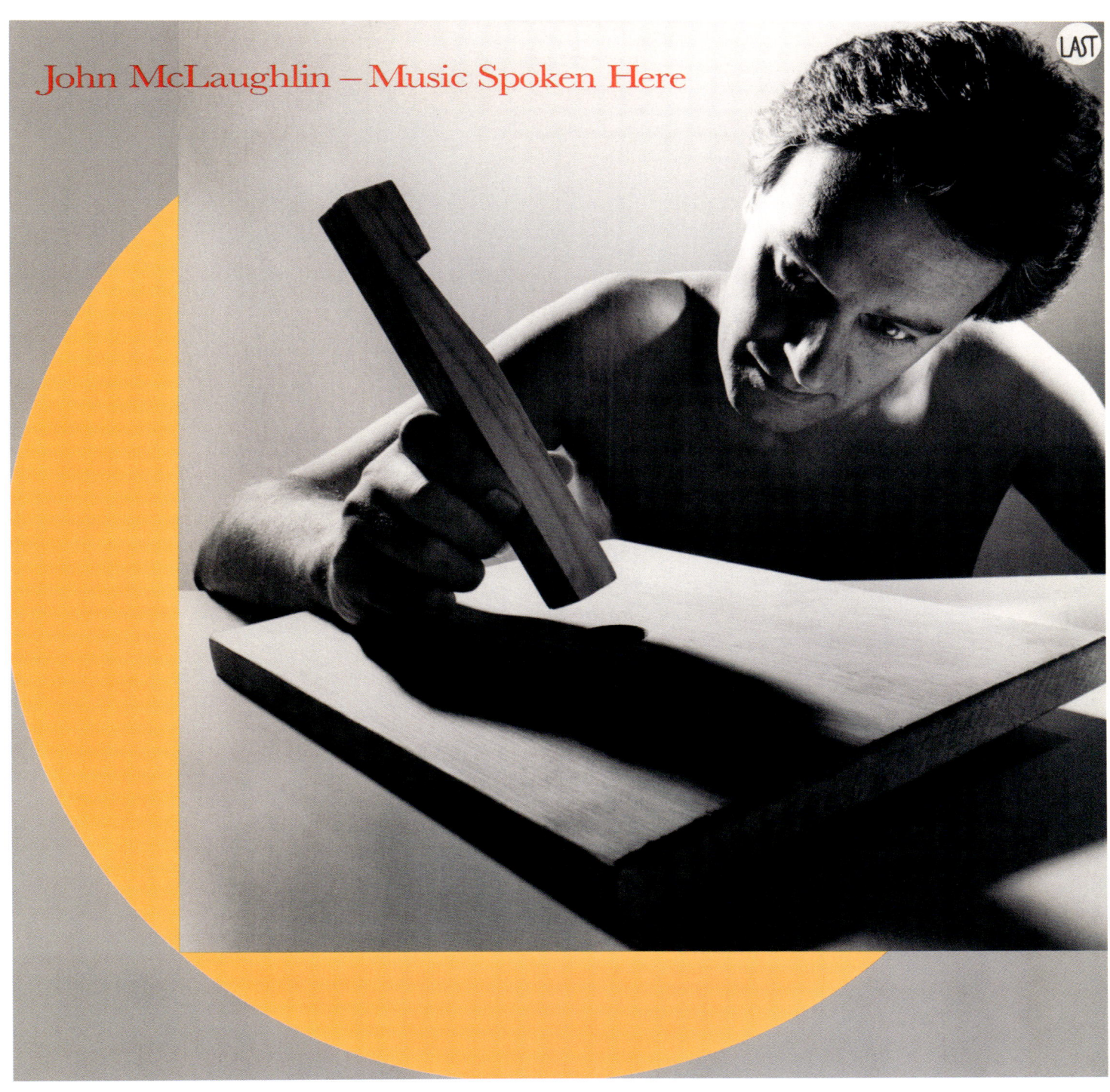

John McLaughlin — Music Spoken Here

LAST

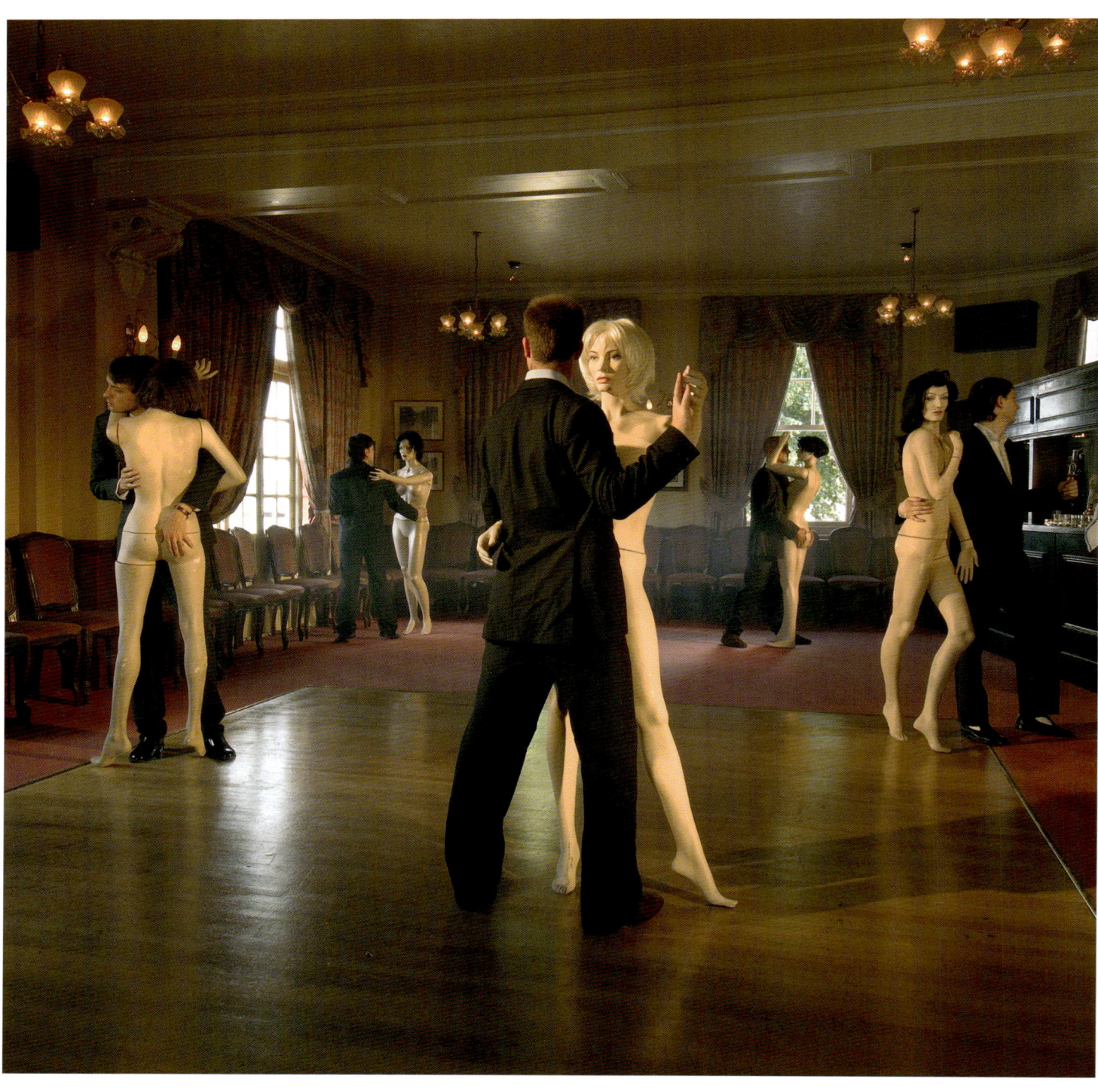

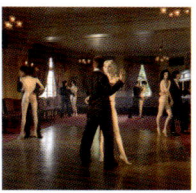

PROGRAM THE DEAD Program The Dead are a hard and heavy rock band from LA, who were very interested in a thing called a 'Verichip'. Their music was deceptive, seeming at first rather aggressive, but on later exposure, revealing a much greater variety and depth (in our humble opinion) feelings of despair, thwarted romance, all set in the future perhaps – shades of the movie *Logan's Run*.

The Verichip, is indeed veri-interesting - it's a chip that can be implanted in the human body and can send out radio information, and is the basis therefore of the electronic tagging of prisoners and of truant children in California. It is favoured by Brazilian businessmen to reduce the threat of kidnapping, and also by Spanish teenagers who obtain illicit alcohol by purloining the Verichips of adult drinkers. The Californian children were initially encouraged to wear Verichips to deter truancy but the parents and the kids themselves complained that it was an infringement of their civil liberties (a complaint which was later upheld). It is much used for pets, about whose rights society is not quite so liberal. This is why the Verichip poses such a complex dilemma - keep track or keep control?

The Verichip business also reminded me of the clones in *Bladerunner*, so we dreamed up this dance where the women, like *Stepford Wives*, are the picture of compliance, and despite appearing to dance normally are seemingly lifeless or dead (as in Program The Dead), naked for God's sake but not giving a damn. Obedient, sheeplike as if programmed. The mannequins lent a sinister jaded atmosphere to the proceedings, like a neutered Helmut Newton, or an Edvard Munch painting, where their movements may be controlled by others, a dance that is not really a dance at all, more a dance of the dead. Program The Dead.

Program The Dead **Program The Dead** *CD album front Universal 2005*
Design & Photos StormStudios Location Putney, London

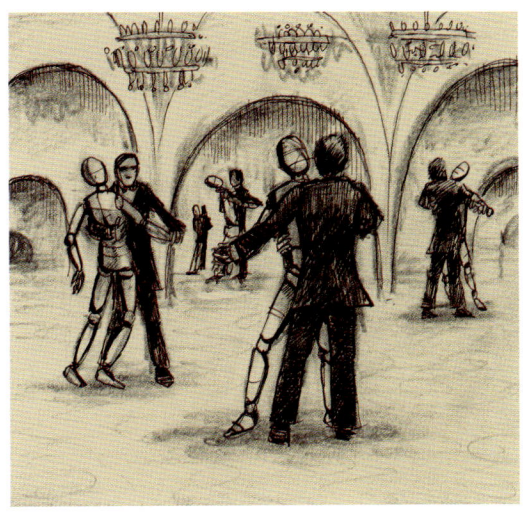

ART VS COMMERCE

ART VERSUS COMMERCE is a continuing area of dispute in the music business, particularly between record companies and musicians, but also between record companies and our good selves. I imagine the same debate rages in the corridors of film land and in advertising, but I know very little of these domains. I don't know much about the music business other than my own experience and that of colleagues; however most record companies and management regularly feel compelled to take issue with us graphic designers over what promotes sales and what doesn't. And without research or statistics to support their case they often assert that certain characteristics like big lettering, big objects, big portraits and big tits improves sales and should be part of cover design, nothing too subtle or highbrow. Dumbing down is their usual m.o.

What gets my goat is that basically if they knew what design attributes improve sales figures they would use them, re-use them and would be proven to be right, but they don't and they aren't. What also gets my goat (such a peculiar expression that) is their reluctance to be consistent and reward accordingly - if a design could be shown to effect sales positively then they could pay the designer extra... but do they hell!

My feeling is that it is mostly a question of hearsay, groundless presumption and prejudice. The record companies and management express views as if widely known and generally recognised, which are merely extensions of their own private opinions, not rooted in any rational argument nor substantiated by data. In my view album covers neither help nor hinder sales, though

I imagine a really ugly or boring visual might deter the purchaser, but I personally assumed that other people like me acquire albums for the music, the cover design being an added pleasure and not an incentive to buy.

Actually the real purpose of an album cover is firstly, to protect the vinyl or CD from scratches or dust and the grubby hands of small children, or the compass point of a jilted lover. Secondly, an album cover identifies its contents - quite handy in the factory or the shop or in one's own collection. Thirdly, a cover provides additional information in the form of credits and lyrics, very useful for those interested in such things (which I estimate to be quite a few). After these requirements comes the issue of taste, representation and sales. Only fools, they say, judge a book by its cover or food by its look, or a person by their clothes. However, these things can help, they can assist judgement and extend the enjoyment. Same goes for album covers... but don't count on it.

What is gratifying about designing album covers is that despite being commercial art, like advertising, they are not enslaved to product, they do not have to show the item for sale as does a car advert or a commercial for trainers or beer. Cover designs enjoy the enviable privilege of being freer and more or less unrestricted. Album art can be concerned with the breadth of emotion that embodies the music and since this constitutes a huge range across the genres of music the accompanying cover designs are equally unfettered. In short, a designer of covers can do anything, can design in any style, use any technique, select any subject matter, subscribe to good taste or bad, be innovative or referential. We can and do get away with blue murder (another peculiar expression). If one likes problem solving then album art can appeal because each time you successfully complete a cover you have solved a problem, not world shattering but satisfying in its small way.

The downsides are the smaller budget (smaller than advertising for example), the conservatism of clients inclined to repeat what was done before, the rigid squareness of the canvas and the whimsicality of musicians. On balance the pros far out way the cons, stress or no stress. Even the insecurity, the sword of Damocles for all free-lance workers is bearable if, and it's a big if, one can do the occasional good piece of work... oh and scrape enough to 'pay the fucking rent!' as Free so memorably said in *All Right Now*.

The major upside of designing covers, which I nearly forgot because it's so obvious, is that it is great to work for music. Everyone likes music of some kind or another, from grannies to guardsmen, from pubescents to politicians. Music is intrinsically a good thing like trees - see pg.14 - one of the wondrous things on this planet.

Working for music feels relatively clean and wholesome, if not spiritually satisfying. I tried working in the commercial mainstream advertising beer and confectionary and felt unclean afterwards, let alone wondering why on earth one would use a lot of energy filming or photographing product items. Can you imagine spending hours and hours refining the lighting on a bottle of beer? And for what? More money? If you want money be corporate... and the best of luck.

Art versus Commerce... clearly what we do is commercial, insomuch as it is commissioned and insomuch as it is usually for a purpose, cover or poster, and it is remunerated, whether it is art... gawd knows. Many a fine artist has been commissioned in one way or another, many a fine piece of art has been executed for a specific purpose as opposed to reflecting the private insights and pains of the artist. However, is what we do art? It's in the eye of the beholder, that's you dear reader, that is, and you probably don't give a monkey's because it only matters if you like it... or not.

The whole issue of Art versus Commerce for sleeve designers may not matter a jot in the face of the internet, where downloading music may obviate the need for album covers and therefore put us poor old sleeve designers out of a job. March of progress... PAH!

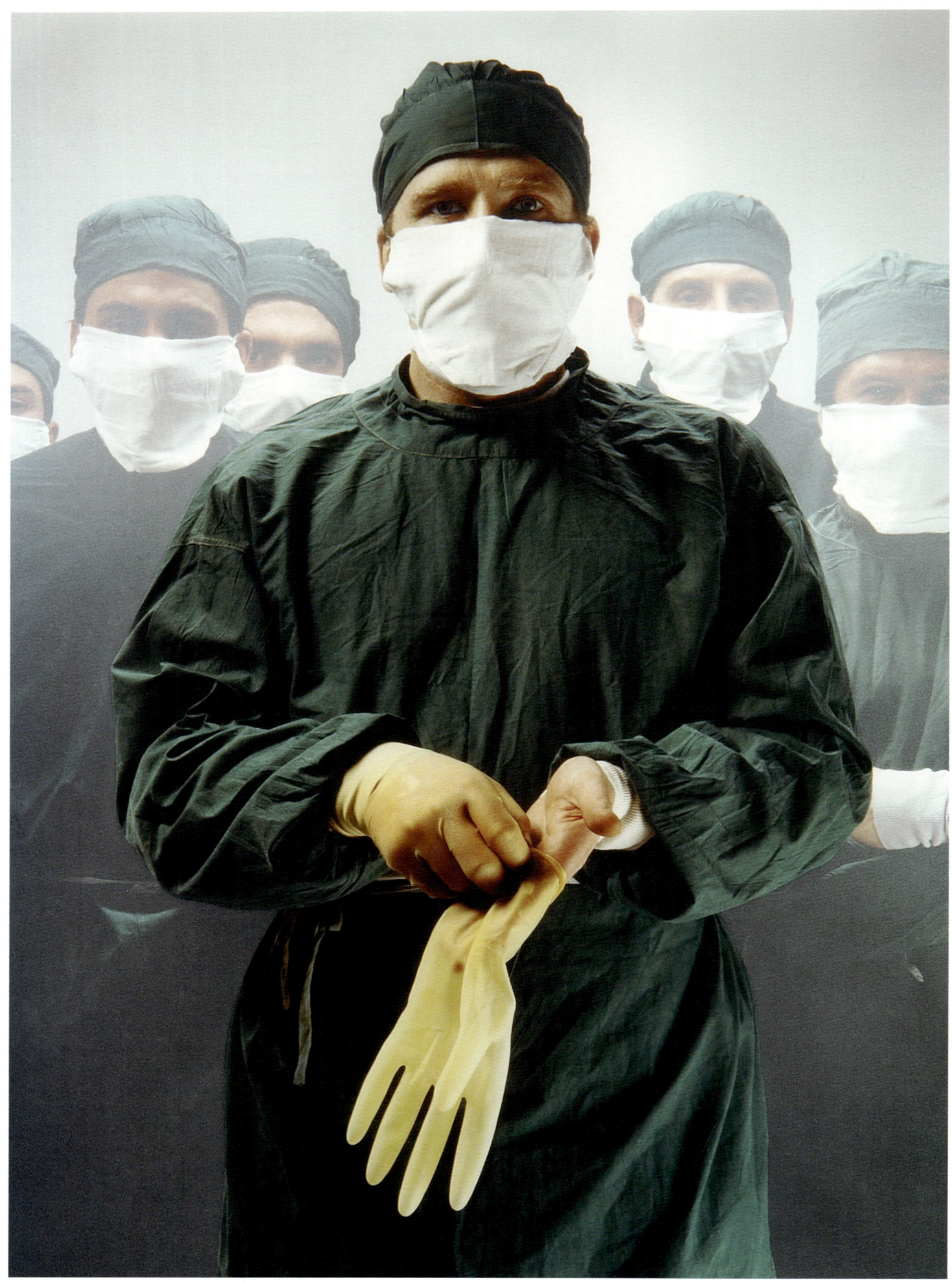

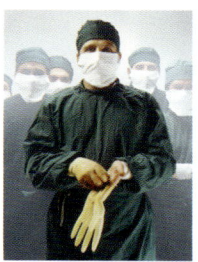

DIFFICULT TO CURE I think it was Rainbow's likeable manager, Bruce Payne, who called us to do this job and said, "All you need to know is the title, boys. The music is Rainbow, what more do you want to know?" So this image is simplicity itself, a bunch of surgeons gather for a team photo, prior to a major operation on a patient who may be 'difficult to cure'. The head surgeon is at the front putting on his rubber gloves while his lieutenants stand behind, back a bit, respectful, of lesser rank but always close at hand. This was not any veiled reference to Richie Blackmore and the band, but rather a good arrangement for a group portrait. In particular I enjoy the technique of 'setting back' the other figures – this is achieved by masking out the front figure and spraying a thin layer of white paint over the other figures, like a mist, literally speaking. Since this was really a one colour picture, *i.e.* green outfits for the surgeons, it was shot in black and white in our studio and then hand coloured.

Difficult to cure? Difficult to spot? Can you tell who are the team players behind the lead surgeon? Answers please with a $10 entry fee to my mum.

*Rainbow **Difficult To Cure** Vinyl front Polygram 1977 Design & Photos Hipgnosis*

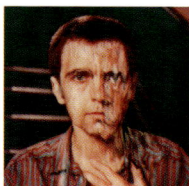

PETER GABRIEL 3 MELT When I was young I wanted to be a painter, probably because of my mother's love of Van Gogh, or because the reputation of painters like Picasso, Matisse etc, was very alluring. Unfortunately my hand wouldn't do what my brain told it. If it said 'draw in this direction', it would not. I don't know if you'd had this feeling – of being unable to do something, not for want of trying but simply because of some whimsical defect of nature (I can't sing either, but I won't go into that). This love of painting stayed with me for years and I had forever wanted to turn photography into painting. When a photo print developed in the developing tray I wanted to put my hand in the developer and smudge or move around the elements on the paper, but I could not, for it had no effect. Making prints and photography in general have a mechanical aspect that is simply not like painting, which is so much more 'hands on'. I have come to terms with this problem now, but my introduction by Paul Maxon to the work of Les Krims sparked the realisation of this design for Peter Gabriel.

It was his third solo album, cleverly entitled *Peter Gabriel 3* but known to us as *Melt* and is a lot about the technique. I had dreamt, which I rarely do, that the cover for Peter's album would show him with a dripping face, like a melting, wax effigy. Peter quipped that he didn't mind being in my dreams, so long as I wasn't in his, and he gamely went along with this facial distortion. What a good sport! ━ ━ ━ ➞

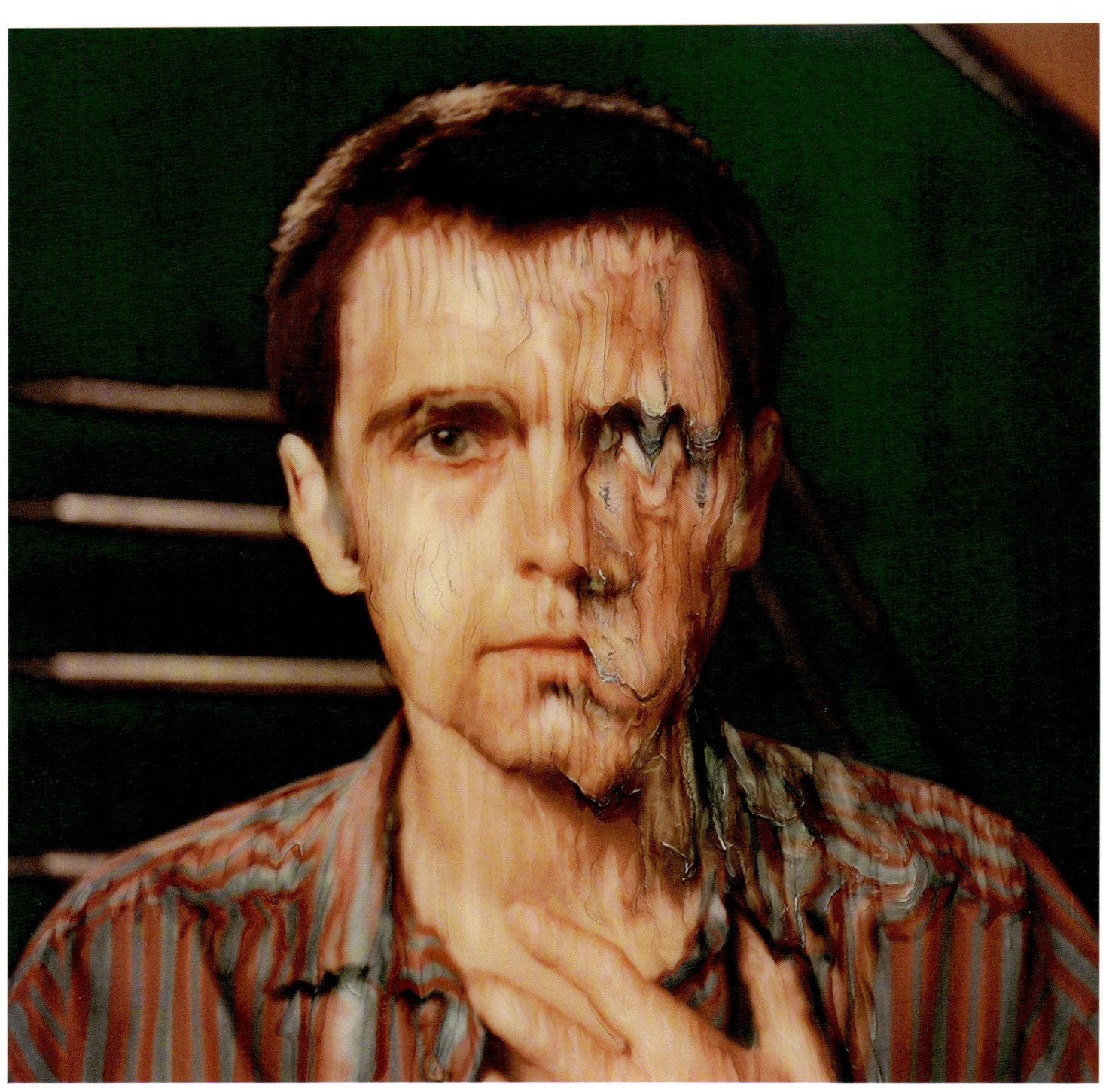

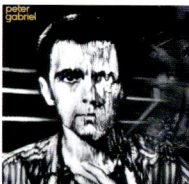

MELT CONT. Les Krims pioneered a process that generated what we came lovingly to call Krimsographs, wherein he took a common-or-garden Polaroid and applied pressure as the picture appeared. Because the developing image was sandwiched between two layers of plastic, the pressure applied by the blunt end of a pencil, for example, would push the developing image in certain directions, stretching and elongating it. If one did this over and over it became like a painting, impressionistic and made of what looked like brush-strokes. What we did at Hipgnosis was to take tons of Polaroids and push and pummel them as they developed. We all did it, including Pete Gabriel as I said, and gathered a vast pile of distorted faces, finally finding one for the front cover, which we then photocopied, enlarged and made black and white, so as to distance it from being a typical Polaroid (thumbnail). We selected another for the single (opposite).

It was all great fun, and involves only an ordinary Polaroid and a blunt pencil or some such, anybody can do it. Unfortunately this was the rub, the breakthrough into 'painting photography' was not pursued because if anyone can do it, then it has no cachet and the thrill is diminished. My desire to be a painter is wearing a bit thin set against the overwhelming evidence of my lack of drawing capability (you should see some of my ideas before either Fin or Dan has re-drawn them properly... then again, perhaps not).

*Peter Gabriel **Peter Gabriel 3 'Melt'** Vinyl front Virgin 1980 Design & Photos Hipgnosis & Paul Maxon*

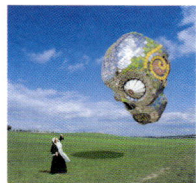

AMPUTECHTURE (overleaf) The Mars Volta told us, in person that is, that one of the big ideas informing their *Amputechture* album, was a story they'd seen on Polish television about the crucifixion of a Catholic nun by fellow Catholic priests because they thought her beliefs and behaviour were heretical. She claimed to have visions which were god speaking to her directly. Her visions were more real than her church, more real than her priests.

She thought them insane to reject her visions but they crucified her all the same, or so Mars Volta told us and when we were incredulous and protested that crucifying in this day and age was primitive, Medieval and cannot possibly be true, they said it was ever so, they'd seen it on TV, Polish TV. The Mars Volta were also very interested in 'landscapers' - Mexican gardeners and domestics in LA who worked in well-to-do white homes and often moved things silently around, re-arranging furniture before disappearing quietly at the end of the day. Another of their preoccupations was with Madame Blavatsky who when she first came to London experienced spiritual guides more real than her fellow men. This concoction of real and unreal, of illusion, of visions, nether figures from nether worlds and a Catholic nun became the background out of which floated, literally floated, a vision in the form of a Mexican Aztec type head made of mirrors (mirrors being portals to other worlds and purveyors of illusion), pursuing the nun, angrily confronting its originator.

And here is her vision, captured secretly by our camera in a gnarled wood and out in the open countryside against a hill known as Dead Man's Hill, a nun dressed in full habit as specified by Voltaic email. The finished art was delivered to the Voltarians in California who turned it down flat without explanation, excommunicated us and our vision as severely as the Polish church excommunicated their visionary nun. What irony!

An intermediary told us we had been replaced, and superceded by another artist, not any old Joe I trust.

*The Mars Volta **Amputechture** CD front, unused Universal 2006*
Design & Photos StormStudios Location Dead Man's Hill, Herts & Wimbledon Common, London

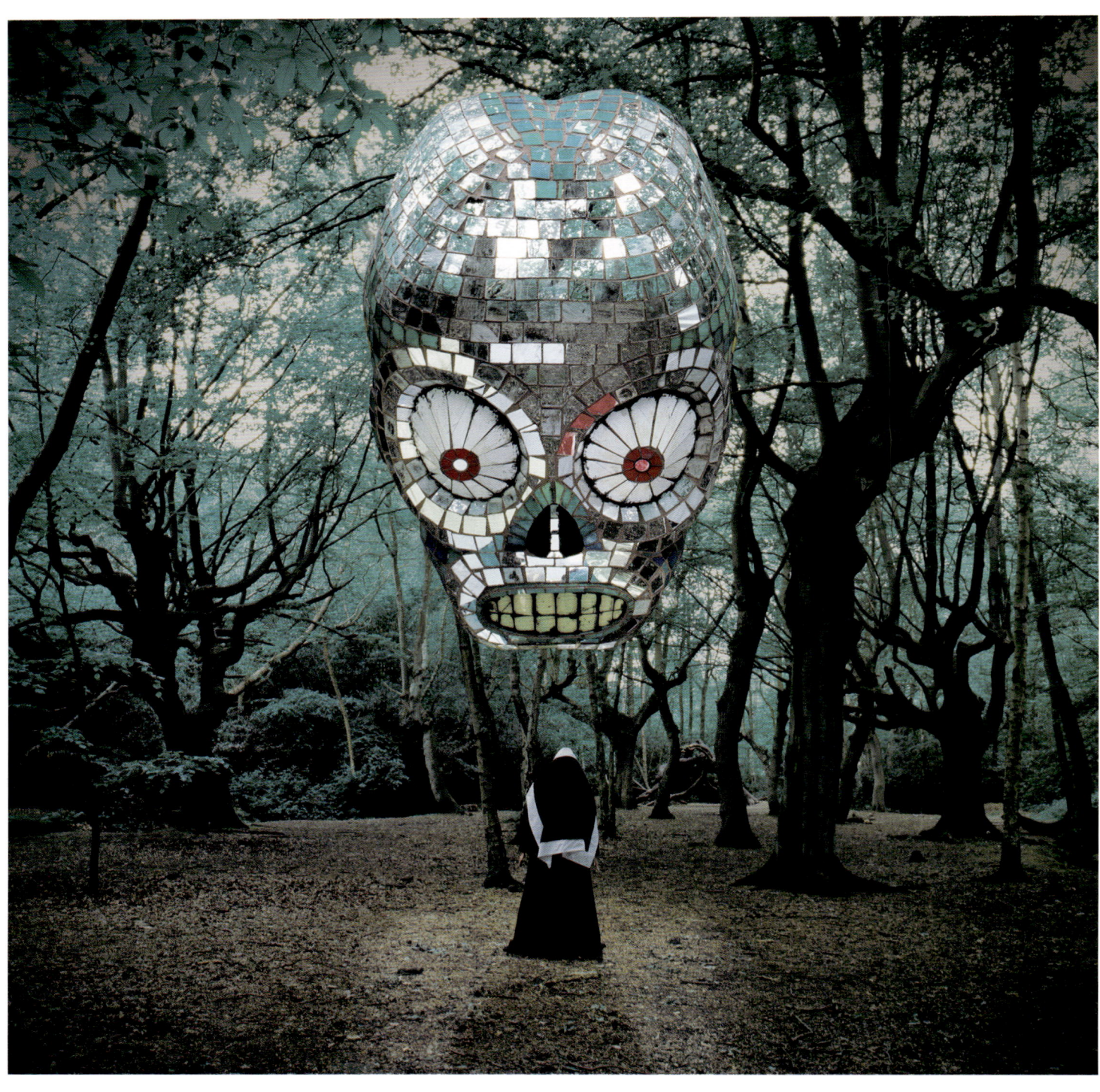

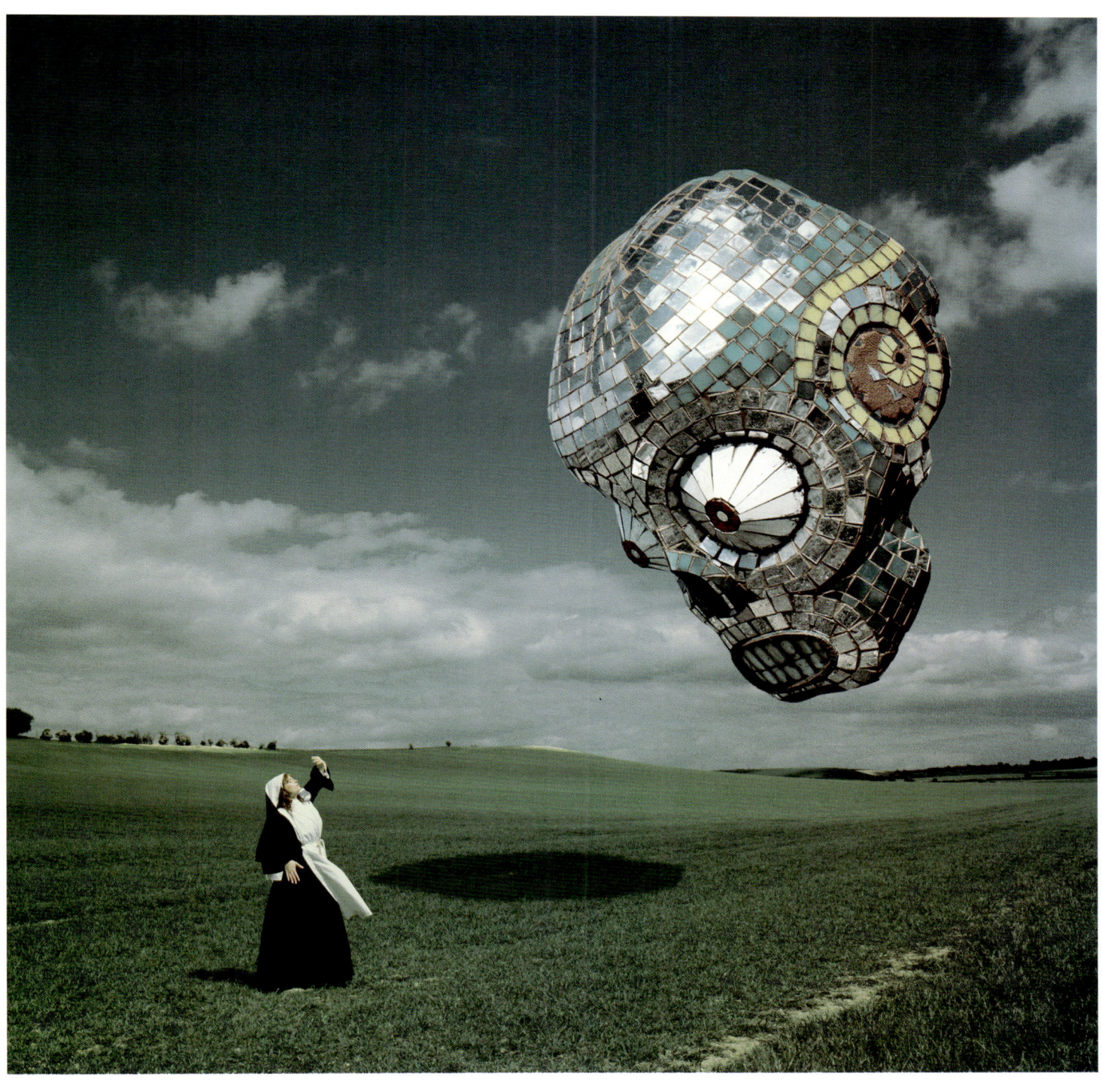

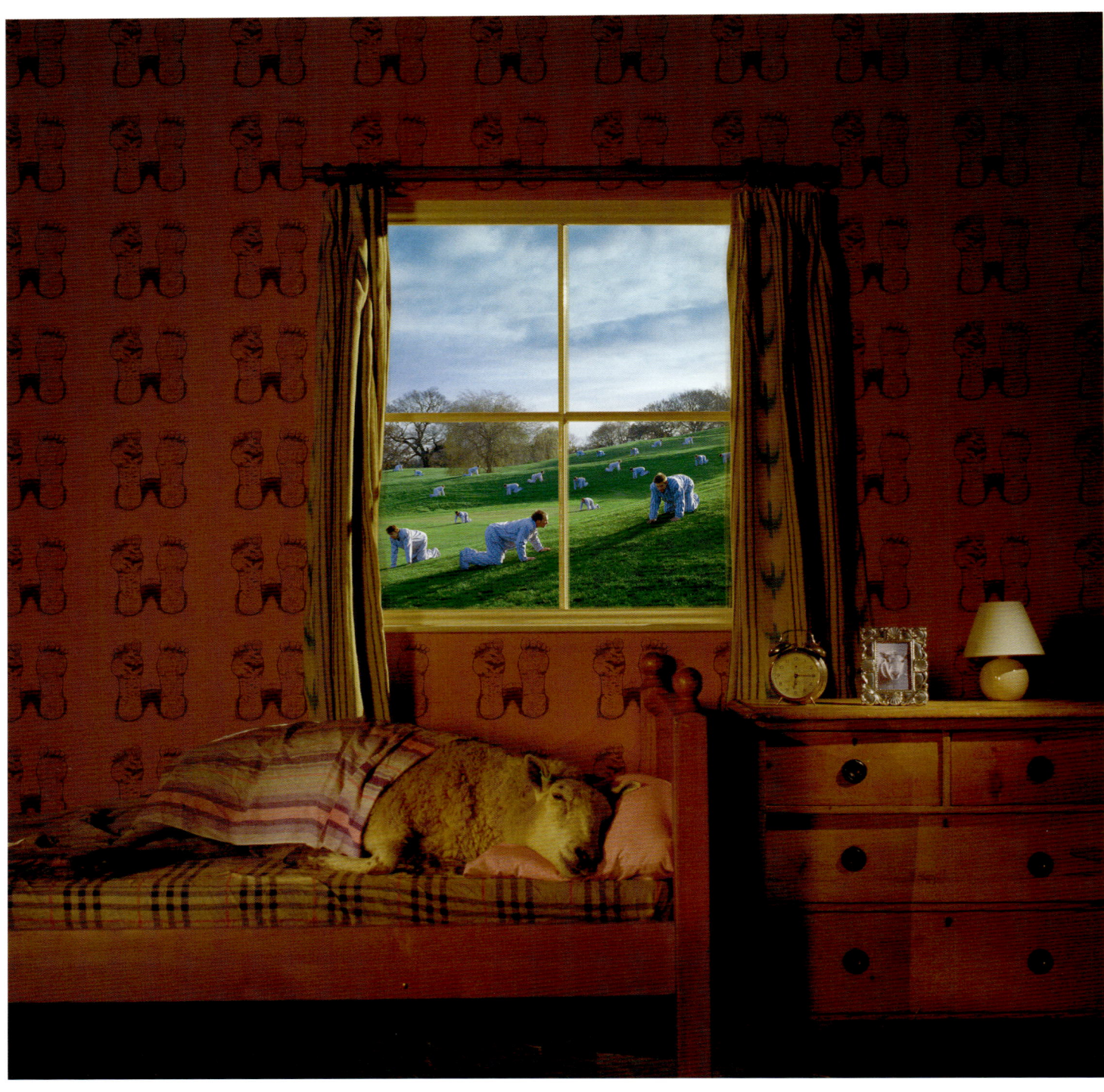

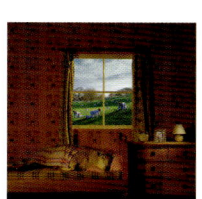

SAFETY IN NUMBERS Umphrey's McGee are a jazz-rock ensemble from Chicago, playing a mixture of improvised and tight material, very nice too. They requested something humourous, but how to be funny in a picture? it's tricky, difficult to raise a good laugh, easier to elicit a chuckle. One aims not for a bellow but for a smile.

I like this image not just because it's the wrong way round but also because the men in pajamas, pretending to be sheep in a field, are daft and were a hoot in real life, stopping the traffic on an adjacent road, passing drivers not quite believing their eyes. Another touch I also like is the family photo on the chest of drawers.

The sheep was called Honey and was very cute. At one point she nearly went to sleep in the bed of her own accord, although at another point the handler had to wrestle her back into bed to keep her in position, which I have to say looked like some weird sexual practice from behind the camera. But it lasted briefly, and Honey laid down again and was a darn good model, I can tell you.

There is an old saying in film and photographic circles 'don't work with children or animals', but I must say this Honey was a honey. I don't know about counting sheep, more like counting blessings.

Umphrey's McGee **Safety in Numbers** *CD front Sci-fidelity Records 2006*
Design StormStudios Location Edgware, London

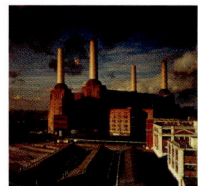

ANIMALS I don't have much to say about *Animals*, partly because it's not my idea, but that of Roger Waters of Pink Floyd, and he'll know the whys and wherefores. It's also because I didn't like it at first, thinking it a bit silly, conceptually speaking. And how wrong was I about that?

Despite these misgivings, we at Hipgnosis were very thorough in selecting a good vantage point from which to shoot (actually we chose 11 just to make sure, being as how the event wasn't easily repeatable), and very fortunate with the weather and suitably conscientious in completing the artwork.

The stories around the event are legion and mostly true. It was a glorious, Spinal Tap-like extravaganza, involving escaping pigs, marksmen, late night rescue and interruption of plane flights into Heathrow. It hit the major national headlines the next day. We couldn't have gotten more publicity if we had tried.

I came later to love this picture for two particular reasons. Firstly, the weather, which was dramatic and Turneresque, lending a magical, painterly quality to the image. Secondly, the robust elegance of the architecture, unappealing, in the sense of being a power station, but nonetheless beautiful and deeply nostalgic. The pig dirigible was dwarfed by them both but works effectively as a great off-set.

Pink Floyd **Animals** *Vinyl gatefold EMI 1997*
Design Roger Waters Photos & Artwork Hipgnosis Location Battersea, London

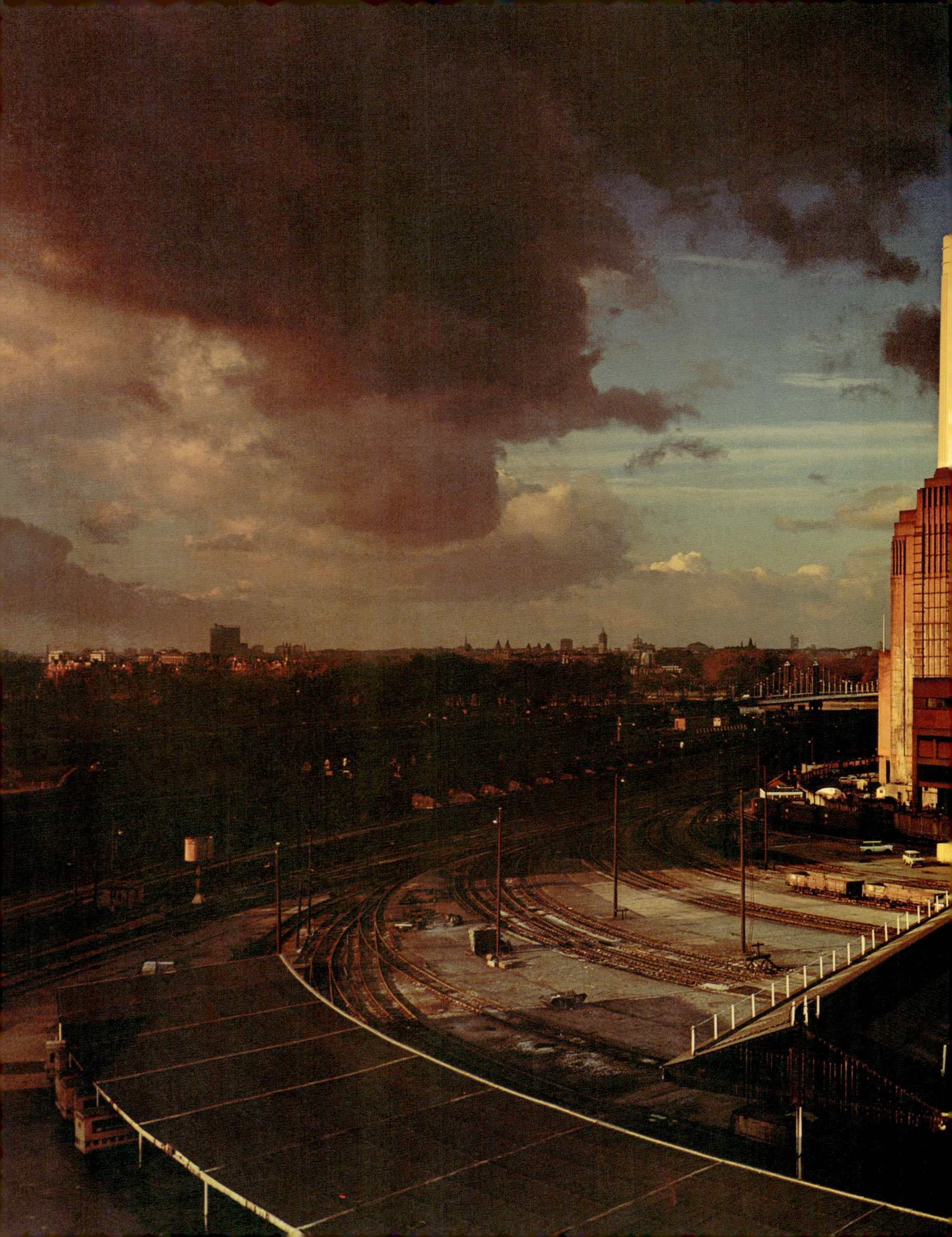

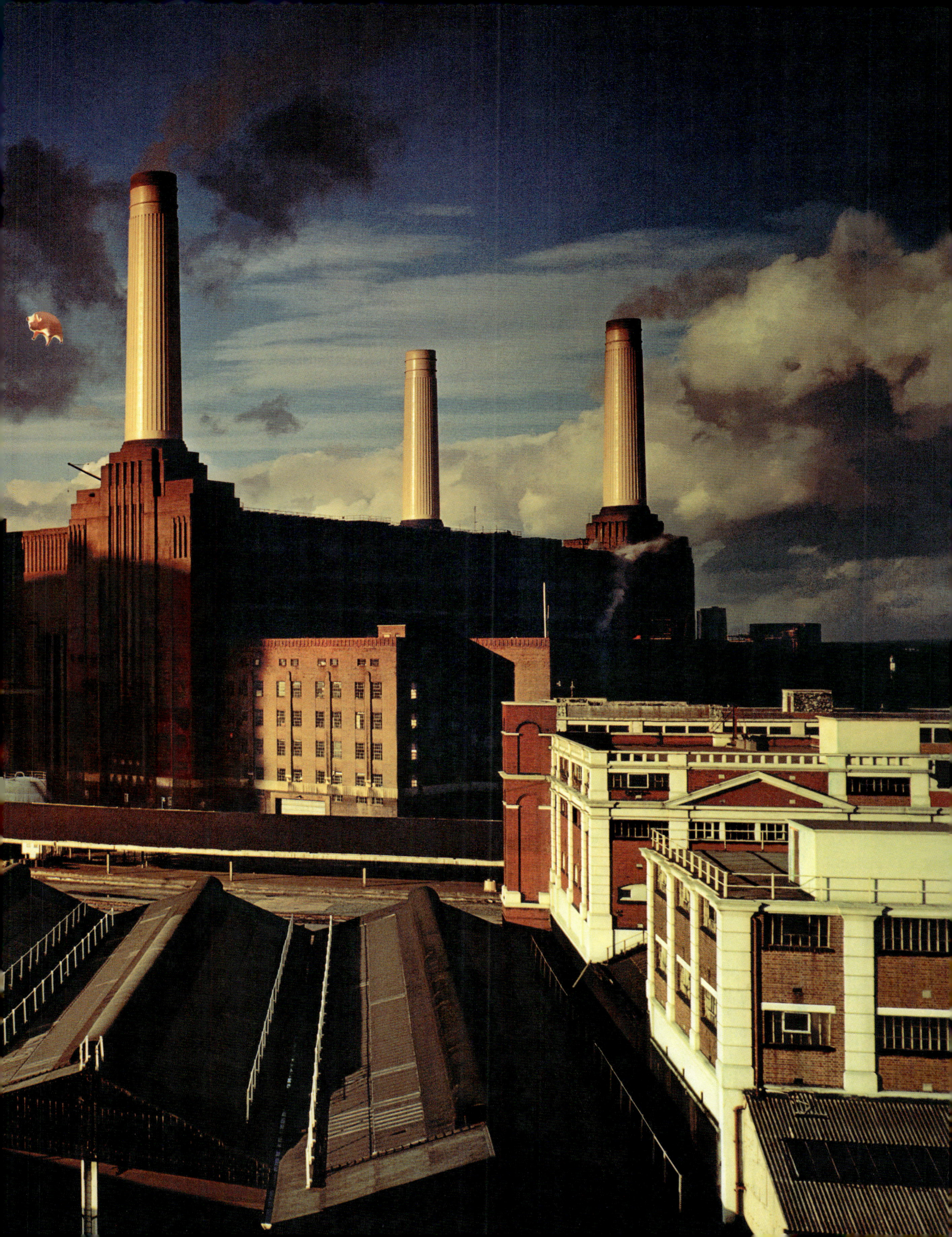

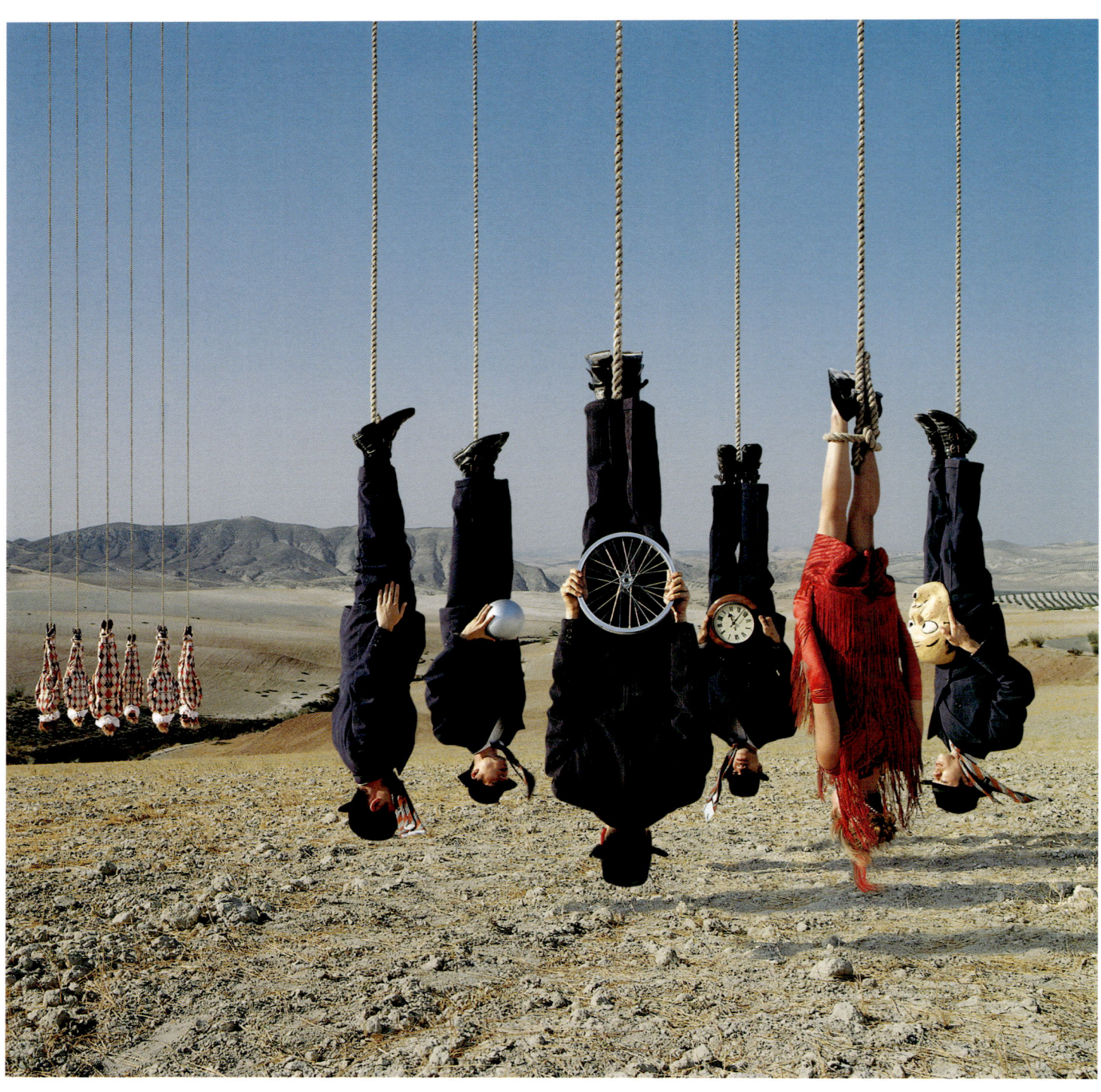

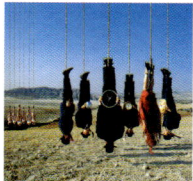

TRY ANYTHING ONCE *Try Anything Once* was the title for Alan's album in 1993 which suggested something a touch reckless perhaps, or at least a departure from normal behaviour. Or more specifically a departure from his usual musical style. We joined this thought with the image of a bungie jump from a high bridge on television – wondering what on earth people would do for a thrill – jumping from a high bridge? Try anything once, I suppose. I find stepping off the kerb threatening enough and getting out of bed in the morning, let alone jumping off a high bridge into nothingness (but 'chacun a son gout' as the great French existentialist said, whilst chucking his beloved cat into the Seine).

So I imagined the great bungie jumpers of the sky dropping in, as it were, at the end of extremely long ropes for some kind of a business meeting. Sky dwellers slumming it close to the ground but maintaining a connection to home seemed a crazy enough experiment to qualify for the *Try Anything Once* approach.. In pursuit of our ideal that 'doing it for real' is worthy the people in our picture are indeed hanging upside down and apart from going quite red in the face, they bore it with great stoicism, though I haven't seen any of them for some time now. The location is in Spain known as Larva Valley about 20 miles east of Jaen sandwiched between two mountain ranges. It's a truly magical spot, as of course it would be when visited by sky dwellers.

*Alan Parsons **Try Anything Once** Arista 1993 Vinyl front*
Design & Photos StormStudios Location Larva Valley, Jaen, Spain

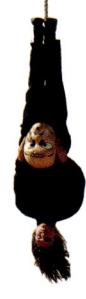

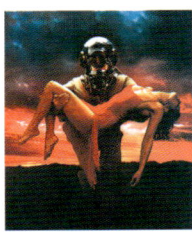

DECEPTIVE BLENDS I think those clever Northern lads, 10cc, relocated from Stockport to Dorking, for reasons I can't divulge, but not I suspect to be nearer us. But on the road coming into Dorking is a warning sign of twisty bends, partially hidden by thick woods, which reads 'Deceptive Bends'. I think 10cc liked this title because of its several meanings. They were always fond of word-play, double entendres, cross-references, associations, etc, etc. Although this record marked the break up of the band into halves (not called 5cc each), these predilections remained.

I thought of bends in terms of a diver, for when he returns too rapidly to the surface, he suffers hallucinations - a kind of petit-mal, a derangement of the senses, provoked I think by some issue with the oxygen up-take in the brain. If a diver, especially wearing one of those old suits with round, brass helmets, were to hallucinate, what would he see? I imagine that he would imagine that he was a hero, a saviour probably, rescuing a damsel in distress, emerging from the waters of the black lagoon, carrying this scantily dressed damsel in his arms, a hero, admired by all, and especially by the said damsel. I imagined that he'd rescued her from some monster of the deep and that our design would be therefore a pastiche of B feature film posters - 'the monster from the black lagoon'... but done photographically, not as illustration.

It was obviously just another way to get a gorgeous woman on the front of an album cover, along with a few subtle undercurrents. The photograph was taken in a studio and stripped together as dye transfer, a photo 'comping' technique now superceded by the ubiquitous computer. Never ones to abjure a happy accident, the dramatic lighting quality of this photograph was partly achieved by one of the flash heads not firing, the effect of which was to increase the dark mood and reflect the ominous skies.

*10cc **Deceptive Bends** In store poster Phonogram 1977 Design & Photos Hipgnosis*

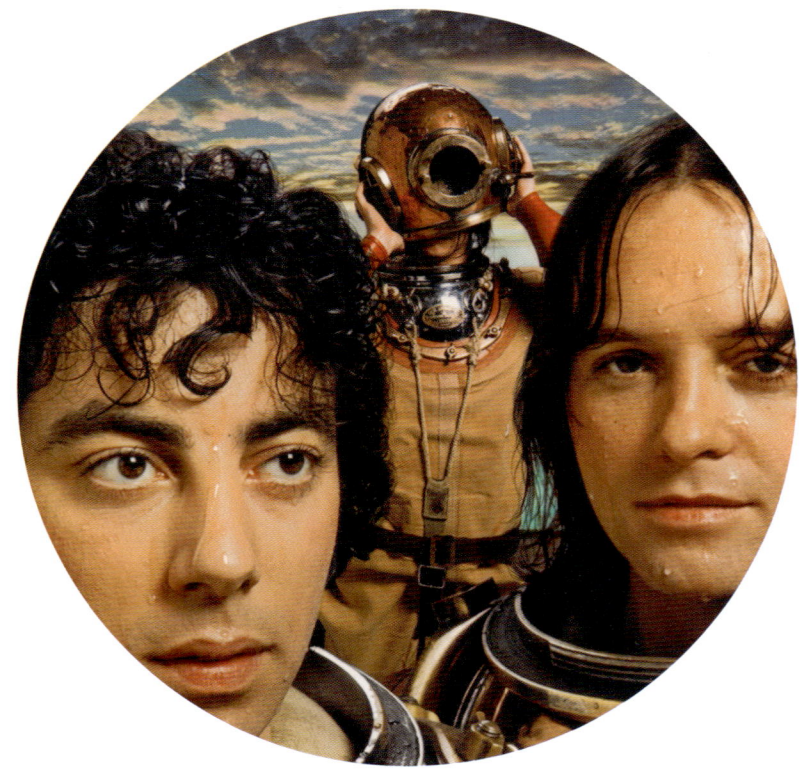

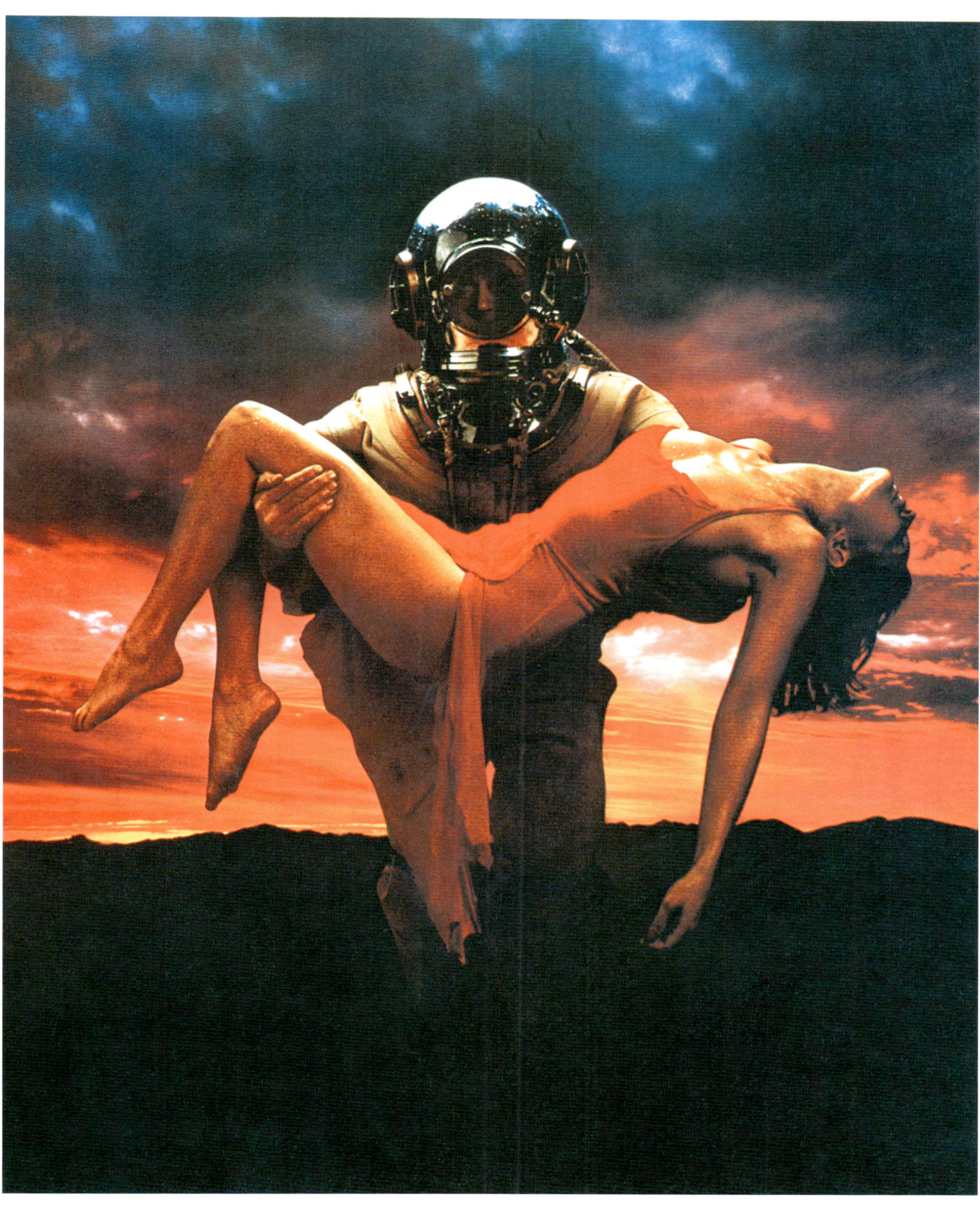

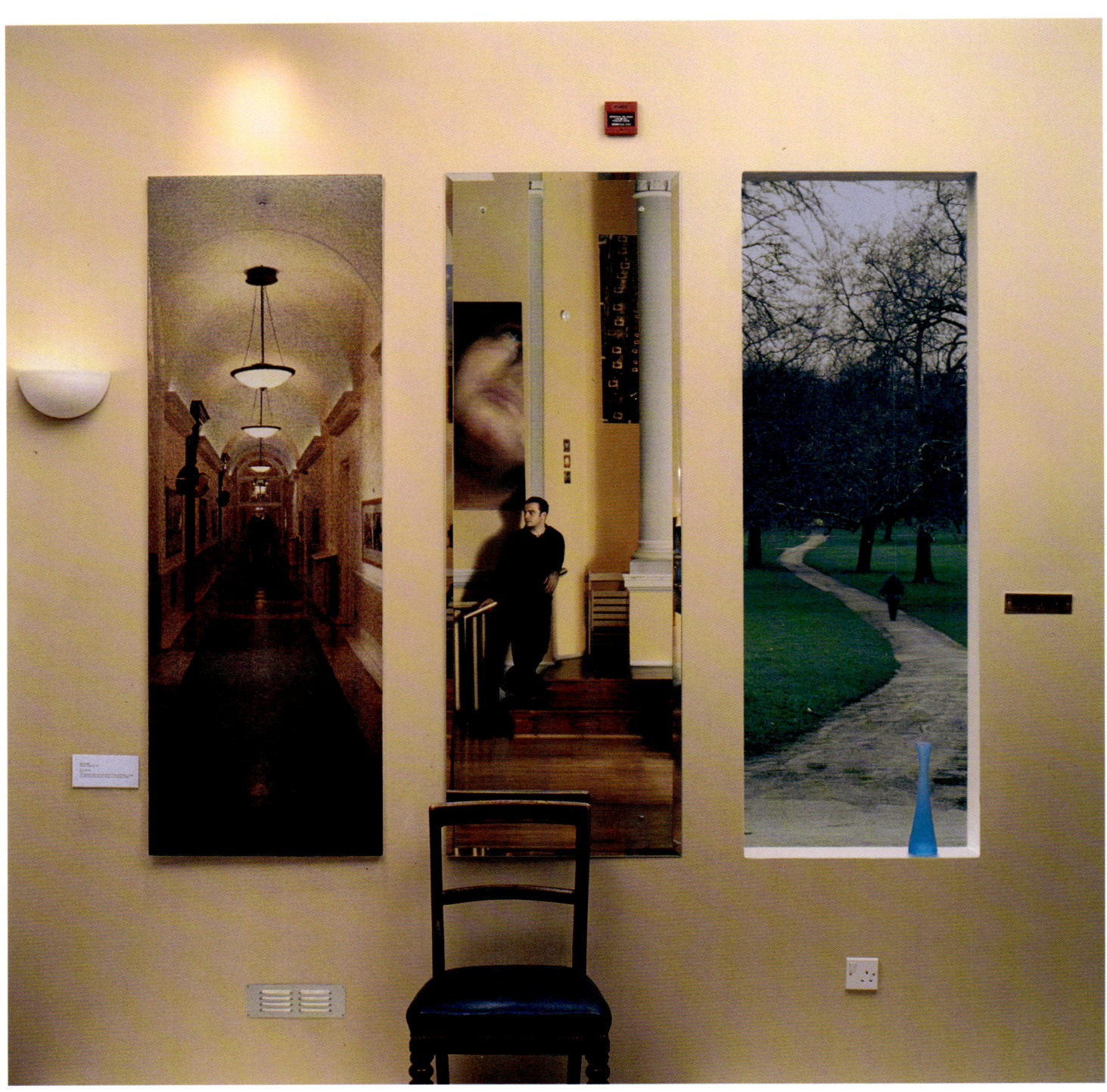

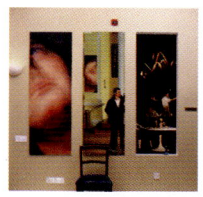

WISHVILLE It's not always clear, even to me, from where our images derive, but my unreliable memory banks tell me that it was the issue of perspective (*i.e.*, how far away things are, what size they are and seen from what angle?) that came to the fore during a rather argumentative design process with the band. I'd had this idea for an installation piece which consisted of a triptych: three identical shapes – one mirror, one picture and one window. How would you know which was which? The viewer is invited to speculate , if they'd be so kind.

We built the installation in a grand old Victorian room in Richmond, south west London, which boasted a big French window through which our new 'window' could look. The 'mirror' reflected Rob Dickinson, the lead singer, whilst the 'picture' was a photo of an adjacent corridor receding from view but only metaphorically, of course, since it was only a picture. The path seen through our 'window' receded from view physically outside into the park and the view in the 'mirror' receded in the opposite direction inside back across the room . All of this seemed jolly interesting to me at the time - what clues tell you what, what shadows, perspectives or sizes keep you correctly informed? Still seems interesting, though I detect that the invitation to explore may not be as persuasive as I'd hoped. But then nothing's perfect, except perhaps in Wishville.

*Catherine Wheel **Wishville** CD front EMI/Chrysalis 2000*
Design & Photos StormStudios Location Richmond and Primrose Hill, London

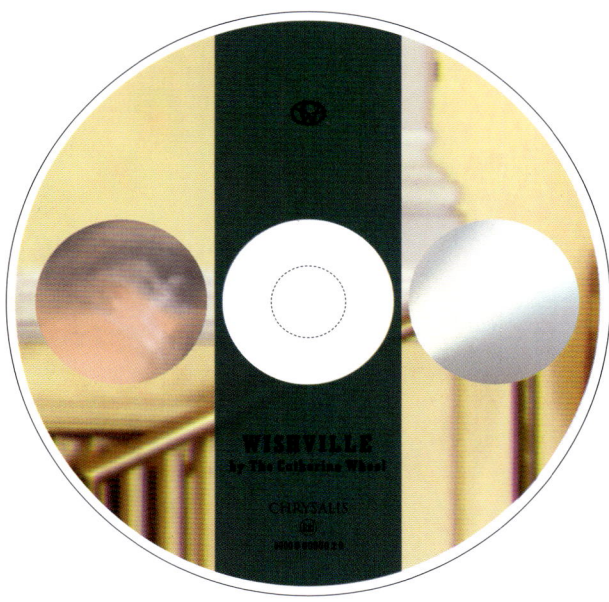

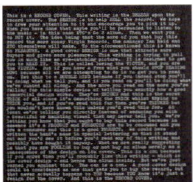

GO 2 XTC were an inventive band from sunny Swindon who had emerged from the punk milieu relatively unscathed. They were finishing their second album, Go 2, and came round to see us in our dishevelled studios in Denmark Street, Soho. One of the characteristics of the Denmark Street studio was its untidiness, not always a virtue, but in this case an advantage. Writer and singer Andy Partridge discussed various thoughts with us but these were quickly dispelled when one of the band stepped on a piece of paper on the floor which was in fact a prototype of an album design originally intended for the likes of Pink Floyd, or 10cc. The design was all about the commercial iniquities of an album cover. He picked up the piece of paper and asked what it was The fact that it had been rejected by others seemed to increase its attraction for XTC who said, they would take it as they found it. By some quirk of fate it seemed that the humour and disrespectful critique appealed to XTC's mindset. I think they liked the sarcasm and aggressive attitude and that it was cheaply and unfussily done, just some typewriting on a piece of paper. If bands like Pink Floyd and 10cc didn't like it, all the better.

I was amazed by this fortuitous turn of events because I'd always liked this idea, its self-sabotage, not to mention the direct attack on record companies and their unseemly commerciality. I also liked the double-bind - it's trying to tell you, you the customer, that you've been had, but you don't know this until you've been had, but you knew it all along didn't you? So it always seemed like a joke on somebody else. It made XTC chuckle, as it did me, not unlike the cow for *Atom Heart Mother* (pg. 188), but visually very different, just a bunch of ordinary type-written text on a piece of paper, no flashy fonts, no lovely leading, no careful kerning.

And finding a cover through standing on it by accident, on the scruffy floor of a Soho studio was, in effect, the coup de grâce.

*XTC **Go2** LP front Virgin 1978 Design & Photos Hipgnosis*

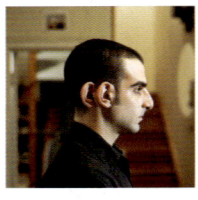

COME AGAIN Canadian band Thornley called their debut album on Roadrunner Records *Come Again* which I surmised had sexual overtones, at least in their minds, but we ignored it all altogether and decided instead to illustrate the English expression 'come again' meaning "Please repeat what was just said because it wasnt heard properly". Perhaps they felt that their music should be revisited and heard again because it wasn't listened to properly in the first place when their first single was released, but knowing rock bands as I do it was most likely sexual innuendo.

I find that when I use the expression I tend to cup my ear, so ears were central. I saw a billboard ad using doubled eyes, one eye close under another, both eyes of a face doubled and found it visually disturbing , like a double take. It was as if the eyes moved, right there in front of my eyes like a winking postcard, but no, just two sets of still eyes, perfectly still, no movement except in my brain.

Without guilt I purloined this repeat technique but used ears instead of eyes, a double take reminiscent of the expression 'come again'. What I like particularly is the shadow of the second ear cast across the first and natural ear to enhance the reality of the second ear, though in your heart you know it's a fake rather than some gruesome mutation or gross birth defect. What I also like is the model, a friendly gent I spotted at my local eaterie who gamely agreed to take part though he'd never met us before. Thornley, on the other hand, didn't particularly like anything and rejected it in favour of the image on pg 73. In fact they refused to use it anywhere in the CD booklet or on the label and at no extra cost...

There's no pleasin' some folks.

*Thornley **Come Again** CD booklet Road Runner 2004 unused Design and photo StormStudios*

This is a RECORD COVER. This writing is the DESIGN upon the
record cover. The DESIGN is to help SELL the record. We hope
to draw your attention to it and encourage you to pick it up.
When you have done that maybe you'll be persuaded to listen to
the music - in this case XTC's Go 2 album. Then we want you
to BUY it. The idea being that the more of you that buy this
record the more money Virgin Records, the manager Ian Reid and
XTC themselves will make. To the aforementioned this is known
as PLEASURE. A good cover DESIGN is one that attracts more
buyers and gives more pleasure. This writing is trying to pull
you in much like an eye-catching picture. It is designed to get
you to READ IT. This is called luring the VICTIM, and you are
the VICTIM. But if you have a free mind you should STOP READING
NOW! because all we are attempting to do is to get you to read
on. Yet this is a DOUBLE BIND because if you indeed stop you'll
be doing what we tell you, and if you read on you'll be doing what
we've wanted all along. And the more you read on the more you're
falling for this simple device of telling you exactly how a good
commercial design works. They're TRICKS and this is the worst
TRICK of all since it's describing the TRICK whilst trying to
TRICK you, and if you've read this far then you're TRICKED but
you wouldn't have known this unless you'd read this far. At
least we're telling you directly instead of seducing you with
a beautiful or haunting visual that may never tell you. We're
letting you know that you ought to buy this record because in
essence it's a PRODUCT and PRODUCTS are to be consumed and you
are a consumer and this is a good PRODUCT. We could have
written the band's name in special lettering so that it stood
out and you'd see it before you'd read any of this writing and
possibly have bought it anyway. What we are really suggesting
is that you are FOOLISH to buy or not buy an album merely as a
consequence of the design on its cover. This is a con because
if you agree then you'll probably like this writing - which is
the cover design - and hence the album inside. But we've just
warned you against that. The con is a con. A good cover design
could be considered as one that gets you to buy the record, but
that never actually happens to YOU because YOU know it's just a
design for the cover. And this is the RECORD COVER.

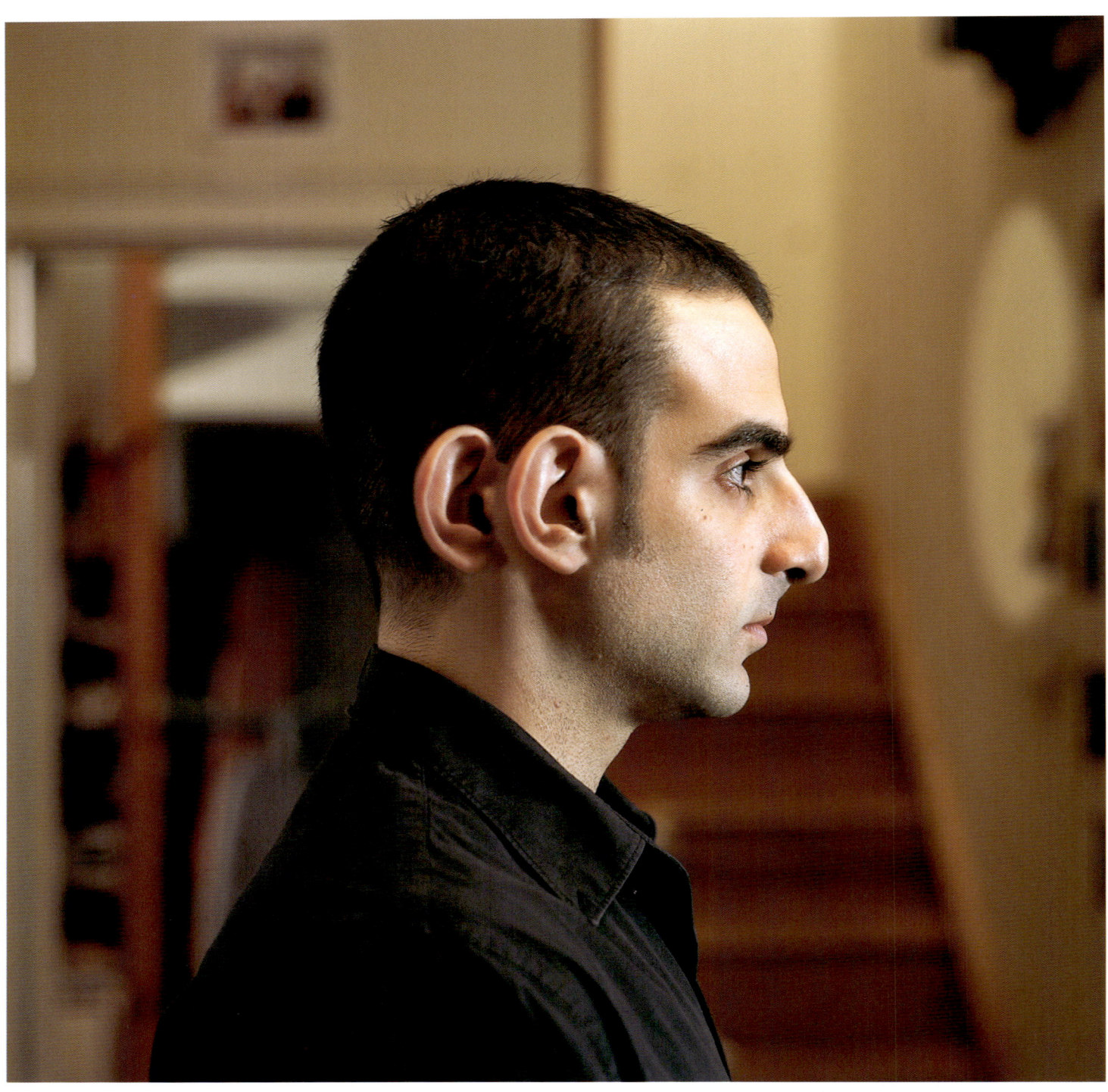

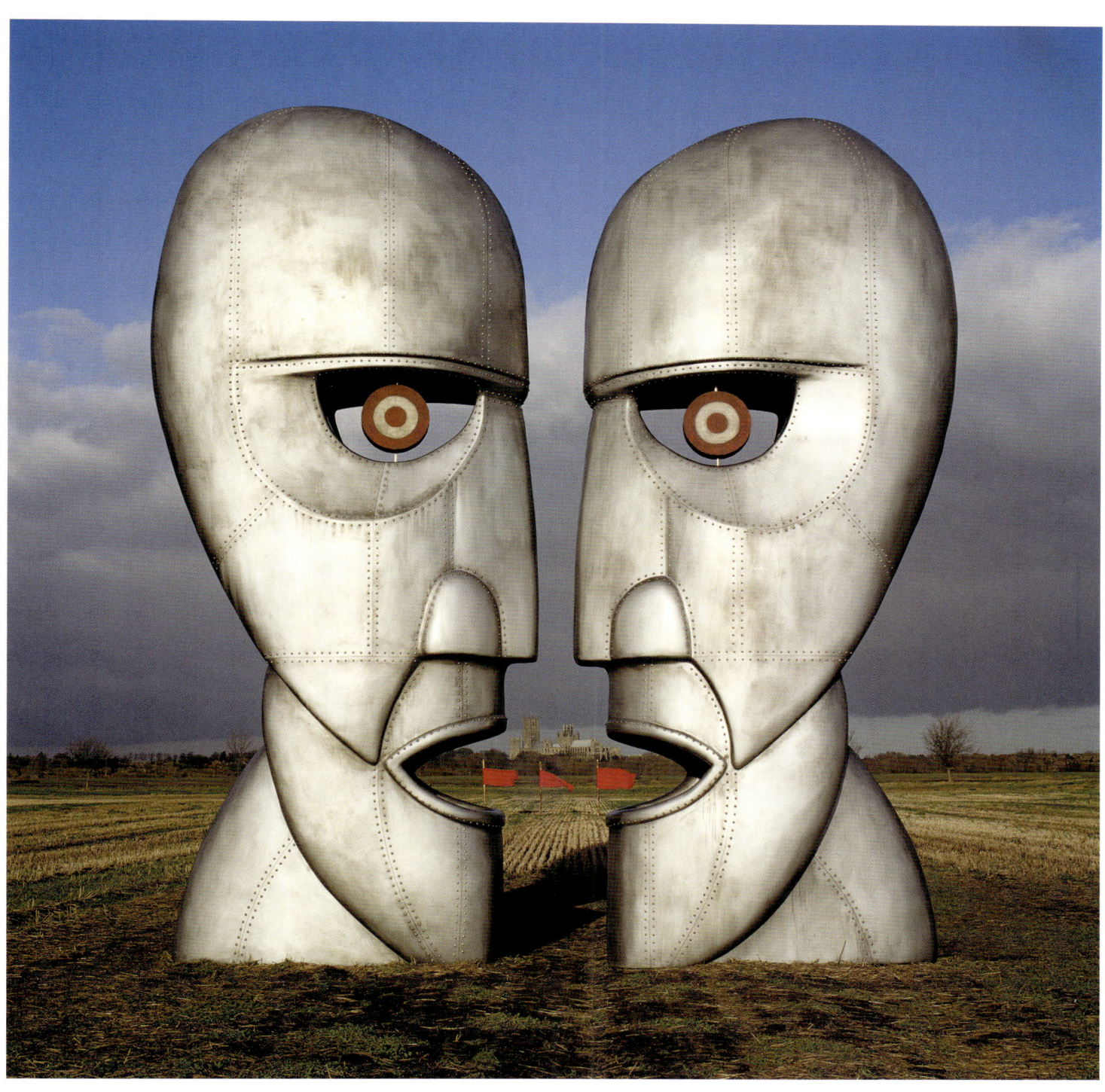

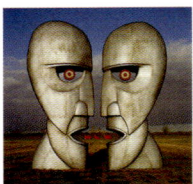

THE DIVISION BELL Rock musicians often record alternate takes or alternate versions of the same song, I guess because they might play it differently or better, or might add another instrument or change the nature of a sound. They don't usually know which works best until they have done it and listened to the playback. We are much the same and here is a good example of an alternate version - flags to replace lights and a heavier cloudscape instead of a lighter one (see pages 64/65). This alternate version was a front runner at the time but did not make the final cut.

Pink Floyd **The Division Bell** *Alternate version 1994 Design Storm Thorgerson & Keith Breeden*

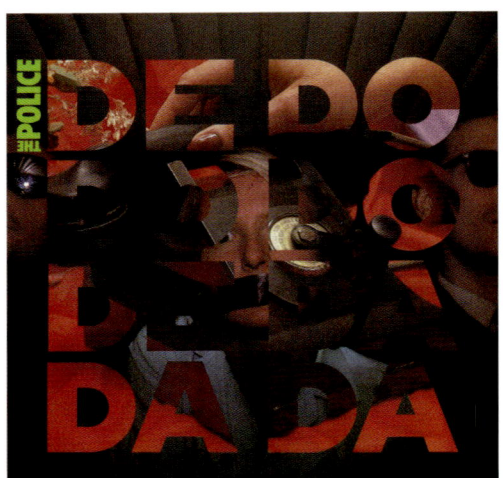
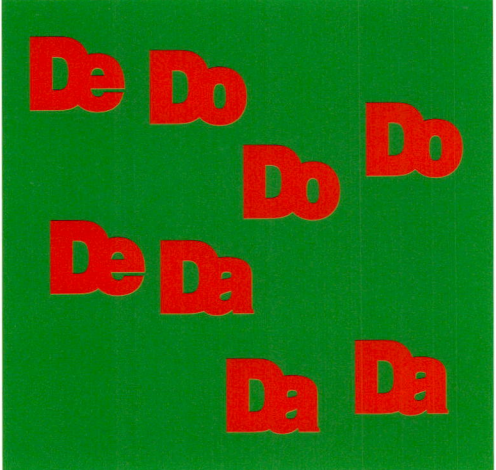

THE POLICE I must confess that this piece is included in part because of the story I'm about to tell, but also because it was, I thought, a good example of the visceral approach, by which I mean a design intended literally to reflect the sound; without great meanings, undercurrents, or elliptical references, just a straight-forward visual attempt to look like the sound of the music.

The Police were hugely popular in the late 'Seventies and produced a string of fantastic singles, starting with Roxanne, and culminating in Stand So Close'. The follow up was 'De Do Do Do, De Da Da Da', for which this was the design - big lettering to emphasise the nonsensical title, and featuring telephones and gagging to highlight the communication, or lack of it, referred to in the song.

This 'postcard lettering' design was used because my favourite idea was rejected and so we have re-created it here, for your edification, the original previously lost in the mists of time. It is based on the retinal qualities of green and red when placed in close proximity. The rods and cones of the human eye cannot handle the boundary so that bright green and bright red, when adjacent, are seen to jump about, oscillate and play havoc with the brain. This jumping-about quality is factual, not a question of interpretation, but of physiology - everyone will experience discomfort. It was this discomfort that seemed to echo the staccato and nonsensical words of the song. The very sound seemed to me to be reflected in this green/red juxtaposition. Except of course, if you were partially colour blind....

Miles Copeland, the fast-talking, straight from the hip, speak it like it is, manager of The Police, said, "Get on a plane Storm, fly to Seattle, where the band are working and present your ideas", so I did. I flew 12,000 miles in a weekend, full of excitement and confidence, thinking that my green and red eyeball twister was a winner. However, the manager, the tell it like it is manager, had omitted to tell me that Sting was slightly colour blind, and guess in what area people have the most difficulty... yes, it's the reds, folks!

My coveted, visceral approach, was about as useless as the the words to which the song refers. Do Do Do, Da Da Da indeed.

More do do than da da.

The Police **De Do Do Do, De Da Da Da** *Reconstructed single front , unused A&M Records 1980 Design Hipgnosis/Halpin*

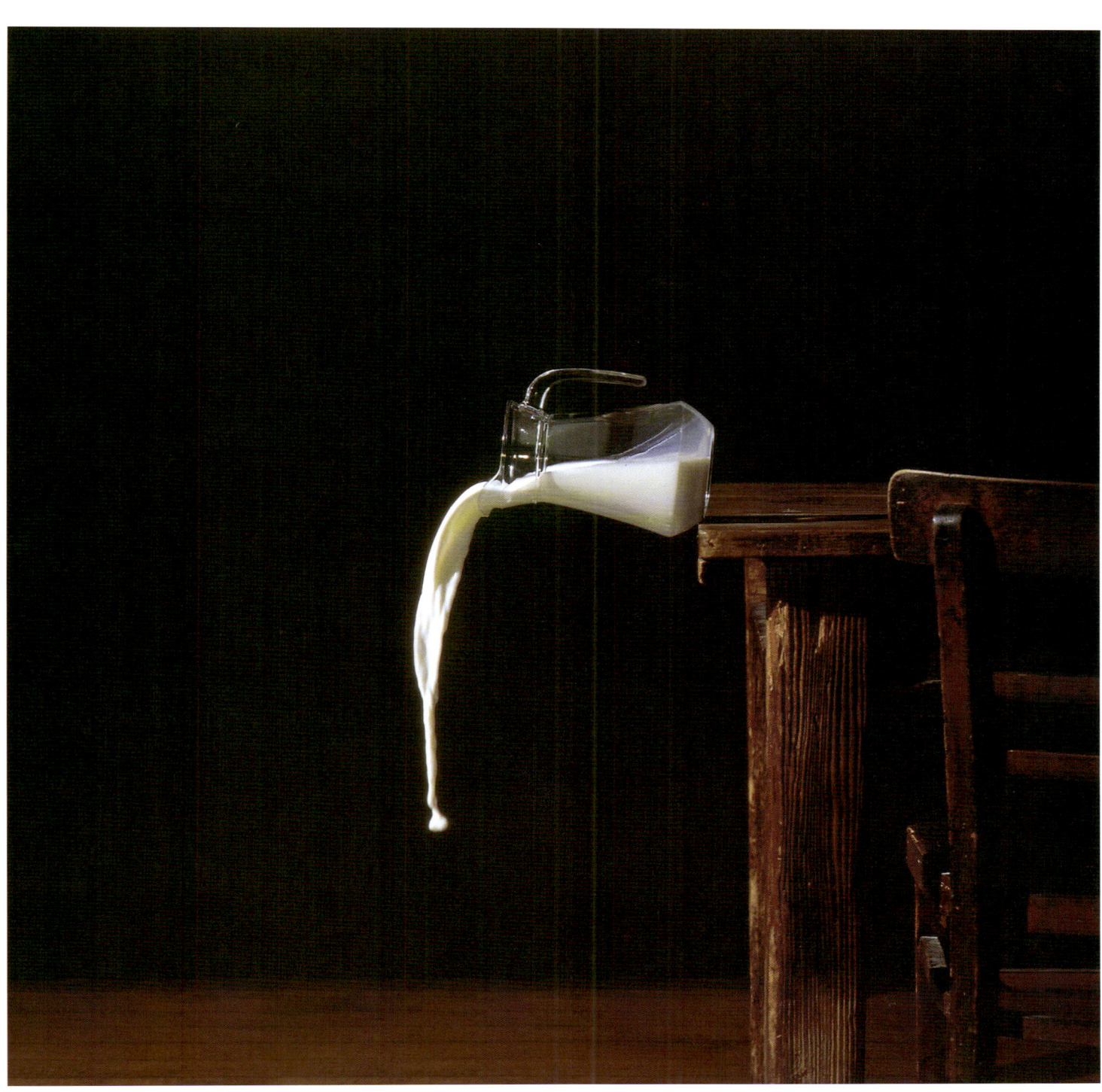

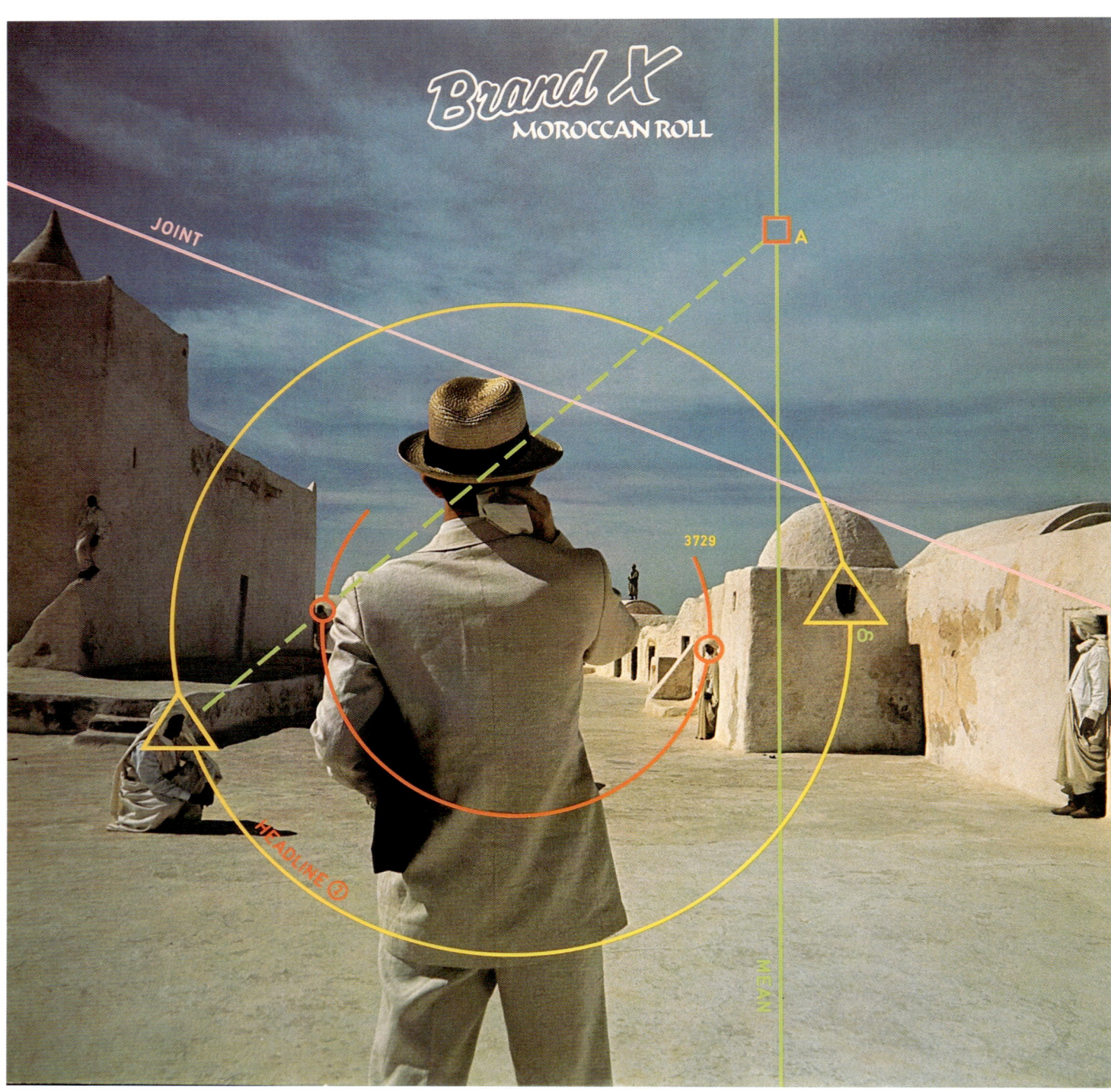

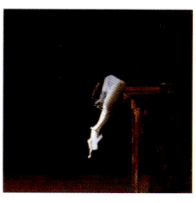

SPARKS ARE GONNA FLY Catherine Wheel produced a single called 'Sparks are Gonna Fly' saying in effect that something is going to happen any minute. We thought, cleverly, of a picture of something imminent, something about to smash, about to explode - but "don't fret," we told ourselves, "dont be alarmed....it'll be alright, dont you worry, dont cry - no point crying over spilt milk" and hey presto! There's our picture - the moment when milk is about to be spilt, the moment before it hits the floor: as the jug is being tipped, starting to fall, caught as only the camera can, in that split second before CRASH! it hits the floor breaking into a thousand pieces and spilling the milk all over the place in an inelegant mess. In a perverse way the precarious angle of the jug and the shape taken by the milk are the opposite, really very elegant, as if that instance before the chaos, the moment of sparks beginning to fly, is quite an ordered moment, though seldom seen.

I always thought there was more power in this idea, in this picture, than in a straight rendition of flying sparks, more power in the suggestion of something about to happen than in the thing actually happening like a large wave about to break see pg. 45. But, then again, I could be wrong. I was twice last week.

Catherine Wheel **Sparks Are Gonna Fly** *CD single Chrysalis 2000 Design & Photos StormStudios*

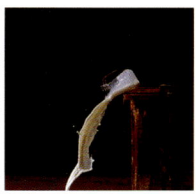 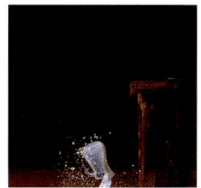

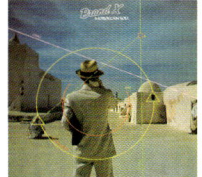

MOROCCAN ROLL Brand X were a jovial but mysterious ensemble of jazz-rock musicians from the late Seventies whose complex music was infused with all sorts of humorous undercurrents and deeper meanings, even clues to the great, cosmic secret, whatever that is. This cosmic key would have, of course, to be visually embedded, lest it be perceived too readily by criminal factions or delinquents, thereby putting the world at unnecessary risk. This cosmic key is represented by the joining up of points in our picture. No happenstance this, but a map leading to The Secret, the secret of the Alchemists.

This kind of thinking appealed fortunately to the mind-set of Brand X, which included Phil Collins at the time. On the surface the picture shows Our Man in Morocco, not Our Man in Havana, about to be 'rolled' by some suspicious-looking Arabs, hence a 'roll' in Morocco or a 'Moroccan roll' or more rock'n'roll. But beneath the surface, as you can see from our map, the secret of the universe is at hand, you just need to look hard enough and begin to unravel it. Same with the music. Whatever is good enough for the alchemists of old, is probably good enough for Brand X, the alchemists of the new.

PS Is this the best title ever of any record? Is it the first time it was ever used?

Brand X **Moroccan Roll** *Vinyl front Charisma 1977*
Design & Photos Hipgnosis with George Hardie Location Hammamet Tunisia

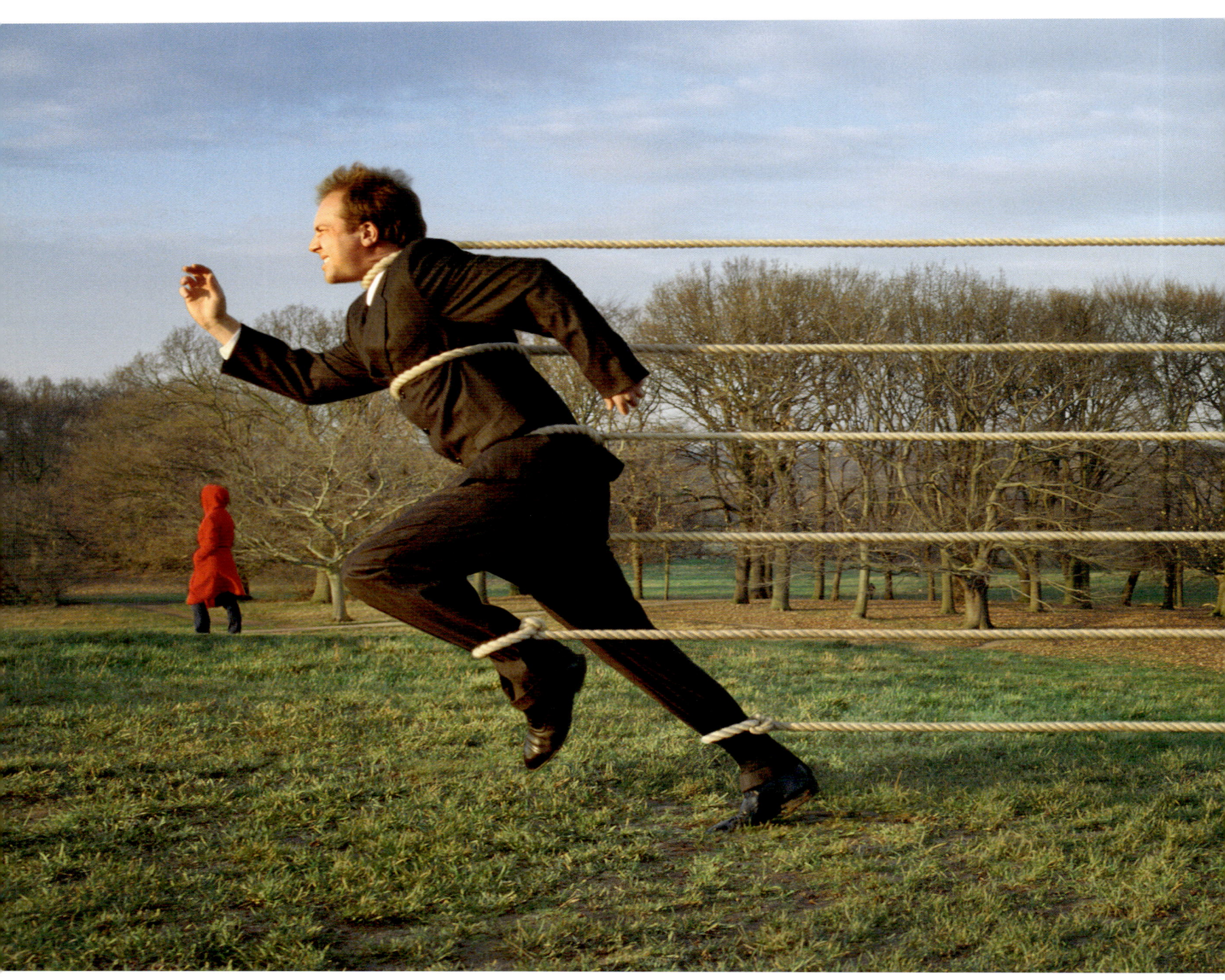

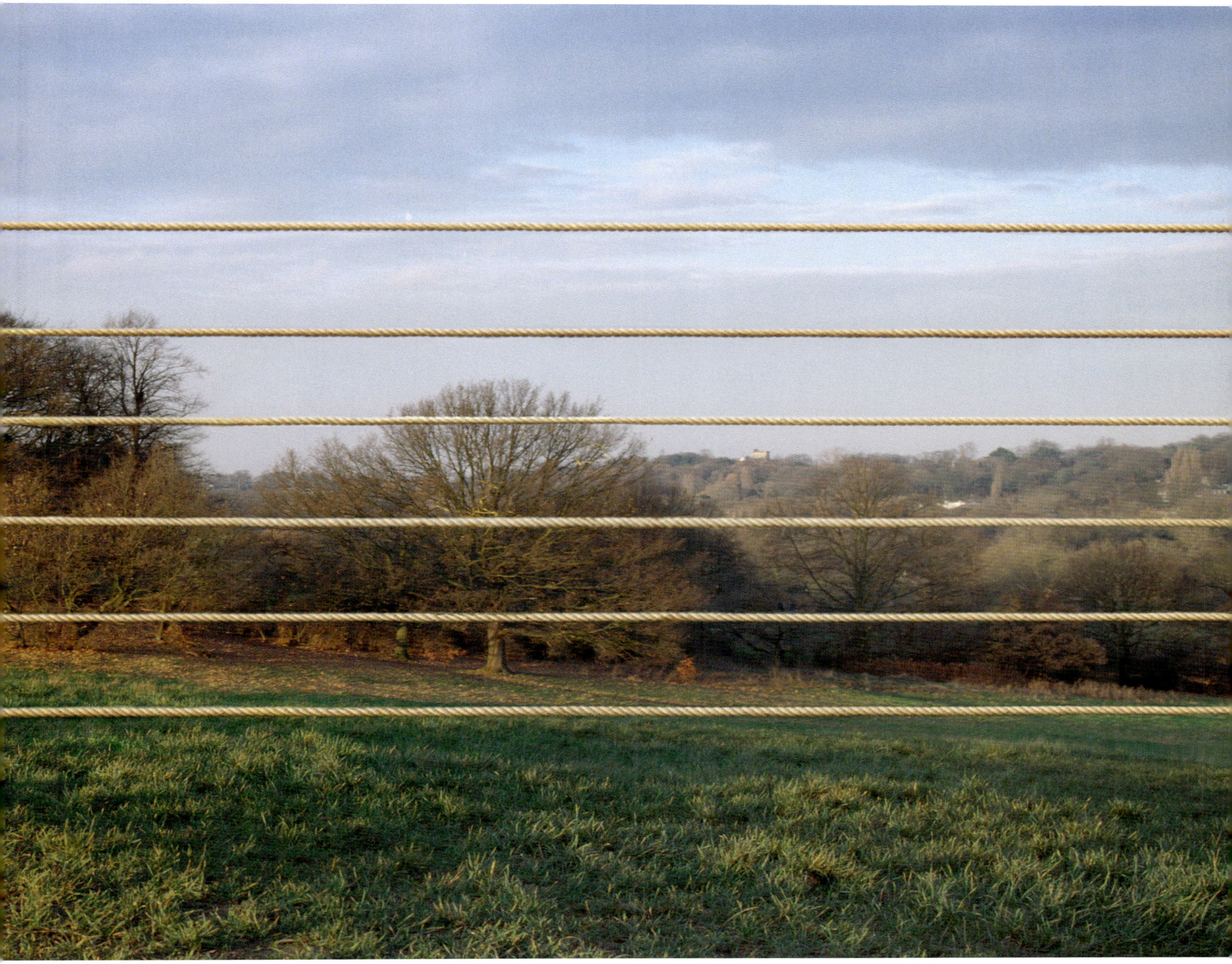

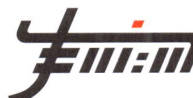

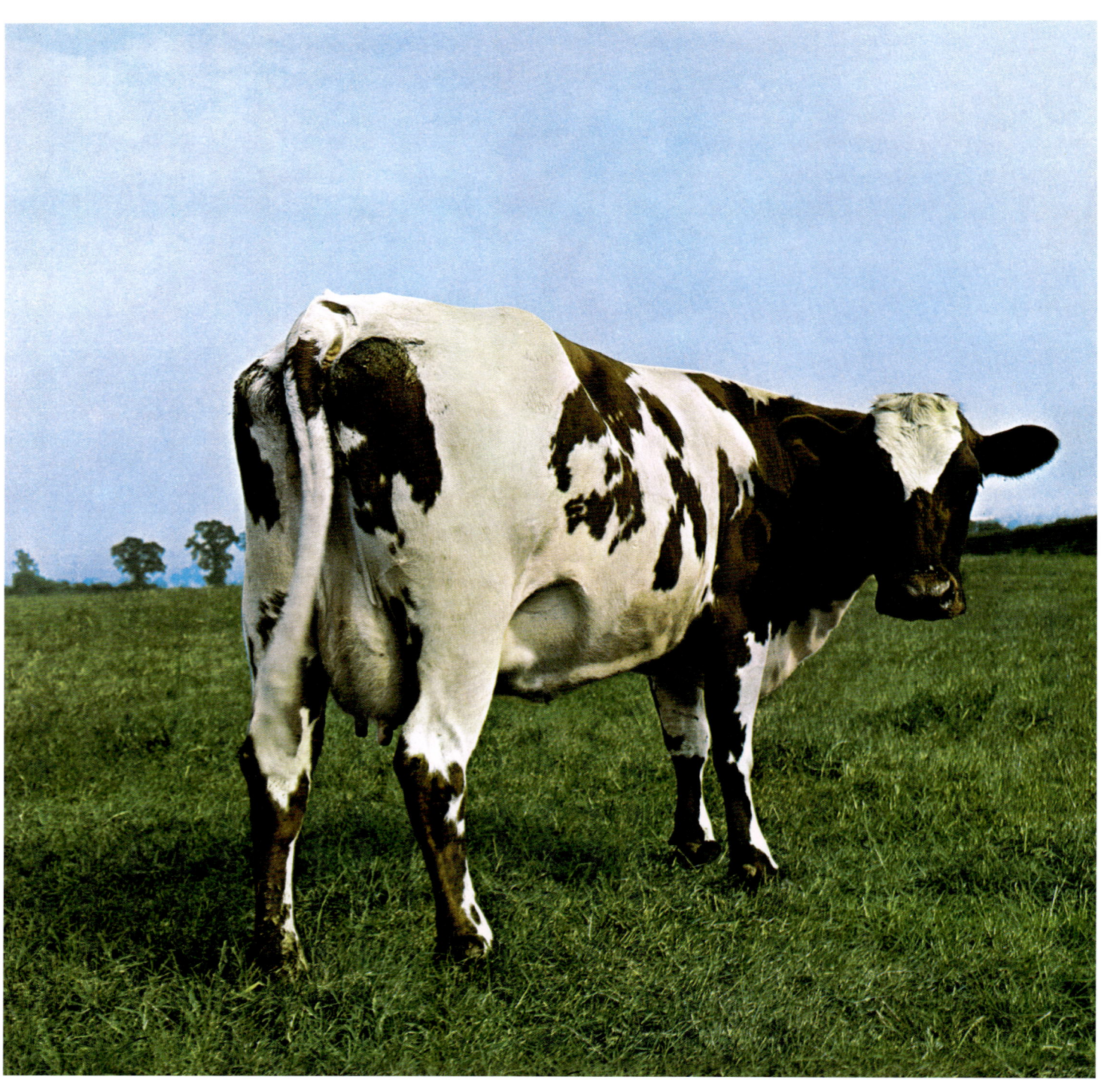

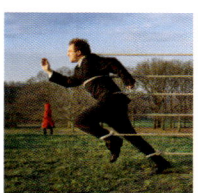

17 The image of the runner going nowhere, striving to get forward, about to be snapped back across the park or across the page, is an extension of the theme of conflict (see Ignoto pg 116). I think the idea came from one of those dog-leads you see in the park or street, which are extendable, so that the dog can run several yards this way and that before being 'snapped back' to the owner, or so I fantasised.

In this case it is a man on his way to work, who is about to be 'snapped back', but who is doing the snapping? Is it his spouse? Or society? His firm? All of which he is trying perhaps to escape rather than to attend. It is a story of a man at breaking point, at the end of his ropes, or rather at the end of his tether. striving to break free, pulling desperately at the binds that tie, stretching them to their limit. Are they about to break? (You'll notice that there are 6 ropes or strings to represent the clashing guitars of a young rock band in full creative conflict).

Yourcodenameis:milo **17** *Fiction 2005 CD single*
Design & Photo StormStudios Location Hampstead Heath, London

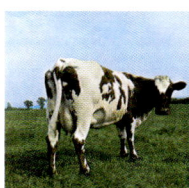

ATOM HEART MOTHER Cows are not so much odd as loveable. What was odd though was the choice of putting an ordinary cow on a Pink Floyd record. It was intended as a non-cover, an unexpected cover, a cover without relevance, a cover unlike other covers. Only Pink Floyd could do this and get away with it, though they nearly didn't because the record company threw a fit, the managing director was apoplectic, and nearly had a coronary right in front of me. "A COW!" He bellowed, "A COW? Why the fuck a COW? What's a COW got to do with it? And no name on the cover? Are you completely barking?" No dogs here, just a cow, I thought to myself, but said nothing.

It worked a treat, the cow was spectacular, even if I say so myself, on its own or in comparison with other records in a record shop. It was like a conundrum, a mystery but not a mystery, for it's only a cow. They love this cover in Japan apparently: now that is a mystery.

PS The title was equally mysterious having little to do with either the music or the cover design. It was filched from a newspaper headline for an article about a heart pacemaker, or so I believe. Also irrelevant is this sketch for a proposed design for Nick Mason's book Inside Out. The relevance is in the liking.

Pink Floyd **Atom Heart Mother** *Vinyl front EMI 1970*
Design & Photography Hipgnosis & John Blake Location Potter's Bar, Hertfordshire,UK

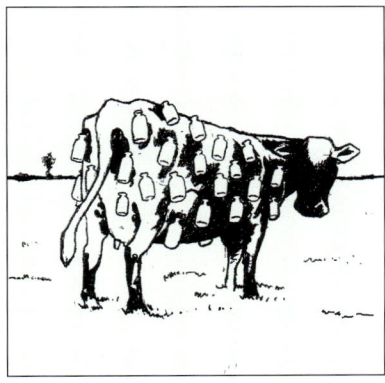

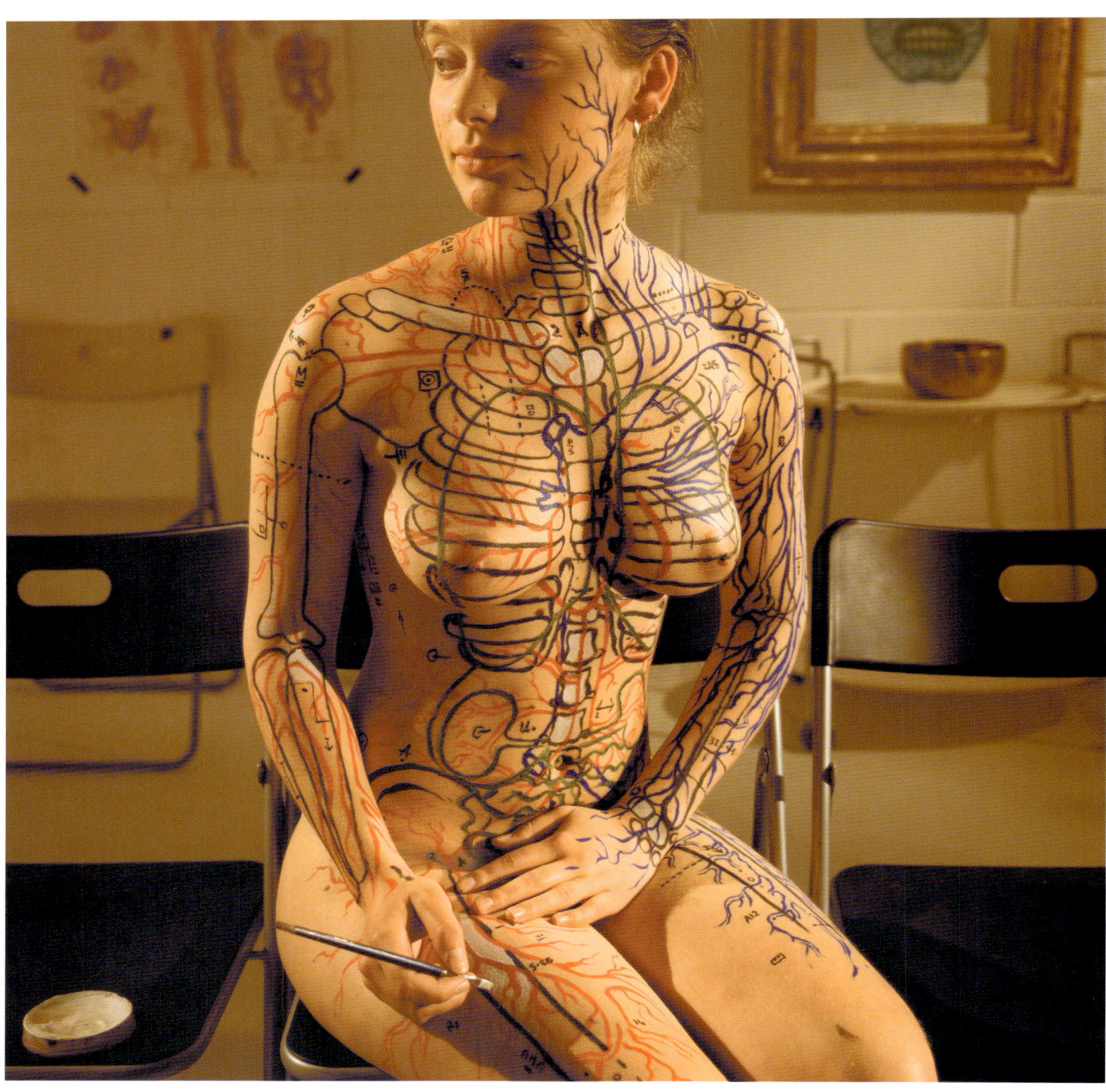

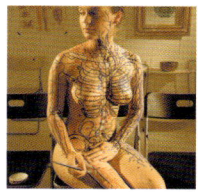

AMPUTECHTURE/BODYMAP/BETRAYAL Variations are an artistic key, exploring variations, changing, amending, developing, rearranging, are all vital ingredients in my ever humble view of the artistic process. If they're good enough for Elgar, they're good enough for us. There's nothing like a re-visit, re-assessing an idea that one had devised sometime previously. It's an enigma, but I'm sure musicians do it just as much as we do. In fact, what is rock'n'roll, but a set of variations?

One day Dan had an idea about someone drawing a map on their body, as an interpretation of the notion of finding one's way, geographically, emotionally or metaphorically. The word 'amputechture' devised by The Mars Volta as a title for their third album seemed very much to apply to the body and its internal architecture - 'ampu' as in the amputation of limbs, and 'tecture' as in architecture. Thus a map of the body delineated by blood vessels, nerves, bones, and the occasional organ seemed a promising variation.

Our nude model, Miriam, sat patiently for several hours whilst Dan and Carolyn Roper inscribed her flesh with all manner of lines, vessels and symbols. An internal map, geographical rather than physiological, but bearing the hallmarks of obsession, and extreme dexterity, since the subject is seen to be painting it herself.

Betrayal is a further interpretation of the tale told on pg 167, namely that of a modern day crucifixion which took place in Poland. I found this story very hard to stomach, but it felt as though a central feature must have been the massive sense of desertion and betrayal the nun would have felt whilst dying at the hands of her religious brethren - 'knifed in the back' hardly does it justice. We decided therefore to render this idea as a trompe l'oeil in order to present it anew, and thus more powerfully (we hope).

What you see is a woman stabbed viciously in the back with several knives or daggers, but not suffering overtly. So why is that? Answers to this conundrum, dear reader, on a postcard please, and addressed to The Mars Volta, Los Angeles, US of A.

*The Mars Volta **Amputechture**/**Bodymap** & **Betrayal** Universal 2006 CD booklet, unused
Design & photography StormStudios*

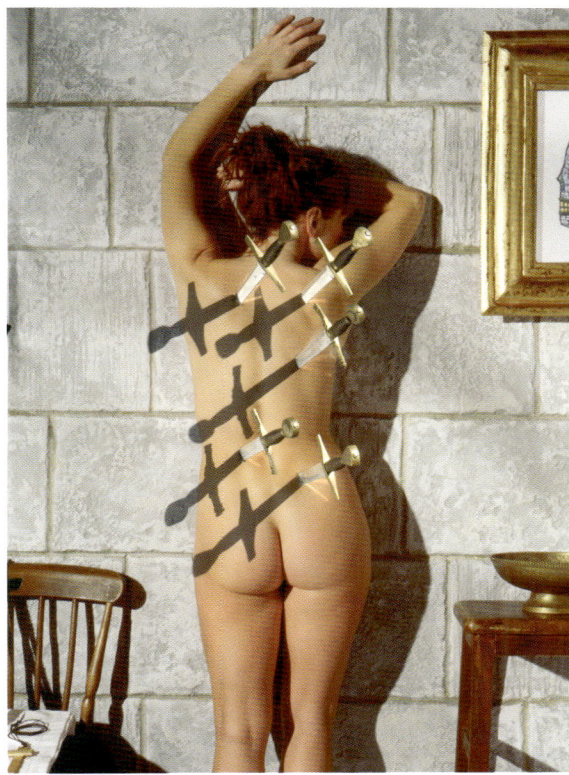

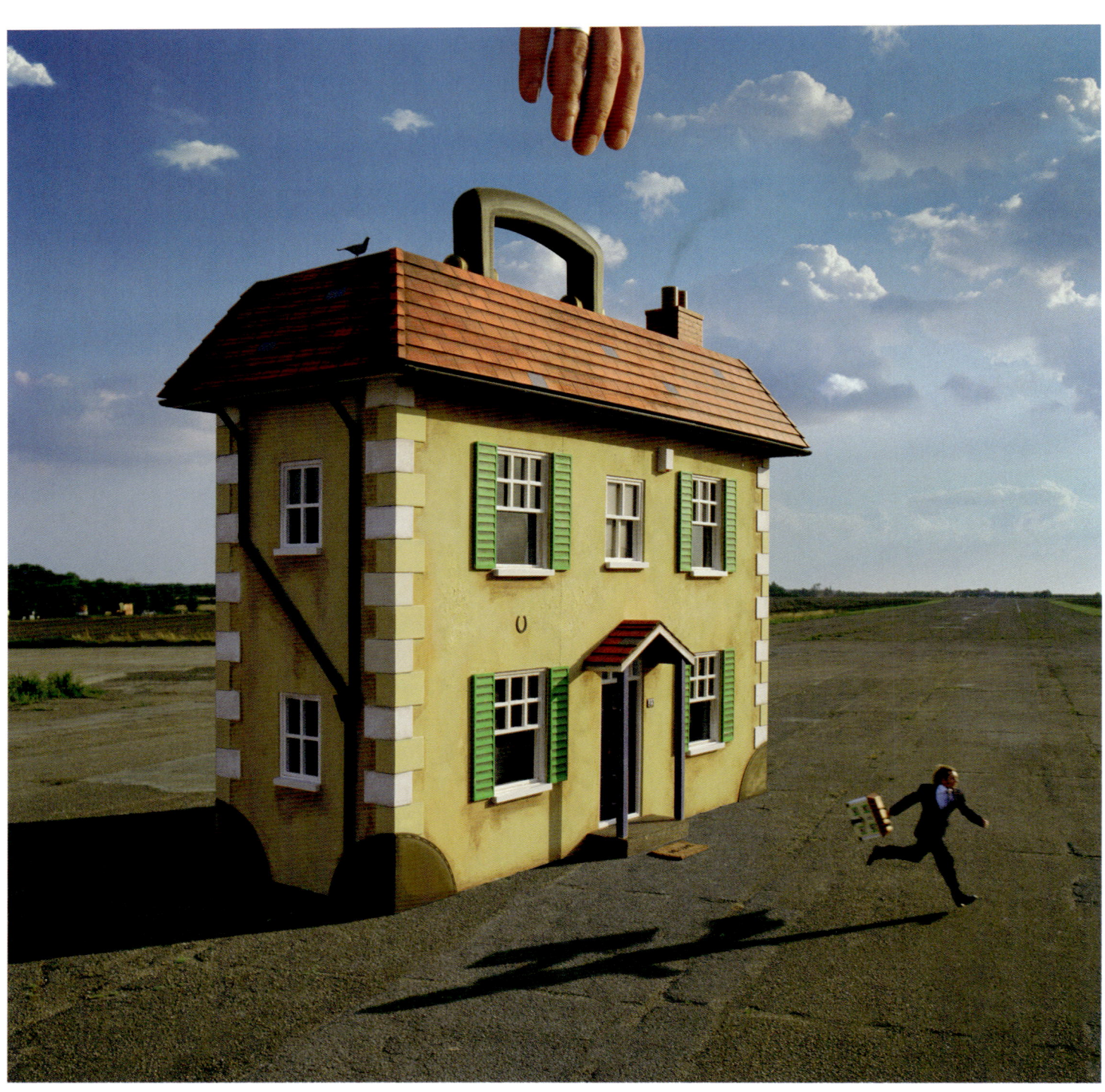

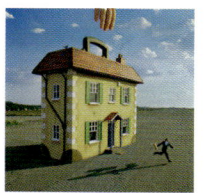

STORIES OF A STRANGER The main preoccupation of O.A.R. (Of A Revolution) at the time of this record was how to balance the life of a travelling musician, a life on the road, with family life, a life at home. One loves both playing and being with one's family, but these can be mutually exclusive. And in trying to avoid the more usual and lurid solutions of outrageous behaviour or over-indulgence - or both (which may provide, of course, for a litany of colourful rock and roll stories but also a trail of fucked-up marriages and abandoned children…steady on) O.A.R. put it instead into their art. I likewise tried to do the same, and see this work/home dilemma as part of an imaginary fairy tale to reflect the old conundrum, do you take your work home or your home to work?

So we see a man running from his house in a hurry, presumably on his way to work - hence the suit and briefcase. But his briefcase is the shape of the house he's just left because he's taking 'home' to work. But the house he's just left is also in fact a huge briefcase belonging to a giant who is reaching down to pick it up on his way to work. And so it goes on, a dilemma that is difficult to resolve. Better to make a record - a piece of art - than plunge your head in a bucket of vomit in a hotel room in Kentucky. Moreover, we're not people to mess around, so we built a giant house/briefcase, took it in sections to the location and erected it, photographed it in late afternoon light, as you can see, then came home (and they call that work). Wait a minute - it is work.

O.A.R. **Stories Of A Stranger** *CD front Atlantic 2005*
Design & Photography StormStudios Location Bourne Aerodrome, Cambs.

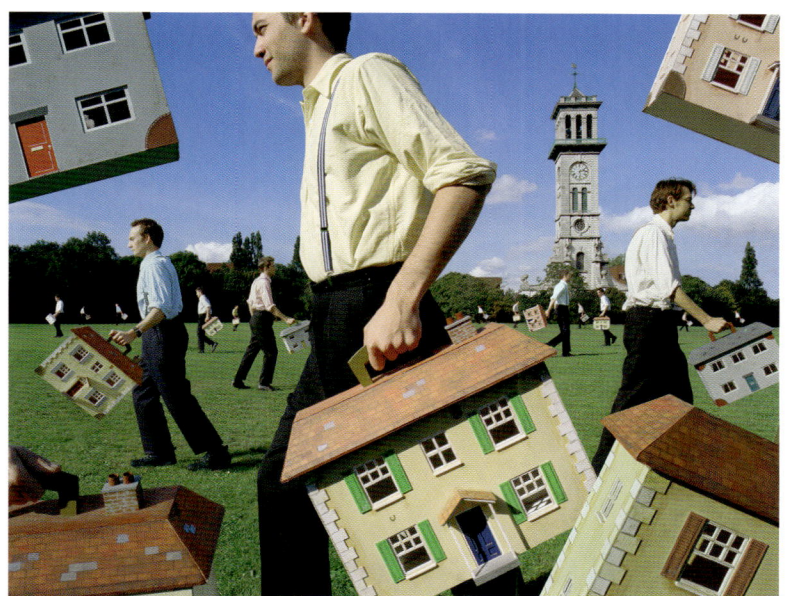

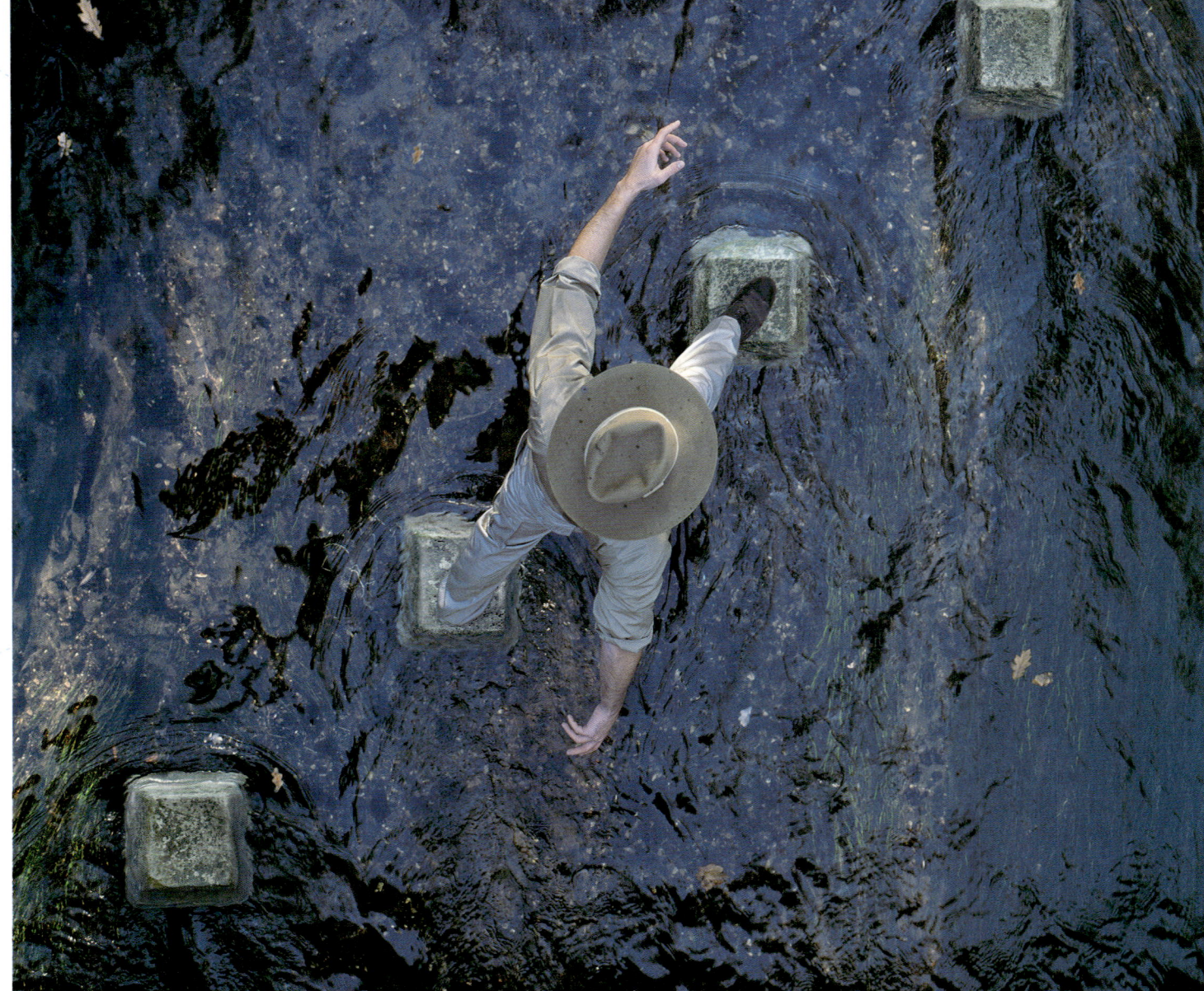

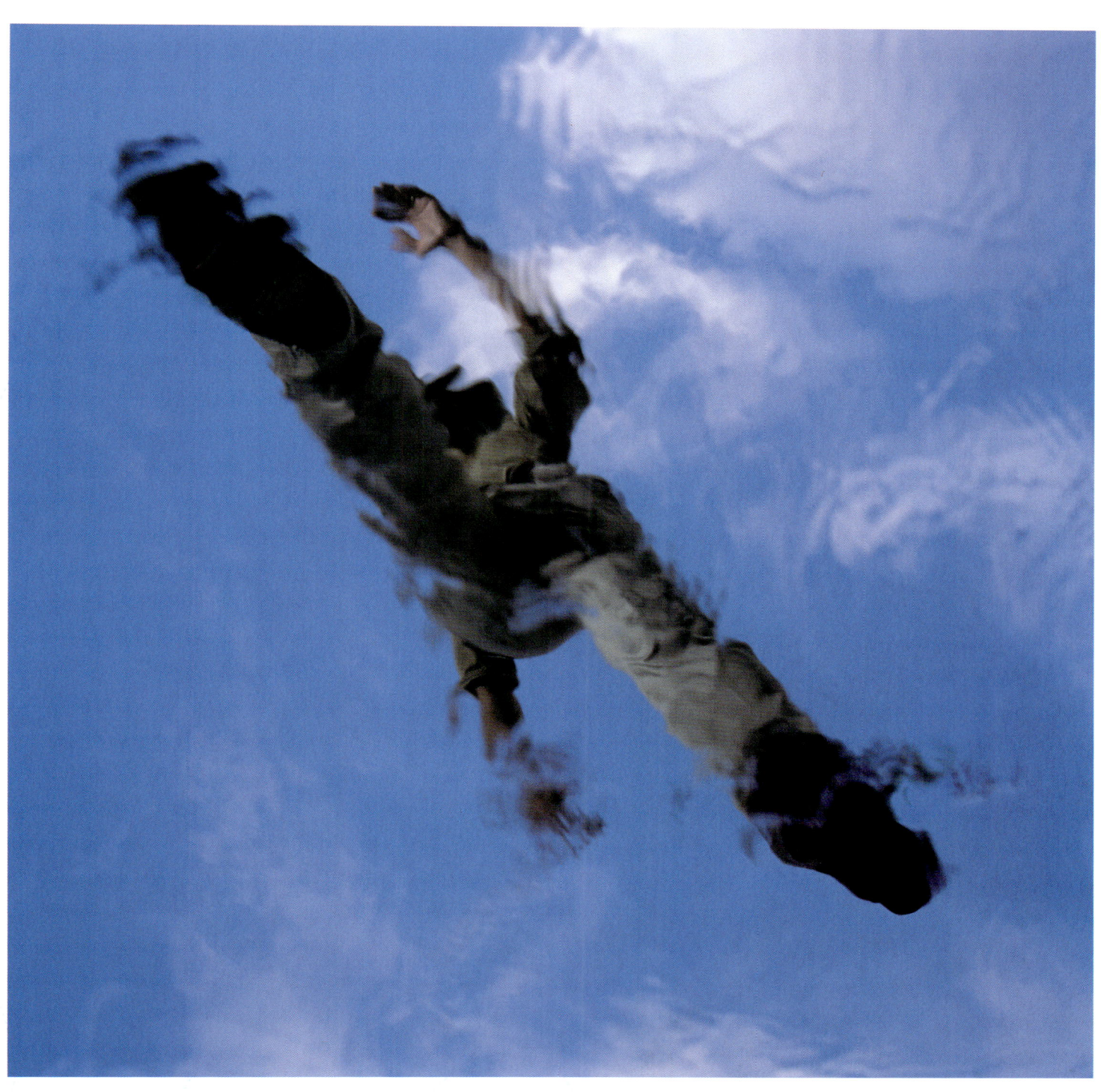

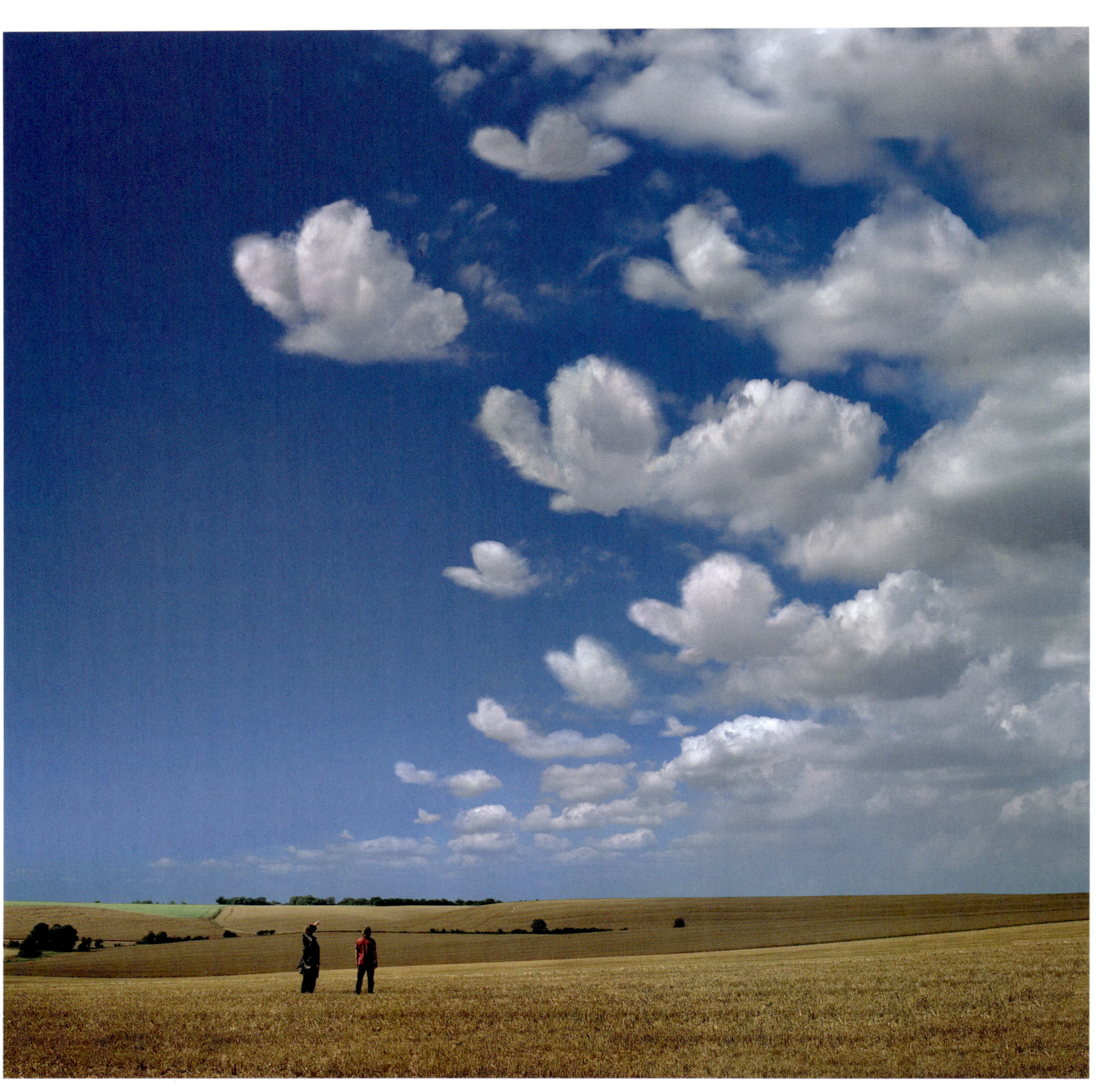

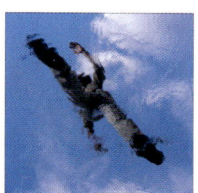

A VALID PATH Alan Parsons was making an album of more experimental music; 'less songs' than his usual offerings – produced in conjunction with some electronic outfits from California namely Uberzone and Spongola and Wise Guys and also his son Jeremy amongst others. He wanted a design which suggested an exploration of new territories, stepping out across new landscapes, taking a different path, setting sail through uncharted seas etc. Our image here derives from the simple idea of stepping into the unknown, walking over literal stepping stones, strung out across a stream high in the mountains of Uzbekistan. By electing to shoot from above the exact location is unbounded and could be anywhere. The aerial POV also allows for a more graphic representation of a line of stones across which the intrepid explorer has to step. It further lends an abstract quality - a backdrop canvas upon which events can unfold. It is also derived from an old idea about taking a photo of a geyser from the six different perspectives: front, back, two sides above and below, which should cover it, if you'll excuse the pun.

The stepping stones are shaped like the keys on a computer keyboard, to echo the electronic nature of the music and the figure is dressed in an Indiana Jones style to indicate that he is an explorer as Alan felt himself to be, stepping into new musical territory, taking a more valid path, perhaps. Though I say it myself, I particularly like the back cover (overleaf) - a picture taken from below (below the water level of the front image that is), a diverting complement to the front cover, repeating the use of diagonals and itself representing an unexpected perspective, much like the music within.

*Alan Parsons **A Valid Path** CD front 5.1 Records 2004 Design & Photos StormStudios Location*

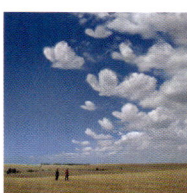

BUTTERFLIES & HURRICANES Somewhere in chaos theory is expressed the idea that merely the flutter of a butterfly's wings in one part of the global system can cause dramatic disturbance (hurricanes) in another part of the global system. We took this all rather literally and imagined storm clouds (forgive the pun) gathering and appearing briefly in the shape of large butterflies. I have to say I thought this idea was a bit simplistic until our intrepid retoucher, the great Badger, wove his magic computer wand and deftly transformed cumulus into butterfly clouds, passing unsuspectingly over the summer fields of Hertfordshire.

*Muse **Butterflies & Hurricanes** CD single Warner 2004 Design & Photography StormStudios Location Baldock Herts*

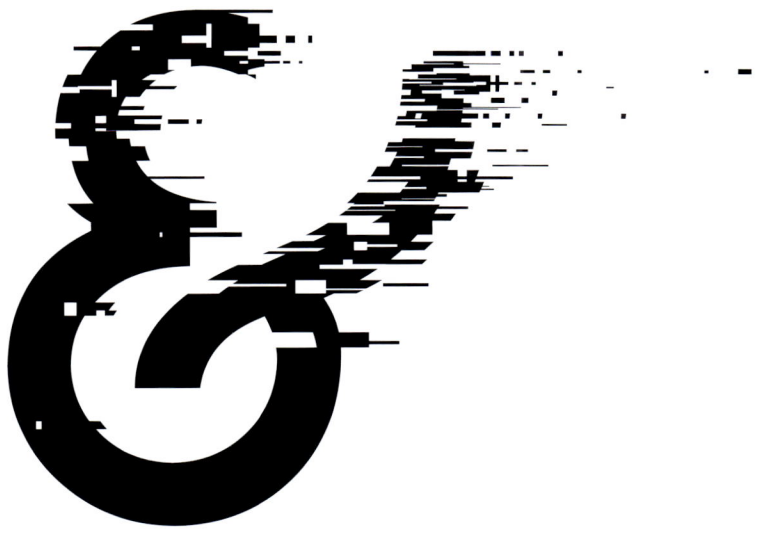

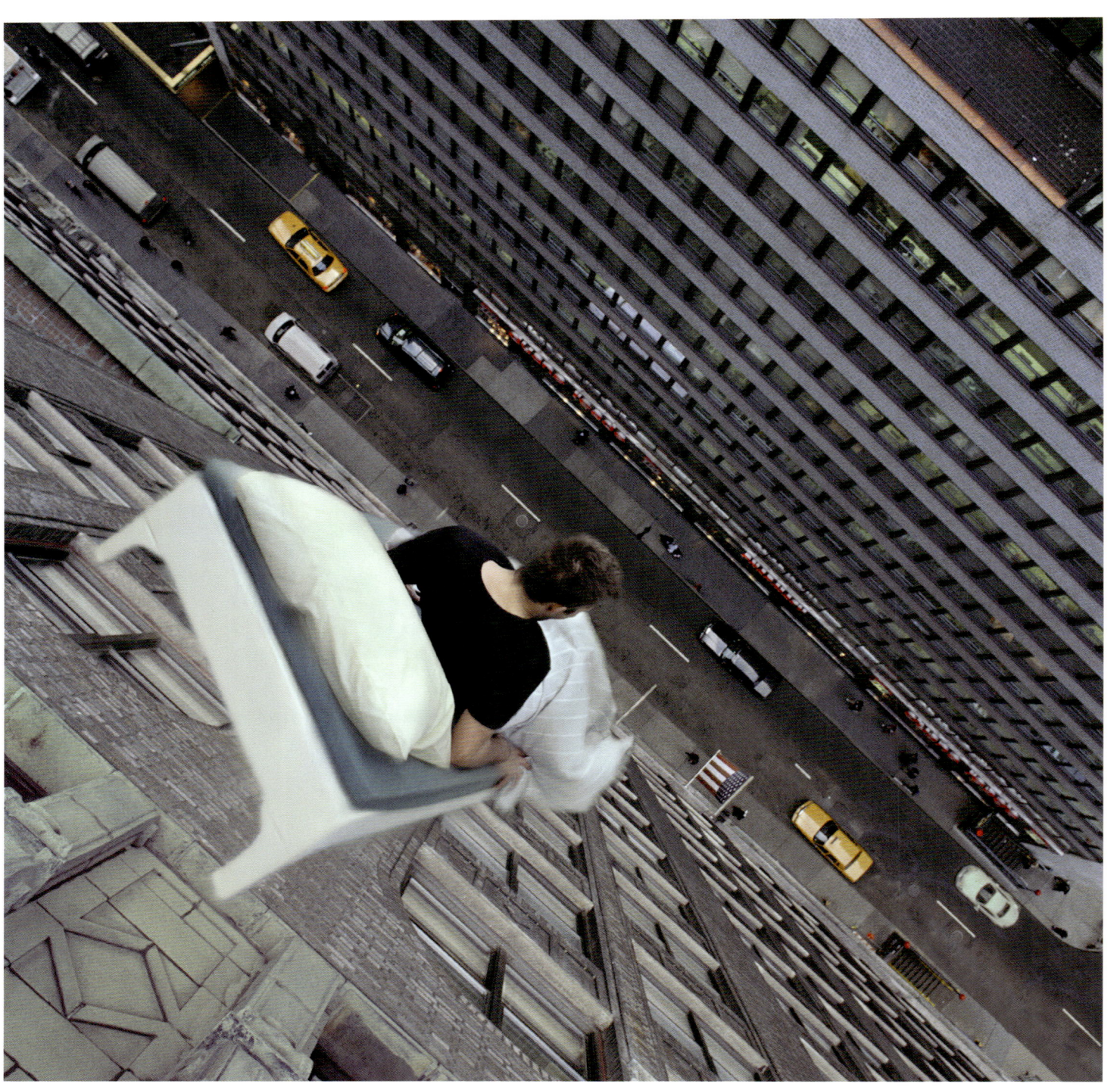

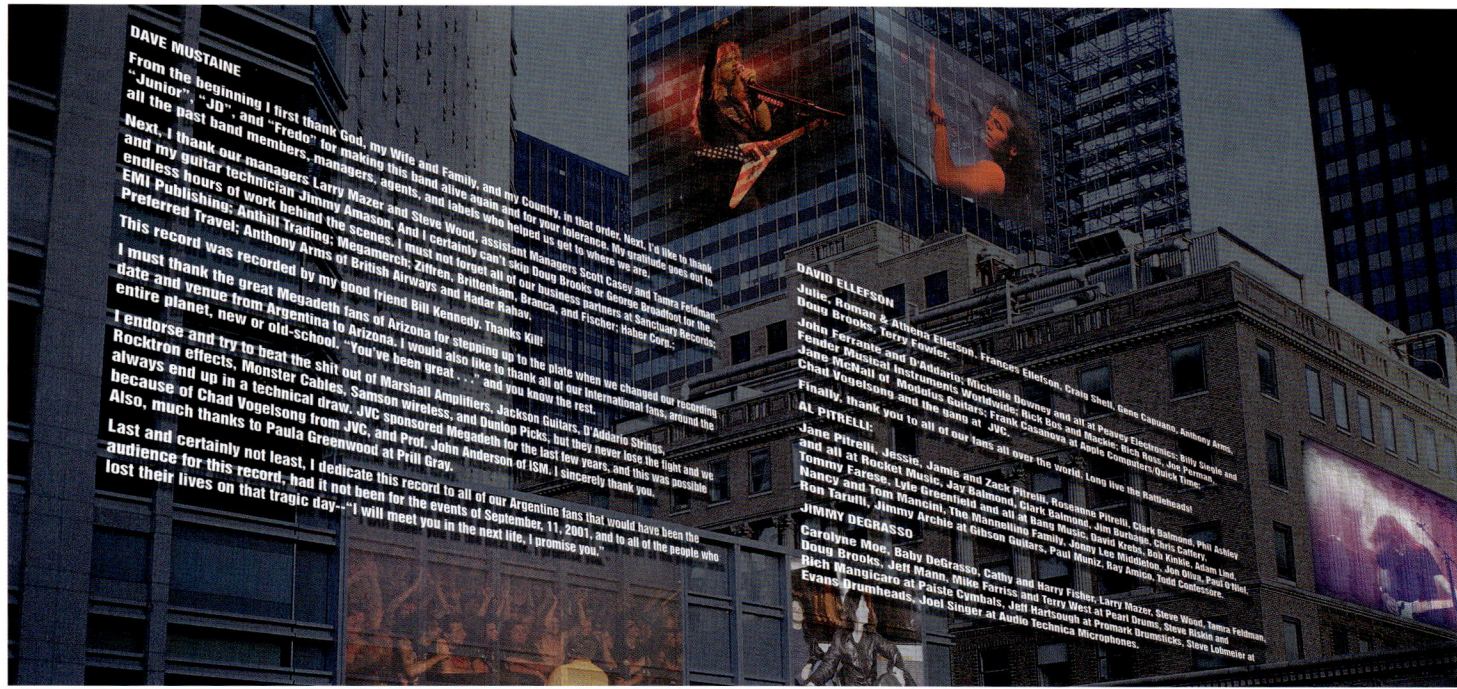

RUDE AWAKENING Just the kind of humour you'd expect from a heavy metal band - being ejected in your bed from your hotel room, high up above the streets of New York, would of course constitute a very serious rude awakening. Clearly there are also references here to trashing hotel rooms and of waking up too pissed to notice anything's wrong until it's too late... references to a mythic life on the road.

I flew one weekend to Phoenix to catch Megadeth playing, and have a chat. They were very friendly, but very loud, in performance that is. Now there's a surprise. Actually there was a genuine surprise in so much as they'd had precisely the same idea as us, though seen from a side angle rather than a top angle. This synchronicity of course meant that other ideas were thrown out when later presented, faster than a bed out of a window.

Although our avowed policy is to do things for real, let's not get stupid - we don't do snuff covers - though it is true that Rupert hung his camera on a pole from the 28th floor, hanging five feet out of a window in order to do the picture. That scared me more than the plight of the guy in the bed, which of course cannot be real, can it? Lest in your nightmare.

Hmm. I've always liked the use of diagonals, which I believe Peter sustained brilliantly in the booklet (that's a fiver you owe me Peter).

*Megadeth **Rude Awakening** CD front and booklet Sanctuary 2001*
Design & Photos StormStudios Location New York

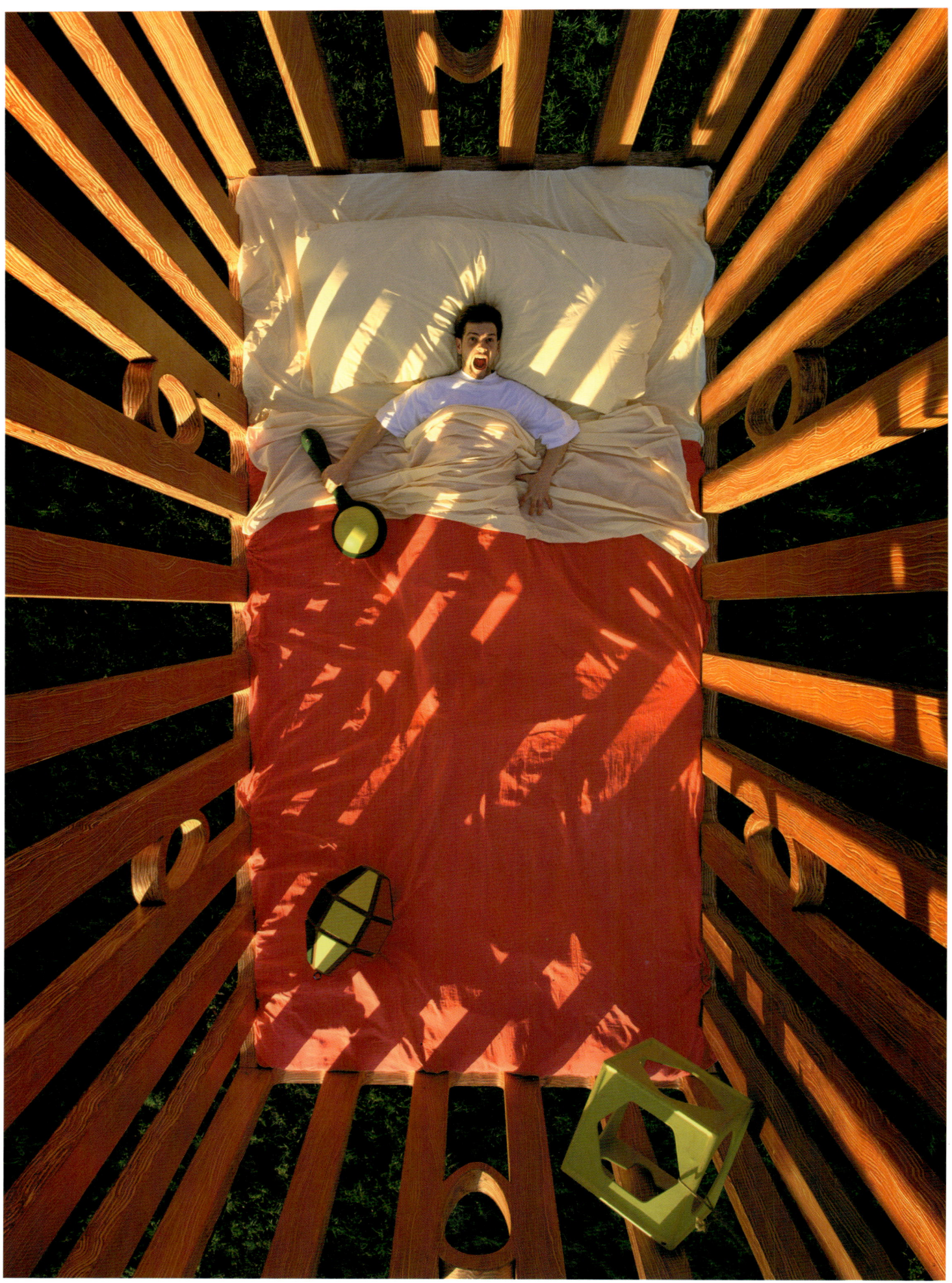

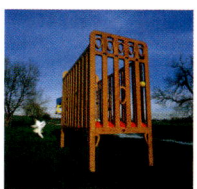

HAPPY DAYS Our adult-as-child, our child-in-adult clothing, is simply but starkly realised by the largeness of the cot around him making him at least child size in comparison. To enhance this Alice-like size conceit we made oversized bedding an oversized baby's rattle and oversized alphabet blocks, and then took the whole lot - baby an' all - to a rural setting and photographed it in evening light from a tall step ladder, the camera looking down at our baby cum adult to emphasize the perspective of the bars and to heighten the sense of menace. The occupant is screaming - is he returning to a particular nightmare of childhood? Or is he simply recalling the giantness of things, parents, cot, trees, everything, seeing the looming world around him from a small person's point of view as intrinsically threatening....though you don't have to be a child to feel that, now do you?

Happy days... are we so sure?

*Catherine Wheel **Happy Days** CD front and Advert Phonogram 1995*
Design & Photos StormStudios Location Grantchester, Cambs.

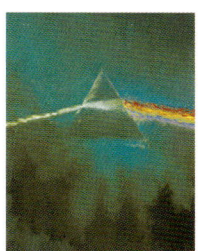

DSOM LIVE (overleaf) Roger Waters toured Europe in summer 2006 and played the entire *The Dark Side Of The Moon*. At the time of writing he is not technically part of Pink Floyd though he played at 'Live 8' in London as part of a reunited Floyd, therefore he does not bill himself as Pink Floyd. Correspondingly it was deemed inappropriate to use the original prism imagery from 1973 to promote his concerts which is, of course, strongly associated with Pink Floyd.

To keep it connected, however, called for a reworking of the prism design. The first concert arranged was in France, thus I rendered it like a painting, obviously a French painting, and thought Monet was a good choice to imitate, because of the song 'Money' which is how this version came to be called 'Green Monet', green being the colour of money, Silly isn't it? We had great fun concocting a gold and a purple Monet and also other prisms in the style of Jackson Pollock, Seurat, west coast psychedelia and Pop Art... our homage to Roy Lichtenstein was used by Italian Rolling Stone when Roger played Rome, in effect a homage to a homager par excellence.

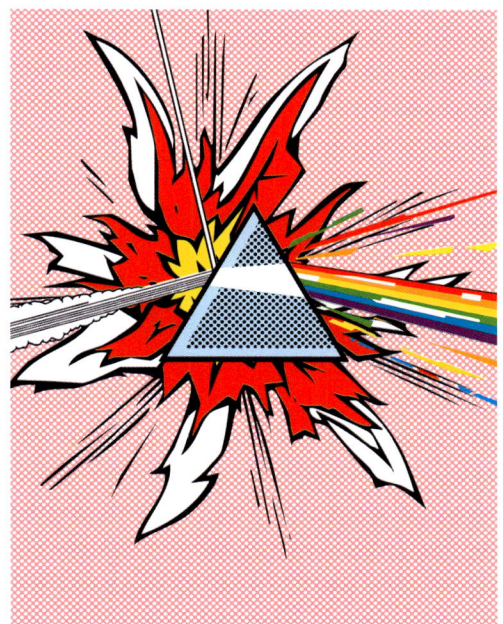

*Roger Waters **The Dark Side Of The Moon Live Tour***
Programme 2006 Design & Photos StormStudios

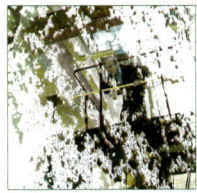

SMALLCREEPS DAY Equally painterly is this image for Mike Rutherford from Genesis, who made a solo album in 1980 based on a book of the same name. Mr. Smallcreep was the preverbial little man, working in a large factory making a big machine. He rarely sees his fellow workers and has no idea what he is helping to manufacture. One day he decides to go and find out. The album describes his adventures. The figure in our image is seen in a Victorian pumping station looking nervously about as he sets off to explore his surroundings.

The splatter technique has no direct relevance – it is something I dreamed up too look like paint splashes or to feel blotchy like a watercolour. The effect is achieved literally by splashing developer on the exposed bromide such that a small part of the photograph appears where the drops of developer fall. It is somewhat of a random procedure, because one is in the dark room and the developer is colourless. I thought this technique was a truly original idea at the time, I had never seen this technique before and I have never seen it since, until very, very recently. Painterly, punkish and original – well not quite as original as I though, more's the pity.

*Mike Rutherford **Smallcreeps Day** Vinyl front & Advert Charisma Records 1980*
Design & Photos Hipgnosis Location Pumping Station East London

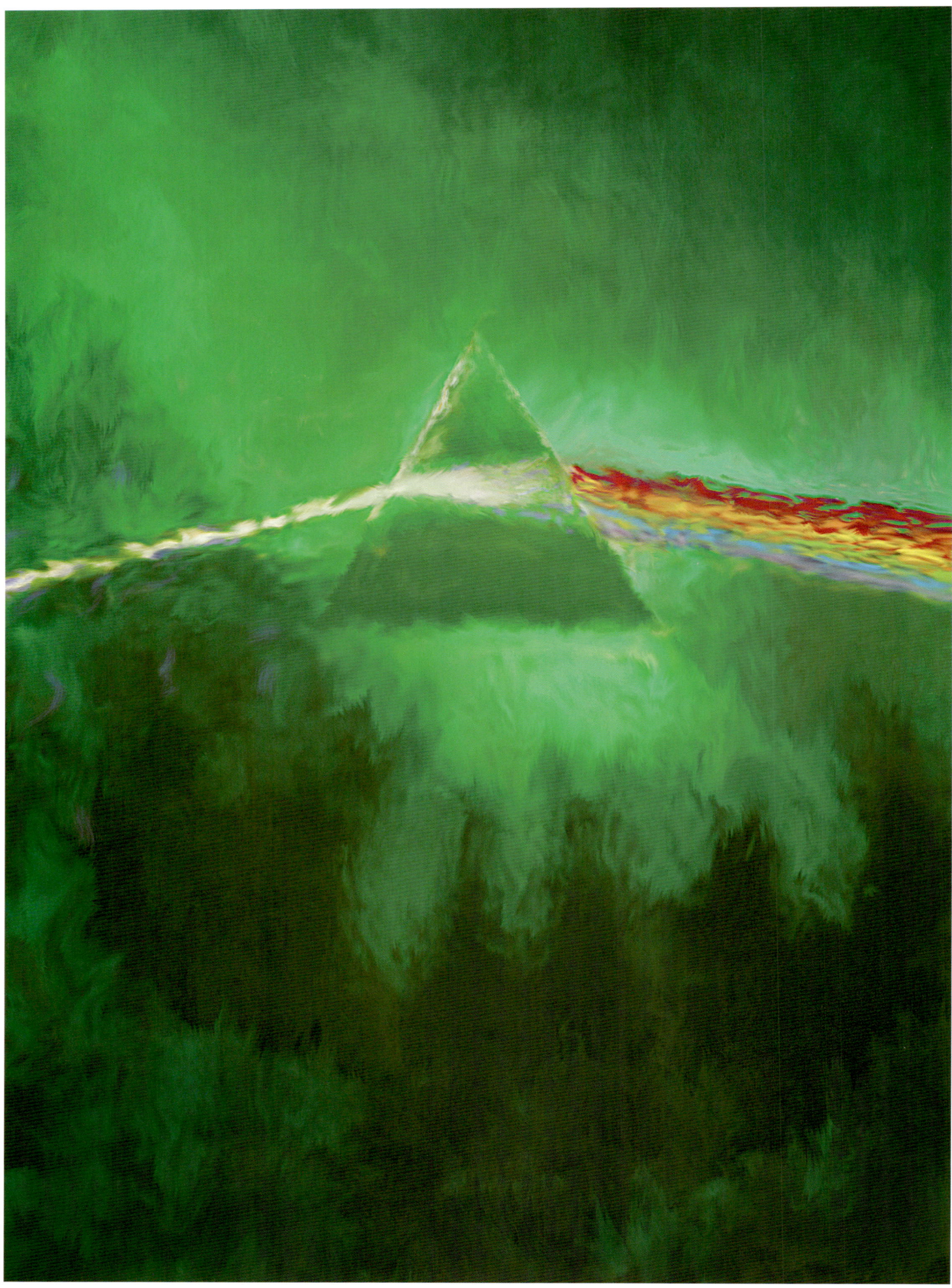

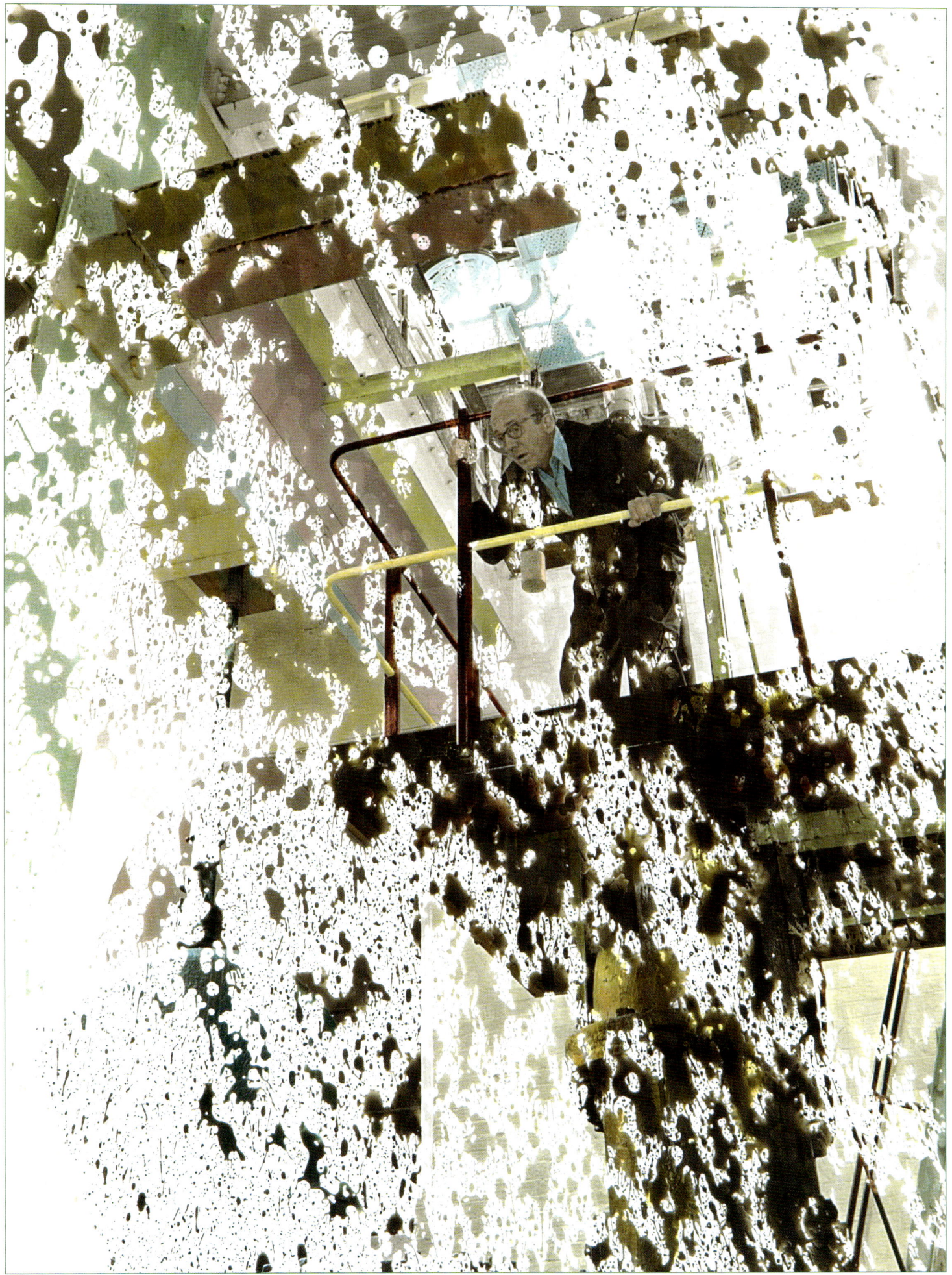

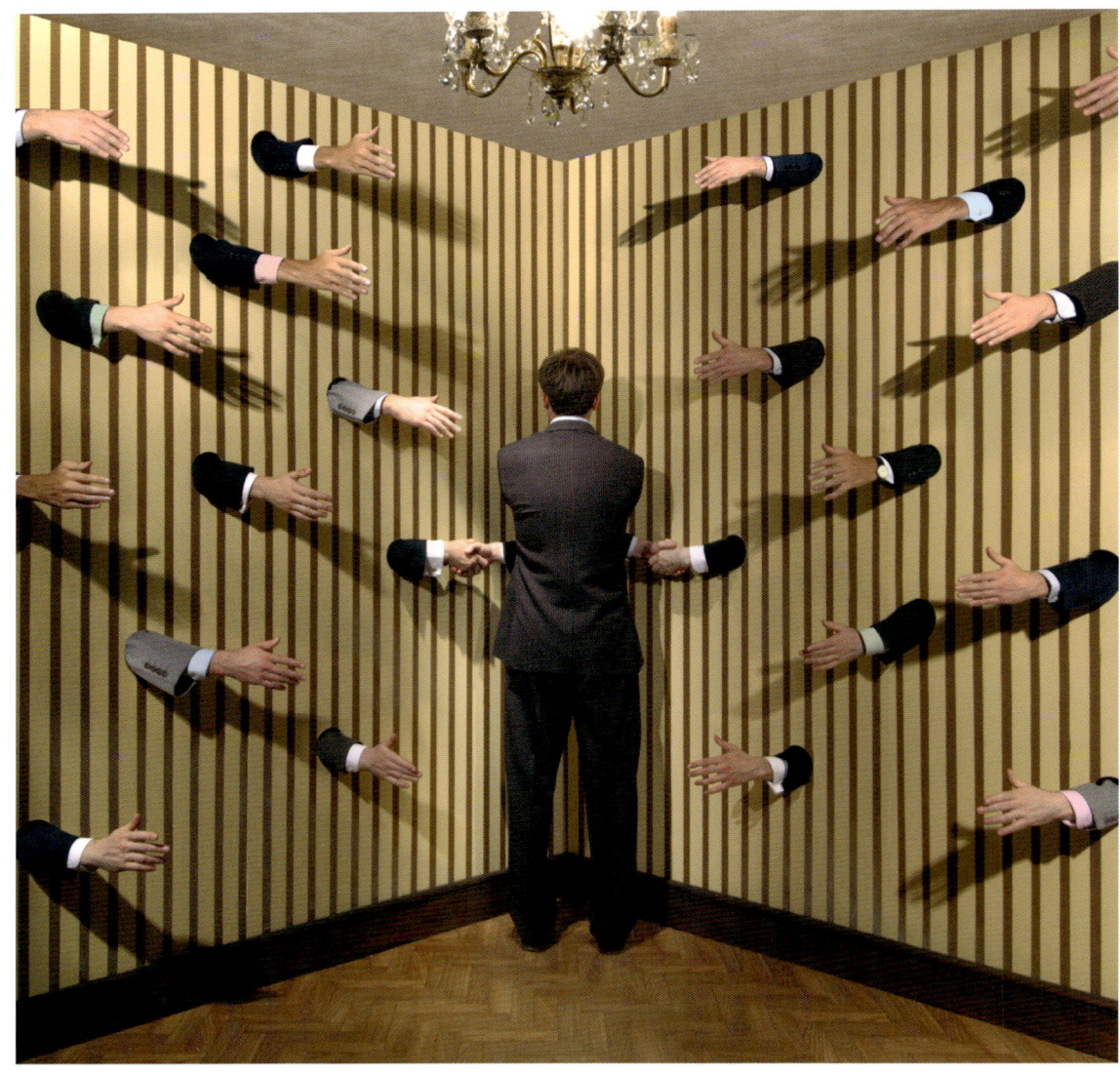

SECRET SOCIETY Not the final countdown but the final image for the book. This design for the band Europe was finished in September 2006 immediatly prior to finishing the artwork for the book. The idea is based on the widely held suspicion that secret societies in business often demand special handshakes, especially in Italy, or so I imagine. The image is a mixture of a scene from *Repulsion*, a film directed by a man from Poland, and an obscure sexual practise that occurs only in Holland so I was told. The band come from Sweden, their manager is from Finland, I am from Norway, the cover was shot in England and the record released by a company in Germany. What could be more European?

*Europe **Secret Society** CD Front Sanctuary 2006 design and photos StormStudios*

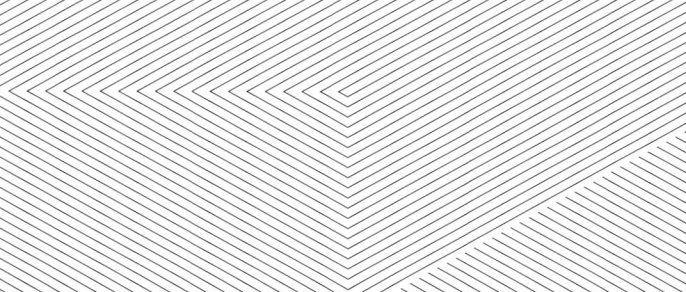

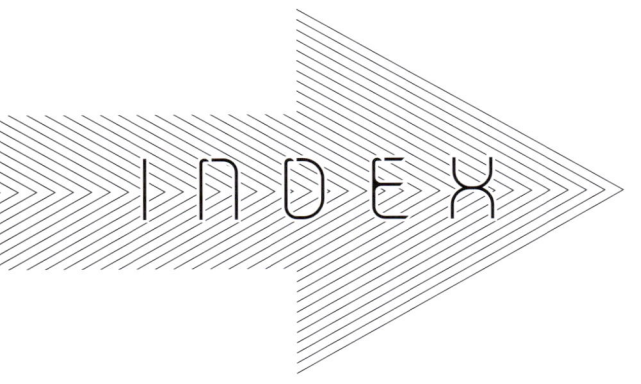

INDEX

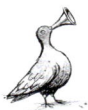

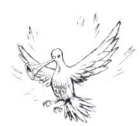

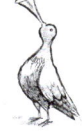

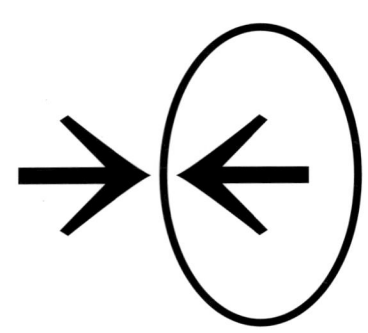